D1083128

Black Religions in the New World

Black Religions
in the
New World

GEORGE EATON SIMPSON

NEW YORK
COLUMBIA UNIVERSITY PRESS

LIBRARY OF CONGRESS CATALOGING IN PUBLICATION DATA

SIMPSON, GEORGE EATON, 1904–
    BLACK RELIGIONS IN THE NEW WORLD.

    BIBLIOGRAPHY: P. 383.
    INCLUDES INDEX.
    I. BLACKS—AMERICA—RELIGION.   2. AFRO-
AMERICANS—RELIGION.   3. CULTS—AMERICA.
I. TITLE.
BL2500.S55   291'.097   78-16892
ISBN 0-231-04540-9

COLUMBIA UNIVERSITY PRESS
NEW YORK   GUILDFORD, SURREY

COPYRIGHT © 1978 BY COLUMBIA UNIVERSITY PRESS
ALL RIGHTS RESERVED
PRINTED IN THE UNITED STATES OF AMERICA
9 8 7 6 5

Contents

Preface

FORTY YEARS AGO a Social Science Research Council postdoctoral fellowship enabled me to study for a semester at Northwestern University with the late Professor Melville J. Herskovits and also to conduct field work for seven months on peasant life near the village of Plaisance in northern Haiti. In 1953, I did field work in West Kingston, an economically depressed area of Kingston, Jamaica, and, in 1960, in Port of Spain and neighboring towns, and in a rural section near Couva, a settlement located about thirty miles from Trinidad's capital. Shorter visits were made to the Caribbean in 1936, 1947, 1957, 1962, 1967, and 1972.

The results of these studies that are cited in this book have appeared in the following journals: *African Notes, American Anthropologist, American Sociological Review, Anthropological Quarterly, Caribbean Studies, Comparative Studies in Society and History, Journal of American Folklore, Phylon, Social and Economic Studies,* and *Social Forces,* and in two monographs: *Jamaican Revivalist Cults* (Kingston: Institute of Social and Economic Studies, University of the West Indies, 1956), and *The Shango Cult in Trinidad* (Rio Piedras: Institute of Caribbean Studies, University of Puerto Rico, 1965). A selection of these papers, as well as the latter monograph, are reprinted as *Religious Cults of the Caribbean: Trinidad, Jamaica, and Haiti* (Rio Piedras: Institute of Caribbean Studies, University of Puerto Rico, 2nd revised edition, 1977). Another selection of articles on the Caribbean area was reprinted as *Caribbean Papers* (Cuernavaca, Centro Intercultural de Documentacion, 1970).

In chapters 3 and 4, I have drawn extensively on these earlier publications. Parts of chapters 2–4 were included in my paper, "Religions of the Caribbean," in Martin L. Kilson and Robert I. Rotberg (eds.), *The African Diaspora: Interpretive Essays* (Cambridge: Harvard University Press, Copyright © 1976 by the President and Fellows of Harvard College). An earlier version of the section on Black Pentecostalism in the United States in chapter 8 appeared in *Phylon,* 35 (1974): 203–11. In a number of places throughout the book, I have utilized materials that I have published heretofore in books issued by Folkways Ethnic Library, Harper & Row, Ibadan University Press, and the University of Pennsylvania. Acknowledgements of these previous publications are given in numerous footnotes, and full listings of them are included in the Bibliography. In the present work, the religions of blacks in the Caribbean, South America, the United States, Canada, and England—cults, sects, and the historical churches—are examined and compared.

I am grateful to the following for permission to reprint materials in this book: *The Black Scholar, Concept,* Cummings Publishing Company, Editions Gallimard, *The Journal of Negro History,* Oxford University Press, The University of Florida Press, and The University of Wisconsin Press. Specific acknowledgements for these permissions are given in the text.

For the financial support that made possible my field work in the Caribbean and in Nigeria, I am grateful to the Social Science Research Council, the American Council of Learned Societies, the American Philosophical Society, the National Institute of Mental Health, and Oberlin College.

I have been extremely fortunate in my contacts with research associates: the late J. B. Cinéas in Haiti, the late Arthur Bethune in Jamaica, Joseph Francis in Trinidad, and in Nigeria, M. O. Ogunyemi, Adekunle Adeniran, and Amos Adesimi. For assistance in the field and helpful criticisms I am grateful to Maurice Dartigue, formerly Minister of Education in Haiti; Sir Philip Sherlock, formerly Vice Chancellor of the University of the West Indies; the late H. D. Huggins, formerly

Director of the Institute of Social and Economic Research, University of the West Indies; George Cumper, Department of Statistics, Government of Jamaica; Pedro Aparicio of Port of Spain; and Joseph Black, formerly Dean of the Faculty of Social Science, University of Ibadan, and now of the Rockefeller Foundation.

In addition to Professor Herskovits, I am indebted to many colleagues for stimulating suggestions and encouragement over the long period covered by these studies. Among these friends are William R. Bascom, Department of Anthropology, University of California, Berkeley; Joseph G. Moore, of St. Croix, Virgin Islands; and Robert I. Rotberg, Department of Political Science, Massachusetts Institute of Technology. I am deeply grateful to J. Milton Yinger, of Oberlin College; Peter B. Hammond, of Washington, D.C.; Harold Courlander, of Bethesda, Maryland; and an anonymous reviewer for reading the entire manuscript and providing many valuable criticisms. The manuscript has greatly benefited also from the expert surveillance of the members of the editorial staff of Columbia University Press. I am solely responsible, however, for the form this work has taken. My wife, Eleanor Brown Simpson, has played an important role in all of my field trips and in the preparation of the materials collected in the Caribbean, Nigeria, and the United States. I am grateful to Paul Arnold, of Oberlin College, for preparing the maps of The Caribbean Area and South America.

I acknowledge with pleasure the tremendous help given me by scores of West Indians, Africans, and Americans who have aided in countless ways and provided invaluable information from their personal experiences and observations.

For competent and conscientious secretarial assistance, I am indebted to Mrs. Betty Berman, Mrs. Jean Hope, and Mrs. Linda Clarke.

GEORGE EATON SIMPSON

Oberlin, Ohio
August 1978

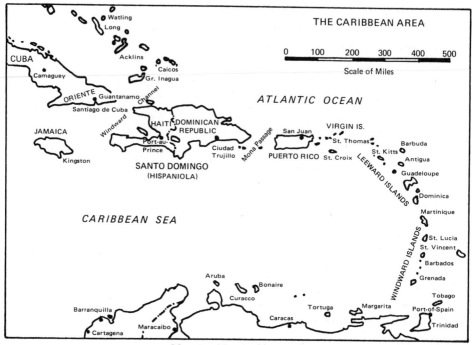

Map 1. The Caribbean Area

Map 2.   Profile Map of Central and South America Showing Cities and Regions Referred to in the Text

Black Religions in the New World

CHAPTER ONE

Slavery, Freedom, and the Religions of Blacks in the New World

The African Diaspora

FOR MORE THAN a century, much has been written about the religions of sub-Saharan Africa; about traditional magical and religious beliefs and practices, about the spread of Christianity and Islam, and about the many messianic, millennial, nativistic, reformative, and separatist religious movements.[1] This book examines a variety of religions found not among contemporary Africans, but among the descendants of sub-Saharan Africans dispersed throughout the Americas during the Atlantic slave trade.

The concern here is with the African Diaspora[2] in North America, the West Indies, and Latin America—and, to a much lesser extent, in Northern Europe—during the past five hundred years. It should not be overlooked, however, that there have been successive dispersals of population out of sub-Saharan Africa to other parts of the world for 10,000 years. St. Clair Drake's suggestion for studying eight situations of the Black Diaspora is shown in figure 1.1.

The earliest dispersals from sub-Saharan Africa were to Egypt and North Africa. Blacks functioned in high positions as well as on low levels in ancient Egypt, and for centuries the terminal points for caravans crossing the Sahara have been in Libya, Tunisia, Algeria, and

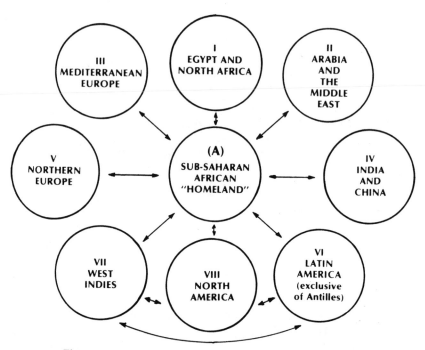

Figure 1. 1.   Dispersals of Population Out of Sub-Saharan Africa
Source: St. Clair Drake, "The African Diaspora in Pan-African Perspective, *The Black Scholar,* 7 (1975), 5. Used by permission.

Morocco. Ethiopians played active roles in the Middle East in antiquity, and Iraqi Arabs made slaves of thousands of black pagans from the interior of Africa.[3] The slave trade to Asia continued for more than a thousand years and left large numbers, perhaps millions, of Africans throughout the continent. For the most part, Afro-Asians continue to occupy the laboring roles that they have always held in Asia.[4]

A recent study examines the Black Diaspora into the ancient Mediterranean, a dispersion that did not result in any permanent communities on the northern shores of the Mediterranean.[5] There have been Negroes in Britain for more than four centuries,[6] but the present black population derives almost entirely from immigration since World War II. Net immigration from the West Indies to Britain increased from 2,300 in 1953 to 66,300 in 1961, but the controls introduced by government in 1962 resulted in declines in West Indian immigration to a net increase of only 700 in 1969 and 1,700 in 1970, and to a net decrease of 1,100 in 1971. In 1966, the estimated West Indian population resident in England and Wales, including both those born overseas and those born in the United Kingdom, was 454,000. Those of West African origin constituted an estimated 50,700.[7]

This study is not limited to "black" religions. It is a study of religions that have been important to blacks in the New World Diaspora. In some religions, all of the participants considered here are black; in others the believers are not limited to blacks; and in still other instances blacks are actually in the minority. In a number of cases, impressive parts of the belief system or the rituals seem to have been derived from traditional African religions; in others there is little or no trace of indigenous African religions.

The Atlantic Slave Trade

Although extended consideration of the slave trade is beyond the scope of this work, a brief background regarding this trade to the New World is essential. Slaves were shipped from eight coastal regions in Africa, even though the actual origins in the interior are often uncertain: (1) Senegambia, including the Gambia and Senegal of today; (2) Sierra Leone, a region somewhat larger than the present country; (3) a region consisting mainly of the present Ivory Coast and Liberia; (4) the Gold Coast, roughly coterminous with the present-day Ghana; (5) the Bight of Benin region from the Volta to the Benin River, the core of which in the eighteenth century was the more limited area known as the "slave coast" of present-day Togo and Dahomey; (6) the Bight of Biafra, centered on the Niger Delta and the mouths of the Cross and Duala rivers to the east; (7) Central Africa, corresponding roughly with the present-day Angola; and (8) southeastern Africa from the Cape of Good Hope to Cape Delgado and including Madagascar.[8]

Prior to the Post-World War II studies, the literature of the slave trade generally gave estimates of total slave imports into the New World of 15 to 20 million. Revisions of these estimates have reduced the total to something like 9 or 10 million, distributed by importing region as shown in table 1.1.[9]

TABLE 1.1
A SPECULATIVE GEOGRAPHICAL DISTRIBUTION OF SLAVE
IMPORTS DURING THE WHOLE PERIOD OF THE
ATLANTIC SLAVE TRADE (000 OMITTED)

Region and country		No.	%
Grand total		9,566	100.0*
Old World traffic		175	1.8
Europe		50	0.5
Madeira, Canaries, Cape Verde Is.		25	0.3
São Thomé		100	1.0
North America		651	6.8
Territory of the United States		427	4.5
British North America	399		4.2
Louisiana	28		0.3
Middle America		224	2.3
Mexico	200		2.1
Central America and Belize	24		0.3
Caribbean Islands		4,040	42.2
Greater Antilles		2,421	25.3
Haiti	864		9.0
Dominican Republic	30		0.3
Cuba	702		7.3
Puerto Rico	77		0.8
Jamaica	748		7.8
Lesser Antilles		1,619	16.9
US Virgin Is.	28		0.3
British Virgin Is.	7		0.1
Leeward Is.	346		3.6
Guadeloupe	291		3.0
Martinique	366		3.8
St. Vincent, St. Lucia, Tobago, & Dominica	70		0.7
Grenada	67		0.7
Trinidad	22		0.2
Barbados	387		4.0
Dutch Antilles	20		0.2
Bahamas	10		0.1
Bermuda	5		0.1

SLAVERY, FREEDOM, AND BLACK RELIGIONS

Region and country	No.		%
South America		4,700	49.1
The Guianas		531	5.6
Surinam & Guyana	480		5.0
French Guiana	51		0.5
Brazil		3,647	38.1
Bahia	1,200		12.5
Other	2,447		25.6
Spanish South America		522	5.5
Argentina, Uruguay, Paraguay, & Bolivia	100		1.0
Chile	6		0.1
Peru	95		1.0
Colombia, Panama, & Ecuador	200		2.1
Venezuela	121		1.3

*Percentages have been rounded.

Sources: Tables 4, 11, 17, 18, 22. Philip D. Curtin, *The Atlantic Slave Trade* (Madison, 1969), 88–89. Used by permission of the University of Wisconsin.

The destinations of the Atlantic slave trade at its peak (1701–1810) are shown graphically in figure 1.2.

Even if a sizable allowance is made for error in estimating the distribution of slave imports during the whole period of the Atlantic slave trade, it is clear that the real center of the trade was tropical America. Approximately half of the slaves were brought to South America, 42 percent to the Caribbean Islands, 2 percent to Middle America, and 7 percent to British North America. Probably the Atlantic fringe from Brazil through the Guianas to the Caribbean coast and islands received 90 percent of the trade.[10]

As examples of the proportions of Negro slaves in the New World by coastal region of origin, estimates for North America, Jamaica, and Saint Domingue (1751–1800) are given in table 1.2. It should be emphasized that these percentages are indeed estimates and should not be taken as hard and fast figures.

SLAVERY, FREEDOM, AND BLACK RELIGIONS

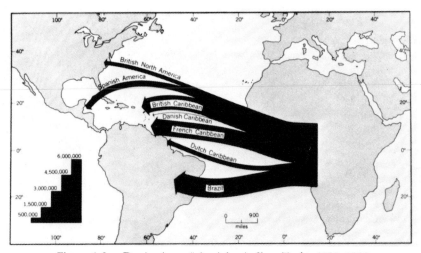

Figure 1.2. Destinations of the Atlantic Slave Trade, 1701–1810
Source: Figure by University of Wisconsin Cartographic Laboratory, data from table
65, Philip D. Curtin, *The Atlantic Slave Trade* (Madison: University of Wisconsin Press,
1969), p. 215. Used by permission of University of Wisconsin Press.

Treatment of Slaves in the New World

Slavery as an institution varied from the Latin to the Anglo-Saxon
areas of the colonial world and within each of those spheres. The controversy concerning the extent of these differences shows no signs of
abating.[11] Tannenbaum and others have claimed that slavery was harsher
in the English and Dutch colonies than in the Latin possessions.[12] In
this view—at least during the early years of slavery—the Spanish, Portuguese, and French governments supported attempts by the Catholic
church to ameliorate the system. The French and Spanish codes of the
seventeenth century prescribed baptism by the priests within a year of
the slaves' arrival from Africa. Also, matrimony between slaves was encouraged, the master of either husband or wife was required to purchase
a slave's mate, and the manumission of slaves was advocated. Confor-
mance, however, often fell short of the standards set in law and ethics.

Genovese points out that the number of priests was never adequate
to the task in Brazilian and Spanish American slave societies, that the
moral quality of the priests did not attain the level expected by Rome,

TABLE 1.2

	Speculative estimate, all slaves imported into North America, by origin (%)	Speculative estimate, slaves imported into Jamaica, 1655–1807, by origin	French slave exports from Africa, 1751–1800: Based on shipping data combined with population samples from St. Domingue
Senegambia	13.3	3.7	5.4
Sierre Leone	5.5	10.9*	0.9
Windward Coast	11.4		2.3
Gold Coast	15.9	25.5	6.4
Bight of Benin	4.3	13.8	28.0
Bight of Biafra	23.3	28.4	8.5
Angola	24.5	17.5	45.2
Mozambique-Madagascar	1.6	—	1.6
Unknown	0.2	0.3	1.6
Total	100.0	100.0	100.0

*Includes Sierre Leone and Windward Coast

SOURCE: Tables 45, 46, and 60. Philip D. Curtin, *The Atlantic Slave Trade* (Madison, 1969), 157, 160, 200. Used by permission of the University of Wisconsin.

and that the priest was subservient to the bishop or the *senhor;* but he agrees with Tannenbaum's assertation that Catholicism made a profound difference in the lives of the slaves. Genovese argues that,

Catholicism imparted to Brazilian and Spanish American slave societies an ethos . . . that profoundly reflected premodern, seigneurial rather than bourgeois ideas of property, class, status, and spiritual brotherhood. Accordingly, the white racism and cruel discrimination that inevitably accompanied the enslavement of black to white emerged against countervailing forces of genuine spiritual power. All the evidence now being accumulated to prove the existence and severity of white racism in Brazil cannot explain away the chasm that separates Brazil from the United States in rates of intermarriage, access of blacks to positions of respect and power, and the integration of people of color into a single nationality. Catholicism does not by itself account for the difference, but from the

SLAVERY, FREEDOM, AND BLACK RELIGIONS

8

beginning it played its part by the force of its impact on society as a whole.[13]

On the other side, instead of the slaves' being substantially affected by the intervention of church or state in the Latin territories, evidence has been cited to show that it was the interests of the colonial planters that counted most heavily in how the slaves were treated. At the middle of the nineteenth century, the reasoning of the slaveholders in Brazil, in the words of a contemporary, was quite straightforward:

> One buys a Negro for 300 milreis, who harvests in the course of the year 100 arrobas of coffee, which produces a net profit at least equal to the cost of the slave; thereafter everything is profit. It is not worth the trouble to raise children, who, only after sixteen years, will give equal service. Furthermore, the pregnant Negroes and those nursing are not available to use the hoe; heavy fatigue prevents the regular development of the fetus in some, in others the diminution of the flow of milk, and in almost all, sloppiness in the care of children, from which sickness and death of the poor children result.[14]

Whether slave owners in the highly capitalistic slavery of the United States generally used force optimally rather than maximally is controversial. In *Time on the Cross,* Fogel and Engerman argue that it was used optimally and for exactly the same purpose as such positive incentives as extra pay, prizes, gifts, bonuses, unscheduled holidays, patches of land for growing crops, working on own account, and limited promotions from one type of work to another on the plantation. Through the application of force and the use of pecuniary and nonpecuniary incentives, they assert, the businessmen who ran the plantations sought to achieve the largest product at the lowest cost. In his critique of *Time on the Cross,* Gutman questions the data Fogel and Engerman cite in support of their contention concerning the relative infrequency of whippings.[15]

In their reexamination of slavery, one school of economic historians presents a list of "corrections" of the traditional characterization of the slave economy, including the following: (1) The purchase of a slave was generally a highly profitable investment; (2) the slave system was not moribund in 1860; (3) slaves employed in industry compared favorably with free workers in diligence and efficiency; (4) the material (not psychological) conditions of the lives of slaves compared favorably with those of free industrial workers.[16]

The methods and the findings of the "cliometricians" are being debated. Haskell's comments on the inherent limitations of Fogel and Engerman's efficiency index are of special interest:

> One can grant that slavery was a profitable institution and that the Southern economy was thriving as a whole. One can also grant that Southern agricultural production was "efficient" in the narrow economic sense measured by the index. All three of these conditions are compatible with indifference and even "day-to-day resistance" by slave laborers. If the demand for cotton was sufficiently strong, even the most cumbersome production process might have yielded a net profit for planters, economic growth for the region, and a favorable "efficiency" rating for slave labor.[17]

Gutman insists that whatever importance *Time on the Cross* has as economic history, it is poor social history. In his view, it uses an inadequate model of slave socialization, and it contains important errors in its use of quantitative evidence essential to its main arguments. His critique sees the principal methodological flaw in the assumption that the existence of the economic factor is sufficient to explain behavior, whereas an adequate study would show the way in which Africans and their Afro-American descendants adapted to enslavement and the changing patterns of enslavement.[18]

The earlier closing of the slave trade may have made slavery milder in the United States than in Brazil in the nineteenth century. After the trade was closed, slavery could survive only so long as it could replenish itself, and that required some interest in the physical care of the slaves.[19]

One measure of well-being is the ability to survive and multiply. Data on natural increase or natural decrease of Afro-American populations during the period of slavery are incomplete, but some general trends are discernible. Conditions in the sugar islands—intense cultivation of the land, high ratios of African-born to total slave population, and high proportions of men to women in the slave group—tended to produce a natural decrease in the slave population. As a rule, this decrease was made up by slave imports from Africa. Later, the slave populations leveled off, and slave imports were only large enough to offset the difference between deaths and births. Still later (Barbados by 1810, Jamaica by the 1840s), the deficit disappeared, and the population began to grow even without further imports.[20]

Although census data are inadequate and the definition of "Negro" or "colored" varies, the broad pattern of Afro-American populations at the middle of the twentieth century is noteworthy (table 1.3). The United States imported less than 5 percent of the slaves, but in 1950 it had nearly one-third of the total Afro-American population. The Caribbean islands imported more than 40 percent of the slaves but now have about 20 percent of the Afro-American population. Specifically, Cuba received about 7 percent of the Atlantic slave trade, but the Negro and mulatto population in that country in 1953 was approximately 1.5 million, or about 3 percent of the Afro-American population of the New World. A more striking example is Saint Domingue. When the slave trade to that island ended in 1791, the total slave imports had been more than twice those of the United States, but the surviving slave population was only 480,000 compared with a slave population in the United States in 1861 of approximately 4.5 million.[21] Likewise, at the beginning of the nineteenth century, Brazil and the United States each had about a million slaves and later importations into Brazil were three times greater than into the United States, but in 1861 there were 4 million slaves in the United States compared with 1.5 million in Brazil.[22] Brazil imported approximately 38 percent of the slaves and now has about that proportion of the Afro-American population.[23] Mexico received an estimated 2.1 percent of the total slave imports during the period of the Atlantic slave trade, but in 1950 those of African descent constituted only .3 percent of the population. The biological and cultural absorption of the African component of the population has been much greater there than in Central America, where an estimated .3 percent of the slave trade to the New World was received in comparison to an estimated .5 percent of the population that was of African descent in 1950.[24]

It is not easy to judge the relative severity of slave systems. It may

TABLE 1.3
RELATION OF SLAVE IMPORTS TO POPULATION OF AFRICAN
DESCENT, C. 1950 (000 OMITTED)

Region and country	Estimated slave imports		Estimated population partly or entirely of African descent	
	No.	%	No.	%
United States & Canada	427	4.5	14,916	31.1
Middle America	224	2.4	342	0.7
Mexico			120	0.3
Central America			222	0.5
Caribbean Islands	4,040	43.0	9,594	20.0
South America	4,700	50.0	23,106	48.2
Surinam & Guyana			286	0.6
French Guiana			23	†
Brazil			17,529	36.6
Argentina, Uruguay, Paraguay, & Bolivia			97	0.2
Chile			4	†
Peru			110	0.2
Colombia, Panama, & Ecuador			3,437	7.2
Venezuela			1,620	3.4
Total	9,391	100.0*	47,958	100.0*

*Percentages have been rounded.
†Less than 0.05%.

SOURCES: Angel Rosenblat, *La población indígena y el mestizaje en América*, 2 vols. (Buenos Aires, 1954), 1:21; consolidation of data in Table 24, Philip D. Curtin, *The Atlantic Slave Trade* (Madison, 1969), 91. Used by permission of the University of Wisconsin.

be true that at some times and in some places slavery was milder in the Latin American colonies. Differences between the treatment of slaves in Latin America and the United States, however, may not have been greater than regional or temporal differences within the countries themselves. At times, an exploitive, capitalistic form of slavery was common in Brazil and Spanish America, and at times North Americans followed a paternalistic model and acknowledged the humanity of their slaves.

Negro slavery may have been, therefore, "a single phenomenon, or *Gestalt,* whose variations were less significant than underlying patterns of unity." [25]

The Slave Experience and the Religions of Blacks

Slavery, a vital fact of the experience of Afro-Americans, was a major force in shaping their religions. Likewise, religious beliefs and behavior were important in the adaptation of blacks to slavery. Blacks born in Africa underwent emotional shock when transplanted to a strange environment. Slaves were economically dependent upon and politically subordinate to the slave-owning class. Generally slaves were in poor health. Blacks, who were largely excluded from the world of the dominant group, found segments of traditional African cultures appealing. In parts of the Caribbean, the services of established churches were unavailable to slaves. In the Catholic countries, permission to organize religious fraternities along ethnic lines encouraged the perpetuation of African religious traditions. In the United States, the conditions under which participation in the rites of the historical churches were offered to slaves in the early part of the nineteenth century were unacceptable to certain black leaders. The existence of these conditions was an important factor behind the formation of the independent Negro churches.

Cult, Sect, Established Sect, Church

The term cult has at least three meanings. One type tends to be small, short-lived, concerned with searching for mystical experiences, and dominated by a charismatic leader such as Father Divine in the United States. A second type of cult appears as a hybrid religion, often during the early stages of a culture contact situation where it is impossible for the members of a subordinate group to reestablish their old religion intact, or to accept fully the religion of the dominant group and be accepted as coparticipants in that religion. Syncretistic religions such as the Neo-African cults, the less African "ancestral cults," the revivalist cults, and the spiritualist cults of the Caribbean and South America are of this type. The third type of cult appears when a society is undergoing severe reorganization and is involved with group as well as individual

SLAVERY, FREEDOM, AND BLACK RELIGIONS

stresses. The Ras Tafari movement of Jamaica and the Black Muslims in the United States are examples of religiopolitical cults.

By sect we shall mean "a religious protest against a system in which attention to the various individual functions of a religion has been obscured and made ineffective by the extreme emphasis on social and ecclesiastical order."[26] The principal instance of the sect in this work is Pentecostalism. The established sect is more inclusive, less alienated, and more structured than the sect. Examples of this religious type are the early Methodists, the Quakers, and the Mormons. With the exception of the early Methodists, this type of religious organization plays little part in this study.

The church is "a religious body that recognizes the strength of the secular world and, rather than either abandoning the attempt to influence it or losing its position by contradicting the secular powers directly, accepts the main elements in the social structure as proximate goods." Of the three widely recognized subtypes of the church—universal, ecclesiastical, and denominational or class—the Roman Catholic Church of the Caribbean and South America comes closest to illustrating a universal church as "a religious structure that is quite successful in supporting the integration of a complex society, while at the same time satisfying, by its patterns of beliefs and observances, many of the needs of individuals on all levels of society."[27] In the United States the Catholic Church became denominationalized to a significant degree by the middle of the twentieth century. As a type of religious organization, the ecclesia serves mainly the dominant elements in a society, thereby failing to meet the needs of large sections of the population, particularly the lower socioeconomic classes. Established national churches tend toward this type; the Anglican Church of the British Caribbean, from the middle of the seventeenth century through the mid-nineteenth century, came somewhat closer to this subtype than did the Lutheran Church of the Virgin Islands during the two and one-half centuries of Danish rule. Although the range among denominations is rather wide, the class church is conventional and respectable. In this book, the major denominations considered are the Moravians, Lutherans, Methodists, Baptists, and Presbyterians.

SLAVERY, FREEDOM, AND BLACK RELIGIONS

A Classification of Religious Cults in the Caribbean and South America

From the viewpoint of cultural content, religious cults in the Caribbean whose membership is made up entirely or mainly of black persons are classified here under five categories: (1) Neo-African religions, (2) ancestral cults, (3) revivalist cults, (4) spiritualist cults, and (5) religio-political cults. Neo-African cults, found in countries which are predominantly Catholic, have incorporated a considerable body of African traditions in their beliefs and rituals. Ancestral cults have fewer African components than those of the first type. Revivalist cults are descendants of the Afro-Protestant cults of the late eighteenth century and, in the case of Jamaica, of the Great Revival of 1861–1862. Spiritualism has been popular in Puerto Rico for nearly a century. Ras Tafari, a religio-political movement which began to take shape in Jamaica in the 1930s, is an offshoot of Marcus Garvey's Universal Negro Improvement Association. A classification of religious cults in the Caribbean is shown in table 1.4.

Although the classification that I use for the Caribbean may be applied to South America, not all of the types are found among the religions we consider there. No instances of revivalism, ancestral cults,

TABLE 1.4
RELIGIOUS CULTS OF THE CARIBBEAN

Neo-African Cults	Ancestral Cults	Revivalist Cults	Spiritualist Cults	Religio-Political Cults
Vodun (Haiti)	Cumina (Jamaica)	Revival Zion (Jamaica)	Spiritualists (Puerto Rico)	Ras Tafari (Jamaica)
Shango (Trinidad)	Convince (Jamaica)	Shouters (Trinidad)		Dreads (Dominica)
Shango (Grenada)	Big Drum (Grenada and Carriacou)	Shakers (St. Vincent)		
Santeria (Cuba)	Kele (St. Lucia)	Streams of Power (St. Vincent)		
	Black Carib (Belize)			

or of religio-political cultism are cited for South America. Spiritualism is represented by Umbanda in Brazil and the cult of María Lionza in Venezuela, and Neo-African and African-derived religions by a number of cults. Although the Batuque of Belém is derived ultimately from African religions, it has become so Brazilianized that the Leacocks regard it as an independent cult. The application of the classification to South America is shown in table 1.5.

TABLE 1.5
RELIGIOUS CULTS OF SOUTH AMERICA

Neo-African Cults	African-Derived Cults	Spiritualist Cults	Independent Cult
Dahomean and Yoruban (San Luiz, Maranhão, Brazil)	Spirit cult (San Antônio, Maranhão, Brazil)	Umbanda (Brazil) María Lionza (Venezuela)	Batuque (Belém, Brazil)
Candomblé (Bahia, Brazil)	Yoruban-derived (San Luiz, Maranhão, Brazil)		
Xangó (Recife, Brazil)	Macoumba (Rio de Janeiro, Brazil)		
Pará (Porto Alegre, Brazil)	Boni (French Guiana)		
Winti (Surinam)			

In chapters 2–6, I contrast the experience of blacks in the historical churches of the Caribbean and South America and in a number of cults and sects which have arisen in those areas since the beginning of the colonial period. In chapter 9, I point out some of the differences between the religions of blacks in the United States and in the Caribbean and South America.

The Development of Caribbean and South American Religious Cults

I attribute the emergence and continuation of religious cults in the Caribbean largely to the interaction of three major factors—cultural, structural or socioeconomic, and psychological. The cultural variable consists of elements of traditional African religions and of Christianity which were syncretized in different ways in various cult groups during the slavery period and later. The second major factor affecting the development of these cults is the social structure of the areas. Most of the devotees of the cults and sects have been dispossessed and powerless—slaves, peasants, low-income, or unemployed people. The third major variable explaining the existence of these cults consists of certain psychological processes—especially the compensatory tendencies, visionary experiences, and inner urges to attain personal or group goals which seem to characterize the behavior of leaders.

Other factors which have influenced the fate of Caribbean religious cults include ecological position, especially the degree of the members' isolation; the amount of continuing contact with Africa; continuity of leadership; group cohesiveness; and the existence of rival cults. The importance of these major and contingent factors is explained in chapter 3.

Psychological and Social Functions of Religous Cults and Sects

Black religious cults and sects in the New World offer rewards of considerable value to their adherents, many of whom are dispossessed persons without rank or power in the societies in which they live.

Religious ceremonies take believers away from the mundane affairs of life and are often exhilarating experiences. The rites take place under optimal conditions: the participants are dressed in ceremonial garb or in immaculate white clothing, the sacred objects are prominently displayed, the familiar and emotionally charged songs are sung, and portions of well-known myths are recited or favorite biblical passages are read or quoted. A well-performed religious cult ceremony in the Caribbean or in South America provides dramatic entertainment for participants. Moreover, some believers gain "understanding" through being possessed by a deity, an ancestor, or some other spirit.

For the rank-and-file participants, *social* consensus, based on such ritual actions as providing offerings for the gods and the dead, dancing, speaking in unknown tongues, singing, and asking the spirits for assistance, does not evoke explanations about supernatural phenomena but leads directly to highly patterned ceremonial behavior. For the leading figures in the group, however, these and other ritual elements are not simply signs or signals which guide them step by step in the performance of the rites. Because of their greater concern with the intricacies of the belief system, these more sophisticated members have elaborated a symbolic, logical, and esthetic structure. Although *cultural* consensus among them is incomplete, there is enough agreement to make communication and discussion possible.[28]

Taking part in the activities of a cult or sect provides emotional support for members who are forced to live in a world that they often perceive as hostile. At the same time, they compete for position within their religious group. In the revivalist cults of the Caribbean, for instance, a major gain from "mourning" and "building" (optional advanced rituals) for persons of low socioeconomic standing is the increased recognition they get because of the physical hardships they have endured, as well as for the accounts which they give publicly of their visions, spiritual travels to distant lands, and other wonderful mystical experiences. One mourns and builds to "take a higher degree." For the ambitious, successful experiences in the "sacred chamber" validate each step up the ladder of the revivalist hierarchy. In many cases, healing services are offered by cult or sect officers, and material aid may be available in time of dire need.

Participation in cults has its costs as well as its gains. Some devotees contribute a substantial part of their economic resources to the upkeep of cult centers and, for some members, cult activities may be emotionally disturbing. The expenditure of time, effort, and money on cult affairs reduces or eliminates the possibility of active participation by cult members in political affairs. For most, however, the advantages of belonging to a cult or sect seem to overshadow the disadvantages.

Spirit Possession

According to traditional religious belief in many parts of the world, the behavior of a devotee during trance in a religious ceremony is due to his being possessed by a god, a dead ancestor, or some other spirit. Such beliefs were brought from parts of West Africa to the New World, where in almost unmodified or modified form they still have a prominent place in black folk religions. In some South American religious cults, similar beliefs have been derived from American Indian traditions, or from both Indian and African beliefs. This phenomenon is discussed more fully in chapter 4, but brief mention of it here seems appropriate because of its importance in a number of Caribbean and South American cults.

During trance an alteration of consciousness occurs which brings physiological and psychological changes in the individual. These changes may affect sensory impressions, memory functions, and concepts in identity. In addition to possession trance, the hallucinatory or visionary trance in which a spirit reveals a message but does not invade and take over the personality of the believer is a minor aspect of some New World religious cults.

Spirit possession does not always involve full dissociation. Possessed persons may experience profound states of unconsciousness or be only partially unconscious. Likewise, some participants pass through two or three stages in possession trance. Regardless of individual and group variations, possession behavior is not spontaneous and idiosyncratic behavior. It is culturally structured, and devotees learn the proper ways of acting when seized by a spirit. Some members of a cult group never become visibly possessed, but they may be mildly possessed "internally." Those whose possessions are observable anticipate being visited by particular spirits during a ceremony and their behavior is in accord with cult beliefs concerning the character and temperament of these spirits.

Blacks in the Historical Churches, Sects, and Cults
of the United States, Canada, and England

Important demographic differences existed between the slave-importing countries of the Caribbean and South America on one hand and the United States on the other. Blacks were the overwhelming majority of the population of the Caribbean during the colonial period, but they constituted a minority of the population of the North American colonies. Plantations in the Caribbean were larger than in the United States. At the end of the eighteenth century, the average sugar plantation in Jamaica was staffed with about 180 slaves; in Virginia and Maryland the average plantation had less than 13 slaves. Because of the smaller percentage of whites living in the Caribbean islands and because of the size of the typical sugar plantation, blacks there had less contact with European culture. Also, through the end of the eighteenth century and the beginning of the nineteenth century, the large majority of the slave populations of the British and French islands were African-born. In the North American colonies, the slaves born in Africa made up only 20 percent of the black population by the end of the American Revolution. By 1860, 99 percent of the slaves in the United States were native-born, and most of them were second- to fifth-generation Americans. These persons had not had any personal contact with Africa, and most of them had no acquaintance with those who did have such contact.[29] These demographic differences help to account for the persistence of a larger number of Africanisms in the religious life of blacks in the Caribbean and in South America.

Evangelical religion appealed to the untutored masses, white and black, on the colonial frontier in North America. During the Great Awakenings (1720–1740 and 1790–1815) the Methodists and the Baptists converted large numbers of Negroes. The major independent Negro churches were not formed until the period 1816 to 1825, and in basic doctrine and ritual they differed little from the denominations from which they originated.

In racially segregated communities in the United States, the Negro church has served as a clearing house for innumerable activities. Vigorous protest against racial discrimination has never been an outstanding characteristic of the Negro church, but it has emphasized social reform somewhat more than has been the case elsewhere in the New World.

During the early part of the twentieth century, a multitude of sects and cults evolved among black people in the United States, particularly among recent migrants to the cities. The Holiness and Pentecostal sects attracted the largest number of black followers. About sixty years ago the Pentecostal movement divided along racial lines, and numerous variations of black Pentecostalism appeared. Cults of the type of Father Divine's Peace Mission flourished in the early part of the twentieth century, as did groups of Black Jews in Harlem. Various Moorish or Islamic cults arose in American cities from the 1920s on, and thousands of small storefront cults prospered by combining deviations from the Christian tradition with healing, counseling, and magical charms.

Black churches in Canada have almost always been conservative theologically and socially. The majority of Canadian Negroes have belonged to the Baptist church, and few cults have appeared. Never outstanding, the Negro church in Canada in the 1970s was moribund.

West Indians who migrate to England seldom join the historical churches, but those who were members of a religious sect in the Caribbean are likely to seek out and join some religious group in Britain. Pentecostal churches are the most popular. Segmentation and proliferation of groups has promoted the growth of these black churches.

CHAPTER TWO

The Caribbean:
Blacks in the Historical Churches

NEARLY ALL of the studies of religions in the Caribbean have been separate accounts of major denominations, esoteric groups, or syncretistic
cults. Most of these reports have lacked the historical or the comparative
dimension—or both. This chapter and the following two provide a historical perspective on religious developments in the region and indicate
some of the important relationships that have existed there among many
of the religions of the past and the present.[1]

In the Latin colonies of the Caribbean, Catholic missionaries baptized and served large numbers of African slaves. In these countries Protestant ministers had little success until relatively recent years.

In the British possessions the Church of England was the religion of
white settlers and officials in the seventeenth and eighteenth centuries; it
was not a missionary church for the slaves.[2] The arduous work of the
Nonconformist missionaries, especially the Baptists and the Methodists,
during those centuries resulted in the conversion of only a small minority of the slaves in the non-Catholic countries. In Jamaica, the Native
Baptists were without serious competition for forty years (1780–1820) as
George Gibb, Moses Baker, and other subordinates in George Lisle's
"leader system" founded their own groups and as these split into still more
new cult groups. During this period a reinterpretation of Christianity

spread throughout the island, and by 1830 the Native Baptists had become "another religion competing with the Christianity of the European missionaries."[3]

Because they were not exposed to Christian doctrine, were only partially instructed, or were not welcomed as participants, many persons of African descent in the West Indies never became members of the churches established by whites. Instead, they participated regularly or occcasionally in syncretistic cults or independent religious movements.

The Roman Catholic Church: Haiti and Grenada

In 1667 Father du Tertre, a priest who came to the Antilles in 1640, asserted: "There is scarcely a Negro in all the French Antilles that is not a Christian, scarcely one that they [the missionaries] have not regenerated in the waters of Baptism." Du Tertre claimed that more than 15,000 slaves had already been baptized in the French islands; he claimed also that these slaves went to Mass, Confession, and Holy Communion.[4] In 1685, the "Code Noir" prescribed that all slaves in the French islands were to be baptized and given instruction in the Catholic religion.

In Haiti, the colonists ignored all parts of the Code Noir, including the sections dealing with religious obligations, that were contrary to their economic interests. Plantation owners were indifferent rather than antagonistic toward the priests, unless they showed a strong interest in the slaves' welfare. Some priests were not too zealous about their duties and attended only to the external aspects of religion. Because the Jesuits were thought to be stirring up the slaves, the members of that order were expelled from the colony in 1764. A report to Rome in 1794 stated that "since the expulsion of the Jesuits, the curés have for the most part led lives so indecent . . . that the citizens and Negroes have lost all the sentiments of religion which the Jesuits gave them." Leyburn comments that while there had been distinguished churchmen in Saint-Domingue before 1750, none appeared thereafter.[5]

From the formation of the Republic of Haiti in 1803 until 1858, a schism existed between the state and the Roman Catholic Church. The Constitution of 1805 provided for the complete separation of church and state, granting freedom to all religions and denying support to any denomination. The Church in Rome refused to recognize Haiti as a state and forbade priests to enter the country. With the passing of time, the people grew farther and farther away from a Catholicism which necessarily had not developed deep roots. Religion in Haiti during the 55 years of the schism "was a strange gallimaufry of Catholicism and folk belief." During those years vodun grew rapidly, and from 1847 to 1859 it "flourished with official approval."[6]

A Concordat was approved in Rome in April 1860, ending the long break between the Catholic Church and the Haitian state. With the consecration of an archbishop of Port-au-Prince the Church was again established as the official church of Haiti. The new Catholic priests encountered no hostility, but they were faced with "an ineradicable folk religion" which had grown up alongside Catholicism. Despite campaigns that have since been waged against vodun from time to time, this is still largely the situation. In the late 1930s a foreign observer concluded that Roman Catholicism plays "as large and as small a part in the thinking of the Haitian upper classes as among members of upper-class French society. . . . It is considered proper to attend Mass and otherwise to pay respect to religious forms; actually one loses nothing in prestige if he is not a practicing Christian."[7]

Grenada, one of the Windward Islands in the eastern Caribbean, was "ceded" by the Carib Indians to the French West Indies Company in 1650 and in 1674 the island came under the domination of the French Crown. The English captured it in 1763, and for sixteen years the British Government permitted Catholics on Grenada to practice their religion without interference. The island was recaptured by the French in 1779, but it was permanently ceded to England by the Treaty of Versailles in 1783. At that time French churches and church lands were taken over and given to the Protestant churches and to the Crown. The rights and privileges of Catholicism were abolished.[8]

Although the end of the eighteenth-century and the beginning of the nineteenth century was a troubled period for the Catholic Church in Grenada, in 1814 Bishop Poynter wrote concerning the work of Abbé Planquais: "In this island there are three chapels and one in a neighboring island called Carriacou, in which this priest exercises the offices of the sacred ministry. He tells me that they are nearly all Catholics in this island, consisting for the most part of negro slaves, that they are pious and devout, but absolutely wanting in instruction, which he with the utmost zeal is striving to give them." [9] Hard times continued for the Catholic Church in the decade 1816–1827. A petition in November 1822, to the House of Assembly for some sort of financial assistance was disregarded. In 1823, all but £2,500 of the appropriations for religion were allocated to the five clergymen of the Established Church and their clerks, who were, Devas asserted, "ministering by comparison to a mere handful of people, though including the wealthy, throughout the Colony." Relenting in 1838, the Assembly voted £500 to Father O'Hannan in remuneration for his labors, including visits to different parts of the island and for his "advice and religious instruction to the negro population which had greatly contributed to their present peaceable condition." [10] By 1842, Catholic priests were again allowed legally to officiate at marriages, baptisms, and burials—rituals which had been the exclusive right of the clergy of the Church of England.

During the difficult days for the Catholic Church in Grenada in the late eighteenth and early nineteenth centuries, the priests established several schools. Although a central school and many other parochial schools were being assisted by the Government, the Catholic schools in St. George's were not given a grant until 1837. The other five Catholic schools around the island depended entirely upon the voluntary contributions of church members, most of whom had only recently been emancipated. When the grant-in-aid system was inaugurated in 1852, the grant to Catholic schools was trebled. At that time there were nineteen Anglican, one Presbyterian, four Wesleyan, and eight Catholic schools, including one established that year in Carriacou. In 1857, the first Board of Education was formed, consisting of five Protestants and two Catholics. But in 1863 the Catholics addressed an appeal to the Secretary of State for the Colonies concerning the unequal distribution of educational grants. In 1875, a law was passed giving aid to the 24 schools in the Colony. [11]

Explaining in 1932 why the reader finds nothing in his book on the Catholic Church in Grenada about Obeah, Shango, or African dances, Devas says:

THE CARIBBEAN

But why should there be? Would a History of the Church, say in the Isle of Man, devote any space to spiritualism, necromancy, or any other form of superstition? Hardly. There is, however, this difference, I suppose, that unlike the Isle of Man (I hope!), so-called Catholics in Grenada still, alas, often relapse into one or other or all of the above-named pagan practices handed down by their forefathers.[12]

The Roman Catholic Church: Jamaica and St. Lucia

Anthony Quigly, the first Catholic priest to serve in Jamaica, came to the island in 1792. Delany attributes this "first installment of freedom of worship" granted to the Catholics of Jamica to the influence of trade—to the increased number of Catholics from other islands and from South America who were settling in Jamaica for commercial purposes. The majority of the Catholics under the care of the Irish Franciscan Friar were either French or Spanish.[13]

In 1829, Father Benito Fernandez, a Spanish priest who came to Jamaica from Colombia in 1812, reported:

> Our congregation consists of Spaniards, French, Dutch, some Italians, and a few Irishmen, scarcely twelve in number. We, however, are endeavoring to do all we can for the advancement of religion, conforming to the rites of the Church, and in keeping with the few means afforded by the condition of the country and the fervor of the parishioners. We have just finished a work on our chapel which will render it much more roomy than before, and it is now sufficiently large to celebrate the divine services with the solemnity and decorum that become them.[14]

Although Roman Catholics constitute only 7 percent of the population today, the church is influential in Jamaican life. It is predominantly urban, with 70 percent of its members residing in Kingston and the surrounding urban area.[15]

The first attempt to settle St. Lucia, one of the Windward Islands, was made by Englishmen in 1605. Fighting over the island between England and France recurred for more than two hundred years. A final cession to England was made in 1814.

According to Breen, Catholic missionaries in St. Lucia were not greatly concerned about the ordinary people of that island during the early decades of the nineteenth century.

> Some of the priests are zealous and attentive; but their zeal and attention are confined within the walls of the church. They catechise and instruct on the week-days, but the Negro cannot quit his work. They preach on the Sundays and holydays, but then the church is crowded, and the devotee who has a seat and understands French may profit by the sermon, while the peasant, who stands at the door, either does not hear one word, or, if he hears, does not understand. . . . In former times the Christian missionary was to be seen travelling in every direction in search of spiritual patients, and he deemed it not derogatory to his calling to court acquaintance with the lowest haunts of ignorance and vice; but in these days of selfishness and sound, he is castled up in towns and cities, surrounded by the fashionable follies of the rich, inaccessible to the vulgar vices of the poor.[16]

French influence on the development of St. Lucia during the latter part of the nineteenth century and in the twentieth century was very great, evidenced in part by the preponderance of the Roman Catholic Church.

The Anglican Church

Although the slaves of the French Antilles in the seventeenth century were allowed, and often encouraged, to become Christians and to practice their religion, a different situation existed in other parts of the West Indies. In Barbados, the early slaves were not permitted to become Christians, and in Antigua and St. Eustatius baptism was denied slaves until they were in danger of death—and it was not always obtainable then.[17] In 1700 the Anglicans organized the Society for the Propagation of the Gospel in Foreign Parts to preach to the heathen—slaves and free men—in North America and the West Indies.[18] The Society held a trust estate and slaves in Barbados, and for many years supported a catechist to train its own slaves in religion and to conduct services for them. Many of the Society's slaves were only nominal Christians, and by 1784, the mission had come to be regarded as a failure.[19]

Between 1745 and 1784, the Bishop of London, who claimed ecclesiastical jurisdiction over the West Indies, licensed 106 clergymen for the region. Twenty-nine churchmen were assigned to Jamaica, fourteen to Antigua, thirty-five to Barbados, ten to St. Kitts, six to Dominica, four to Grenada, three to Monserrat, two each to Nevis and Tobago and one to St. Vincent. Actually the bishop had no way of directing the clergy's work and his right to exert any control was challenged by local laws.[20]

The Church of England in Jamaica in the eighteenth century was the religion of the white settlers and officials; it was not a missionary church for the slaves. It was regarded

> as little more than a respectable and ornamental adjunct of the State, the survival of a harmless home instituion which would cease to be tolerated if it showed any signs of energy or activity outside its own particular groove. The Church at home was willing to provide chaplains for white settlers, but its missionary zeal in the first half of the eighteenth century was only beginning. C.M.S [Church Missionary Society] did not then exist, and S.P.G. [Society for Propagating the Gospel] . . . had for its object to establish and conduct missions in foreign parts. Jamica was not foreign; it was a British colony. The probability is that the Bishops of London in sending clergy gave no instructions as to missionary work among negroes, about whom they cared little or nothing, but . . . exercised in many cases their office or patronage to oblige a friend or to find a home and an income for some family encumbrance.[21]

At this time the Assembly in Jamaica was made up almost entirely of slaveowners and those who were sympathetic with slavery. These persons believed that the teachings of Christianity produced feelings of disaffection, and they attributed the more or less severe slave outbreaks that occurred about every five years to these teachings.[22] Since West Indian planters opposed any activity that might stimulate unrest among the blacks, any religious work among them had to be sponsored by groups that had outside support.[23] The few Anglican clergymen who showed an interest in the slaves were treated in much the same manner as the dissenters. For preaching two sermons in 1800 urging slaveholders to adopt equitable measures for dealing with their workers, a Dominican rector was summoned before the local council and soon resigned his post and left the island. A local paper called him "a diminutive wolf in sheep's clothing."[24]

THE CARIBBEAN

Although the Jamaican population of 400,000 was almost half of the total of the British West Indies in 1800, there were only twenty Anglican churches in the island. The places of worship were small and probably not more than 300 persons attended religious services each Sunday. In 1788 one writer commented that "the planters seem to have no religion at all."[25]

Some Anglican ministers had as many as 18,000 persons, white and black, in their parishes. To the suggestion that he instruct slaves, the rector of Clarendon Parish, Jamaica, replied: "I have little more time than sufficient to discharge the common functions of my office, in burying, marrying, christening, and attending on Sundays my church, which is situated at least ten miles from my rectory." In some islands rectors were required by law to devote two hours every Sunday to instructing the slaves in religion, but these laws were not enforced.[26] During the eighteenth century many of the churches were seldom opened; in 1811 the Lieutenant Governor of Jamaica reported that many of the clergy refused to officiate at a church service when no white person was present.[27]

In addition to clerical understaffing and lack of interest in the slaves on the part of most of the clergy, many of the rectors were incompetent or dissolute. An eighteenth-century writer described the majority of the Anglican clergy as being "of a character so vile that I do not care to mention it; for, except for a few, they are generally the most finished of all debauchees."[28]

Many clergymen in the British West Indies held civil and political offices—commissions of the peace, appointments as Councillors, and seats in the Assembly. Most of the regular clergymen shared the views of the dominant class. The organizers of new missionary movements, including the Society for the Conversion and Religious Instruction and Education of the Negro Slaves in the British West Indian Islands, sought the approval of the governing classes. Through its President, Bishop Porteus, in 1794 this organization sent copies of its charter and a letter of explanation about its proposed policies to the islands. According to this letter, all missionaries and teachers sent out by the Society would be told " 'to confine themselves to the proper Business of their Mission, and not to meddle with the political and commercial concerns of the Island,

nor to give the least Offence or Umbrage in any respect to the Proprietors or the Established Clergy.' " The letter said further that religious
instruction would cause the planters' slaves " 'to be faithful, honest,
quiet, peaceable, diligent, humble, submissive, and obedient to their
Masters.' "[29]

The temper of early-nineteenth-century Jamaica was reflected in a
resolution of the Assembly in 1815 to consider at its next meeting the
state of religion among the slaves, and especially to investigate the "dark
and dangerous fanaticism of the Methodists, Moravians, and Baptists."
Rather than abandon the 350,000 slaves in the island to the dissenters,
the Jamaican legislature enacted a law in 1816 providing for the ap-
pointment of Anglican curates to instruct the Africans. Clerical assistants were to teach the slaves on Sunday afternoons and on two other
days on estates where the owner's permission had been obtained. The
minister was to receive a fee for each slave who was baptized and registered as a member of the Church. One rector baptized and registered
5,000 of the 24,000 blacks in his parish in six months. Slaves regarded
baptism as a charm against sorcery, and many were baptized several
times. Within a short time, this program ended in failure.[30]

In 1823, the British Government attempted to inject some vitality
into the Anglican Church in the West Indies. Two new bishoprics were
established, one for Jamaica, the Bahamas, and Honduras; the other for
the Leeward Islands. In addition, a special grant provided the new
bishops with funds for work with the slave populations. Also at this
time, Anglican societies, including the Church Missionary Society, the
British and Foreign Bible Society, and the Society for the Conversion
and Religous Instruction of the Negro Slaves in the British West Indies,
were becoming interested in the slave population of the West Indies.[31]

Between 1824 and 1832, thirteen Anglican churches were built in
Jamaica, and nine were under construction, with funds provided by the
Assembly and the vestries. In the Diocese, there were 45 clergymen, 32
catechists and school masters, and instruction in religion was being
given to slaves on 280 estates. It was claimed that on 70 of these estates
more than 18,000 slaves were receiving instruction.[32]

The years 1831–1834 were critical ones in the slavery period. Slave
uprisings in Cornwall in 1831 led to the proclamation of martial law

throughout Jamaica. Teachers of religion were persecuted by the planters, but most of their hostility was directed toward the Nonconformist missionaries. An Anglican church historian has claimed that during these years the Church of England ministers and teachers did not incite to rebellion but worked quietly at gaining power and influence over the people.[33]

The Jamaican Assembly protested that the Emancipation Act passed in London on August 28, 1833, was unconstitutional, but in the end accepted it and apprenticeship began in 1834. After 1834, the churches in Jamaica competed for followers among the freedpersons, and the Assembly provided more generously than it had in the past for churches and schools.[34]

At the time of the inauguration of Crown Government in 1865, the population of Jamaica was estimated at 480,000 and the position of the various religious bodies was as follows:

	Accommodation	Average Attendance
Church of England	48,824	36,300
Wesleyan	41,775	37,570
Baptist	31,640	26,483
Presbyterian	12,575	7,955
Moravian	11,850	9,650
London Missionary Society	8,050	6,780
Roman Catholic	4,110	1,870
American Mission	1,550	775
Church of Scotland	1,000	450
Hebrew	1,000	500
	162,374	128,333

Disestablishment of the Church of England was accomplished in most of the colonies between 1868 and 1870, but in Barbados the legislature refused to take this action. In Trinidad the Church of England and the Catholic Church both received grants from the government; in British Guiana the Church of England, the Presbyterians, and the Dutch Reformed Church had all received subsidies, and these arrangements were continued.[35]

In 1898, an Anglican writer asserted that the Baptists had found that it was dangerous to admit blacks too rapidly to the pastorate or the responsibility of congregations, and that the Methodists had had a similar experience. On the other hand, he claimed that the Anglicans had made quiet advances by means of minor orders: cathechists, lay readers, Sunday School teachers, schoolmasters, church officers, and workers in missionary and temperance societies. In time, he thought, training in these posts would provide a corps of people who could make the Church self-sufficient. In addition, he favored "elasticity in worship." To offset the greater appeal which many observers believed the Moravian and Methodist, as well as the Catholic, modes of worship had for West Indian Negroes, Caldecott advocated some modification in the eighteenth-century Anglican type of worship to suit the "special features in West Indian character and West Indian circumtances."[36]

The Moravian Brethren

New efforts at Christianizing the slaves in the West Indies were started in the second third of the eighteenth century. Three groups undertook this work: the United Brethren, or Moravians, from Germany; the Methodists from England; and the Baptists from North America. The first Moravian missionaries in the West Indies were David Nitschmann, a Moravian carpenter from Zauchtenthal and Leonard Dober, a Lutheran potter from Wurtemberg. They arrived in St. Thomas in the Virgin Islands on December 13, 1732.[37]

The work of the first Moravian missionaries began quietly and pleasantly. Public meetings were not allowed, so Nitschmann and Dober both worked as carpenters and visited the homes of the slaves after dark. The official language of St. Thomas was Danish, but the Negroes spoke Creole and the Brethren spoke "in a jargon of Dutch and German." Despite the problems of communication, the missionaries made it clear that "Christ had died for blacks as well as whites [and] the poor slaves clapped their hands for joy." Dober remarked that the slaves "felt the truth rather than understood it."[38]

One of the five points given by Count Nikolaus von Zinzendorf, a German religious and social reformer and the founder of the Moravian missions, when he addressed the converts at a mass meeting in St. Thomas in 1739 was a justification of slavery. He exhorted the converts to "be true to your husbands and wives and obedient to your masters and bombas [foremen]. The Lord has made all ranks—kings, masters, servants, and slaves. God punished the first negroes by making them slaves, and your conversion will make you free, not from the control of your masters, but simply from your wicked habits and thoughts, and all that makes you dissatisfied with your lot." Zinzendorf did not favor the emancipation of the slaves. With other theologians, he held that "the negroes were descended from the Canaanites. The whole argument . . . ran as follows: Ham insulted his father Noah. For this sin, Ham's descendants, the Canaanites, were condemned to slavery. The Negroes were descended from the Canaanites. Therefore, slavery is a Divine institution." Zinzendorf even opposed teaching the slaves to read and write.[39]

In the beginning, the Brethren met considerable opposition from the planters. On one occasion a missionary named Martin and one of his co-workers were imprisoned because Martin had married his co-worker, Freundlich, to a free mulatto. Such an act was unlawful at that time and strengthened the belief of whites that "the Brethren were not only fanatical visionaries but were also seriously planning to carry through a social revolution." In a memorandum sent to Governor Moth on February 23, 1739, the planters asserted that "when the Moravians get permission to spread their harmful doctrine" it was to be feared "that our slaves might revolt against us and murder us." The government in Copenhagen paid little attention to the planters' opposition. For example, the missionary Feder was given permission to work with Martin provided "that he does not interfere with followers of other confessions but confines his work to those Negroes who of their own free will will be instructed by him." The officials on St. Thomas were told to protect Feder and Martin "as long as they do not exceed the already designated royal limits."[40] Despite the early opposition encountered by the Brethren, the zeal of the missionaries, aided by the friendly assistance received from the Danish government and some of the planters, resulted in the rapid growth of the mission after 1740. In 1774 the King of Denmark issued an edict in support of the Brethren. The cost in lives of the early missionaries, however, was high. In St. Thomas alone during the first fifty years, illnesses led to the deaths of one hundred and sixty missionaries.[41]

Under the leadership of Martin Mack, a Moravian missionary from

1762 to 1784, a system of using "native helpers" was quite successful. An outstanding example was a slave named Cornelius, a stonemason who had purchased his own freedom. This man preached in Creole, Dutch, English, and Danish, and his sermons and conduct were reported to be on a high level.[42]

Most of the planters in the British West Indies despised the first Moravian missionaries, but on each island there were a few who were deeply interested in missionary work among the slaves. Most of the governors and higher officials were favorably disposed toward the missions. The Brethren missionaries built their first stations on the estates of sympathetic planters. Some of these churchmen were given tracts of land, became plantation operators themselves, and preached mainly to their own slaves.[43]

Moravian missionaries arrived in Jamaica in 1754 and were the first to attempt seriously to Christianize the slaves of that island. The Brethren accepted a gift of the estate of New Carmel from absentee planters on the condition that they would also work among the slaves on four other estates belonging to the same owners.[44] But the Brethren had greater success on some of the other islands; by 1800 they had baptized less than one thousand Negroes in all of Jamaica.[45]

The Brethren's first efforts in Jamaica were a failure for several reasons: the slaves disliked most of the missionaries because they preached the Gospel to them on Sunday but punished them for laziness at other times; the missionaries "lost caste" because they earned their own living; the multiplicity of rules laid down by Christian Rauch, originally an inspector sent by Zinzendorf but later director of the mission, was deeply resented; and the missionaries' incidence of illness and death was high.[46]

In the tense period in Jamaica prior to emancipation, the Moravians, who had always stressed law and order, were charged with being seditious. Following a report by a Committee of Inquiry, the House of Assembly issued a declaration that the preaching and teaching of Moravians and Methodists had a seditious tendency. In reply, the Moravians issued a statement concerning the teaching of their converts and the behavior of these persons during the rebellion that was so convincing the Brethren were then praised for their loyalty.[47]

After his visit to Jamaica in 1887, J. A. Froude asserted that the

Moravians had greater influence over the islanders than either the Anglicans or the Nonconformists, and added that they did the most good. According to Hutton, if that conclusion was correct, it could be accounted for by the Moravians' stricter discipline and high ethical standards, as well as the closer attention they paid to the individual, their study of the people's social requirements, and their great stress on education.[48]

A mission station established by the Brethren in St. John's, Antigua, in 1756 eventually became quite successful, as did a settlement at Bassetere, St. Kitts, in 1774. The mission established in Barbados in 1765, and another at Tobago in 1790, were much less successful.[49] The hurricane which devastated Antigua in 1772 is said to have caused a religious awakening among the slaves and to have brought many new adherents to the Moravians. With Nathaniel Gilbert's death soon after the hurricane, the Methodists' work, which had met with great success, declined. Meanwhile the Moravian cause proceeded energetically. In 1775 the Unitas Fratrum had more than 2,000 members in Antigua; by 1793 it was estimated that more than 5,000 Negroes, one-sixth of the total population, were under the care of the Moravian Brethren.[50] According to church records, 9,609 adults and 2,178 children had received baptism in Antigua from the estabishment of the mission to the middle of 1798. By 1795 the Brethren had obtained permission to preach on 52 plantations in St. Kitts, and the number in their congregation had risen to 1,689.[51]

A paragraph concerning the work of the Moravian missionaries quoted by Edwards from his abridgement of the 1787 report of the Lords of the Committee of the Council of the Legislature of Antigua on the slave trade throws some light on the strict code of the Brethren.

> The believing negroes are not suffered to attend any where, where the unconverted meet for the sake of feasting, dancing, gaming, etc. and the usual plea *of not entering into the sinful part of these diversions,* is never admitted, inasmuch as the least step towards vice and immorality, generally plunges them by degrees into gross sins. The hankering after the vain traditions of their forefathers, is considered as a falling off from that love to the Lord Jesus and his doctrines, which once prompted them to forsake all ungodliness, and devote themselves unto God; and if they persist in evil ways, the faithfulness due to the rest of the flock on the part of the missionaries, demands their separation, lest they seduce others.[52]

In Paramaribo, Dutch Guiana, in the first half of the nineteenth century, blacks frequently formed associations. In an effort to keep the town Negroes from the public-houses and gambling establishments, the Brethren organized a large number of Christian clubs. These clubs also served to raise money for religious and charitable purposes. There was a society for the poor, a sick club, an insurance society, Young Men's and Young Women's Christian Associations, prayer unions, singing clubs, and a reading society. According to Hutton, the clubs in Paramaribo became almost as important as the Church. Another special circumstance in Surinam was the disagreement between the Government and the missionaries over language. The Government would not provide state-aid unless the teachers used and taught the Dutch language. Since the missionaries spoke Negro-English, a pidgin language, they could not at first comply. Although the Brethren brought a few headmasters from Holland, their schools never achieved the success of those in the West Indies.[53]

At the request of the Dutch Government, the Brethren revived their work among the Bush Negroes (descendants of fugitive slaves) who lived along four rivers: the Surinam, the Saramacca, the Coppername, and the Cottica. In the region on the Surinam where the Saramakkers lived the climate was so bad that the missionaries could pay only short visits, leaving most of the work to local helpers. A missionary's widow, Mrs. Hartmann, was an exception to that rule; she lived alone among the people and taught Bible history in many villages. Among the Matuaris of the Saramacca river the chief preacher for 37 years (1862–1899) was a local evangelist, John King. By 1922, most of those of African descent in Paramaribo were Christians, but most of those who lived along the four rivers were still "heathen." Their resistance to Christianity was due in part to their suspicions of whites in political matters.[54]

In 1899, a General Synod discussed the question of the management of missions, and the following year important changes were made by the Moravian missionaries in Surinam. In the past, the missionaries had done nearly all of the work—money-raising, preaching, teaching in day-schools, caring for lepers, providing for orphans, and visiting the distant Bush Negro stations. From 1900 on, the responsibility for these tasks was to be shared by the people. Business and preaching were separated. No longer were missionaries required to serve their time with

Kersten & Co., the general business organization of the Brethren. In this change, the missionary exchanged the earning of his own living for a ministerial salary, and his followers were charged with contributing to his support. In 1899, the first local minister was fully ordained, and by 1912 there were eight such ministers.[55]

The Lutheran Church

During the two and one-half centuries of Danish rule in the Virgin Islands, the Lutheran church was the state church. The first Lutheran congregation in the Western world was established in the Danish West Indies in 1666, and the congregation on St. Thomas is the first Christian church of continuous existence in the Virgin Islands.[56]

In 1666, there were no Negroes on St. Thomas. In 1673, the white population, made up of Danes, Germans, English, and French, numbered 100. Arriving in the following year were 55 Negro slaves, who had accompanied their owners from other islands. In 1688, the first official census showed a population of 317 whites and 442 Negroes. Not more than 50 of these inhabitants were Danish Lutherans—about one-sixth of the local whites.[57]

The West Indian Company purchased the island of St. Croix from France in 1734. Denmark purchased the West Indian Company in 1754. Four hundred slaves were included in the transfer of property to the Danes. Two Moravian missionaries had arrived in St. Thomas in 1732 to work with the slaves, and now sentiment favoring the opening of a Lutheran mission among the blacks developed rapidly in Denmark. On February 3, 1755, a royal ordinance issued by King Frederick V provided that God's word shall be preached to the slaves; they shall be instructed in the Christian religion; and their children shall be baptized like other people's children. The ordinance stated that the owners would suffer "strong and exemplary" punishment if they placed the least hindrance in the way of the slaves' appropriation of their religion. Within a few years ten missionaries were dispatched to the colony.[58] After the ordination of a missionary pastor in Christiansted in 1771, the Lutheran missions on the three islands increased their Negro membership to a thousand persons. Many had to stand outside the churches for lack of space. In 1781, church officials were amazed at the confirmation examinations in Danish Creole, a pidgin language, which, it was said, "could not have been better in the most enlightened European congregations."[59]

By 1785, the Lutheran mission in the Virgin Islands was small only in comparison to the work of the Moravians. On St. Thomas there were 208 confirmed members; the congregation in Christiansted, St. Croix, was almost as large; and there were 40 members in the newly established Negro congregation in Fredericksted, St. Croix. The Negro congregation in the latter town was led by the clerk, Michael Samuelson, himself a slave. In 1788, the Lutherans instituted a system of helpers to assist in mission work, and mission (and government) schools conducted by black teachers were established.[60]

Danish was never predominant in the Virgin Islands. Dutch was the chief language until eclipsed by English at the end of the eighteenth and the beginning of the nineteenth century. The Negro Dutch Creole was used for conversation between Europeans and African slaves for nearly two centuries. After 1815, English gradually took the place of the Negro Creole dialect. According to Larsen, in the Lutheran schools for Danish children, Danish was taught, but in the school for slaves and free Negroes, instruction was first in Creole and later in English. The Negro Dutch Creole literature produced by the Danish Lutherans and the German Moravians had a remarkable cultural influence on the Negro slaves of the Virgin Islands, giving them "a new sense of dignity" and helping "to mold them from a number of diverse groups into a homogeneous people."[61]

At the beginning of the nineteenth century, there were two Lutheran congregations in each parish—both with the same minister, the same church building, and the same government supervision. The Danish Lutheran "missionary pastor" conducted services and ceremonies in both congregations—in Danish in one, in Creole in the other. He also supervised the schools maintained for Danish children and the Creole school conducted by black teachers, and he taught religion in these schools.[62]

By the time of the emancipation proclamation in 1848, many slaves and nearly all people of mixed descent had already become free. In the Creole Lutheran congregation on St. Thomas several years before emancipation, only one-sixth of the children baptized were not free.[63]

After the transfer of the Virgin Islands to the United States in 1917, the Americanization of the Lutheran Church was achieved slowly and cautiously. In each congregation, the first step taken was the introduction of the American Lutheran hymnal and Sunday-school literature; organization of the congregations, the church councils, and various societies after the American pattern came later.[64]

The Methodists

Methodist missionaries began their work in the West Indies in Antigua in 1770. Reverend Thomas Coke visited the British West Indies in the 1780s and was one of the founders of the Methodist Missionary Society in 1789. The first missionaries who asked permission to visit the slaves were met with reluctance and hostility by the planters. Some planters, however, were converted to Methodism. After hearing John Wesley preach during a visit to England, Nathaniel Gilbert, a lawyer, planter, slave-owner, and Speaker of the House of Assembly in Antigua, joined the Methodist Society and opened his house to Methodist worship by whites and Negroes alike.[65] The attempts of Gilbert and his brother Francis to uplift the slaves provoked alarm, and they were ostracized by upper-class Antiguans. Nathaniel Gilbert's death soon after the hurricane of 1772 and the departure of Francis Gilbert from Antigua in 1774 weakened the Methodist Society, but its class meeting organization held it together until new personnel arrived. Two Negro women confessors of humble status took the lead by carrying on meetings in their own cottages.[66]

Daddy Baxter, a white workman at the shipyard, was one of the most effective Methodist lay preachers in Antigua. Recognized as the successor to Nathaniel Gilbert, he preached and carried on pastoral work among the slaves and the less prosperous whites. Baxter was aided by Mrs. Gilbert, the widow of Francis Gilbert, who met the women's classes and became a general instructor to the slaves. In addition, she conducted a public reading of the Scriptures weekly in her home for whites and blacks.[67]

Both the Methodists and the Baptists used a system of slave leaders to supervise their followers. Because it was difficult for missionaries to gain permission to enter the estates, they relied on black assistants to visit the sick, hold prayer meetings in the evenings, and oversee the conduct of the members in their charge. Usually the missionary would talk to his charges quarterly when their membership cards were renewed.[68]

In Nevis and in the British Virgin Island after 1793, the Methodists enjoyed friendly relations with the planters. In both areas, however, they ran into difficulties toward the end of the eighteenth century. In Nevis in 1797, the whites suspected that the missionaries were supporting Wilberforce's parliamentary campaign. Attempts were made to intimidate the missionaries, and a chapel was burned. Eventually hostility died down. A similar crisis in the British Virgin Islands in 1799 followed a slave revolt, but an investigation cleared the missionaries of any blame for the rebellion.[69]

The revolt in Haiti in the 1790s frightened the white populations of the other islands, especially those in neighboring Jamaica, and strengthened their misgivings about missionary enterprises. Every uprising of the Negroes produced new expressions of anger against the missionaries, and the local legislatures enacted extreme acts of repression. The antislavery campaign in England increased the hostility of the colonists toward the Wesleyan and Baptist churches and their agents. On many estates, instruction of the slaves was forbidden and Negroes were not allowed to attend church services. In 1793 the Assembly of St. Vincent prohibited the holding of religious services by unlicensed, itinerant preachers, but the home government disallowed this act. In Dominica, a Methodist missionary was ordered to report for militia service on Sunday and later was ordered to leave the island. In 1799, Wesleyans in St. Vincent were accused of provoking insubordination among the blacks. In 1800, the legislature in Barbados forbade individuals other than officials of the Church of England from conducting religious services in the island, and fined and jailed a Methodist missionary who continued his work. This law remained in effect for three years.[70]

The Methodist missionaries were careful to teach their slave-converts patience and obedience, and to avoid offending their masters.[71] John Wesley's cries of the early 1770s against slavery gave way "to the more complaisant mysticism of Dr. Coke, . . . who saw, even in slavery and the slave trade, the hand of a beneficent Providence, turning evil into good."[72]

A Negro slave known as "Black Harry," who had been converted to Methodism in North America, had such a powerful influence upon the slaves in St. Eustatius in the 1780s that the planters became alarmed and persuaded the Governor to forbid him to continue preaching. In 1787, the Council of St. Eustatius passed a flagrant law against religion, which stated

> that if any white person should be found praying with his brethren, for the first offence he should be fined fifty pieces of eight; for the second, one hundred pieces; and for the third he should be whipped, his goods confiscated, and he should then be banished from the island. That if a coloured man should be found praying, for the first offence he should receive thirty-nine lashes; and for the second, if free, he should be whipped and banished; but if a slave, be whipped every time.[73]

In the 1780s, William Hammet, a Methodist preacher in Kingston, had succeeded despite persecution in providing a chapel large enough to hold 1,200 worshippers. His life was frequently endangered, and Mr. Bull, his associate, several times barely escaped being stoned to death. A campaign of slander and abuse was carried on in local newspapers against Methodist preachers. In 1802, the House of Assembly in Jamaica published an act aimed at persons described as "ill-disposed, illiterate, and ignorant enthusiasts," who addressed "meetings of Negroes and persons of color, chiefly slaves, unlawfully assembled," inciting them to "concoct schemes of much private and public mischief." In June, 1804, the King disallowed this Act.[74]

In 1807, the Kingston Council prohibited the holding of religious meetings in Kingston and its precincts before sunrise or after sunset, that is, during the only free time that the slaves had. This act also prohibited all preaching, teaching, the offering of public prayer, and the singing of psalms by unauthorized persons of any sect or denomination, and in unlicensed places, within the boundaries of Kingston. By adopting this act on November 28, 1807, the House of Assembly virtually reenacted the act of 1802. The oppressed Methodists appealed to the

Throne, asserting that 400,000 slaves were effectually excluded from all public worship. The second act was annulled on April 26, 1809.[75]

By the end of 1823, there were 9,000 Methodist church members in Jamaica. More than half of the Society in Kingston were slaves; almost all the others were Negroes and colored people (persons of mixed descent). Fewer than 60 of the 4,000 church members in the Kingston Circuit were white. Religious persecution arose again in Jamaica in 1826 when the Code of the Slave Laws was revised; new provisions prohibited the holding of religious services "by sectarian Ministers or other teachers" before sunrise or after sunset. Since Presbyterians, Roman Catholics, and Jews were exempted from this rule, it applied only to Baptists, Moravians, and Methodists. Despite religious harassment preceding the Act of Emancipation (1824–1833), Methodist church membership grew to almost 13,000.[76]

Slave uprisings in Cornwall (Jamaica) in 1831 led to the proclamation of martial law throughout the island, and on January 26, 1832, an association called the Colonial Church Union was formed in the rectory of St. Ann's Bay. The objects of this organization were said to be the defense by Constitutional means of the interests of the Colony, exposure of the falsehoods of the Anti-slavery Society, and the support of the Established Church, but its real purpose was to attempt to drive out the Free Church missionaries.[77] In the wave of vandalism that followed the founding of this organization, a number of Baptist and Wesleyan chapels were destroyed, and several ministers were imprisoned and mistreated. Even clergy of the Anglican church who had been friendly with the slaves were suspected and abused.[78]

In 1833, slaves made up 23,000 of the 32,000 Methodist church members in the West Indian Districts. No other church had so large a slave membership. Within a few months of Emancipation, the Missionary Committee of the Wesleyan Methodist Missionary Society sent reinforcements to the West Indies. The staff of 54 in 1833 became 85 by 1840, and by 1844 the church membership had reached 54,552.[79]

Within a decade after Emancipation, a period of decline set in for West Indian Methodism. The Jamaica District lost 1,000 members during 1845, and the Antigua District half that number. The enthusiasm accompanying Emancipation had been expended and disappointment followed the previous excitement and high hopes. A major reason for the disillusionment of the former slaves was the continuing gulf between white and black after 1833. With some exceptions, the propertied and official classes continued to regard the Negro as "fit only for subjection." The Methodist Church became increasingly the church of the black and colored people. Whites were not excluded; they withdrew. The estrangement had begun during the struggle for emancipation, and when, after 1833, the Church of England increased the number of clergy for West Indian parishes, many middle and upper class white families became Anglicans.[80]

Following Emancipation, the Methodist church played a leading role in establishing elementary and secondary schools.[81] The Methodist enterprise in the West Indies revived somewhat after 1866. The excesses of the Great Revival of 1861–62 had passed, and the reports of the missionaries became more hopeful.[82]

The Baptists

George Liele (Lisle), a manumitted slave who came to Jamaica in 1783 with his fugitive former master, was one of the first Baptist missionaries in the West Indies. Lisle had preached in Virginia, and he soon organized a church in Kingston. By 1791 his church had 450 members—all Negroes and most of them slaves. Thirty years after Lisle's arrival in Jamaica, the Baptist Missionary Society began to send out missionaries from England. In Montego Bay they worked in a hostile atmosphere, were stricken with malaria and other diseases, and served an average of less than three years. Regular services were started nevertheless, and schools were opened at Kingston, Falmouth, and Spanish Town. The Baptist missionaries acquired a growing following among the slaves, and by 1831 they had built 24 churches, enrolled 10,000 members and claimed another 17,000 "inquirers."[83]

After Emancipation in 1834, Baptist congregations in Jamaica quickly grew. By 1837, there were 16 Baptist missionaries and school masters serving 16,000 church members and an equal number of "inquirers." Three thousand people had been baptized the previous year. The Emancipation Act provided for a period of indentured labor—called a period of apprenticeship—for seven years. Slaves were to work for their old masters for three-quarters of the time and were still subject to punishment. To the freed laborers, there was little distinction between slavery and apprenticeship; the system was a failure and the British Parliament reduced the period of indenture to four years.[84] With an end of the apprenticeship system, 800,000 Negroes became fully and unconditionally free on August 1, 1838. No real preparations had been made for the sudden termination of the system, and few people seriously undertook the training of the former slaves for their new situation. Almost immediately there was confusion, disillusionment, and suspicion throughout Jamaica. Missionaries played a role in the attempt to reconstruct economic and social life. When some planters demanded exorbitant rents for the cottages and grounds occupied by Negroes, William Knibb and his associates established free townships and villages where blacks could have their own smallholdings. Those who obtained these freeholds supplemented their incomes by working for neighboring planters.[85]

The Baptist church in Jamaica continued to grow in the late 1830s and early 1840s and, in response to repeated missionary requests, two dozen new missionaries were sent from England within four years. In 1842, the Jamaica Baptist Association asked that the work of their church be made self-supporting. Enthusiasm for self-support led to the launching of several new projects: the establishment of a training college for native ministers, the beginning of a mission to Western Africa, and the starting of a program in other West Indian islands (Haiti, Cuba, the Bahamas, and Panama).[86]

The Presbyterians

The Scottish Missionary Society, a nondenominational body, sent three pioneers to Jamaica in 1800, and like other missionaries already in the field, they met with much opposition. In 1819, the established Church of Scotland initiated its work in Kingston, and in 1823 the Scottish Missionary Society began the program that was carried on later by the United Presbyterian Church. The missionaries from Scotland were active in teaching the people in the rural districts of Jamaica. In

1841, a secondary school was opened near Goshen, and in 1846 the Montego Bay Academy was established. In 1846, the Presbyterian workers in Jamaica sent a band of missionaries to Calabar, West Africa.[87]

The United Presbyterian Church was formed in 1847, and by the end of 1865, the Presbyterian mission in Jamaica included 26 congregations with a total membership of 5,124 and 467 candidates. Members of this denomination had been active in education for 25 years and at the end of 1865 were operating 29 day schools with 2,326 students enrolled. In 1869 the Mission Board in Scotland decided that efforts should be made to train a native ministry and that European missionaries should be withdrawn from the field. In 1894 the Presbyterian Synod in Jamaica established a mission among East Indian immigrants, and in this work they were assisted by two catechists sent to Jamaica by the Canadian Presbyterian Church in Trinidad. In 1911, there were 7 East Indian stations, 1 school, 6 catechists, 9 helpers, and 261 communicants; 1,389 East Indians had been baptized since the founding of the mission.[88]

During the apprenticeship period (1836), a Presbyterian missionary was sent from Scotland to Port of Spain, Trinidad, and within a few years, additional appointments were made to Arouca and San Fernando. In 1911, the Foreign Mission Committee in Scotland discontinued its work in Trinidad and the Presbyterian program there became fully self-sustaining.[89]

The Presbyterian church in Jamaica experienced difficulties in the first half of the twentieth century. A survey made to find ways to make the church effective in social programs, including cooperating with Government and semi-Government agencies and assisting in social reconstruction, found that "the Church was in no spiritual state to lead any movement, that ministers were losing heart, that congregations were dwindling, that our leadership—elders, managers, teachers—was poor and sparse."[90]

Summary of Christian Churches through the Nineteenth Century

Within the framework of the system of slavery, colonial society, and a diversity of religious formulations, the slaves and free men and women of color attempted for centuries to work out their salvation. In the British Caribbean, the Established churches were closed to the black slaves for a century and a half. During the eighteenth century the nonconformist missionaries attempted, not altogether successfully, to destroy the African cultural traditions among the slaves. To secure toleration for their efforts to Christianize the slaves, the missionaries accepted the need for the subordination of blacks which the system of slavery created. At the same time, the establishment of predominantly Negro churches provided certain emotional satisfactions for the converts and they gave some Negroes opportunities for leadership which they had previously lacked.[91]

Despite the prodigious labors of the nonconformist missionaries, only a small fraction of the slaves in the non-Catholic colonies were converted to Christianity. After Emancipation, the Protestant denominations increased their missionary staffs throughout the West Indies in their drive for converts. Large numbers of persons of African descent were added to the rolls of the Anglican, Methodist, Baptist, Presbyterian, and other Protestant churches in the non-Catholic countries, and rapid population increases in the twentieth century have swelled their memberships. Little attention was paid by Protestants to the black and colored populations in the Catholic countries so long as they were slaves, but after 1834 serious efforts were made to proselytize them. Protestant ministers, however, met with little success in these countries, and one hundred years later Catholics constituted approximately two-thirds of the population in such places as Grenada, Carriacou, and the Grenadines.[92]

Recent Developments: The Rise of the Pentecostal Movement; Changes in the Historical Churches

The economic depression of the first three decades of the twentieth century bankrupted many large estates in the West Indies and made it difficult for the churches to support ministers and large church and school properties. Gradually the major financial responsibility for schools shifted to government.[93] Between 1925 and 1952, however, the number of Protestants increased more rapidly in a number of areas in the Caribbean than in preceding periods of similar length. Nine countries showed the following growth:[94]

	1925	1952	Approximate Increase
British Lesser Antilles	134,420	343,947	2½ times
Trinidad	113,839	318,247	3 times
Guatemala	11,117	75,845	6½ times
Jamaica	128,783	915,726	7 times
Cuba	15,942	165,622	10½ times
Mexico	31,138	334,756	11 times
Haiti	12,198	259,523	21 times
Venezuela	400	13,775	34½ times

In parts of the West Indies, there was a multiplicity of churches in the 1930s and 1940s. In Savanna-la-Mar, Jamaica, a town of 3,500 inhabitants, churches and church-groups included: Anglican, Baptist, Methodist, Presbyterian, Roman Catholic, Church of God, Salvation Army, Seventh-Day Adventist, Plymouth Brethren, Pentecostals, Jehovah's Witnesses, Millennium Dawn, Holiness, Samuels, Gospel Trumpeters, International Bible Students, and three revivalist groups. At that time, the Anglican church had 500 members, and the first five churches listed above accounted for three-fourths of the Christians of the town. Three to five churches were found in a large number of Jamaican rural villages and hamlets inhabited, at most, by a few hundred people. None of them could support a resident pastor; each church was a mission visited once or twice a month by the minister of a larger church elsewhere. In 1941, a Protestant pastor commented that new forms of religion had grown rapidly in the previous 25 years in Jamaica, and added: " 'Our sober and unemotional type of service cannot compete with the drumming, dancing, and emotionalism of these sects.' "[95]

For two decades after 1930, Protestants attempted to obtain a majority of West Indian ministers over expatriates. Theological schools had been established by the Anglicans in Barbados and in Jamaica, and the Baptists, Moravians, Presbyterians, Methodists, Congregationalists, the Churches of Christ, and the Society of Friends cooperated in providing theological training in Jamaica for all the West Indies.[96] Nevertheless, at the middle of the twentieth century, after more than two hundred years of work in the West Indies, the majority of Protestant ministers came from the outside. In 1956, British ministers numbered 585; American, 776; and locally ordained, 897 (Bahamas, British Guiana,

British Honduras, British Lesser Antilles, Costa Rica, Cuba, Dominican Republic, El Salvador, Haiti, Honduras, Jamaica, Netherlands Guiana, Netherlands Lesser Antilles and Curaçao, Panama, Puerto Rico, Trinidad and Tobago, and the Virgin Islands).[97] A noteworthy development by the 1960s was the Haitianization of the Roman Catholic clergy by President François Duvalier. Over a long period of years, the French clergy had tended to side with the privileged upper class and with foreign political and economic interests. Duvalier cleared Haiti of foreign Roman Catholic bishops and priests.[98]

In the 1950s, the churches of the Caribbean sought to overcome a sense of isolation. For years the Salvation Army had been the only Christian organization to treat the Caribbean as a unit. Little coordination existed among the eight dioceses of the Anglican Church. An Anglican Council of Bishops and a Provincial Advisory Council of the Methodist Church were formed to combat the feeling of isolation. In some of the islands little denominational cooperation had been evident on social and political issues.[99] In November 1973, representatives of fourteen autonomous churches met in Jamaica to inaugurate the Caribbean Conference of Churches. Among the denominations represented were the African Methodists, Anglicans, Baptists, Lutherans, Methodists, Moravians, Presbyterians, Roman Catholics, and the Salvation Army. The delegates agreed "to join together in a regional fellowship of churches for inspiration, consultation and cooperative action."[100]

Since the end of World War II the most rapid expansion of Protestantism in the West Indies has been in the Pentecostal and related movements. In 1955, the president of New York's Union Theological Seminary was impressed with "the omnipresence and the relative inconsequence of the Christian church" in the West Indies and South America.[101] He was struck particularly with the weakness of Protestantism in this area. Of the three main branches of Christianity, he found it to be the least vigorous, while in some of the islands and in parts of South America, he discovered the influence of the Roman Catholic Church to be very great. But his principal finding was the extent and influence of the so-called "fringe sects"—"Pentecostal," "Adventist," "Holiness," "Church of God," or "Church of Christ" groups. Ecumenical Protestants in the countries he visited expressed concern about these groups, as had Protestant spokesmen he had met on a trip through twenty countries in Asia and Africa in 1953, and they asked for advice on what to do about these sects. Van Dusen commented:

> "Fringe"? On the fringes of what? Of *our* sects, to be sure, of ecumenical Protestantism. But on the "fringe" of authentic Christianity, of the true church of Christ? That is by no means so certain, especially if the measuring rod is kinship of thought and life with original Christianity. . . . Many of its marks are strikingly, unmistakably, undeniably reproduced in this "new Christianity," as they were in historic "sectarian Protestantism" in its beginnings.[102]

This observer concluded that ecumenical Protestants were rationalizing their annoyance over the reality of the new sectarianism with two illusory assumptions: (1) that this development was a dangerous phenomenon, sub-Christian in theology and ethics, and (2) that it was a temporary and passing phase which would soon be domesticated within traditional Protestantism.[103]

The past three decades have shown that the new sectarianism was no passing phenomenon. In 1943 the Church of God in Jamaica stood seventh in membership with 43,560 members (3.5 percent of the total population). By 1960, it was the third largest denomination in the country with a membership of nearly 200,000 (12 percent of the population). By 1970, it had become the second largest religious group in Jamaica with a membership which constituted nearly 340,000 (17 percent of the total population).[104] Table 2.1 shows the proportions of the population of Jamaica in the major religious groups between 1943 and 1970.

The two Pentecostal groups (Church of God and Pentecostal) constituted 4 percent of the total population of Jamaica in 1943, but 20 percent in 1970. The Seventh Day Adventists, another rapidly growing sect, increased their membership from 2 percent of the population in 1943 to 6.5 percent in 1970. Together the two Pentecostal groups and the Seventh Day Adventists made up approximately 27 percent of the Jamaican population in 1970.

In 1973, Gerloff found that the Holiness, Pentecostal, and Adven-

TABLE 2.1
MAJOR RELIGIOUS GROUPS, JAMAICA, 1943–1970

	Percent of Population 1970	Percent of Population 1960	Percent of Population 1943
Baptist	18	19	26
Church of God	17	12	3.5
Anglican	15	20	28
Roman Catholic	8	7	5
Seventh Day Adventist	6.5	5	2
Methodist	6	7	9
Presbyterian/Congregational	5	6	9
Pentecostal	3		.5
Moravian	3		4
Brethren	2		.5
Other and Not Stated	16.5	24	12.5
	100.0	100.0	100.0

tist movements in Jamaica "not only talk about poverty but work with the poor, and present as well as preserve their values and their dignity. . . ."[105] In 1955, a Protestant church spokesman in Puerto Rico said that the total Protestant constituency in the island was approximately 200,000, but that the membership of the historic Protestant churches did not exceed 50,000. The phenomenal growth of the new sects there occurred between 1935 and 1955. In 1974, Francisco Martinez, President of the Christian Pentecostal Church in Cuba, claimed that the Pentecostals had grown more in recent years than any other church in that country.[106]

As a political tactic, François Duvalier, dictatorial president of Haiti from 1957 to 1973, encouraged the growth of various Pentecostal churches as a balance against the power of the Catholic Church and the vodun cult. The movement spread through the segmentation and proliferation of cells. When members of one Pentecostal cell moved to another city in search of jobs or to join family members, they often formed new units and converted local residents. This "geographic peel-off" was repeated again and again as "daughter" churches reached out to residents

THE CARIBBEAN

of villages farther in the interior, and many leaders in government, the Catholic Church, and the vodun cult were led to underestimate the size and potential of the movement.[107]

For thirty years, then, Pentecostalism has been the fastest growing religion in the Caribbean.

ઌૐCHAPTER THREE ௧ை

Neo-African Religions and Ancestral Cults of the Caribbean and South America

*Major and Contingent Variables in the Development
of Religious Cults of the Caribbean and South America*

THE EMERGENCE and perpetuation of the various types of religious cults in the Caribbean and South America—Neo-African, ancestral, revivalist, spiritualist, and religio-political, cannot be attributed simply to economic conditions during slavery and the post-slavery period, the presence of persons sensitive to the stresses of disadvantaged classes, the existence of diverse cultural traditions, or indeed to any other single factor.[1] Instead, these cults owe their existence in large part to the interaction of three major variables: cultural, socioeconomic, and psychological.

In the social structure of slavery, economic decisions were made, rules promulgated, the necessities of life distributed, and discipline administered by the master class. Those who were brought into the system from the outside had to conform to the regime of work and they were exposed to the ways of the dominant class in realms other than the economic. Those who were born into the system were enculturated by conditioning, subtle or otherwise. The same points may be made for those who have been involved in the systems of peonage and sharecropping which followed slavery.

During the colonial period a rigid dualism of white and black did not exist in the social structure. Rivalries and competition were present everywhere within as well as between classes: the state versus established religions or against dissenters, landed proprietors versus traders, whites against mulattoes, black freemen versus slaves, and "nation" against "nation" among the blacks (Yoruba versus Dahomean versus Muslim versus Congo versus Angolan, and so forth). In adapting to the realities of the social structure in ways that were permitted, blacks found niches where they could insert parts of their African heritage. In Brazilian society, these niches included *batuques* (dances), *confréries* (religious societies), organizations of *Negroes de ganho* (Negro street merchants), and the "nations" of the large cities—each of which was under the authority of a king or governor.[2]

Societies based on ethnic descent enacted segments of traditional African religious rituals and provided amusement and recreation in many parts of the Caribbean and South America. In Haiti, associations of Rada, Congo, and other ethnic groups were formed. In Cuba, the "nations" were organized into *cabildos:* Arara (Rada), Lucumi (Yoruba), Congo, Mandingo, Nãnigos (Calabar), and so forth, each of which held private festivities, and, twice a year, led masked processions publicly in Havana. In Brazil, ethnic groups formed religious associations, and there were even societies for mulattoes and for Creoles. Elsewhere in the New World, Catholic fraternities were founded along ethnic lines, and these also helped to perpetuate African religious beliefs.[3]

Gatherings other than those sponsored by religious fraternities made use of religious rites for their own purposes. In Haiti, such revolutionary leaders as Macandal, Jean-François, Biassou, Romaine Rivière, Hyacinthe Ducoudray, Halaou, and Boukmann performed religious and magical acts to inspire and unify their followers during the half century before Independence.[4] In Jamaica, obeah (witchcraft) groups, probably following Fanti-Ashanti traditions, existed in the seventeenth century. The Maroons, who fled to the mountains soon after the British conquest of the island in 1655, practiced Myalism (magic) and enlisted African spirits in their battles against the British. For generations the Maroons valued their independence, rejected innovations from European culture, stressed their Africanness, and developed a separate Maroon religion.[5] Much later, Sam Sharpe, a Baptist slave who was also a leader among the

Native Baptists ("spirit Baptists") became the outstanding leader of the Jamaica Slave Rebellion of 1831.[6]

Perhaps the situation can be clarified by seeing it in terms of a general theory of change, a theory proposed by Yinger. This theory starts with a model of a "balanced" society in which the social structure is reinforced by the existing culture and by techniques of socialization that produce character structures harmonious with the social system. For several reasons, there is always some "wobble" in each of the three elements of the system. Some individuals are "poorly socialized"; new cultural elements are invented or borrowed; and the usual patterns of interaction are upset by unusual events. This theory is applied to the processes of change in the rise of Protestantism and the development of capitalism. In contrast to Weber, who saw a new cultural force—Calvinism—as causing realignments both of character and of social structure, Yinger sees Calvinism as coming last in the structural-character-cultural sequence.[7]

During the experience of blacks in the New World, I see the shift to religious cults of one kind or another as coming in the first instance from the nature of the slavery system and the system that followed it, and the social, economic, and political treatment which those at the bottom of these systems received. Over time, these conditions modified character in a stressful direction, and those who were most sensitive to the stress advanced new religious and secular systems to deal with their anxiety. Some of these systems reached many persons who were receptive. Once significant changes in the total system of social structure, character, and culture were underway, influences flowed from each point to the others.

Successful religions spread and persist after the conditions which gave birth to them have changed, or changed to some extent, and individuals are socialized into accepting their beliefs and procedures.[8] This has been the case with such Neo-African cults as Cuban santeria, the Brazilian candomblés, and Trinidadian shango. It has also been true of the ancestral Cumina cult in Jamaica; revivalism in Jamaica, Trinidad, and St. Vincent; the Pentecostal movements in parts of the Caribbean and South America; and spiritualist cults such as Umbanda and the Batuque in Brazil and María Lionza in Venezuela. When this happens,

NEO-AFRICAN RELIGIONS AND ANCESTRAL CULTS

as Peel points out, a religion acquires new meanings and functions for its members, the most universal of which is the satisfaction that comes from group activities.

In this chapter, brief accounts of the social structures of Haiti, Trinidad, Grenada, and Jamaica are given to show the socioeconomic contexts within which cult beliefs and rituals have developed and continued to exist. The relationship between social structure and Neo-African religions in Brazil is presented in chapter 6. Data on personality tendencies of early leaders of Neo-African cults are lacking. A number of the gods in vodun and other cults are of local origin, and it seems likely that these divinities, like some of those deified in recent times, were once powerful religious and magical leaders. At the end of chapter 4, brief accounts of two cult leaders, Norman Paul and Marcus Garvey, are presented to indicate the role of personality factors in groups that have been formed in recent decades.

Changes in the interplay of these three interacting variables—the structural or socioeconomic, the psychological or personality, and the cultural—at a certain time and place have not necessarily resulted in the appearance of a religious cult, nor has the emergence of such a cult meant that alternative means of adaptation have not been utilized alongside or without it. Among other factors that have helped to bring some of these cults into existence or to preserve them are physical isolation, continuing contact with Africa, continuity of leadership, group cohesion, and the presence of competing cults. After considering these contingent factors briefly, we shall examine more fully in this chapter, and the next, the major variables whose interaction largely account for cult life in the Caribbean and South America.

Physical isolation, especially in the early days of a cult, furthers its development. In the Caribbean and in those parts of South America where the ratio of persons of African descent in the total population was highest during the period of slavery, and where these persons were most severely isolated from Europeans, the likelihood that African religious traditions would persist in easily recognized form was greatest. Physical isolation continued in many places after slavery was ended. In the case of the African immigrants who came to Grenada in 1849 and their descendants, the original settlements were closed communities at Concorde, La

Mode, and Munich. In 1870, the Rada, Yoruba, Ibo, Congo, and Mandingo peoples in Port of Spain, Trinidad, lived in separate communities, and the Rada cult was an integral part of the life of those who traced their ancestry to Dahomey. In Jamaica, the Convince cult seems to have developed among the Maroons, who fled to inaccessible regions of the island in the 1830s, or among neighbors of these fugitives who were only slightly less isolated. Likewise, the Cumina cult may be derived from the religion of the Blue Mountain Maroons.[9]

Where physical isolation was less extreme, social isolation existed in varying degrees. The slaves had greater freedom to conduct their own religious services without white supervision than they had in work or in African-type political activity. African styles of singing and dancing were tolerated in slave quarters when they did not interfere with work or were performed on holidays; at times, white onlookers enjoyed them as much as the participating slaves.[10] Sometimes the "amusements" of the slaves provided channels for the enactment of segments of West African religious rituals and for the planning of revolts.

In Brazil, Trinidad, and Grenada, continuing contacts with Africa furthered the retention of Africanisms. The Herskovitses noted in Bahia, Brazil, that such contacts were continuous until the outbreak of World War II: "To the Afro-Bahians, Africa is no vague, mythical land. . . . It is a living reality, whence many of the objects they use in their rituals are imported, where people they know have visited and where other acquaintances live, where their fathers or grandfathers came from."[11] Slavery was abolished in the British West Indies in 1834, and the abolition of the apprenticeship system followed in 1838, but African immigrants continued to settle in Trinidad until at least 1855. More than 1,000 Africans came to Grenada from Ijesha in Yorubaland (Nigeria) in 1849.[12]

Caribbean cults vary greatly in continuity of leadership. Where units of a cult are closely tied to extended families, as is the case in rural Haiti, the groups are quite permanent. In northern Haiti, ritual mechanisms exist for ensuring the continuation of the vodun cult. When a houngan (vodun priest) dies, it is necessary to arrange for his "degradation." Catholic chants and prayers are interspersed with African-type chants and dances as the officiating houngan supplicates both the Catholic saints and old African deities. Eventually, the principal loa (deity) that the dead man had served is withdrawn from his head. This ceremony is followed by the rite of "transmission" or "transference" to discover the successor to the dead leader.[13] In Trinidad, a shango leader may arrange before his death for his spouse or for the second in command to succeed him. The person who takes over must be a follower of the same "power" as his predecessor. If a leader has appointed no one to succeed him, an amombah conducts a rite of drumming, singing, and praying during which the spirit of the dead leader is dismissed. Whoever gets a message from the "power" of the dead leader then takes up the work. If no one takes over, the ritual objects in the chapelle are given away and the cult center disappears.[14] To take the other extreme in stability, the revivalist cults in Jamaica (Revival Zion and Pocomania), the Shouters or Spiritual Baptists in Trinidad, and the Shakers of Grenada and St. Vincent are highly unstable. All of these groups are intensely competitive, and the survival of a given "church" depends mainly upon the personality and ingenuity of the leader. Shifting memberships and secessions are common, and a leader who loses all or most of his following simply tries to recruit another.[15]

M. G. Smith argues that the displacement of the Big Drum Dance in Grenada shows the importance of group cohesion in the persistence of a culture complex. Although Shango was a late arrival, it had a priesthood and a formal organization.[16] In Jamaica, the struggle of the rebellious Maroons to maintain their independence promoted social solidarity among them. Rejecting Christianity, they utilized African spirits to assist in that struggle, and the present day Cumina cult seems to have some connection with the Maroon religion which developed in the eighteenth and nineteenth centuries.[17] Undoubtedly, group cohesion has been influential as well in the continuation of vodun in Haiti, shango in Trinidad and in Recife, Brazil, santeria in Cuba, and the candomblé in Bahia, Brazil.

Where two or more Caribbean cult-types—Neo-African religions, ancestral cults, revivalist cults, spiritualist cults, and religiopolitical cults—exist in one area, cultural borrowing and social interaction occur, and some persons rely on more than one cult-group. In Trinidad, many shangoists attend Shouters ceremonies during the intervals between the annual ceremonies of the numerous Shango groups. Moreoever, Shango priests and priestesses go to a Shouters leader to be baptized and to be guided in advanced spiritual experiences known as "mourning" and "building." Or, to take another example, despite the hostility of Rastafarians toward revivalists in West Kingston, Jamaica, participants in the former cult are acquainted with and have been influenced by revivalist rituals.

My interpretation of the emergence and continuation of Caribbean and South American religious cults through the interaction of major and contingent variables does not account for the greater retention of Africanisms in the Catholic countries. Thus far the explanations given for this difference are not entirely satisfactory. As I have pointed out, Catholic missionaries baptized and served large numbers of African slaves in the seventeenth and early eighteenth centuries. In the Catholic countries of Brazil, Haiti, and Cuba, slaves were permitted to form ethnic associations ("governments," "nations," cabildos, religious fraternities) where African languages, dances and religious beliefs could be perpetuated.[18] Herskovits suggested that Catholic theology and ritual may have been "too fixed" to satisfy the religious needs of transplanted Africans within the church.[19] In any case, the possibility of intercession on behalf of devotees by the numerous Catholic saints was understandable and congenial to Africans who were acquainted with dozens of divinities in tribal pantheons. Bastide, who studied Afroamerican culture and particularly African religions in Brazil extensively, attributed the syncretism of African gods and Catholic saints in Afro-Brazilian cults to the necessity of concealing from whites the African nature of the religions by covering the altar with statues and lithographs of the saints—by placing white masks on the black faces of ancestral divinities.[20] Still another element that may help to account for this difference is that in many of the Latin areas where blacks are found and where Catholicism has been predominant, white settlement was never very extensive.

A related question is why some Catholic countries—most notably Cuba, Haiti, and Brazil—have Afro-Catholic cults while others—including Martinique, Guadeloupe, and Puerto Rico—do not have them. Such rituals did exist in Martinique and Guadeloupe at one time, but, with the exception of remote rural areas, after 1750 the "wild dances" of the early eighteenth century disappeared from the cities of those islands.[21]

The cults referred to here are from forty to two hundred years old.

NEO-AFRICAN RELIGIONS AND ANCESTRAL CULTS

Specific cult-groups have been revised, replaced, or transformed, but none of the five cult-types has disappeared from the region. Among the revised cults in the Caribbean are the Neo-African religions: vodun, candomblé, santeria, and shango. Greater modifications of African religions are found in the ancestral cults: Cumina, Convince, Big Drum, Kele, and the ancestral cult of the Black Carib of Belize. In Jamaica, Trinidad, Grenada, and St. Vincent one revivalist cult has replaced another, and the same is true of spiritualist groups in Puerto Rico. Garveyism has been transformed into Rastafarianism in Jamica, and in the United States into the Black Muslim and black power movements.

The Meaning of "African Elements"

Bastide discerned a double diaspora for blacks in the New World: that of African cultural traits which transcend ethnic groupings, and that of blacks themselves who have lost their ethnic distinctiveness through interbreeding and have been absorbed to a considerable extent by their social environments—English, Spanish, French, or Portuguese. On the first phenomenon, there is a dominant African culture for each area, but the predominance of that culture is not directly related to the preponderance of a given ethnic group in the shipment of slaves to the area concerned.[22]

In Haiti, the various "nations" have been transformed into divinities—for example, Congo Mayombé, Ibo, Badagri, Bambara, Caplaou, and Mahi. In the process of syncretization, these loa, and the cultural patterns they represent, have been absorbed by the dominant Dahomean religion. In vodun, they are subordinated elements of Fon Culture.[23] Although Yoruban and Yoruban-derived centers are found in northern Brazil (São Luiz do Maranhão), the leading cult is Dahomean (in this case, Fon). In Cuba and Trinidad, in northeast Brazil (Alagoas, Recife, Bahia), and in southern Brazil (from Porto Alegre to Pelotas), Yoruba culture predominates. Gêgê (Dahomean), Angolan, and Congo candomblés still exist in Bahia, Brazil, but the Nago (Yoruba) candomblé alone "has inspired all the rest with their theology . . . , their ceremonial ritual, and their basic festivals."[24] Fanti-Ashanti (Ghana) culture is found in its purest form among the Bush Negroes of Surinam and French Guiana. These cultures contain traits taken from Dahomean traditions (the vodous) and Bantu religions (such spirits as the Loanga Winti), but these are subordinated to Fanti-Ashanti culture. In Jamaica, the predominant African cultural pattern in folk religion, names, and folklore is that of the Kromantis (Ghana). Among the Black Caribs, the process of syncretization has been so thorough that it is almost impossible to distinguish the African and Indian elements.[25]

Other students of Neo-African and African-derived religious cults in the New World are in agreement with Bastide's views on the predominance of an African culture in a given area. Métraux points out that the most important deities in Haitian vodun belong to the Fon and the Yoruba, especially the Fon—Legba, Damballah-wèdo, Aida-wèdo, Hevieso, Agassu, Ezili, Agwé, Zaka, Ogu, Shango, and many others. Herskovits and Bascom have made similar comments.[26] Courlander found that in isolated regions cult centers devoted exclusively to Nago deities are still in existence; elsewhere Mahi (Dahomey) or Ibo (Nigeria) services are held separately. Some cult centers have several temples, one for Dahomey, one for Nago, one for Ibo, and so on, with a separate building for Gèdé, the deity for the dead. More frequently, however, one temple contains several altars. In certain regions, the Petro cult groups (Congo-Guinée family), which included the Pétro, Bumba, Moundongue, Bambara, Congo Loangue (Loango), and other "nations," held separate services. In places such as Port Au Prince, however, major differences between vodun and Congo-Guinée rites have disappeared, and altars to both Pétro and Dahomean gods are found within the same *houmfort*. Many of the original deities of the Dahomean earth, sky, and thunder pantheons have not survived in Haiti. In addition to Yoruba deities and those of other West African tribes which have been brought into the cult, a very large number of divinities have originated in Haiti itself.[27]

In the worship of African deities in Cuba, Bascom states that "the African elements of santeria are predominantly Yoruba." In these ceremonies, animals are sacrificed to Yoruba gods, Yoruba music is played on African types of drums, songs with Yoruba words and music are sung, and dancers are possessed by the orishas. Beads of the proper colors are worn by the devotees, Yoruba foods are cooked for the participants and the orishas, and leaves with Yoruba names are used in preparing medicines and in washing the sacred stones and the heads of the worshippers.[28] Ortiz and others have documented the African authenticity of santeria rites.[29]

In northern Brazil (São Luiz do Maranhão) Yoruban cult groups have perpetuated Yoruba worship in less pure form than the Dahomean groups in that city. In groups which Eduardo calls "Yoruban-derived," Nago rites are even more attenuated.[30]

Bascom concludes that Yoruba religion in the city of São Salvador de Bahia is the purest of any place in the New World. Not all of the traditional Nago cults are equally pure, however, and the traditional cults are reported to be declining. At midcentury, Carneiro found that only a few candomblés in Bahia were dedicated to the gods of only one "nation."[31]

Herskovits was one of the first social scientists to assert that the Shango cult of Trinidad is derived mainly from the Yoruba. The Herskovitses' field work of 1939 showed that Shango and many other deities of Yoruba derivation were worshipped in Port of Spain in "the African mode of worship." Mischel has referred to the same derivation of this cult. In a comparison of the Shango cults of the Yoruba of southwestern Nigeria and of lower class people of African descent in Trinidad, Simpson found interesting similarities and differences in the form and meaning of a number of culture elements. In my view, these are not accidental or random parallels, but represent continuities and changes in a historic stream of culture. In his study of Gasparillo, a village in southern Trinidad, Elder found that the Yoruba group stood out among the people of African descent as the major group, numerically and in culture strength. The Yoruba ancestor cult (Shango) of the village is "anchored among the Yorubas," but the ritual has undergone considerable modification over the years because of the incorporation of Judeo-Christian, Congo, Dahomean, and Hausa elements.[32]

The last immigrants from Africa arrived in Trinidad about 1855, and after several years of residence on the island, one of these newcomers founded the Rada compound in Port of Spain. Around 1870, groups of settlers made up mainly of Rada, Ibo, and Congo peoples lived along the Belmont Valley Road at the northeastern corner of the city. According to Carr, in 1952 the Rada community had retained "a large measure of ancestral religious beliefs and rites."[33] I do not know whether Rada rites are still performed, but in 1960 the only Neo-African cults that I observed in Port of Spain and neighboring towns were predominantly Yoruban.

The Acculturative Processes

Acculturation operates by means of three analytically distinctive but interrelated processes: retention, syncretization, and reinterpretation. Through these processes, a sizable number of African cultural elements have been incorporated into the belief systems and rituals of religious cults of the Caribbean and South America. These traits include the names and characteristics of African deities, "soul" concepts, ritual objects, drum rhythms, song styles, dance steps, spirit possession, the ritual use of herbs, stones, and water, seclusion and "mourning," animal sacrifices, belief in the immediacy of intervention of supernatural beings in human affairs, utilization of spirits of the dead, and ritual words. These traits have been blended with Christian elements—including the names of Catholic saints, Catholic and Protestant theological concepts, hymns, prayers, Bible verses, the cross and crucifixes, and with spiritualist doctrine—in diverse ways which are set forth in this and subsequent chapters. In addition to the intrinsic interest which these rich materials have, they show, in the case of the Neo-African cults, that Cuban santeria, Haitian vodun, Brazilian candomblés and shango, and Trinidadian-Grenadian shango developed along the same general lines in isolation from one another. Variations in the operation of the acculturative processes are seen in the accounts of cults which emphasize ancestor worship: Cumina-Convince in Jamaica, the Big Drum Dance in Grenada and Carriacou, Kele in St. Lucia, and the ancestral cult of the Black Carib in Belize. Similarities and differences in acculturation as found in the beliefs and ceremonies of revivalist cults in Jamaica, Trinidad, and St. Vincent are set forth in chapter 4, and in chapter 5 the differences in the development of spiritualism in Brazil and Venezuela are traced. In chapter 9, I compare briefly selected aspects of religious cults within and between countries in the Caribbean and South America.

NEO-AFRICAN RELIGIONS AND ANCESTRAL CULTS

NEO-AFRICAN CULTS

Haiti's Social Structure

Marked social distinctions in Haiti antedated independence. The principal social divisions prior to 1804 were the French colonial officials, the white planters, employees of the colonials, free men of color, and slaves. In the original agitation of free men for political and civil rights, the black masses were given no consideration. The successful termination of the Revolution brought freedom and small tracts of land to the masses and a new non-white aristocracy came into existence. This elite was composed of military chiefs with their legitimate and "natural" children, the free men of the old regime, and the mulatto descendants of displaced white proprietors. The emergence of this post-Revolutionary ruling class did not alter materially the situation of the peasant mass.[34] Probably the mulatto elite and the black elite together have never constituted more than 5 percent of the total population of Haiti. The great majority of these persons live in the capital and in the few principal towns.

Haiti's miniature middle class is made up largely of artisans, small shopkeepers, rural coffee buyers, and lesser government employees; it is not much larger than the elite. Members of this class are predominantly nonrural, and some are to be found in every town as well as in Port au Prince.[35]

The lower class in Haiti, which makes up 85 or 90 percent of the total population, is divided into the large rural mass and an urban proletariat that has been increasing in size for several decades. The latter group consists of those employed in personal and domestic service, unskilled workers, the unemployed, and the underemployed. The chances for peasants to climb into the elite, first by passing into the middle class and then into the upper stratum, are slight. The peasants speak a patois called Creole while the language of the elite is French. While practically all of the children in the elite receive formal education, only a small fraction of all Haitian children are in school. Most members of the upper class rely on medical doctors and remedies purchased at pharmacies; the majority of the peasants still depend on vodun practitioners for the treatment of disease. Overpopulation on badly eroded, overworked land, ignorance, isolation, and economic stagnation characterize the life situation of the masses in Haiti. Métraux points out that the average peasant "is in debt, in possession of doubtful title-deeds and can neither read nor write. Unable to speak French as do the town-folk, he falls an easy prey to their cupidity. And to all these causes of anxiety is added the dread of illness. Tuberculosis, malaria, and hookworm are endemic and their threat is always present in addition to that of accidents which may ruin him." [36]

Throughout the post-slavery period, Haiti has been among the least developed countries economically in the West Indies. The average per capita gross national product is about $67, and the country "ranks at the bottom of the Latin American and near the bottom of most global scales." Public service deteriorated early in the history of the Republic, evidence of neglect is seen everywhere, life expectancy is low, agricultural production is in decline, the system of education is inappropriate, the peasants are cut off from modern developments in the capital and the coastal towns, and child-rearing patterns seem to occasion complicated tensions. [37]

Haiti is supposed to have a representative form of government, but actually it has been a democracy in name only. The peasants have no conception of political issues and they have very little to do with government. Some of them vote, but this means nothing because it is impossible for a candidate for any office to win unless he has the endorsement of the President. The President uses the various forms of power—force, domination, and manipulation—to attain his ends and these are applied to the members of the elite as well as to the peasants. [38]

The teaching of Christian doctrine by the Catholic church has not been accompanied to any extent by programs of rural education, health programs, better rewards for labor, rising expectations, and alternative activities to vodun that meet the emotional needs of ordinary Haitians. In the absence of such alternatives, vodun has provided the peasant with meaningful explanations of reality and a basis for relationships with others. As Courlander states, if there is failure in Haitian life, it is not a failure of vodun, which offers something essential, but a failure of the society at large to provide any other satisfactory choices. [39]

NEO-AFRICAN RELIGIONS AND ANCESTRAL CULTS

Haitian Vodun [40]

Columbus landed on the northern coast of Haiti in 1492, and his successors established settlements on the island soon thereafter. By 1513 African slaves began to be imported to replace the aboriginal population that was declining because of mistreatment and disease. The Spanish developed the western third of the island, later call Haiti, less extensively than they did the eastern portion, which subsequently came to be known as Santo Domingo. In the middle third of the seventeenth century, French buccaneers established a position on the plains of northern Haiti, and the Treaty of Ryswick in 1697 gave France possession of the western part of the island. At that time, Haiti's inhabitants consisted of about 6,000 adult white and mulatto males and about 50,000 black slaves. [41]

Undoubtedly, elements of African religions were transplanted to Hispaniola, the name by which the entire island was known to the Spanish, in the early part of the sixteenth century. Unfortunately, no details are available concerning the nature of such beliefs and rituals. The Code Noir provided that assemblies of slaves for purposes other than Catholic worship were illegal, and masters could be punished for permitting such gatherings. African dances, however, were performed by the slaves, and, presumably, religious beliefs of the Dahomeans, Senegalese, Congolese, and others were combined with certain beliefs about Catholic saints as a Neo-African religion gradually developed. Leyburn refers to the period 1730 to 1790, when the importation of slaves was steadily increasing, as the stage of emergence of vodun, with a gradual ascendancy of Dahomean ideas. [42] Finding the rites useful for their cause, revolutionary leaders brought about further religious syntheses.

According to Moreau de Saint Méry, a French priest stationed in Haiti during the latter part of the eighteenth century, the initial aspect of the rites consisted of the officiant's interpretation of the wishes of the divinity, symbolized by a snake. Dancing followed, and the service also included singing, fainting, evidence of intense nervous excitement, and some rather violent behavior. At this point the Catholic elements in the ritual were practically nonexistent. Gradually more or less standardized sets of rites emerged. During the next 150 years the beliefs and rituals of the cult became more elaborate, the number of Catholic components increased, and regional differentiation developed.

NEO-AFRICAN RELIGIONS AND ANCESTRAL CULTS

The most prominent supernatural figures in the cult are the *loa* (also called *Zanges, Les Esprits,* and *Les Mystères*). Many of the loa are old African gods, including Damballa, Erzilie, Obatala, Legba, Ogun, and Shango. In the list of 152 loa that I collected in 1937 in the village of Plaisance in northern Haiti, 27 bore the names of African gods, 18 appeared to be variations of names of African gods, 6 had names derived from African tribal or place names, 9 were probably names of African origin, 57 seemed to be names of Haitian origin, 16 were names of Catholic saints, and 19 were of uncertain origin. All told there are hundreds of loa.

In the Plaisance region, there are three schools of thought concerning the relationship between the loa and the Catholic saints. One view is that there is a spirit "under the water" to correspond to each saint of Heaven.[43] Since God is too busy to listen to the pleas of men, the loa and the saints meet at the halfway point on the road between Heaven and earth, and the loa tell "their brothers" what their human followers want. The saints then return to God and report on the appeals of men, and God grants or refuses the various requests. This group does not believe, however, that the loa are limited to those who correspond to the saints. A second group believes that the saints are loa, although they hold that not all loa are saints. A third point of view is that the saints and the loa are bitter enemies. According to these vodunists, the loa are fallen angels who are worshipped by those who have been chosen by them.

The characteristics of selected loa are shown in table 3.1.

Most of the loa of Haiti belong to two groups—Rada and Petro—but in an earlier period there may have been seven or more pantheons. In Mirebalais in 1934, Herskovits found that some of the *humforts* (vodun temples) had separate rooms with special sacred objects for Rada, Petro, and Congo gods. Most of the Rada divinities are of Dahomean or Yoruban origin; most of the Petro group come from other parts of Africa. In northern Haiti, separate ceremonies are not held for Rada (Dahomean), Nago (Yoruban), Congo, Ibo, "Petro" and other African tribal gods. With the exception of groups in isolated places, by the middle 1950s cult groups and ceremonies other than Rada and Petro were rare anywhere in Haiti.[44]

TABLE 3.1

CHARACTERISTICS OF SELECTED LOA IN NORTHERN HAITI

Loa	Physical Traits	Favorite Foods and Drinks	Colors	Powers	Behavior of Devotee When Possessed by Loa
Legba (St. Anthony the Hermit)	Handsome old man with flowing beard.	Meat and alcoholic drinks.	Black and yellow.	Guardian of crossroads and barriers.	Limps. Carries a cane and walks carefully.
Agoum Tonnere or Loa St. John or Shango (St. John)	Stern and nervous.	Black cattle, white sheep. Champagne and fine liqueurs.	White.	Guardian of thunder. Causes earthquakes.	Both haughty and conciliatory.
Damballa (St. Patrick)	Ugly and strong.	Pork and goat meat. Loves alcohol.	Red.	Loa of snakes and floods. Powerful. Cures serious illnesses.	Consumes quantities of alcohol. Violent behavior includes rolling on ground.
Erzilie (Mater Doloroso)	Beautiful brown woman. Very amorous.	White chicken, fine cakes and desserts. Non-alcoholic drinks.	Rose and white.	Grants favors like a queen.	Tranquil, aristocratic, and coquettish. A learned loa who speaks several languages. Personifies gentleness, sensitiveness, and health. Shows dislike for alcohol, houngans, and bad people.

Loa St. Peter or Papa Pié (St. Peter)	Military appearance. Never laughs.	Goat meat and cocks. Taffia (raw rum).	Red, black, and white.	Powerful loa. Makes rivers overflow.	Energetic, authoritative behavior. Speaks with piercing voice.
Gédé	Resembles a dead person.	Fish with pimento. Black chickens. Fried plantains.	Black.	Loa of death. Important figure in magic intended to kill human beings.	Talks continuously in a nasal tone. Always armed with a knife with which he beats possessed persons.
Ibo	Handsome man.	Goat meat, chickens, vegetables.	Rose and white.	A secondary loa.	Friendly loa who jests with children. Sometimes acts like a dog, and may eat dog meat.
Sousou Pannan	Very ugly. Body covered with sores.	Blood, pork, and red cocks.	Red.	A wicked and cruel loa who does evil deeds.	Drinks much alcohol and also blood of animal sacrifices. Breaks drums and furniture.
Congo	Handsome, but apathetic.	Mixed foods with pimento. Mixed drinks.	Mixed colors.	Subordinate loa.	Quiet and shy.

Vodunists believe that if one observes the taboos imposed by one's chief loa-protector, as well as those of any other loa that one may follow, and if one is punctilious about giving offerings and ceremonies, the loa will be generous with their aid. It is believed also that neglect of one's loa will result in sickness, the death of relatives, crop failure, or other misfortunes.

In the vodun cult of northern Haiti, the dead rank second only to the loa. Some of the dead eventually become loa, but those who do not achieve that distinction must also be treated with respect. Although there is no separate cult for the dead or for the twins in the North as there is in central Haiti,[45] neither the dead in general nor the dead twins may be overlooked in any vodun service.

In West Africa, "soul" concepts are highly elaborated. In Dahomey, all persons have at least three souls, and adult males have four.[46] In Haitian vodun every man has two souls, the *Gros-bon-ange,* which animates the body and is similar to the soul in the Christian sense, and the *Ti-z'ange,* or *Bon-ange* that protects a person against dangers by day and by night. Witches operate on the *Gros-bon-ange,* and the famous zombies in Haiti are people whose *Gros-bon-ange* has been captured by some evil *bocor* (conjurer). In a sanctuary near Port-au-Prince, a *mambo* (cult officiant) showed Métraux five white pots on her altar, which contained the souls of her dead relatives; and on the steps of the altar in the same temple were three jars sheltering the souls of unrelated persons that had been entrusted to her. The *mambo* said that she summoned the latter souls for the families who wanted to consult them.[47]

On the day of a major ceremony the vodun altar is fitted out with a collection of flags, chromolithographs of Catholic saints, crucifixes, holy water, choice foods and liqueurs, flowers, rosaries, candles, thunder stones (neolithic celts widely believed in West Africa and many parts of the African diaspora to be stones hurled by Shango, god of thunder and lightning, during a thunder storm), and various objects thought to have some magical properties. About 4:00 P.M. the officiating priest (*houngan*) appears in the garb which symbolizes his chief loa. First he rings a small handbell and traces cabalistic designs on the ground with cornmeal, syrup, tafia (raw rum), and liqueur. He then prepares food offerings for the dead twins and invites them to come to the ceremony.

NEO-AFRICAN RELIGIONS AND ANCESTRAL CULTS

The drummers beat a rhythm for the twins as the priest places food for them in calabash dishes. While singing several songs in honor of the twins, the officiant places offerings for them under the trees, and at springs and crossroads that the twins are believed to visit.

About 7:00 P.M. the priest consecrates the places which are thought to be the abodes of the gods or the sites which they frequent. These places are sprinkled with holy water, and libations of white flour, fried corn, and liqueur are thrown to the gods. The drumming which has accompanied these ritual acts ceases as the houngan begins an introductory address in which he says that the ceremony is being offered to the gods of the water, the gods of the sky, and the gods of the forest. With his handbell and whistle, as well as the *chachas* (rattles), *ogans* (iron bars which are struck with pieces of iron), drums and flags of his assistants, the gods are saluted. A mixture of songs and prayers follows, including the Lord's Prayer, the Apostle's Creed, morning and evening prayers, a Hail Mary, and the Magnificat (all rendered in distorted form) and a number of songs and prayers peculiar to the vodun cult. The latter prayers are addressed to all the Saints, all the angels, all the loa—known and unknown, all the dead, and all the twins. All of these beings are asked to cease persecuting the members of the family giving the service and to deliver them from tribulation. Legba, the guardian of the crossroads, is now summoned with appropriate drum rhythms, songs are sung in his honor, and a chicken is sacrificed and offered to him. After a lull, the priest starts a song for another god. One possession follows another, but not more than ten to twenty percent of the devotees ever become possessed at a ceremony. After several hours of drumming, singing, dancing, and spirit possession, the sacrificer cuts off the head of the principal offering (a goat, a sheep, or a bull) and the animal's blood is caught in the proper utensils. Catholic and vodun chants are smoothly interwoven as three or four chickens are added to the main sacrifice. After an intermission, the priest concludes the ceremony with a final series of songs and prayers, places portions of the cooked food at nearby sacred places, and oversees the distribution of the rest of the food to the participants.[48]

In addition to the annual ceremony, other important vodun rites include special ceremonies for the loa, the services for dead relatives and family ancestors (including the nine-night ceremony given nine nights after the death of a vodunist), the "degradation" ceremony intended to remove the special talent or "spirit" of a dead houngan or other person thought to have an occult ability in dealing with the forces of the other world, a "transmission" ceremony which transfers the talent of a dead houngan to his successor, a ceremony of renunciation for the heirs of a houngan who does not wish to continue the maintenance of a humfort, and a ceremony of dismissal for vodunists who become converted to Christianity.[49]

Although magical beliefs and practices cannot be considered as integral parts of vodun as a religious system, they are closely related. Most houngans engage in healing, and some are involved in divination and in sorcery, as well as in conducting ceremonies in honor of the gods and the dead. Since it is believed that the loa or the ancestors may be responsible for the misfortunes of the living, appeals for help may be made to these figures publicly or privately. In many cases, the distinction between houngans and bocors (those who deal in harmful magic), is a distinction without a difference. In short, a houngan may use his knowledge to prepare *ouangas* (evil charms) as well as to counteract such devices.[50]

As I point out earlier in the present chapter and again in chapter 9, for nearly two hundred years vodun has met the religious and emotional needs of a multitude of ordinary Haitians in a situation where such needs have been meagerly provided for by other social and religious institutions.

Vodu and Magic in the Dominican Republic

Because of the large number of fugitive slaves from Haiti who sought refuge in Santo Domingo, the migration of many workers to the sugar plantations after the period of slavery, and the strong commercial activity among the bilingual inhabitants of the frontier zone, much of Dominican vodu has been derived from Haiti. It is not, however, simply a copy of that cult, and it is not known whether it was originally a parallel development.[51]

In Haiti, vodun's magical aspect does not constrain the religious side of the cult; in the Dominican Republic, vodu is intimately and substantially tied to magical procedures, including sorcery, divination, and healing.[52] Some differences are found in the gods of the pantheons of the two cults. A large proportion of the *lua* in Santo Domingo coincide with loa in Haitian vodun, but there are also local lua, and there is one category of lua which pertains exclusively to Dominican vodu—the divinities of the Indian division.[53] Finally, in the Dominican cult, prayers in Spanish and the selection of a queen have been incorporated in the ceremonies.[54]

Dominican vodu sessions are generally private, but collective meetings are held occasionally. In Haiti, possession trance is occasioned by the religious "atmosphere" of a vodun ceremony; in Santo Domingo, the magical character of the lua makes it necessary for the officiant to induce spirit possession. The induction of that state involves purifying his body through fumigation and the use of ointments, the drinking of rum and the smoking of tobacco, and the repetition of Catholic prayers and incantations devised locally. To call the Barón del Cementerio, one cult leader limits himself to praying three Our Fathers and Ave Marias. After lighting a candle and striking the floor three times with his right foot, another officiant implores: "Come spirit to me and give me strength, will, and valor to resist your weight upon my neck; open my mind and put me in contact with my client so that I may triumph. This I ask of you in the name of the Father, the Son, and the Holy Ghost." In addition to prayers and songs, the oral part of the rites may include oaths, curses, and magical *holófrasis* (short words that condense the meaning of a phrase or prayer).[55]

Social Stratification in Trinidad

Unlike the black populations of many islands of the Caribbean, Trinidad's Negro people are only secondarily of African derivation.[56] In 1876, there were 4,250 persons of African birth living on the island; in 1881 the number was 3,035, and in 1931 only 164 resided there. Although a few of the persons of African descent in Trinidad's population came from the South American mainland and the United States, most of its Negro people have come from other West Indian islands. After slavery was abolished in 1838, indentured workers from India were brought to the island to work as laborers on the sugar estates. By 1960, those of East Indian descent constituted 36.5 percent of the total population.[57]

NEO-AFRICAN RELIGIONS AND ANCESTRAL CULTS

Trinidad became British in 1787, and during the 175 years of the colonial period the main divisions in the island's social system consisted of an upper class of Europeans headed by the Governor (the political appointee of the Secretary of State for the Colonies), the white Creole group, the colored middle class, and the black lower class.[58] The difference between the "white" creole and the British immigrant was long emphasized. In 1866, the Civil Service was predominantly British, even for the most junior appointments. Gradually, the British and the creole planter class fused. The colored middle class is not of recent origin either biologically or socially. It emerged biologically during slavery, and was so small at the time of emancipation "that the subsequent immigrant groups quite swamped it." Most of the present middle-class groups had their origin in the other islands of the Caribbean. Until recently, at least, a sharp line, "almost a caste line," has been drawn between the white and the colored sections of Trinidad's population.[59] As is the case between the white upper class and the colored middle class, there is a minimum of social mobility between the middle class and the lower class. Although the lower class is predominantly black, it includes a strong representation of light-skinned and brown-skinned elements. Light-skinned persons, particularly women, have greater chances of mobility than do those whose skin color is darker. Economic discrimination against the dark-skinned rests upon an ascriptive basis, but also upon the particularistic ties of kinship and friendship. Usually, middle-class colored children have been sent to private schools, while most lower-class children have attended the free public schools. Typically, middle-class children have been forbidden to have informal contacts with lower-class children. The "frien'ing" relationship, as well as common-law unions, always widespread among the lower classes, have been until recently rare among the middle class.[60]

Braithwaite's analysis of social stratification and ethnic stratification in Trinidad is incisive. The stratification system of Trinidad was founded on an ascriptive basis that evaluated the white group positively and the black group negatively.[61] As other groups entered the social system, they tried to differentiate themselves as much as possible from the blacks. Since the social stratification system was based on ethnic affiliation, non-Negro groups attempted to retain their ethnic identity. The result was that immigrant groups remained partially outside the social

NEO-AFRICAN RELIGIONS AND ANCESTRAL CULTS

system. The Portuguese were looked down upon because they could not speak English. As indentured laborers, the East Indians were despised. As house-to-house peddlers, the Syrians were regarded as outsiders. Unlike the local population, these newcomers did not have to maintain "standards of living." They acquired wealth more easily than the local people and in time a middle class appeared in the ethnic groups which could not be regarded as outside the stratification system. Although members of these groups gave up a considerable part of their cultural heritage they sought to retain their ethnic identity by prohibiting intermarriage except with the white group. Among the various ethnic groups, the Chinese were the first to enter the lower fringes of white society, but Syrians and East Indians have also broken into the white group. Because of their skin color and hair texture, they appear to be more acceptable to the white group.[62]

Some members of the lower class are affiliated with the Roman Catholic, Anglican, Presbyterian, and Methodist churches. Among the religions which draw their support entirely from the lower class, the Pilgrim Holiness, Gospel Hall, Seventh Day Adventist, and Jehovah's Witnesses are relatively "respectable" compared with the Spiritual Baptists and the Shango groups.[63] As I point out earlier, some shangoists attend the Catholic church or a Protestant church with some regularity, and some lower-class persons who belong to orthodox denominations at times consult shango leaders about personal problems. There are lower-class persons, however, who are highly critical of both the Shouters and the shangoists and who emphatically dissociate themselves from everything related to the cults.[64]

For small segments of the lower class in Trinidad, the Shouter and shango religions provide satisfactions that they have not been able to obtain elsewhere. Occasionally, a middle-class person seeks the help of a shango practitioner about a serious problem. Quite a number of East Indians have joined Spiritual Baptist groups, but relatively few have become shangoists.

Trinidadian Shango

The Shango cult of Trinidad developed during the nineteenth century as persons of African descent, mainly Yorubas, from the west coast of Africa and from other West Indian islands, combined traditional tribal beliefs and practices with elements of Catholicism.[65] In 1960, 70.4 percent of the population of Trinidad and Tobago was recorded as Christian. Denominational percentages were: Roman Catholics, 51.4; Anglicans, 30.0; Presbyterians, 5.6; Methodists, 3.2; Baptists, 3.2; Seventh Day Adventists, 2.2; Jehovah Witnesses, .7; Pentecostals, .7; other Christians, 3.2. (In 1960, 6 percent of Trinidad's population was Moslem, and 23.1 percent was Hindu.) The 1960 Census of Population of Trinidad and Tobago (Vol. 2, Part A, 1963, Table 6) does not list separately the number of Baptists who call themselves Spiritual Baptists, and no reference is made to shangoists. It is impossible to estimate accurately the number of shangoists in Trinidad. Some devotees attend a number of the large annual ceremonies given in different cult centers. Some persons attend a Shouters church regularly but participate from time to time in shango ceremonies. Some shangoists attend the Catholic church or a Protestant church with some regularity. The only connection that some persons have with shango is through the healing or the conjuring that certain cult leaders offer. There are several dozen shango cult centers in Trinidad with a total of thousands of devotees; additional thousands are marginal participants and clients.

The basic establishment of a Shango cult center consists of a shrine area where five or more "stools" (shrines) for the most important "powers" (deities) are located, a *chapelle* or small cult house, and the *"palais"* or "tent" where ceremonies are held and some healing is done. The chapelle houses statues and lithographs of Catholic saints, crucifixes, rosaries, candles, "thunder-stones" (neolithic celts or stones which resemble such celts, but believed by shangoists to be stones hurled by Shango during a thunderstorm), vases of flowers, pots of water, bottles of olive oil, and such "tools" of the powers as swords (steel or wooden), double-bladed wooden axes similar to the dance clubs (carved ritual axes decorated with heads and thunderbolts in western Nigeria [Frobenius *Voice of Africa* 1: 211–14]), cutlasses, hatchets, daggers, whips, wooden guns, wooden spears, bows and arrows, anchors, boat paddles, drums, keys, banners, wooden crosses, *shay-shays* (ceremonial brooms), *chac-chacs* (rattles), and shepherds' crooks. African symbols are not kept in a separate room, a practice followed in many *vodun* shrines in Haiti and in many cult houses of the *candomblés* in Brazil. Nearly all of the objects on the altar and on the upper half of the wall space in the chapelle, how-

75

ever, are Catholic symbols. The inside "stools" (shrines), thunder-stones, and "tools" are arranged on the floor or stand against the lower half of the wall space.[66]

In southern Nigeria, each Yoruba deity, including Shango, god of thunder and lightning, has his own priests, societies, and cult centers. In Trinidad, Shango is only one of dozens of "powers," including twenty or more Yoruba divinities, that are followed by devotees of "African work." Among these gods are Alufon (Olufon), Béji (Ibeji), Emanja, Erelay (Erinle), Eshu (Esu), Ogun, Obatala, Osain (Osanyin), Oshun (Osun), Oya, Shakpana (Sonponna), Shango (Sango), and Yaibo (Yao). Among the most popular of the non-Yoruba powers are Gabriel and Mama Latay. In Trinidad, as in Haiti, parts of Brazil, Cuba, and in some other countries in the New World, old African gods are equated with Catholic saints. The same equivalences are not found everywhere; in fact, there are variations from region to region in the same country and even from one cult center to another. Among these pairs in Trinidad are Obatala and St. Benedict, Béji and St. Peter, Emanja and St. Anne or St. Catherine, Oshun and St. Philomena or St. Anne, Oyá and St. Catherine or St. Philomena, Shakpana and St. Francis or Moses or St. Jerome, and Shango and St. John.

As conceived by Trinidadian shangoists, Ogun, the god of iron and of war, is thought of as a warrior who prefers rams and cocks as offerings and whose colors are red and white. He "works" with a sword and is violent and "outrageous" when he possesses a follower. Oshun, mistress of the ocean, prefers female goats and hens as offerings. She "works" with an oar or a double-bladed wooden axe (as one of Shango's wives she may carry one of his symbols). Temperamentally she is very placid and those possessed by her behave mildly. Shakpana, often referred to as a doctor, is thought by some to control all evil spirits. His color is red and the correct offering for him is a goat or a rooster of mixed colors. He "works" with a shayshay, is said by some to be a cripple and to have a cross disposition. Shango, god of thunder and lightning, is given a variety of sacrifices, including bulls, rams, red or white cocks, and white pigeons. His colors are red or red and white. He "works" with a *pessie* (whip), dances in fire, and appears at ceremonies in different forms: Abacuso, Guroon, and Saja.

The Yoruba in Nigeria generally distinguish at least three separate "souls": *emi* (the breath), *ojiji* (the shadow), and the *ori* (*eleda, olori*), or guardian soul.[67] According to Talbot and to Forde, an evil person can summon by incantation the shadow of a deceased person and interrogate it, a procedure considered quite different to communicating with the spirits of the ancestors in a reverent way or in seances during which priests or attendant mediums are possessed by departed spirits of men.[68] The Yoruba attribute many misfortunes and illnesses to the anger of the spirits of the dead.[69] In Trinidad, many shangoists believe in two aspects of the human spirit: the soul and the shadow. They hold that a "good" member of the shango cult can obtain remedies from the dead for the treatment of the sick, and that an evil operator can capture an evil spirit and use it for his own purposes.[70]

Each Shango cult center in Trinidad holds an annual ceremony at approximately the same time each year. That ceremony begins on Tuesday night with a prayer meeting. Original prayers by prominent members of the cult-group or by important visitors follow several repetitions of the Lord's Prayer; Hail Mary; and the Apostle's Creed. These prayers are known by nearly everyone and are recited in unison. For prayers which are not so well known—for example, St. Francis's prayer, St. George's prayer, and Blessed Martin's prayer—the leader recites the whole prayer and then goes through it line by line with the others repeating each line after him.

Eshu, also known in West Africa as Elegba or Elegbara, is the divine messenger among the deities and a trickster who enjoys causing trouble. Identified to some extent with Satan, Eshu must be dismissed before the other powers can be summoned. A ritual assistant brings a calabash filled with water and ashes (Satan's food) into the palais and places it on the ground while a song for Eshu is sung. The calabash is then carried outside the palais and emptied, symbolizing the ejection of Eshu from the ceremony. After Eshu's dismissal, Ogun (St. Michael) is summoned by playing one of his rhythms on the drums and by singing one or more songs in his honor.

As a rule, other male powers are invited immediately after Ogun's arrival as the ceremonial leader starts a song for Shakpana, St. George, or St. Raphael. Following the coming of a number of male gods, several female powers are summoned. Special attention may be given to certain

NEO-AFRICAN RELIGIONS AND ANCESTRAL CULTS

powers each night, but no night is reserved exclusively for one or a few gods. The language used in Trinidadian shango includes a sprinkling of Yoruba words such as *kere* (attention), *omi* (water), *ile* (house), *l'aiye* (in this world), *orisa* (deity), *aduro* (we wait), *emi* (I am), *aloco* (the name of a bird), *airi* (we do not see), *a loc ba ree* (Yoruba— *a lo ba re o* [go home and find good fortune]) and the names of at least twenty Yoruba gods. It includes many English words, some French Creole expressions, some words which seem to be of purely local origin, and a few undecipherable sounds.

From time to time a person possessed by a god, or one of the ceremonial assistants, pours water or rum in each of the four corners of the palais. Shortly after the onset of possession, a devotee may run to the chapelle, seize the implement of his principal god, and return to the palais brandishing it. Alternatively, he may take the implement, rush to the stool of the power possessing him, and dance on or near the shrine. Drumming, dancing, singing, and spirit possession continue all night, the climax coming at dawn with the sacrificing of pigeons, doves, chickens, ducks, agoutis, morocoys (land turtles), goats, and sheep. Similar rites are performed on the following three nights, often including at some point the sacrifice of a bull. Other noteworthy shango rites include the initiatory rituals of headwashing and headgashing, "laying" (establishing) a stool for an orisha, "planting" a flag near a stool, "feeding the children" (a thanksgiving service), moving a stool to another site, the consecration of a new set of drums, and the dismissal of a power.

The acculturative process in Trinidadian shango may be thought of in terms of full or nearly full African retentions, reinterpretations of African cultural elements, Afro-European syncretisms, and European-borrowed traits and reinterpretations of European cultural elements. Among the most important items in the first category are animal sacrifice, thunder stones, dancing as a part of religious ceremonies, the use of drums and rattles, emphasis on rhythm and polyrhythms, the presence of supernatural beings who intervene in the affairs of men, and revelation by the gods of procedures that will be helpful in dealing with illness and other misfortunes. Included in the reinterpretation of African traits are the polytheistic orientation of the cult, the names and some of the characteristics and powers of Yoruba deities, initiatory rites, the

NEO-AFRICAN RELIGIONS AND ANCESTRAL CULTS

multiple soul concept, the ritual use of blood, the use of leaves, divination by throwing *obi* seeds, public possession by the spirits, and utilization of the spirits of the dead. Among the syncretisms found in Trinidadian shango are the equatability of selected African gods and Catholic saints, the ritual uses of water, the extensive use of charms, numerous death rites, belief in witches, and the use of dreams in divining. The outstanding European and reinterpreted European cultural elements are the Bible, Catholic prayers, books of magic, "spontaneous" prayers of the "Baptist" type, candles, the cross and crucifixes, incense, and divination by gazing into a crystal ball, a glass of water, or the flame of a candle.

Aspects of Trinidadian cult life that are closely related to religious behavior include divination, conjuring, and folk medicine, often strikingly similar to West African procedures. There is, however, one notable difference between some Neo-African religions in the Caribbean and the traditional religions from which they are derived. Orunmila, the deity of divination, is absent in the Shango pantheons in Trinidad and Grenada. This is not the case in the *santeria* cult in Cuba, a religion which is also derived from Yoruba traditions. Perhaps fear of the gods served by the *babalawo* (priest-diviners in the Ifa tradition of the Yoruba) caused very few of these officiants to be sold into the West Indian slavery.

Since full knowledge of the Ifa geomantic system of divination requires years of study, it is highly unlikely that those who were sent to the Caribbean could have trained competent assistants under the conditions of slavery. The lack of a fixed mode of Ifa divination has driven devotees of Shango in the British Caribbean to find their own substitutes for determining the causes of events in order to learn which ritual actions must be taken. These substitutes include "looking" or "seeing" with crystal balls, cards, or leaves, as well as reliance on dreams, visions, and prophecy. Ifa techniques gave indirect access to a knowledge of the causes and sequence of events, but West Indian techniques through visions and messages to possessed individuals are direct and immediate. As M. G. Smith points out, this factor "allows progressive individualization of cult practice and organization, hence increasing variability of belief and rite over time in Shango worship as practiced by West Indians."[71]

Nearly every shango leader engages in healing. Some of the old "orisha" people insist that they seldom or never seek the services of a physician. Some of them consult only medical doctors; others go to healers for certain complaints and to physicians for other illnesses. Some use medical and nonmedical personnel at the same time for the same or for different diseases. Leaves are extremely important in popular healing formulas in Trinidad, and they are often boiled or crushed in water and mixed with one or more oils (palm, olive, coconut, castor, whale, shark, and so forth). Sometimes drums are beaten in Trinidad when a healer undertakes to cure a person who is seriously ill, especially one who is thought to be possessed by an evil spirit.[72]

Due to some industrialization, further urbanization, the expansion of education, the growth of health and welfare services, and the increased influence of mass communication on tastes and beliefs, traditional religious and medical beliefs have been undermined to some extent in recent decades. Also, Trinidadian shango has been diluted (or enriched) at an accelerating rate in recent times by the intermixture of some of its aspects with the Shouter (Spiritual Baptist) complex. In addition to their annual ceremonies and the other shango rites mentioned above, some leaders hold "prayer meetings" two or three times a year or conduct Spiritual Baptist services on Sunday evenings or preside from time to time over rituals which combine shango and Shouter elements. Ordinarily a shangoist is baptized and "put to mourn" by a Spiritual Baptist, but one widely known shango leader admitted that she had been conducting "mourning" rites.

Grenada's Social Structure [73]

Located in the southernmost part of the eastern Caribbean, Grenada was colonized by the French but passed into British hands in the 1770s. Its indigenous population of Carib Indians had already been replaced by Europeans, African slaves, and their hybrid offspring. Under the British, the colony's slave population and its sugar exports increased rapidly. In 1808, however, further imports of African slaves were prohibited, and

thirty years later slavery was abolished. With the decline of the Caribbean economy based on the production of sugar by slaves, many hold-
ings were abandoned and many former slaves acquired land by squat-
ting, purchase, or some form of tenancy. The latter arrangement enabled
Grenadian proprietors to shift to the cultivation of cocoa.

I point out in chapter 2 that the Roman Catholic church was well
established during the French colonial period, but that Protestantism
spread after it became a British colony. When M. G. Smith studied the
variety of Shango called the "African Feast" in 1953, approximately 1
percent of Grenada's population of 76,000 persons was white, 5 percent
East Indian, 17 percent "colored" hybrids, and 77 percent Negro or
black.

Until 1877, Grenada was administered politically by English governors responsible both to the local legislature, made up of white merchants and planters, and to the British Crown. In 1877 the colonial
legislature asked the Crown to assume all the responsibilities of government. Grenada remained a Crown Colony until a new constitution in
1925 provided for a limited elective section in the local assembly. Universal suffrage was introduced in 1951, but less than one-sixth of the
island's adult population was eligible to vote under the terms of the
property franchise; and only a fraction of those who were qualified to
vote could stand for election. The Governor controlled a permanent majority in the legislature through nominated and official appointments to
it, and Government concerned itself with routine administrative functions. Government programs reflected the interests of planters and merchants, and no trade unions or political parties of any consequence
existed.

Following the development of cocoa as an export crop, the cultivation of nutmegs was introduced into Grenada, and frequently the two
were intercropped. Until World War II, labor relations in Grenada were
customary rather than commercial; they were relations between planter
and peasant rather than between employer and employee. The Second
World War served to improve Grenada's economic situation. Demands
for labor increased, and prices for exports and for imported goods rose.
Unionism was still absent, and many of the dissatisfied emigrated to

Trinidad, Curaçao, or Aruba. For some time after World War II, Grenada's economy continued to benefit from conditions caused by the war. Gradually economic conditions worsened, and a trade union of estate workers was formed. Wage increases were won, and a strike of all farm-labor followed. Universal suffrage was introduced at the end of the 1940s, but the legislative power of labor's majorities in the legislature was limited by the Governor's executive power. Riots and strikes took place in 1951, and the old socioeconomic order seemed to have broken down. Decisions made by Eric M. Gairy, the leader of the labor union and party, alienated many workers, and his influence declined after October 1951. In 1952–53, Gairy attempted to regain his political strength by a militant trade union program which included the threat and calling of strikes. As Smith points out, Norman Paul represented an earlier tradition. His Shangoism (the African Feast) "proposed no social program, but relied on ritual and faith to protect or promote individual well-being."

Goveia's conclusions concerning social structure in the Leeward Islands of the northeastern part of the Caribbean apply to other sugar producing and agricultural islands in the region, especially to the smaller islands. Color and status were closely linked in the social structure of the Leeward Islands at the end of the eighteenth century. The small, almost exclusively white ruling class "held in subordination a predominantly brown middle class of free people of color, a mixed group of brown and black privileged slaves, and a dispossessed laboring population of field slaves, who were almost all black." After emancipation, "the density of population, which had helped to destroy the slave system in these islands by making it increasingly expensive to maintain, now helped to preserve the social structure built up under the slave system, by reviving the sugar economy on which it was based." Holding that the social system of the Leeward Islands combines incompatible elements of democracy with the heritage of slavery, Goveia asserts that the existence of political democracy provides "the hope of appealing to the large majorities still suffering from the effects of poverty and lack of opportunity to vote for effective reforming policies based on universalist social values."[74]

NEO-AFRICAN RELIGIONS AND ANCESTRAL CULTS

The Shango Cult in Grenada

In 1849, more than 1,000 postemancipation immigrants arrived in Grenada from Ijesha, Nigeria. After completing their indentures, these Yoruba people settled at Munich, Concorde, and La Mode. Within these communities, the Yoruba language was spoken, and many aspects of Yoruba culture were preserved, including elements of the kinship system and concepts and rites basic to Yoruba polytheism. Shango was originally the religion of these Africans. Years later, when they and their descendants began to move away from their closed communities, their religious cult attracted many followers. Smith writes that as the cult spread, it "was marked by syncretisms of form and content, numerous traits being taken over from the Nation Dance as well as from Catholicism, until Shango is now the representative form of African ritual among the Grenadians." [75]

There are many similarities between the Shango cults in Grenada and in Trinidad.[76] The majority of the "powers" have the same names and functions as they do among the Yoruba, and most of them are associated with Catholic saints. Each god has his own devotees, persons dedicated to him at birth or who have received revelations during visions. As in Trinidad, altars are called "stools," and the emblems, colors, and sacrificial animals are the same as in Africa. Usually, the time of a deity's annual feast coincides with the birthday of the saint with whom the orisha is identified. Separate annual ceremonies are not held for each god; all of the deities are invited in succession to the same ceremony. A deity is summoned by a particular drum beat or song, and, when the Queen of Shango (the cult leader), rings a bell, a worshipper of that god becomes possessed by him. The advice of the powers is sought, and at times they are asked to heal the sick. To send a power away, the possessed person is placed on the ground and covered with a sheet. The sign of the Cross is made on the forehead with chalk and the devotee's name is called. After the Queen has tapped her shoulder three times with a bell and blown a whistle, the worshipper gets up, but she does not become her normal self immediately. As in Brazil and Trinidad, there is a transitional period during which the person who has been possessed behaves in a childish way. In Grenadian Shango belief, minor deities, called *were,* possess cult members after the major powers have departed.

In Grenada, "Shango Dances" take place in the home of a Queen and are given on such occasions as thanksgiving at the end of a harvest, the consecration of a new house, payment for a vow, or requests for the powers to intercede in a financial venture. According to Pollak-Eltz, the Queen "organizes the dance, initiates the novices, and casts the kolanuts to find out if a given sacrifice pleases the deity." Initiation ceremonies are less elaborate in Grenada than in Nigeria, but they follow the African pattern. A short period of seclusion is followed by head-washing with an infusion of sacred herbs, anointment with olive oil, and the pouring of the blood of a sacrificial animal over the head of the initiate. The ceremony is known as "baptism of the power"; Christian baptismal words are used.

The Shango cult in Grenada has been influenced by practices followed in Shouter (Shaker) sects and by spiritism. Shangoists often attend "mourning rites" held by Shouters (Shakers) in the hope that they may obtain special "gifts" through prayers and visions. Some Protestant hymns are now sung during Shango rites, and some who call themselves Shango priests are also Shouter preachers.

The African Feast Cult in Grenada

A cult founded in Grenada in 1948 by a man named Norman Paul combines Adventism, Shango, Shakerism, and magical beliefs taken from such books as the Sixth and Seventh Books of Moses.[77] At an early age, Paul heard his father relate stories about ceremonies which had been performed by the Munich Africans. When he was seven, Paul went to live with his mother's mother, and from her he learned to "sing Big Drum and dance." At sixteen, he was baptized in the Seventh Day Adventist church. When he travelled to Trinidad, he met a man who told him stories about Egungun, a Yoruba deity. Both in Grenada and in Trinidad, he had had opportunities to acquire some knowledge of Shango and of the Spiritual Baptists (Shakers in Grenada, Shouters in Trinidad). Paul had experienced visions from time to time during his youth and early manhood, and he had devoted considerable time to studying the Scriptures, giving feasts, and going out on the road to preach. It was not until 1945–46 that he received instructions during a visionary experience to prepare a thanksgiving table and to "feed the children" (a Shango ceremony). In 1948, at the age of fifty, Oshun asked him to get three drums and prepare a feast for her. According to Paul, from that time on, Oshun (St. Philomena) directed him in everything he did.[78]

Denying that he staged Shango feasts, Paul called his religious activities "an African feast."

> The first time I wanted to beat drum, I went for a permit in the police station at Point Fortin [Trinidad], and the sergeant asked me what it is I am carrying on, if it is Shango or an African feast. I told him I doesn't know anything about Shango, what I know of is an African feast, and I related to him how it happened that I should give that feast; he told me well, he would not oppose me if it was an African feast, but if it is Shango I could not carry it on. He brought the logbook, he showed me that a Shango feast is for people that used chalkmark [magical signs], and they invoke the evil spirit and they will throw somebody down and they will beat up themselves, they will roll in the mud, they will remain there, some of them, some of them sometimes will even dead. This is what they call Shango, but mine is something quite different.[79]

Paul claimed that he never had anything to do with "other African Dance people." He operated from his home on the basis of instructions from Oshun and other "powers." Presenting his offerings at a place in the river designated by Oshun, he watched the big fish come and feast on them, and he received messages from his protector and other gods.

Despite Paul's protestations, the belief system of his "African feast" strongly resembles that of the Shango cult in Trinidad.[80] In his account, Paul mentioned most frequently Oshun, Yemanja, Ogun, Obatala, Oba, Shakpana, Oya, Erile, Osayin, Legba, and Abakoso (Shango). All of these gods are of Yoruba origin except Legba, a Dahomean deity. Apparently Legba had been substituted for Eshu; Legba was referred to as the "prince of darkness," a view, as Smith points out, that was simpler than the original African conception of Legba or Eshu. He spoke also of various Indian powers, among them Baba (found also in Trinidadian shango), and an unidentifiable spirit called Gurun (another name for Shango—Simpson, *The Shango Cult*, 19). He referred to *wereh* (*wéré*), a state of semi-possession, as another Yoruba deity.[81]

In the African feast cult, several of the Yoruba divinities were

NEO-AFRICAN RELIGIONS AND ANCESTRAL CULTS

equated with Catholic saints—Oshun with St. Philomena, Yemanja with St. Anne, Ogun with St. Michael, Osayin with St. Anthony, and Abakoso with St. John. These identifications closely resemble those found in Trinidadian shango, Haitian vodun, Cuban santeria, and in the Brazilian candomblé. All of these powers, and others such as Shakpana, had certain days of worship and preferred certain sacrifices, ritual objects, perfume, and types of dress when they possessed devotees. These preferences were close to their Nigerian originals.[82]

In Paul's religion, Shango (Abakoso) used the *sheshere,* a broom made of palm-leaf spines, to repel and punish evil. Persons possessed by Shango were said to be able to dance in fire and to eat burning coals without being harmed. Shakpana was associated with illness and misfortune, but not exclusively with evil. Paul considered him as a potent healer. Osayin and Erile (Erinle) were also associated with medicines and magical help.[83]

In keeping a three-day feast, Paul began his "work" on a Tuesday night, praying for "all the saints first, but I don't call in the people who are dead." The ceremony was continued on Wednesday by honoring Ogun (St. Michael). Following prayers from seven until twelve on that night, drumming and dancing caused Ogun to "manifest" on a believer. At 4:00 A.M., the sacrificial animals were bathed and taken to Ogun.

It is outside there where I go and pray first, put salt and ask anything; I would take the goat there for sacrifice. And when I kill the goat, you can't put it down and saw its neck and it keep on bellowing all the time. It must face the East, and it must be one cut. If you missing with that cut and it start to bleat and run about, you have more distress and trouble in that sacrifice. Ogun not any blind man, is a watchman, and if he displease with his work, he leave you in trouble. You will have to get a next feast and have a next goat, because it is spoilt. And when you kill the goat one cut, you have to get the obi (kolanuts). To satisfy the people I have to get the obi and ask the Powers if they are satisfied.[84]

Paul gave a general feast of thanksgiving every Easter, starting on Sunday and lasting through Saturday. So long as his followers were pleased with the results of that feast, they did not ask for another ceremony until the next year. Occasionally, when he felt satisfied with whatever "work" he had been doing, Paul gave a thanksgiving feast. As an example of such an occasion, he mentioned going to Carriacou to give a feast at the home of a woman whose child had been troubled by an evil spirit. After finding through the obi that a power was satisfied with the offerings, Paul placed the meat from the sacrificed animal in the hands of the participants and told them to eat it. He said he did not place offerings on the table in the hall of the house for the purpose of feeding "people's dead," a practice he attributed to the Nation Dance people and some Shango people.[85]

Cuban Santeria

Afro-Cuban religion is known in Spanish as *santeria*. Most of its non-European elements are derived from Yoruba beliefs and rituals. In the town of Jovellanos, Matanzas province, Bascom witnessed many ceremonies in which animals were sacrificed to Yoruba deities, Yoruba music was played on African types of drums, songs with Yoruba words and music were sung, and dancers were possessed by the orisha. Beads of the proper colors were worn by the devotees, Yoruba foods (*eko, amala, olele, akara* and *fufu*) were cooked for them and the gods, and leaves with Yoruba names (*botjue, ewe Ifa, pompola,* and *atori*) were used in making medicines and in washing the stones of the orishas and the heads of cult members.[86]

Among the Yoruba orisha found in Cuban santeria are Shapana (Babaluaiye), who is identified with St. Lazarus and is associated with all skin diseases. He is known for his favorite food of maize (*agabdo*), his clothes of jute, and his crutches. Elegba, who is equated with St. Peter, opens the road, prefers rats (*ekute*) and pigs (*elede*) to eat, likes to drink and to smoke cigars. Shango, god of thunder, wears red and white beads, prefers ram (*agbo*) as food, and is associated with St. Barbara. The Catholic equivalent of Oya, one of Shango's wives, is St. Teresita. Oya wears maroon beads, and, in Cuba, has become the owner of the cemetery. Our Lady of Mercy is Obatalá or Orishanlá, whose beads and other objects are white and for whom alcohol is forbidden. Yemajá, the owner of salt water, wears crystal or blue beads and is identified with the Virgin of Regla (the town is a suburb of Havana). The Virgin of Cobre (the town is in eastern Cuba) is Oshun, the owner of fresh waters and of brass and gold, and a deity who is famous for her beauty and her love affairs. Osanyin, "the doctor" and the owner of all the leaves of the forest, is associated with St. Raphael and prefers the tortoise (*ahun*) as food. Ifa or Orunmila, the deity of divination, is equated with St. Francis of Assisi. St. Michael is Erinle or Inle, a doctor who specializes in surgery. St. Comas and St. Damien, the twin saints, are the Ibedji, who behave like small children. St. John the Baptist is associated with Ogun, the Yoruba god of war and iron, who is noted in Cuba for his bravery in battle, his ability as a blacksmith, and his love of alcohol. A Cuban myth reconciles the discrepancy between the Catholic chromolithograph depicting a young boy with a ram in his arms and Yoruba ritual. According to this myth, Shango tricked Ogun into exchanging the ram for a dog (*aja*), Ogun's favorite sacrificial animal.[87] Other sacrificial foods for Changó include a red or white cock, ochra stew (*quimbombo, amala ila*), bean fritters (*akara*), cornstarch porridge and gruel (*eco; eko* in Yoruba), and tortoise.

The ethnographic studies of Herskovits, Price Mars, Courlander, Ortiz, Bascom, Bastide, Métraux, Simpson, and others have stressed the syncretisms represented by the identification of African deities with Catholic saints, the African pattern of possession, the retention of animal sacrifices, African drumming, singing, and dancing in African-derived rituals in the New World. In the minds of santeria cult members in Jovellanos, Cuba, in 1948, Bascom found that the stones, the blood, and the herbs were the foundations of their form of worship. Each *santero* (santeria priest) takes an oath to protect his sacred stones and to feed them at least once a year. When the orisha are fed, the blood of the sacrificial animals is allowed to flow onto the stones. Many possessions following the blood sacrifices and the drumming, singing, and dancing are an indication that the gods are well fed and satisfied, and the invisible fluid and the power of the stones are increased by the presence of the orisha at the ceremony. Each deity has its own special herbs, its own type of stone, and animals which are its favorite food. The herbs serve to cleanse, refresh, and prepare devotees and ritual objects for contact with the orisha. The blood is the food of the deities, and the stones are the objects through which they are fed and in which their power resides.[88]

Bascom has described the striking similarities between two forms of

NEO-AFRICAN RELIGIONS AND ANCESTRAL CULTS

Afro-Cuban divination and Yoruba divination. Among the Yoruba in Nigeria, the priests of Ifa are called *awo* or *babalawo;* in Cuba, they are known as *aguo* (*awo*) and *babalao.* The Yoruba diviner "selects the particular figure pertaining to his client's case out of 256 possible figures by manipulating sixteen palm-nuts or a chain of eight seeds. . . ." The figure is marked on a wooden divining tray with wood dust, and a "bell" is tapped on the tray to get the attention of Ifa. All of these objects are used in Afro-Cuban Ifa divination, but since few diviners in Cuba know the use of the sixteen nuts, most of them use the divining chain known as an *opele,* a device which is also employed more frequently among the Yoruba than the palm-nuts. In Cuba, as among the Yoruba in Nigeria, each figure is associated with a set of verses which contain the predictions and which are memorized and recited by the diviner. According to Bascom, the introductory sections of Ifa divination among the Lucumi [Afro-Cubans of Yoruba extraction] "refer frequently to previous divinations, naming the diviners or the figures, the clients, and the sacrifices made. Many of the verses also include an illustrative myth or folktale, known as *historia* in Spanish and as *itan* (myth, or literally, history) in Yoruba, which expands upon the case serving as a precedent. The verses end with an explanatory section, introduced by 'Ifa says,' which states the problem facing the present client and prescribes the sacrifice necessary to insure a successful solution, unless this is the same as in the precedent previously cited."[89]

Although it is not as highly regarded as Ifa divination, the system of divination which employs sixteen cowry shells and is known in Cuba as *dilogun* or *eridilogun* (from the Yoruba *erindilogun,* meaning sixteen) is the most frequently used system of divination in the Afro-Cuban cults. Among the Yoruba, the same system of divination, known as *elegba,* is considered as the female counterpart of Ifa.[90]

In his detailed account of lucumi dances, Ortiz demonstrates the African authenticity of the rituals. The lucumis honor each of the gods with choral dances and pantomime in accordance with orthodox tradition. Dances are given for each god and for each important episode in the mythical life of each deity. The dances are numerous, but many of the sacred African dances have not been preserved in Cuba.[91]

Elegbara or Echú is honored first in a santeria ceremony. In Cuba, this restless god personifies destiny or luck, and his attitude can make it easy or difficult for a devotee to realize a particular desire. Elegbara tells jokes, sometimes harsh ones, and engages in mischievous caprice. Cuban Christians, like Christians in some other places in the New World, err in saying that Eléggua is the devil; Yoruba mythology does not include a person like Satan who is always wicked. In Africa, Eléggua is an erotic god, but in Cuba he has lost his character. This change may be due in part to the fact that the rituals of fertilization have lost their social function in Cuba. Also, in the Cuban social environment, all symbolism that was regarded as obscene was eliminated. The copular pantomime, circumcision, human sacrifice, and other elements of African social and religious rituals have not been continued.[92]

In santeria, Ogun also is mischievous and very shrewd. The inventor or the inheritor of the blacksmith shop is now associated with everything made of iron, including railways, automobiles, tanks, and airplanes. The symbols used in dances for Ogun include shovels, machetes, picks, hammers, chains, keys, and other iron objects. In Cuba, he is identified with St. John the Baptist (Bascom, *The Yoruba,* 15), or, because he holds in his hands keys for opening the sky, with St. Peter.[93]

Ochosí, the Yoruba god of the hunt, becomes excited when he attends a ceremony and shouts like a hunter during the chase. In the pantomimic dances of hunting his emblem is the bow and arrow. Oko, the god of agriculture, is not excitable by nature and so does not have a special pantomime. Obatala, the African deity who created the world, is androgynous. In Cuba, his feminine personality predominates, but he appears in various forms.[94]

The Ibedji do not take possession of devotees, but instead engage in childlike play during a ceremony. They provide numerous songs and, in dancing, imitate the capricious antics of children. Changó is thought of in Cuba as the god of virility and sexuality. In a ritual, he manifests himself like a bull as he butts with his head. He opens his eyes widely, sticks out his tongue as a symbol of fire, shakes his sacred axe, and holds his testicles in his hands. No other oricha goes through such violent contortions nor stages such an unusual pantomime. His dances are warlike or erotic; in the latter, pantomime emphasizes his sexuality through obvious gestures.[95]

NEO-AFRICAN RELIGIONS AND ANCESTRAL CULTS

Yemayá is a mythological figure exemplifying femininity and maternity, a wise and virtuous deity. Her emblem, a fan called *agbégbe,* is made of palm leaves or of peacock feathers, with ornaments of snails and bells that tinkle. Her colors are navy blue with white that symbolizes the foam of ocean waves. Like the other female oricha, she wears a dressing gown with a cloth belt around the waist. During a ceremony, Yemayá laughs heartily and whirls like waves of the sea. She bathes herself between the waves and is carried back and forth by them. Sometimes she swims from one side of a wave to the other; at other times she dives under the water for snails, seaweed, and fishes for her sons. Sometimes she rows to the other shore where she is awaited by Ochun. Her dances start with gentle undulations, but quickly change to violent movements symbolizing angry waves blown by strong winds.[96]

When Ochun, the goddess of coquetry, of lewdness, and of luxury, comes to a ceremony, she laughs like Yemayá and whirls around in circles. Then her vain coquetry makes her look at the participants with haughtiness and disdain. She combs her hair, using the water as a mirror, and adjusts the necklaces and bracelets which she wears. Sometimes she carries a fan of her favorite color, yellow like the sandy shores of the river. Her yellow gown bears an ornament in rhomboidal form, and on the side of her dress she wears a festoon from which little bells are suspended. The music and dances in honor of Ochun are the most sensual, and the verses that are sung are salacious.[97]

Orúnla or Ifá doesn't dance in a santeria ceremony. If his devotees dance in his honor they do so without any unusual steps. Egungun, the oricha who symbolizes all of the dead ancestors of a lineage in traditional Yoruba belief, is known as Egun in Cuba. The lucumis have no confraternity of Egun or Egungun, but they honor Egun during a santeria ceremony. This dance resembles that performed in the funeral rites that are celebrated for important dignitaries of santeria. In the most spectacular part of the dance, a masked person represents a superhuman being who occasionally visits the earth. The Egungun talk in a falsetto, supernatural voice, and they perform magical games under the direction of a master of ceremonies called *atogún.* This guide carries a decorated whip and guides the Egungun to prevent them from stumbling and serves as an interpreter, translating messages for mortals from this oricha. Usually

NEO-AFRICAN RELIGIONS AND ANCESTRAL CULTS

Egungun dances with only drum rhythms to accompany him, and only the largest drum "talks" and produces the principal sounds.[98]

Especially in the province of Matanzas, Oro and Güelede (Gelede), deities from Nigeria and Dahomey, appear in santeria dances. Like Egungun, they represent the spirits of ancestors. Oro is feared because his activities are related to the administration of justice.[99]

The Abakwa Society in Cuba is a lineal descendant of the Egbo secret society of the Ekoi and Efik peoples of the Calabar Coast of West Africa. Among the many secret societies of this region, the Egbo Club was the most powerful, and its influence in social life and government continued after the arrival of colonial administrators. There were seven grades in the ancient Egbo society, the achievement of each of which necessitated the paying of fees, but the deepest mysteries were not revealed until middle age had been reached. According to Talbot, the chief of Nkanda, the seventh and highest grade of the society, was by far the most powerful man of the town. Each grade had its own dances and songs, as well as its own image (Okum Ngbe or Egbo).[100]

> The so-called image is a figure robed from crown to heel in a long garment, of the color proper to the grade, and pierced with eyeholes. It usually bears on its head a wooden framework covered with skin and shaped like a human head, often with two faces, one male and the other female. This represents the omniscience of the Deity looking both ways, into the future and back to the past, as also the bisexual character shown in the oldest conceptions of Obassi Osaw and Obassi Nsi, Sky Father and Earth Mother.
>
> The Okum runs up and down accompanied by two attendants clothed in gorgeous, close fitting garments, usually of red, yellow and white. One of these carries a rod or whip, the symbol of the power of the society, with which, under native law, he had the right to flog to death any nonmembers who had seriously offended against its rules. The other bears the symbolic green boughs, which play so great a part in the lives of the Ekoi. At almost every important occurrence, from birth onward, green leaves of the kind proper to the event are used, and at the last are gently drawn over the face of a dying man, that his spirit may pass peacefully and without pain from this world to the next.[101]

During the "plays" performed by the Egbo society the principal characters carried wands or whips, the symbols of power which could be used to beat to death nonmembers who were found outside their houses on one of these occasions, or who had committed a serious offense. Minor offenses were punished by fines, the main source of revenue for the club. The society also acted as a collection agency in recovering debts for its members.[102]

In 1941, Courlander observed an Abakwa ceremony in Guanabacoa, a town near Havana. Four drummers played on three small, shallow drums (*encómo*) and a long goatskin drum (*boncó*). Singers were tightly packed around the drummers, and first one brother (*ocobío*) then another took over the singing, with the chorus coming in responsively. Most of the words of the songs were "Carabali" (Calabari), and the drumming was African. Later, a man who played a bell, a hand-made instrument made of two pieces of metal fastened together with rivets, joined the drummers. The bell, held inverted and struck with a bolt, also was played in a manner that was African. Preceding the main event, a singer near the drummers broke into a dance, accompanied by vigorous drumming and handclapping. Many of the brothers and spectators were white.[103]

Finally, the lodge house doors swung open and a black man wearing a turban descended to the court walking backwards. In his hands he held a quadruple ceremonial rattle made of gourds. A masked dancer then appeared in the doorway.

He had a conical "head" which ended in a little tassel, and holding tight to it in the back was a disk-like hat which gave a certain air of comedy. A single green eye glared from the forehead. He wore a raffia skirt, and there were raffia cuffs around his ankles and wrists. Around his waist was a heavy leather belt strung with countless bells. Only his black feet and hands were bare. In one hand he clenched a cylindrical broom-like bundle of straws. He crouched, postured, and sprang forward, descending the stairs after the *morwa* [rattle carrier] who "controlled" him with the multiple rattle. He came, first slowly and cautiously, then bounded down three of four [steps] at a time. He advanced and retreated, his green eye fixed upon the *morwa*, who seemed to draw the *iremé* dancer along with him and yet force him to keep at a distance. Every movement and posture of the *iremé* was pure African dancing. He followed the *morwa* to the drums, where he seemed to go into a momentary rhythmic frenzy, then he turned and fled, danc-

ing with knees wide apart and toes pointed outward, into the sanctuary of the lodge.[104]

Because the occasion for this gathering was an initiation, six blind-
folded men were now brought from the lodge. An officer of the society
marked their chests and backs with the following symbols:

$$+ \mid + \\ \overline{ \mid } \\ + \mid +$$

And their arms and legs with:

This way of marking initiates is similar to the procedure reported by
Talbot in 1912 for the Calabar Coast.[105] The functionary then sprayed
rum on the initiates from his mouth, and another official brought a tray
of burning incense which he held before each of them. During much of
the ceremony, the sound of a bull-roarer (called *uyo* by the members of
the Abakwa society in Cuba) could be heard coming from beneath the
lodge.[106]

Carrying a baton in one hand, and in the other, a live rooster, the
iremé danced out of the building. When the first *iremé* reappeared he was
in the center of a procession which came from the lodge. The bare backs
of the initiates were now marked with blood and their heads were covered with yellow symbols. The *ocobíos* carried candles, torches, a ceremonial drum dressed with the tailfeathers of a rooster, and a tile of
burning incense. One of the brothers held between his teeth the head of
the sacrificed cock. The *morwa*, carrying a tray decorated at each corner
with a quiver of feathers, walked backwards, leading the *iremé*. About
4:00 A.M. the procession retired to the lodge.[107]

In 1951, Ortiz wrote that members of secret societies in Cuba
which honor the *abakuá* ("diablitos", *ñáñas, ñáñigos, írime* or *íreme*), a
class of spirits capable of harming human beings, impersonate this type

NEO-AFRICAN RELIGIONS AND ANCESTRAL CULTS

of supernatural spirit exactly as in Africa. Dramatic rites staged by masked spirits consisted of mimicry, singing, cryptic language, dances, offerings, magical acts, sacrifices, fearsome oaths, ablutions, processions, blood rites, and mortuary commemorations. Ortiz calls these rituals "Supreme Theater." Members of a group of *ñáñigos* are bound by solemn initiatory oaths and are governed by a hierarchy of many functionaries.[108]

In 1966, Barreal stated that the *abakuá* secret society of single men was probably the only one of its type which had survived in the New World. He called this syncretistic development a mutual aid society with a ritual markedly African in its language, music, and dances, but with some Catholic elements.[109]

To some extent, the worship of the oricha has been altered by the Cuban revolution and Fidel Castro's rise to power. Castro is opposed to santeria, as he is to Catholicism and other forms of religion, and the cult has declined in recent years. However, as Bascom points out, he has unintentionally stimulated the worship of Shango and the other Yoruba deities by dispersing Cuban refugees. Santeria has helped to meet the emotional needs of uprooted Cuban refugees living in the United States. Today many priests and priestesses officiate in Miami and materials needed in santeria rites are sold in a number of shops in Florida. In New York City, which may have become even more important than Miami as a center of santeria, a Shango temple has attracted Puerto Ricans and New York Negroes as well as Cuban exiles. Santeria has expanded also to Newark, New Jersey, Savannah, Detroit, Chicago, and Gary, Indiana.[110]

African Influences in Religion and Magic in the British Leeward Islands, Martinique, and Guadaloupe

Bourguignon asserts that there is some evidence to suggest that African-derived religions existed in the eighteenth century in areas where they are not found today. Such areas included the British Leeward Islands (Antiqua, Anguilla, Barbuda, Montserrat, Nevis, St. Kitts, and the British Virgins), Martinique and Guadaloupe.[111]

In the folklore of Martinique, *voduns* continue to appear as apparitions and guardian spirits. *Damballa Quedo,* the sacred serpent of Whydah, has become Demba Rouge. Fishermen venerate Maman D'Eau instead of the African water deities. The African names of the deities called locally Baton Volant and Cheval de Trois Pattes have disapeared, and other deities have been replaced by Catholic saints. The saints of popular Catholicism have some of the characteristics of ancient deities. St. Miguel (Michael) removes misfortune, San José (Joseph) and San Benito bring good luck, and San Antonio (Anthony) is called upon in helping to attract women. French books of magic are still used by conjurers. In Martinique, where medieval European witchcraft and African magical traditions are combined, syncretism is more apparent in magical usages than in religion. In Martinique and Guadaloupe, conjurers are called *quimboisseurs,* and many of them also practice healing. Their principal work, however, consists of manufacturing *quimbois* (charms which are used for both defensive and offensive maneuvers) for their clients.[112]

ANCESTRAL CULTS

Introduction

In the religions of many of the peoples of West Africa, the great gods, usually headed by a creator, control major aspects of nature—sky, sea, earth, thunder and lightning, and so on. Besides nature divinities, there are many specialized and local gods—deities of divination, war, medicine, childbirth, and agriculture, as well as deities of villages and towns. Each deity has its own followers, priests, shrines, and ceremonies, and in addition the ancestors are worshipped. The ancestral cult consists of a few essentials—the importance of the funeral, the need to assure the benevolence of the dead, and concern with descent and kinship.[113] In some New World religious cults, worship of the old African deities has disappeared, but the practice of honoring and propitiating the ancestors, including African ancestors, has persisted in modified form. The Cumina and Convince cults of Jamaica, the Big Drum Dance (Nation Dance) of Grenada and of Carriacou, the Kele cult of St. Lucia, and the ancestral cult of the Black Carib of British Honduras (Belize) are among the principal ancestral cults of the Caribbean.

Social Stratification in Jamaica [114]

For most of the more than three hundred years of British rule, the main social classes in Jamaica were an upper rank consisting of the Governor and the senior civil servants who came from England; the white Creole group; the colored middle class; and the black lower class. The correlation between color, wealth, and power has not been perfect, but generally the poorest people have been black and those with the highest status have been white or near-white. The proportion of whites in the total population decreased from about 4 percent in 1844 to less than 1 percent a century later. While the political influence of this group has declined sharply in recent years, it has retained much of its economic dominance. [115]

Today the indigenous elite of Jamaica is made up of those in the professions, government, business and commerce, and members of the faculty of the University of the West Indies. In recent decades this elite has included a somewhat larger proportion of darker-skinned persons than it did in the past. The lower middle and lower classes, constituting at least four-fifths of Jamaica's population, include unskilled and semi-skilled workers in agriculture, domestic service, small factories, the bauxite industry, the hotel and tourist business, higglers, and small shopkeepers. [116] The heavy concentration of blacks and East Indians in agricultural labor largely accounts for their disadvantageous position.

At least 15 percent of the labor force is unemployed, with particularly high rates in the case of women and young persons. An even greater proportion of the labor force is underemployed. A steady flow of migrants from the country districts to the cities, particularly to the Kingston-St. Andrew metropolitan area, in the past thirty years has greatly expanded the island's urban slums. [117] As Bell says, Jamaica moved into independence in 1962 "with a social structure containing gross inequalities of status and opportunities." [118]

The Chinese, numbering about 19,000, came to Jamaica toward the end of the nineteenth century. After a brief period in agricultural labor, they entered the grocery trade, a field that had been poorly developed. Kinsmen were recruited, trained, and integrated into family economic enterprises. The Syrians, numbering about one thousand, are also involved in commercial enterprises built on a kinship network. The

NEO-AFRICAN RELIGIONS AND ANCESTRAL CULTS

presence of skilled ethnic groups such as the Chinese and the Syrians has had two consequences for lower-class Jamaican Creoles: first, the latter get some training for business; second, the movement of Creole blacks "is retarded and even forestalled by cartel-like domination of large parts of the economy." According to Broom, the privileged position of these minorities in Jamaica is not likely to be permanent. In the long run, three alternatives appear to be open to them: "first, to leave the field as the Creole whites have done for more than two centuries; second, to assimilate with the Creole Africans (probably the Colored); or, third, to defend a vulnerable and conspicuous if privileged status as long as it will last."[119]

The Jews in Jamaica have never exceeded a few hundred. Important in the entrepôt trade with the Spanish Caribbean, they were discriminated against in taxation and civil rights in the seventeenth and early eighteenth centuries. The special taxes were removed in the eighteenth century and their remaining disabilities in the nineteenth century. Jews are widely distributed through the urban occupations, with about half in business activities and most of the others in the professions or the civil service. Broom says that the Jewish group is the most fully integrated of all the ethnic minorities into Jamaican society.[120]

Since emancipation lower class individuals have struggled continuously against exploitation in Jamaica. Higher wages, civil and political rights, and other gains have come slowly and often against bitter opposition. Uprisings have occurred now and then, but much of the hostility on the part of those who have sought social and economic advancement has been repressed. For more than a century, Afro-Christian cults—Native Baptists, Revivalist, Pocomania, Cumina, and Convince—provided one kind of outlet for the expression of repressed resentment.[121]

Lower class discontent and alienation have been evident in recent years, but these dissatisfactions have been primarily economic.[122] Following the extension of political rights, including voting, to every adult in the society in 1944, many of the demands of the lower class have been expressed through political action; others have been expressed through trade union action.[123]

A recent profile of Jamaica provides a summary of the island's social and economic situation.

NEO-AFRICAN RELIGIONS AND ANCESTRAL CULTS

Jamaica's population is rapidly increasing. The birth rate is high but has shown a slight decrease over the last two years. The death rate is low and falling very slowly. Emigration, except among skilled and professional workers, has been considerably reduced. The economy is expanding but efforts to move swiftly are hampered by the high rate of population increase. High rates of natural increase and rural-urban migration are contributing to a rapid rate of urbanization, but this is not accompanied by rapid industrialization and economic development. Thus, the unemployment rate remains high, slums increase, social dislocations and societal alienation grow, and poverty becomes more obvious. The concern for betterment of living conditions and economic development has led to increased expenditures in education, health, provision of jobs, and more recently, in a family planning program aimed at reducing the rate of population growth.[124]

Cumina

In Jamaica, some Cumina gods serve groups which appear to belong to tribes or "nations," among which the most frequently mentioned are *mondogo, moyenge, machunde, kongo,* and *mumbaka.* Other groups sometimes mentioned are *gaw, ibo,* and *yoruba.*[125] Cumina is primarily a family religion, and each group honors a number of family spirits in addition to other divinities. Some of these "ancestral zombies" have attained the status and power of gods.[126]

In Cumina the three ranks of spirits (known widely as zombies) are the sky gods, earthbound gods, and ancestral zombies. Among the 39 sky gods listed by Moore, only one (Shango) clearly has the name of a West African deity (others include Oto, Jubee, Bebee, Belgium, Judee, Fee, Flash, Obei, Faha, and Twiss).[127] Of the 62 earthbound gods named by Moore, at least seven have biblical names: David, Ezekiel, Moses, Cain, Shadrach, Meshach, and Abednego (others include Ajax, Alec, Augustus, Ivan, Davis, Atlas, Mabell, Cynthia, and Brownie). The 21 ancestral zombies are the spirits of men and women (Jimmy Snate, Margaret Miller, Archie Pierce, Obi Backford, Sophie Bartly, James Grasset, Grace Bailey, and others) who, in their lifetimes, were dancing zombies (persons who experienced possession by a god and who danced while possessed), drummers, and obeah men.[128]

Cumina dances are held for several specific purposes, but approximately three-fourths of these ceremonies are related to paying respects to the dead ancestors of the participants. Memorial dances (sometimes called "black and white dance"), given in honor of a deceased member of the family, entombment dances (a service added to a memorial dance), and "crop-over dances" marking the end of "nine nights" after a death (crop-over dances are also given to celebrate the end of a cane cutting season) are among the major Cumina ceremonies. At certain points during a Memorial ritual, the participants dance around and over the graves of the ancestors, rites are performed at the grave of the recently deceased person, and the ancestral zombies predominate in the possessions.[129] The aim of a Memorial dance is to put at rest the spirit of the departed zombie and to make certain that he and all the other ancestors are satisfied. If the dead are not properly honored, their spirits will wander about and constitute a menace to the living.

The second type of Cumina ceremony given in the Morant Bay area, the public Cumina, attracted from 100 to 400 persons in the 1950s. This rite usually began at sundown on Friday night and lasted 24 hours. Other Cuminas are held to celebrate a betrothal or greet a new baby. In addition to these rituals, private "working" ceremonies for a variety of ends are conducted by obeah men in their own "yards."

All zombies are invoked through drumming[130] and singing. Songs are of two similar types—*Bilah* and country. *Bilah* songs are sung in a dialect which is primarily English, but Jamaican country songs are sung in a language referred to in the Morant Bay area as *african*. All of the songs are "lined out"; that is, a song-leader sings each verse line by line, followed each time by the chorus. Male singers are drummers or obeah men; female singers are strong dancing zombies. The female singer is called Mother of the Cumina, or she is referred to as the "black and white girl." The Master of Ceremonies wears a black and white cord around his neck as the badge of his office. At times during the ceremony, the female singer wears this officer's insignia, especially when he is not present or is possessed. Besides dancing to several zombies (becoming possessed by them) during an evening, the black and white girl spends a great deal of her time in attending cult members who are in possession trance.

Several kinds of dancing can be distinguished at an *african* Cumina.

NEO-AFRICAN RELIGIONS AND ANCESTRAL CULTS

The basic *african* dance, participated in by everyone in the ring, is a walking step in time with the basic beat of the *banda* drums. According to Moore: "Because of the counter rhythms, the hips, shoulders, arms, and head are presented with infinite opportunities for variation in posture and movement. Dancing is always counter-clockwise around the ring, and can be done alone or with a partner. . . . Sky and earthbound gods differ widely in the pattern and style of their dances. Ancestral zombies each have distinctive dance styles more closely related to the basic *african* dance."[131]

The sacrifice of the goat and the dance of the Queen of the Cumina take place at 5:00 A.M. Generally, the Queen is related to the direct family line of the sponsors of a cumina dance. She is an important officer because she and her procession dance for the ancestors and the recently deceased persons who are being honored. The dance of the Queen and her attendants functions as a formal conveyance of the wishes of the living members of the family to the ancestors.[132]

The Convince Cult in Jamaica

Convince has a restricted geographic distribution in the two easternmost parishes of St. Thomas and Portland, is limited in its membership exclusively to the lower socioeconomic classes, and has declined in numbers and popularity during the past three decades.

Although the Convince ritual includes a number of Christian elements, the devotees of the cult (called Bongo Men) are little concerned with God and Christ. They deal exclusively with the ghosts of persons who belonged to, or are believed to have belonged to, Convince during their lifetimes. The most powerful Bongo ghosts come from Africa, but the ghosts of ancient Jamaican slaves and the Maroons (descendants of runaway slaves) who perpetuated the cult until recent times are also of importance. The ghosts of Jamaicans whose deaths have occurred more recently are less powerful than the others, but those who practiced Obeah while alive are used by Bongo Men as partners in the practice of necromancy.[133] This ancestral cult is organized on the basis of the sharing of common beliefs rather than kinship.

A Bongo Man feeds his ghosts annually with animal sacrifices. In return, the ghosts teach him spiritual secrets, protect him, bring him good fortune, and assist him in performing magic (Obeah). The cult has little formal organization. Each Bongo Man operates independently, but each also attends meetings of other cult leaders. In the role of guest, the visiting Bongo Man must dance as well as possible and induce his ghosts to perform spectacularly. He is obligated also to assist in maintaining order among the spectators. Lesser followers of Convince are called "apprentices" or "grooms," and each Bongo Man has at least one such assistant. Others who participate in the cult are called "well-wishers," and include women who cook and serve food for visitors, men who look after the sacrificial animals, a helper who collects the sixpence admission fee from each spectator, and, usually, a young girl who reads passages from the Bible and "traces" hymns (reads each line before it is sung) when the ghosts request them. Among these followers, only the apprentices are actually members of the cult. Many of the others are devout Christians, and some are members of the historic churches. These persons enjoy their participation in the ceremonies and understand quite well the ulterior purposes of the rites, but they do not regard Convince as a religion.

With the exception of the sacrificial ceremony held annually by each Bongo Man, Convince rituals occur irregularly as the need for them arises. Memorial services for deceased cult members, held one year after death, offer opportunities for the new ghosts to acquire devotees. At other times, minor rites are performed to pacify ghosts and to thank spirits for help they have provided. Other gatherings are held mainly for purposes of recreation and money-raising. Some Bongo Men conduct special Obeah rites when hired to solve difficult problems. All Convince ceremonies follow a basic pattern.

A Christian prayer meeting at dusk, conducted by well-wishers and consisting of a few prayers, the reading of some Bible passages, and hymn singing, usually precedes the main ceremony. Later, the Bongo Men join the crowd and the Convince rites begin. Well-wishers call the spirits by singing well-known hymns in a slow tempo and special Bongo songs, and by handclapping during the latter. The Bongo Men dance individually to these songs and later the ghosts arrive and dance in similar ways. When possessed by one of his ghosts, a Bongo Man recites a Christian prayer, calls for hymns and psalms to be offered as he dances, leads Bongo songs, and smokes constantly. During possession trance, a

NEO-AFRICAN RELIGIONS AND ANCESTRAL CULTS

Bongo Man may leave the crowd and seek to climb a tree, or at least to get onto the roof of the ceremonial booth or house. After a series of possessions, a ceremony which does not involve a sacrifice ends quietly. At a larger ceremony, the ghosts possess their followers day and night for three or four days. A feast consisting of curried meat, rice, and other foods is held during a sacrificial ceremony. The dancing and spirit possessions which take place after the feast may continue for two days or longer.

Convince includes fewer Africanisms than Haitian vodun and Trinidadian shango, but it shows greater African influence than the Bedwardite, Revival Zion, Pocomania, and Ras Tafari cults of Jamaica.

> Features like blood sacrifice, worship of ancestral ghosts, violent trance behavior conceptualized as spirit possession, the belief in amoral spiritual power, the frankly materialistic purposes of ceremonies, and the involvement with necromancy almost certainly have African antecedents. So also do such practices as religious dancing, providing houses for spirits, phrasing possession as horsemanship, and propitiating potentially malevolent beings. The other Jamaican cults . . . also exhibit various of these traits, but none includes them all or emphasizes them as heavily as does Convince.[134]

Hogg suggests that the more African character of Convince may be due to its development in relative isolation from Western influence. He concludes also that the cult probably has Maroon origins, as is the case with the only other Jamaican cult (Cumina) that has retained more African elements. The decline of Convince since the 1950s is attributed to improvements in social and economic conditions in Jamaica, to the resentment of many Christians of the existence of the cult, and to the growth of Ras Tafari as a protest movement. Once a nativistic movement, Convince now provides only "jollification" and catharsis.[135]

The Big Drum Dance in Grenada and Carriacou (Windward Islands)

An ancestral ritual called the Big Drum Dance (the Nation Dance, or simply *saraca* [sacrifice]) is found in Grenada and Carriacou, a small island north of Grenada. According to M. G. Smith, this dance was the representative African cult of Grenada at the beginning of the twentieth century, and it still flourished as "the representative folk ritual" of Carriacou in the 1950s. These rites do not include spirit possession.[136]

On the island of Carriacou, many residents can still relate the African "nations," traced patrilineally, to which they belong. They retain a strong sense of the continuing power of their deceased ancestors. The Big Drum Dance is given as a sign of respect for them, and as a means of avoiding their disfavor.[137] Usually this ritual is a family occasion, but a special group—fishermen, for example—may give one annually as a joint affair. The reasons for organizing a festival are cases of ill-health or misfortune (usually after a friend or relative has dreamed of an ancestor's desire for the ceremony); a "Stone Feast" (the raising of a tombstone to a deceased member of the family); the launching of a schooner (or the start of any other critical undertaking); and the marriage preparations of a son or a daughter.

The Dance itself has three parts, all of which serve as a symbolic evocation of the life of previous generations in the "yard" where the ritual takes place. First, the "parents' plate," a table containing food for the guests, is set in the best room of the house during the course of the night. Next, the ancestors are called by beating a hoe with a spoon to the accompaniment of the Cromanti "opening song"; libations are offered by members of the family, with the men of the household sprinkling rum and the women water, to bless and prepare the ancestral "yard"; a "free-ring" is provided where the spirits of the ancestors can dance;[138] and the "Beg Pardon" dance is performed, with the members of the family kneeling and singing, asking the ancestors to pardon them ("If I deserve it punish me, if I don't deserve it, pardon me"). The ceremony concludes with the "international," the music and dances of several "nations" given in a certain order of preference by members of these groups.[139]

The Kele (Changó) Cult in St. Lucia [140]

The kele ceremony in St. Lucia resembles the Shango ritual in Trinidad and the Afro-Christian rites found elsewhere in the Caribbean and South America.[141] However, the belief system associated with kele seems to be much simpler. The ceremony is given to ask the African ancestors of present devotees for protection in matters of importance—good crops, good health, and good fortune. In the course of the ceremony, the ancestors are thanked for past favors.

The paraphernalia essential for the kele rite consists mainly of Amerindian polished stone axes, drums, and agricultural implements, including cutlasses, axes, hoes, and forks. The stone axes, often referred to, as they are in Haiti and Trinidad, as *pierres tonnerre* (thunder stones), are believed to have fallen from the sky during a storm when there were loud claps of thunder and blinding flashes of "forked" lightning. One of the drums used in a kele ceremony is long, small in diameter, and single headed; the other is large and double headed. No altar is constructed. Several of the stone axes are placed on the ground in the form of a cross, and additional axes may be arranged around the central grouping. The animal to be sacrificed is tied to a picket nearby. Unlike vodunists in Haiti and shangoists in Trinidad, the participants in kele rites make no use of ceremonial swords, double headed wooden axes, brooms, or whips. Statues and lithographs of Catholic saints and crucifixes have no place in kele. No special clothing is worn by the participants, but the leader may wear a robe that suits his taste.

The stone axes, called Changó (Shango), symbolize the African ancestors of the St. Lucians who celebrate kele. This is a point of great importance, because thunder stones constitute one of the principal symbols of Shango in West Africa, Haiti, Trinidad, Cuba, Brazil, Grenada, and in some cities of the United States. In West Africa, the Shango religion has its own shrines, priests, rites, and devotees. Elsewhere in the Caribbean and South America, Shango is worshipped in remodeled African cults, some of which are named for him. Present-day kele devotees in St. Lucia have no knowledge that Shango is the deity of thunder and lightning in traditional West African belief. In St. Lucia, Changó is simply the name of the thunder stones that enable the living to get in touch with their African ancestors. One informant said that Changó "means sacrifice."

As is the case in parts of West Africa, Haiti, Cuba, Trinidad, and Brazil, the thunder stones are washed in water containing certain leaves and are rubbed with oil to purify them before the ceremony opens. After some preliminary drumming, singing, and dancing, the leader addresses the ancestors, asking them to intercede with God in behalf of the person or family sponsoring the occasion. Kele devotees believe that an African language is used during a ceremony. Actually, the main participants speak, as do the shangoists in Trinidad, a patois that includes some African words. The sacrifice to the ancestors, a ram, must be killed with one stroke of a cutlass. Ordinarily, the principal participants drink some of the blood as it flows from the head of the ram or they drink from a special calabash. Blood is sprinkled on the thunder stones, the link between the devotees and their forbears in Africa, to give them more power "to find the ancestors." Blood is also poured on the agricultural implements to bless them, thus ensuring that no one can be injured while using them.

All of the active male participants in a kele ceremony are supposed to become possessed by the ancestors; certainly this is expected of the leader. Among those who do not achieve a high level of dissociation are some who believe, nevertheless, that they are possessed—and some of these persons may experience "light" possession trances. Communication with God is achieved through possession by the ancestors; the ancestors then transmit the appeals of living human beings to God.

No one who is harboring an evil spirit can become possessed by an ancestor, and no possessions can occur if evil spirits (*loups garous, diablesses, sukuyans, bolams, l'espwit, zombies,*[142] and so forth are in the vicinity. The leading *mauvais esprit,* known to kele devotees as Akèshew, is dismissed at about the midpoint in the ceremony in exactly the same way that Eshu is dispatched in a Shango rite in Trinidad. "Someone who knows how to do it" holds a calabash filled with food and ashes in one hand and a cutlass in the other. The calabash must be smashed into bits.

After the cock and the ram have been cooked,[143] morsels of the meat, as well as portions of yams, rice, and other foods that have been prepared for the ceremony, are thrown on the ground for Changó, that is, for the African ancestors. In addition, Changó receives offerings of water and rum poured out on the earth. These procedures are derived from West African rituals, but in Africa offerings of food and drink are thrown on the ground for deities as well as for ancestors. The latter practice is followed also in Haitian vodun and Trinidadian shango.

Kele is not an alternative to Catholicism. St. Lucia is a predomi-

NEO-AFRICAN RELIGIONS AND ANCESTRAL CULTS

nantly Catholic country and some devotees of the cult are active Catholics. The situation in St Lucia is essentially the same as in Carriacou where Christianity and the ancestor cult (Big Drum Dance) each supplement the deficiencies of the other. As M. G. Smith points out: "The church deals directly with God through its hierarchy of priests, saints and Madonna, while the folk deal with their ancestors and other spirits, who are also the servants of God.[144]

Ancestral Cult of the Black Carib of British Honduras (Belize)

The Black Carib are descended mainly from Africans brought to the West Indies as slaves, but who escaped and settled among the Island Carib in Saint Vincent. Gradually they adopted the language of the Caribs and a considerable part of their culture. By the beginning of the eighteenth century, the Black Carib had developed a distinct society, and by the end of the century they had largely supplanted the native Indians. At that time they were deported by the English to Roatán, an island in the Gulf of Honduras, and from there they spread out along the coast of the mainland. According to Taylor, the Black Carib of British Honduras are today "a negroid people who speak a South American Indian language, and whose outward cultural manifestations differ but little, in the main, from those of their neighbors."[145]

The supernatural beliefs, rites, and practices of the Black Carib consist of a mixture of African and non-African elements. The words for the three spiritual entities possessed by the living individual: *iuani* ("heartbeat," "vitality," "courage," "animating spirit"); *iaua* ("shadow," "reflexion," "image,"); and *áfurugu* ("spirit-double") are Carib,[146] but the idea that the individual possesses several "souls" is African[147] or is derived from both African and South American Indian sources. At the middle of the twentieth century, there seems to be no agreement among the Black Carib concerning the relationship of these three spiritual entities to the various types of disembodied spirits. Two categories of the latter were distinguishable: 1) those who did little except to plague human beings, and who were, for the most part, feared; and 2) those who both reward faithful attention and punish neglect, and are esteemed as well as feared. The spirits in the first class have no cult behind them but offerings of food and drink, or simple magical acts, may be used to appease them. Many of these spirits are female water spirits, similar both to river-spirits still found among Guiana Indians and to water spirits in traditional West African belief. One of these spirits, the *agaiuma,* resembles the *diablesse* of Haiti, a beautiful woman who lures men to horrible deaths. The most feared of the many supernatural beings known to the Black Carib is the *ogoreu* (devourer). This creature may take the form of a small animal (snake, crab, hen, armadillo, or iguana or other lizard) in order to gain entrance to a home. It disappears after its arrival, but its presence may cause serious troubles in the household, including the devouring of the first-born in the family and, if it is not appeased, all subsequent children of the line.[148] It seems likely that beliefs in such spirits as *ogoreu* are derived from and reinforced by both American Indian and African traditions. Taylor cites similarities between certain Guiana Carib spirits and the *ogoreu,* and in some respects this malignant spirit resembles the *baka* of Haiti. *Baka* are evil beings who enter into an *engagement* to provide a person with some important gain. They appear as small bearded human-like figures with flaming eyes, or as cattle, horses, asses, goats, dogs, cats, and pigs. When a baka's claim falls due, he kills one by one the members of the family of the one who entered into the compact, and finally he kills the principal himself.[149]

Most Black Caribs believe that the spirit-double of the dead enters into a state of suspension following the ninth-night ceremony, but there is disagreement concerning the fate of the heart-soul. The usual view holds that the latter entity is the origin of the good spirits—*áhari* (the spirit of a person who has died recently), *áhambue* (a later form of this spirit), *gubida* (a collective name for the family dead), and *hiúruha* (the spirits from which the shaman draws his helpers). The *áhari* tend to pursue their surviving relatives and friends, but the latter take all kinds of precautions to avoid trouble and give offerings to be left in peace. Few among the Black Carib do not believe that their fortunes in this life depend upon the goodwill of their deceased ancestors.[150]

Ancestral rites are given as a result of dreams or other warnings, whose neglect may cause—or have already caused—illness, derangement, or death. A special ancestor-house is build for the *dogó,* the most important of the three ancestral rites. After songs of invocation led by

NEO-AFRICAN RELIGIONS AND ANCESTRAL CULTS

the shaman, the call is answered by the shaman's helper and, accompanied by the latter, by the ancestral spirit or spirits for whom the rite is being given. The women, who outnumber the men by four to one, generally spend the rest of the night dancing *abaimahani,* gestured songs of appeasement sung in unison. Before six the next morning, a crowd waits to watch for the appearance of the *adugahatiu* (men and women sent out to the Cays in three canoes several days earlier to obtain crabs, fish and other seafood for the rite) with their catch. Led by the shaman and three drummers, the procession then enters the ancestor-hall to a traditional refrain. Singing and dancing to a monotonous rhythm of the drums continues for some time. For the *malí,* or the part of the ceremony devoted to placation, the shaman announces: "heart-drummer, thou'lt placate our grandmother." The number of placations during any particular *dogó* depends upon the wealth of the family giving it, but it must be a multiple of eight. For each placation performed, each of the drummers receives a quarter pint of rum and a candle. When the placations of the family giving the ceremony have been completed, or even before then if time permits and the drummers are willing, "extras" may be given by members of other families wanting to placate their own ancestors, but unable or unwilling to meet the expense of an independent rite at that time.[151]

Although spirit possession is not essential to the success of a *dogó,* it is rarely absent from its performance. Those who appear to be most susceptible to possession are young women from 18 to 25 years of age, and possession is most likely to occur among those dancing in the ancestor-house during the latter part of the first of the three days of the ceremony. It is noteworthy that those who become possessed outside the ancestor-house, unless they are noticed and immediately brought in to dance before the drums, always rush to throw themselves into the sea. Usually it is a dancer who becomes possessed, and ordinarily her possession passes gradually through two or three stages. A watcher, however, may suddenly enter upon a full possession. The possessed girl may interrupt her dance to impersonate the deceased ancestor whose spirit has entered her. In the midst of an impromptu song, one possessed girl shouted in Carib: "They're MY ancestors—YOUR ancestors!" If possessions threaten to become too violent, or if persons who are not members of the family become possessed by their own dead ancestors, restraint may be used. "This is done by rubbing the face of the possessed persons with rum, by fanning them with the cotton-strip fans to placate the possession spirit, by giving them a drink called *líhigu,* which is generally held in readiness by the officiating *búiai,* and by other methods." [152]

About midnight of the first day, the first sacrifice of a cock occurs and other sacrifices are made at regular intervals. Dancing is interrupted at daybreak on the second day for another offering. The ancestors' favorite dishes, without salt, are arranged by the cooks on the offering tables. The shaman and the persons giving the rite decide which portions of the food and drink shall be reserved as a sacrifice to the spirits, and what may be allocated to the living participants. A special "pillaging" ceremony of the children takes place that evening, a feast that is similar to the "feeding of the children" in the shango cult in Trinidad. [153]

Dógo dancing continues throughout the second night, interspersed with placation rites, the sacrifice of cocks, and spirit possessions by the ancestors. On the third day, a deep round hole is dug by the edge of the sea or some distance behind the houses and offering-baskets of food and drink are lowered into it. Most of the third day, however, is taken up with songs sung by the women and the corresponding men's songs. According to Taylor, both types of song "contain complaints of loneliness or of sickness, appeals to family solidarity and love of grandchildren, or recount the faithful performance of the singers' everyday toils." [154] Some *dógo* rites include joking by clowns. Before the ceremony is brought to an end, the "scattering" rite is performed by taking the remaining offering-baskets, as well as the debris from the ritual, out to sea in canoes and throwing these offerings into the water. On the evening of the last day, a gathering of the family is held for the final "bringing down" of the spirits. At this time, both grandfathers indicate whether they are satisfied with the sacrifice and the "work," and voice any complaints they may have of the way the rite proceeded. Every night for nine days after the *dógo,* a light must be kept burning in the sanctuary of the ancestor-house. [155]

In many of its details, the ceremonies performed for the ancestral dead among the Black Carib correspond with elements in traditional rituals in West Africa, as well as in Haiti and other places in the Carib-

NEO-AFRICAN RELIGIONS AND ANCESTRAL CULTS

bean. The Black Carib do not become possessed by deities, but their possession by ancestors is not significantly different from African concepts in which some of the deities are deified ancestors. In a vodun ceremony in Haiti, a houngan may talk with ancestors along with the loa, and, as I point out earlier in this chapter, the ancestors possess devotees of Cumina and Convince in Jamaica, the Big Drum in Grenada and Carriacou, and Kele in St. Lucia. The position of the Black Carib shaman in supervising the calling down of the spirits and his control of possessions parallels that of the houngan. The stages of possession and the behavior of possessed persons in Black Carib rituals are similar to those in Africa and in a number of Afroamerican ceremonies. In addition, there are parallels in the ways of feeding the ancestors among the Black Carib and the offering of food to the deities and the dead in Africa and in other parts of the Caribbean, including throwing food on the ground, placing it in a hole, and sinking offerings in the sea.

Most of the Black Caribs are professed Christians, and, in the main, Catholics. They see no inconsistency between their Christian faith and non-Christian beliefs. The protective spirits, ancestral and other, are regarded as subordinate to the Christian God, and the evil forces of the universe are simply manifestations of the Devil.[156]

❦ CHAPTER FOUR ❦

Revivalist and Other Cults
of the Caribbean

IN THE Revivalist category I include Revival Zion and Pocomania in Jamaica, the Shouters (Spiritual Baptists) of Trinidad, the Shakers and the Streams of Power cult of St. Vincent.

Revivalist Cults in Jamaica

Revival, Revival Zion, and Pocomania cults are similar in most respects, but the term Revival Zion is used more often in Kingston and Revival in the Morant Bay area and other parts of Jamaica. Pocomanians seem to place more emphasis on singing and "spiritual" dancing and less emphasis on preaching and biblical explanations, to make greater use of conjuring, and to have more emotionally unstable leaders than Revival Zionists.[1]

The cult groups described here were located in two parts of Jamaica—in West Kingston, an economically depressed, densely populated area on the edge of the capital, mainly in the sections known as Trench Town, Jones Town, Delacree Pen, and Denham Town; and in Morant Bay, a marketing center in the southeast part of the island whose population of 4,000 to 5,000 includes a large number of frequently unemployed laborers.[2]

As indicated earlier, for nearly a hundred years after Britain acquired Jamaica in 1654, no missionary work was carried on in the island, and the official missionary movement did not get underway until the 1820s. For forty years after 1780, the Native Baptist movement, led in part by slaves and freedmen who had lived in the United States, was without serious competition. During this period, according to Curtin, "a reinterpretation of Christianity was created, organized, and spread throughout the island. By 1830 the doctrine and organization of the Native Baptists had become a thoroughly integrated part of Negro culture—another religion competing with the Christianity of the European missionaries." Curtin asserts that by 1860 the Native Baptists were stronger than orthodox European denominations.[3]

Interest in separatist churches as well as in regular missions was greatly stimulated by an emotional religious revival which swept the island in 1861–62. The demand for religious leadership resulted in the formation of hundreds of new "churches," but the enthusiasm dwindled within a short time. The Great Revival "turned African" and "became more and more a mixture of myalism [positive magic] and Christianity, ending as a permanent addition to the Afro-Christian cults.[4] Present-day revivalist cults are descended from the Native Baptists and the Afro-Christian cults of the eighteenth and nineteenth centuries. They are revivalistic in the sense of religious awakening or enthusiasm; they are not, however, revitalistic movements attempting to restore the customs and values of an ancient culture.[5]

Revivalists believe in the existence of many supernatural beings. God the Father, the creator and ruler of the universe, never comes to a service. Some adherents believe that Jesus Christ comes down to Revival but never reveals his presence by taking possession of a devotee. The Holy Spirit does attend services and "manifests on" (possesses) followers. Among the favorite spirits of revivalism are such Old Testament prophets as Jeremiah, Ezekiel, Isaiah, Samuel, Daniel, Solomon, and Joshua; New Testament Apostles and Evangelists, including Matthew, Mark, Luke, John, Peter, and James; archangels, Michael, Gabriel, and Raphael; Moses, Miriam, Caleb, David, Shadrach, Meschach, and Abednego; Satan and his chief assistant, Rutibel; such beings from Hebrew magical tradition as Uriel, Ariel, Seraph, Nathaniel, and Tharsis;[6] Casuel (probably Casziel, one of the four main astral spirits associated in astrology with the malefic planet Saturn); such assorted figures as Constantine, Melshezdek, and the Royal Angel; and, finally, the dead, especially great shepherds and shepherdesses (revivalist leaders) of the past. Most revivalists "travel under" (follow) one spirit, but some of the leaders claim that they receive messages from and are protected and assisted by many spirits.[7]

Dreams and visions in which one or more spirits appear play important roles in the lives of revivalists by validating the positions of officiants, providing warnings about the evil intentions of enemies, predicting coming events, rationalizing conversion to the cults, and reinforcing traditional beliefs about the supernatural world.

The ritual paraphernalia of a revivalist church is concentrated on or near an altar. The principal ritual objects usually include one or more Bibles, white candles, flags made of colored cloth, wooden crosses, drums, jars of leaves, vases of flowers, glasses of consecrated water, a shepherd's crook,[8] swords or machetes (wooden or steel), and, in some cases, polished stones. In West Kingston, it is more common to find sacred stones of one kind or another in the homes or yards of leaders, or near pools of consecrated water or elsewhere inside the churches, rather than on the altars.

The most frequently held revivalist ceremony, known as "divine worship," occurs on Sunday evening and one or two weeknights. Singing (both collective and antiphonal), accompanied by drumming (and, in some cases, by rattles and tambourines), handclapping, praying by the leader and individual prayers by the members speaking simultaneously, Bible-reading, counterclockwise "spiritual" dancing around the front part of the church, preaching interspersed with hymn-singing, spirit possessions, and, on some occasions, public healing constitute the main features of this type of service. Special revivalist ceremonies include baptismal rites, the numerous death rites, the dedication of a new church, and the installation of a new officer. "Tables" (special services) are given from time to time for several purposes: to offer thanks to the spirits, to seek deliverance ("uplifting") from trouble, and to raise money.[9]

In addition to conducting religious services, many revivalist leaders practice healing and conjuring (obeah). In West Kingston, Shepherds

REVIVALIST AND OTHER CULTS

heal publicly in regular or special church services and in private. Illnesses are diagnosed by several methods, including "sounding the patient" (practitioner touches patient with his head), "concentrating" to get a message from one of the spirits, dreaming, acquiring information about the client's history and behavior, and studying the patient's symptoms. Among the techniques employed in healing are the laying on of hands, drinking consecrated water, prayer, Bible reading, singing, fasting, "lecturing," giving moral support, bush teas, purity baths (consecrated water), bush baths (leaves), blood baths, anointing with oil, flagwaving and swordswinging to drive away evil spirits, removing foreign objects that the practitioner himself has placed in a sore, pouring coconut milk over a patient's head, tying a white cloth around the client's head with a piece of tuna leaf, and using perfumes, incense, nutmegs, stones, and candles.

Jamaican witchcraft involves the "putting on" and the "taking off" of duppies (spirits of the dead)[10] and utilizing other spirits for good or evil purposes. Each conjurer has his favorite method of summoning a duppy, feeding it, and instructing it concerning the nature of the work to be done. The evil intentions of enemies and conjurers may be nullified by such techniques as fasting, praying, hymn-singing, drinking consecrated water, bathing (consecrated water, the blood of an animal, or a bush bath), anointing with oil, flogging with a rod, charm-wearing, repeating benedictions, ordering a duppy to leave, and performing special rituals which include drumming, tracing symbols on the ground, and the use of fire and water.[11]

Jamaican revivalists do not equate old African gods such as Ogun, Oshun, Shango, Legba, Obatala, Erzilie, and Damballa with Christian saints as do the members of syncretistic cults in Haiti, Cuba, Brazil, Trinidad, and other parts of the New World which have sizable black populations and where the Roman Catholic church is a dominant influence. Revivalists believe that there are many spirits who take an active interest in the affairs of the living and who intervene in those affairs. The form of the gods has changed in their migration from West Africa to the New World, but the polytheistic orientation and the belief in the constant and direct intervention of divinities in human concerns have been retained. The African tradition that nothing is entirely good or entirely bad, and, specifically, that "each Vodu has his gifts to man and his punishment when angered" [12] has been reinterpreted in the revivalist belief that most of the spirits are capable of aiding or harming men, depending upon the way they are treated. [13]

Elements of West African ancestral cults and of Protestantism have been syncretized in beliefs about the dead and in the death rites observed by Jamaican revivalists. Coming first in the sequence, the wake differs little from its early-nineteenth-century forerunner. This rite is accompanied by " 'every kind of tumult and festivity'—dirges, drumming, horn-blowing in the West African style, praise-songs for the deceased, 'or a recital of the valiant deeds of him or his ancestors.' " [14] The wake is followed by the funeral and, if the family's resources permit and it is desired to honor the deceased fully, a nine-night service, a forty-day mourning table, and the annual preparation of a memorial table. The practice of having a series of death rites parallels custom in parts of West Africa where a temporary burial preceeds the permanent burial, or where the spirit of the deceased would not be at rest until the elapsing of a definite period of time. [15]

The multiple soul concept of West Africa has been reinterpreted in the Jamaican belief that each person has a duppy in addition to a "soul." The ability of a West African conjurer to capture and use a "soul" is found in reinterpreted form in Jamaica in the power of a revivalist leader or obeah man to command the spirit of a dead person to appear and assist him in his work.

The public nature of spirit possessions, the methods of inducing and controlling possessions, and the behavior of possessed persons are reinterpretations of West African elements. [16] The religious and magical uses of stones and herbs also appear to be reinterpretations of African practices. Polished stone celts, and other types of stones, found in the homes, yards, and churches of nearly all revivalist leaders, are believed to "carry" power. They are used to invoke particular spirits, to guard against evil spirits, to add potency to the consecrated water used in healing, and to accomplish certain ends through sympathetic magic. [17] Herbs are important in African magic. Leaves are found on revivalist altars and "tables" and frequently the remedies prescribed for illnesses and other misfortunes are "bush teas" or "bush baths."

REVIVALIST AND OTHER CULTS

Water is a major ritual element in West African religions, and visits to "living" water (a river or the ocean) to obtain sacred water are parts of ceremonies among the Yoruba, the Ashanti, and in Dahomey. The principal syncretisms involving the use of water in Jamaican revivalism are found in baptismal rites. Revivalists do not run into the water under possession by a god, as novitiates often do in Africa, but as a baptismal candidate is immersed the spirit may descend on him and produce a possession hysteria that—at least in its outward appearance—is almost indistinguishable from that brought on by the African water deities (Herskovits, *The Myth,* 234; Simpson, *Jamaican Revivalist Cults,* 422–23). Among the religious and magical uses of the ubiquitous glasses, jars, and pools of consecrated water kept in a revivalist center are attracting a spirit to a service, driving away evil spirits, healing, divining, duppy-catching, and gaining favors from the "river maids" (Simpson, *ibid.,* 423–24). The ritual use of blood in revivalism is much less important than it is in Haitian vodun, Cuban santeria, or Trinidadian shango, but some leaders sprinkle goat's blood on the ground and on "healing" stones during a major ceremony, and blood may be used in a special type of "uplifting" rite or in private healing rituals.[18]

European-borrowed traits and reinterpreted European elements include the Bible as a ritual object, the cross, crucifixes, candles, inscriptions and placards on the walls of churches, and incense. The words and melodies of most revivalist songs are derived from Protestant hymns, but the emphasis on rhythm in singing, the use of drums and rattles, the polyrhythmic drumming, the handclapping, foot patting, and dancing as a part of religious ceremonies are African retentions.[19]

Jamaican magic, like other West Indian magic, represents a combination of the folk traditions of West Africa and Europe. The best example of this amalgamation is seen in the way the use of charms has been reinforced by both traditions. The de Laurence books of magic, published in Chicago, have been popular in the Caribbean because the numerous magical devices and formulas which they depict have fitted into the world view of many lower-class persons. Revelation by the spirits of remedies for treating illnesses, a fundamental West African belief (Herskovits, *The Myth,* 241–42), is found in Jamaica. Reference is made above to the importance of herbs in African and in Jamaican

REVIVALIST AND OTHER CULTS

magic. The interpretation of dreams in divining future events, common in West Africa as well as in European tradition, is popular among revivalists.[20]

The Shouters (Spiritual Baptists) of Trinidad

Apparently the Spiritual Baptist cult in Trinidad spread there from St. Vincent.[21] The age of the Shaker cult in St. Vincent has not been determined, but it goes back at least to the early part of the twentieth century.

The Shouters are lower-class men and women, mainly of African descent, but a few East Indians participate in the cult. Shouters services were forbidden by law from 1917 until 1951, but since that time this demonstrative, fundamentalist cult has flourished. Most of the Spiritual Baptist churches are small, but memberships run from a few dozen to three hundred or more.[22]

A Shouters church is dominated by an altar filled with candles, vases of flowers, crucifixes, placards, and religious pictures. The "center" of the church may or may not include a post decked with flags for the "spirits" and used as a support for a "chariot wheel," a ritual object which is spun from time to time during the service. The "center" of the church invariably includes a large, brass handbell, one or more vases or jars of flowers, and lighted candles. During a meeting, lighted candles are also placed in the four corners of the church, at the entrance, and along the sides. Usually the floor is made of packed earth, and benches to accommodate from thirty to a hundred or more persons are spaced around the building. In addition to the main structure, many Spiritual Baptist leaders construct a small separate room or "sacred chamber" where "mourning" rituals are held. While a Shouters church revolves around a leader, variously called a "Pointer," "Pastor," "Mother," or "Brother," the typical congregation has many officers, including Shepherd, Prophet, Healer, Diver, Prover, Nurse, Matron, and Interpreter, and the affairs of the group are handled to some degree on a democratic basis.[23]

The basic Shouters ceremony, held on Sunday evening, consists of hymn-singing, accompanied at times by handclapping but not by drums or rattles, praying (both standardized prayers such as the Lord's Prayer, and long, original but stereotyped prayers), Bible reading and reciting, chalking symbolic marks on the floor or on the walls of the church, bell-ringing, possessions by the Holy Spirit, preaching by the pastor and two or three guest speakers, and taking the collection. Street meetings, conducted for the purpose of gaining converts, as well as prayer meetings, are held at regular or irregular intervals.[24]

Baptism is a high point in the ritualistic activities of the Shouters. In true fundamentalist belief, baptism is thought of as being born again. Conversion from another faith or a shift of allegiance from one Shouters church to another, symbolized by an attenuated water rite, is regarded as a reconsecration to the right way of life. Although procedures vary from group to group, candidates may be asked to come to the church twice a week for three weeks for religious instruction prior to baptism.[25]

At the end of the period of instruction, the "pilgrims" take their places on the "Mercy Seat," a front bench which has been "signed" with mystical symbols. If the Holy Spirit does not "manifest" soon on one of the candidates, the Leader or the Mother begins to "rejoice" (sing and pray). When the spirit comes to one of the candidates, the Mother places a band around that person's eyes, and then around the eyes of the others. The candidates are told to stand, the congregation starts to sing and rejoice, and additional manifestations of the spirit on the pilgrims occur. Early the next morning, the baptismal procession procedes to the riverside for the rite of immersion. Returning to the church an hour or so later, the baptized "children" are anointed with oil.

One of the connections between the Shango cult-groups and the Shouters churches in Trinidad lies in the baptismal, "mourning," and "building" rituals. Shangoists as well as Spiritual Baptists need to be baptized, and only a Shouters pastor of some standing can perform this service. "Mourning" and "building" are optional, but "putting people to 'mourn' " is done by leaders in the Shouters group both for Shouters and for shangoists, unless the Shango leader also carries on Spiritual Baptist work.

"Mourning" has nothing to do with death rites (wakes, Third Nights, Nine Nights, Forty Days, and Annual Memorials), but refers to one's stay in the "sacred chamber" (usually a small, separate structure near the church). It is conceived of as temporary death. The "pilgrims" are said to be lying "in the tomb," and there is rejoicing on the third day when they are "lifted" and "released." Subsequent trips to the mourning house to "build" involve essentially the same procedures as those followed on the first visit, but on these occasions one tries to increase his spiritual understanding and "to take a higher degree." This phrase means that the devotee hopes to receive a new "gift" (new office or new responsibility in the cult) through a dream or vision.[26]

One influence of Shango in some of the Shouters churches is the giving of offerings to the spirits. At the end of a baptismal ceremony I witnessed at Maracas Bay on August 14, 1960, offerings of food and a live pigeon were tossed on a fire that had been lighted on the beach, and a tray of food and flowers was thrown into the sea for the spirits "of the sea, the land, and the river." Noteworthy also is the participation in one or more annual Shango ceremonies of many persons who are members of Shouters groups. Finally, it should be pointed out that occasionally a Shango power possesses a person who is taking part in a Shouters service.

At the beginning of the "mourning" ritual, the Pointer prepares the cotton bands to be used as blindfolds by "signing" (making designs on the cloth with chalk) and "sealing" them (letting wax from a lighted candle drip along the chalk lines). Prayers and exhortations (usually reading and interpreting Romans 6) by the officers of the church are followed by washing the "child's" hands and feet and anointing her head with olive oil. The "pilgrim" is then taken to the mourning room for a three-day period of seclusion. During this time she fasts and prays. At the conclusion of the mourning rite early Sunday morning, the pilgrim faces the congregation and "reads her tracts" (tells about her spiritual travels while in the mourning room). One may say that she "traveled" to Africa, to India, to Japan, to a Catholic church in Rome, or to the "Thunder House" in the sky. During mourning one hopes to receive a "gift," that is, to find out what her "work" is. One who reports a "vision" in which she bathed a woman whose body was covered with sores will be told by a church officer that she is now a Healer or a Nurse. Some "come out" as Teachers, others as Trumpet Blowers (singers or song leaders), Divers, Hunters, or Shepherdesses. One who does not receive a gift is not barred from trying again. A successful trip to the mourning house may be followed by a later visit to "build," a procedure that is essentially the same as "mourning."

The Herskovitses saw the Shouters as "a point of transition between African religion, represented in Trinidad by the Shango cult, and undiluted European forms of worship, as found in the Church of England, among the Moravians, and, to a lesser extent, the Seventh Day Adventists and the Baptists.[27] These anthropologists observed the following African cultural influences in the Shouters cult.

1. The hymn, psalm, and chapter that the initiate acquires during baptism parallel, in Protestant terms, the specific songs and drum rhythms and modes of speech which, in the Shango cult of Trinidad and in West Africa, cause the devotee "to receive the spirit."
2. The rites of seclusion in the mourning room hold many resemblances to initiation into African cult-groups.
3. Talking in "tongues."
4. The rhythms of the transmuted Sankey hymns.[28]
5. Hand clapping and foot tapping accompaniment of singing.
6. The bodily movements of possession trance, and the theory of possession, with the exception that the concept of becoming the possessing spirit is absent, are African.
7. Pouring of water three times at each corner of the church and at the center post.
8. Chalk marking on the floor.[29]

For the rank-and-file participants, the *social* consensus, based on such ritual elements as ringing the handbell, throwing offerings to the spirits, anointing with oil, dancing, being possessed by the Holy Spirit, speaking in unknown tongues, making chalk marks on eye-bands (blindfolds) or the Mercy Seat (the bench where the neophytes sit), receiving "memoranda" from the Holy Spirit, foot-washing, citing favorite chapters in the Bible, immersing baptismal candidates, and so on does not "evoke explanations and associations but lead[s] directly to highly patterned behavior." On the other hand, for the leading figures among the Shouters these and other ritual elements are not simply signs or signals in continuing social interaction. Because of their concern with matters

REVIVALIST AND OTHER CULTS

beyond the present moment, they have elaborated and articulated a symbolic, logical, and aesthetic structure. This *cultural* consensus is incomplete, but there is enough understanding to make communication and discussion possible.[30] Since, as Parsons has pointed out, integration in the two systems—social and cultural—is not of the same type, tension exists between them.[31]

The Shakers of St. Vincent

English rule began in St. Vincent in 1783, and the Church of England became the established church. It served only the white upper class; Anglicans ignored the slaves religiously. Although the Quakers, the Lutherans, the Catholics, and the Moravians carried on early missionary work in the Caribbean area, the first direct religious influence intended for the slaves of St. Vincent was brought by a Methodist missionary in 1787. By 1960, the Anglicans had 37,671 members; the Methodists numbered 26,537; 8,843 were Roman Catholics; and 2,195 belonged to the Presbyterian, Baptist, Seventh Day Adventist, Jehovah's Witnesses, or Pentecostal churches. Although there were 3,289 "other Christians" in St. Vincent in that year, the Shakers, who had been confirmed in one or another of the established churches, were recorded as members of those churches in the census.[32]

The Shaker cult was outlawed in 1912, but the policy toward it became less harsh in the 1930s. The law against Shakerism was repealed in 1965, and today the pastor of a Shaker church has the right to christen, conduct funeral rites, and perform marriage ceremonies if he has obtained a license. Although St. Vincent has a "poor white" population, all of the Shakers that Henney, an anthropologist who studied this cult in 1966, observed were dark-skinned.

Shakerism appears to be a blend consisting of a Methodist base; some elements borrowed from Anglicanism, Catholicism, and Pentecostalism; some modified African religious traits; and some elements invented locally. An outstanding feature of this religion is the mild states of dissociation, attributed to possession by the Holy Ghost, that some of its believers experience.[33]

A regular meeting of the Shakers opens with hymn-singing, and is followed by rites of sprinkling water (previously prayed over) at the four

REVIVALIST AND OTHER CULTS

corners of the praise house, the center pole, the four corners of the altar, and the doorways, and of ringing the altar bell three times at each station. The person who sprinkles the water repeats the words "in the name of the Father, the Son, and the Holy Ghost," says a silent prayer, makes the sign of the cross with her lighted candle, and curtsies. The members of the congregation then recite the Apostles' Creed, kneel, repeat the General Confession, the Lord's Prayer and another prayer, stand and sing the Gloria Patri again; the same procedure is followed for a biblical lesson taken from the New Testament. The rest of the service consists of a sermon by the pointer, interspersed with hymns led by him and with prayers by members of the congregation. Possession trance rarely occurs during the first part of the service, when the Methodist Order of Morning Worship is being closely followed, but it does occur in the latter part of the service. A benediction and another singing of the Gloria Patri close the service.[34]

In addition to the regular Wednesday, Friday, and Sunday evening services, Shakers hold "thanksgiving" meetings at the homes of members to bless or "christen" a house. Also, lower-class individuals may invite a group of Shakers to conduct traditional ceremonies on the third, ninth, and fortieth night after a person has died. As in the case of the Shouters of Trinidad, baptismal, "mourning," and "building" rites among the Shakers are of great importance. A successful spiritual journey during "mourning" admits the sojourner into the Shaker elite, but these rites also divide this in-group into various classes of elders.[35]

Henney found, as have other observers of possession cults in other parts of the Caribbean and elsewhere, that some individuals achieve dissociational states at almost every meeting, but others never show symptoms of such states. The Shaker explanation of this seeming lack is simply that the Holy Spirit enters some persons, but only shakes them from within.

Streams of Power Cult in St. Vincent

The Streams of Power movement was founded in Holland about 1952 by an artist who had promised to preach God's word if he were cured of an illness. It has spread to the Dutch West Indies, Surinam, Trinidad, St. Lucia, Martinique, St. Vincent, and to parts of Europe and

Africa. A branch of the movement was started in St. Vincent in 1965.

The Streams of Power group, led by an evangelist from Holland, receives outside funds to supplement local collections and gifts. The evangelist, better educated than his followers and his counterparts among the Shakers, is a foreigner of a different race and does not speak the language of the members of his church in his home.[36]

About three-fifths of the congregation of Streams of Power is composed of women, about one-fifth of men, and one-fifth of children. The first third of each service consists of loud and fast singing of evangelistic hymns, with piano and instrumental accompaniment, handclapping, stamping of feet, and gesturing. The singing is followed by "speaking in tongues," a quiet period during which there is no music, singing, handclapping, or drumming. On Sunday, a sermon by the evangelist, hymn singing, the taking of an offering, a prayer and a benediction complete the service. Monday and Thursday evening services are devoted to Bible teaching and a prayer meeting, and some night meetings are followed by healing sessions conducted by the evangelist. In general, Streams of Power meetings are shorter, simpler, and less ritualized than Shaker services.

Like the Shakers, Streams of Power adheres to a fundamentalist approach to Protestant Christianity. The members of both groups are possessed by the Holy Ghost and speak in tongues, but the Streams of Power disapprove of shaking behavior. The Streams of Power evangelist "projects a 'Pollyanna' type of image," but the Shaker pointer admits that "the way is hard." Not surprisingly, the Streams of Power attracts devotees who, on the average, are of slightly higher socioeconomic status than the Shakers.

Summarizing the differences between the orientation of the Shakers and the Streams of Power, Henney states:

> there seems to be a greater emphasis among the Shakers on individual seeking and individual involvement: each person's main concern is his own relationship with the deity and his eventual fate. With Streams of Power, these are important considerations also, but a stronger emphasis seems to be placed on the current situations of its worshippers and on fostering good relations among men.[37]

REVIVALIST AND OTHER CULTS

Spiritualism in Puerto Rico

In a study of spiritualism in Puerto Rico, skin color is mentioned frequently as being correlated with social class. In their Survey Sample of the entire San Juan metropolitan area, Rogler and Holingshead found that two-thirds of the 5,326 individuals were in class V, the lowest socioeconomic group, and only one-eighth of the total were in II and III, the middle classes. All of the families (40 husbands and 40 wives) included in their intensive study fell within class V. These informants referred to the rich as "the whites," the middle classes as "the little whites," and the poor as "the darker ones." Many of those attracted to spiritualism are professed Christians. Two-thirds of the Catholics and half of the Protestants included in the survey believe in spiritualism. Almost as many well as sick persons seek this type of religious help.[38]

The Puerto Rican spiritualist medium's claim to competence is based on the assumption that all individual problems are material or spiritual, or a combination of both. Since most problems are classified as at least partially spiritual, the medium attempts to deal with a vast range of problems, including disorders of personality in the broad, nontechnical sense of the term, by summoning, interrogating, and manipulating spirits of the dead. Contacts between the medium and a client take place mainly in private consultation or in a session involving some fifteen to twenty participants. A group meeting is organized around four social roles: those of the head medium, of the auxiliary medium(s), and of participants with and without "faculties" (an alleged degree of influence over spirits).[39] According to Rogler and Hollingshead, spiritualism is "the one institution to which the people turn for help in their hours of need."[40]

A Religio-Political Cult:
The Ras Tafari Movement in Jamaica

During the period 1914 to 1940, the philosophy of Marcus Garvey (an early black nationalist leader) was regarded by many Negroes in the United States, the West Indies, and elsewhere as a religion—a religion led by the "black Moses." Writing in the Negro World, the Reverend R. R. Porter asserted that a true Garveyite "is true to himself, others and his religion—through the right understanding of One God, One

Aim, One Destiny (the Universal Negro Improvement Association motto) he shall enjoy life and live abundantly in the Kingdom of Heaven on earth, and know that Africa shall once more become the land of the Good, Strong, and Wise."[41]

According to Garveyite theology, blacks are the chosen people of God, and Garvey's followers often likened themselves to the Jews, especially the Zionists. Rabbi J. Arnold Ford, the UNIA's musical director, was a black Jew from Barbados who had adopted Judaism before he joined the Association. Most of his Beth B'nai congregation came to the Garvey movement with him, and he had hoped that Judaism would become the official religion of the UNIA.[42]

Garvey, born in Jamaica, had been brought up as a Roman Catholic. To further the religious side of his movement, he persuaded the Reverend George Alexander McGuire, an Antiguan Episcopal clergyman in Boston, to accept the post of Chaplain General of the UNIA. Ordained a bishop in a service conducted by an archbishop of the Greek Orthodox Church, McGuire became the head of the new African Orthodox Church.[43]

Amy J. Garvey, second wife of "the black Moses" and his close associate in the Garveyite movement, asserts that her husband taught all peoples of African descent "to visualize Christ, the Redeemer of all Mankind, as a man of color," and she asks "who can best portray 'the man of sorrow, and acquainted with grief,' but the down-trodden Negro in modern times?" According to her, the wandering Jew portrayed this figure many years ago when "he was the persecuted, the spurned, the wanderer on the face of the earth, seeking a return to his homeland. Today . . . the New Negro's Icon is of dusky hue."[44] Garvey was not, however, the first advocate of a black God; many religious cults and sects among American Negroes had rejected the worship of a white god before Garvey came to New York.[45]

During the August 1924, Convention of the UNIA, Bishop McGuire asked Negroes to set a time for burning any pictures of the white Madonna and the white Christ they might own and to encourage Negro painters to start supplying "a black Madonna and a black Christ for the training of our children." At the same time, McGuire declared that henceforth the Negro's devil would be white. For various reasons,

REVIVALIST AND OTHER CULTS

including economic considerations, three-fourths or more of the regular Negro preachers opposed the new black religion, and the majority of Garveyites never joined the African Orthodox Church.[46]

An offshoot of the UNIA, the Ras Tafari movement in Jamaica, began to take shape about 1930. Rastafarians consider Marcus Garvey as the forerunner of their movement. His slogans—"Africa for the Africans, At Home and Abroad" and "One God! One Aim! One Destiny!" are proclaimed frequently at Ras Tafari meetings. The basic Rastafarian doctrines are: first, black men, reincarnations of the ancient Israelites, were exiled to the West Indies because of their transgressions; second, the wicked white man is inferior to the black man; third, the Jamaican situation is a hopeless Hell; fourth, Ethiopia is Heaven; fifth, Haile Selassie is the Living God; sixth, the invincible Emperor of Abyssinia will soon arrange for expatriated persons of African descent to return to the Homeland; and seventh, in the near future black men will get revenge by compelling white men to serve them.[47]

The Rastafari movement might be called a religio-political cult. Despite the hostility of the Rastafarians toward clergymen and their congregations, passages of the Bible are read or quoted at meetings and interpreted in ways that give support to Rastafarian doctrines, and many of the cult's songs are adaptations of Methodist or Baptist hymns.[48]

In the early 1950s, participation in Ras Tafari meetings was an escapist-adjustive activity. These occasions provided lower-class and disaffected Jamaicans with opportunities to denounce the enemies of the people: "the white man" and the Jamaican "traitors": politicians, businessmen, clergymen, and the police.[49] The movement grew rapidly between 1953 and 1960, and it became a more complex phenomenon. As a result of their association with criminals during long jail sentences on ganja (marijuana) or other charges, many Rastafarians became habituated to crime, and this development strengthened the Niyabingi subcult of violence. Smith, Augier, and Nettleford (*The Ras Tafari Movement in Kingston, Jamaica,* 18) assert that the expansion of this element "took place at the expense of the more reasonable and orderly section of the Ras Tafari movement." Some groups became committed to a political struggle; others remained escapist. Psychologically, the nonviolent groups resemble the revivalist cults of Jamaica. The violent groups insist

REVIVALIST AND OTHER CULTS

that deliverance from poverty and humiliation must come from within Jamaica and not from Haile Selassie in Ethiopia. Their members have shifted from earlier Rastafarian doctrine, and they share with the secular "rude-boys" the belief that the social system must be changed, by violence if necessary.[50]

The religious doctrines of Rastafarianism constitute one of its most persistent features. Central in the belief system of this cult is the divinity of Haile Selassie. Selassie stands "as a symbol of black glory and ancient African lineage dating back to Solomon and the Queen of Sheba." Nettleford points out that it is the Rastafarians who have deified Selassie, and adds—"The implication for the Jamaican society will continue to turn on whether Rastafarianism can be accepted as a legitimate form of religious worship. It is somewhat tolerated now but . . . there are those who view as blasphemous the belief in the divinity of Haile Selassie."[51]

Just as others have declared the man Jesus to be the son of God, so the Rastafarians have declared the divinity of Haile Selassie. They assert that the histories of other religions prove that eventually they will gain legitimacy for their creed. As other cultists have done, they reinterpret the Old Testament in claiming that they are true present-day prophets, the " 'reincarnated Moseses, Joshuas, Isaiahs, and Jeremiahs.' " They believe that they are " 'destined to free the scattered Ethiopians who are black men.' "[52] It seems likely, however, that it will be a long time, if ever, before Jamaican society will accept Rastafarianism on its own religious terms.

Although our concern here is primarily with Caribbean cults, some reference to Garvey's influence on Father Divine's movement and on the Black Muslims in the United States may be of interest. On the relationship between the UNIA and Father Divine's movement, Vincent comments:

> Though the Divine Peace Mission's only tie to the UNIA was through its large ex-Garveyite membership, the movement's lifestyle was not unlike that of the UNIA. Whites were present, but the Peace Mission was run by blacks under a black God. Grassroots followers in both movements found spiritual escape from established Christianity, and sought to build separate economic insti-

REVIVALIST AND OTHER CULTS

tutions and overcome white racism primarily by developing independent power bases within black society. Many Garveyites were
no doubt reluctant to join a movement which officially rejected the
concept of race, and many more rejected the spiritual aspects of the
Peace Mission, but a sizeable contingent of Garveyites saw in Divine's movement the opportunity to continue building a world of
their own.[53]

Many Garveyites joined the Moorish American Science Temple of
Noble Drew Ali in the 1920s. Later, in recruiting for the Black Muslims, Elijah Muhammad declared: "I have always had a very high opinion of both the late Noble Drew Ali and Marcus Garvey and admired
their courage in helping our people (the so-called Negroes) and appreciated their work. Both of these men were fine Muslims. The followers of
Noble Drew Ali and Marcus Garvey should now follow me and cooperate with us in our work because we are only trying to finish up what
those before us started."[54] Mrs. Garvey asserts that all of the "freedom
movements" in America in the 1960s "were initiated by the work and
teaching of Marcus Garvey," and she adds that the "entire Black Muslim
philosophy . . . is feeding upon the seeds that were planted by Marcus
Garvey."[55]

Changes in the philosophies and policies of the Ras Tafari movement in Jamaica and the Black Muslim organization in the United States
occurred in the 1970s, in part because of changes in the larger societies,
and in part because of the dethronement of Haile Selassie in 1974, followed by his death in 1975, and by Elijah Muhammad's death in 1975.
These changes are discussed in chapter 9.

The Dreads of Dominica

Formerly a British West Indian colony, Dominica is located about
halfway between Puerto Rico and Trinidad. Its total area is about 290
square miles; its population approximately 72,000. In 1975, it was
called "the poorest and most underdeveloped of the Associated States" of
the British Commonwealth.[56] Less than ten families and corporations
control 60 percent of the arable land, and the wage for an agricultural
laborer working on an estate is $3.00 or less per day. Schools are poorly
equipped and staffed, and the unemployment rate is extremely high.

REVIVALIST AND OTHER CULTS

The Rastafarian-type youths in Dominica seem to have taken the name "Dread" from the language of the Rastafarian cult in Jamaica. "Dread" means "the Power that lies within any man." It is a philosophy "of getting the most out of life, of using one's potential for living as fully as possible." They reject "Babylon," the present-day Dominican society, dress simply and are vegetarians. Marijuana is regarded as "essential spiritual food." Formerly, members did not comb or cut their "locks" (hair).

There is no fixed religious ideology to which all the Dreads subscribe. Some adherents believe that Haile Selassie was the living God on earth; others claim that Selassie personified corruption. Those who worship the late Emperor maintain that Africa is their homeland and insist that to attain fulfillment they must return to Africa. Others argue that Dominica is their homeland and say that they will remain on the island and try to redeem the society. All believe that Babylon will fall, but the followers of Selassie expect the fall to come by the direct intervention of God on Judgment Day. The more militant faction advocates the overthrow of Babylon by any available means. Both groups think of socialism as the alternative to capitalist society.

Those who sympathize with the Dreads assert that they have become a scapegoat for anti-socialist groups in Dominica. They claim that blame for six of the nine murders and attacks against expatriates, tourists, and local persons in 1974 and early 1975, attributed to the Dreads, is based on speculation. Strong public opinion has developed against the Dreads, and on November 19, 1974, the Prohibited and Unlawful Societies and Association Act was unanimously passed in the Dominica House of Assembly. Section 5 of this Act states: "Any member of an unlawful association who appears in public or elsewhere wearing any uniform, badge or mode of dress or other distinguishing mark or feature or manner of wearing their hair, shall be guilty of an offense, and shall be arrested without warrant by any member of the Police force." Under this Act, a number of the more militant Dreads were arrested in 1974–75 and given nine-month sentences in prison. Ostensibly, by the middle of 1975, the Dread movement no longer existed. On July 25, 1975, however, a thirty-day amnesty was granted by the government so that the Dreads could surrender arms and discuss current

REVIVALIST AND OTHER CULTS

problems with officials. Members of the Dreads were reported to view the order with mistrust and no meetings were held during the thirty-day period. Later, the amnesty was extended and a committee headed by a Methodist minister was appointed to meet with the Dreads and to recommend solutions to social and economic problems to the government.

THE PSYCHOLOGICAL FACTOR
IN CARIBBEAN CULTS

Participation in the rituals of religious cults provides one avenue of escape from the anxieties and frustrations generated by life in the lower socioeconomic class in Caribbean countries. Among the psychological attractions of the cults are obeisance to the gods, rapport of the group, the drama of well-performed rituals, support and guidance by the leaders, healing, the building up and release of emotional tensions, and the recognition that is accorded to those who have special qualities, especially the ability to go into trance.

Spirit Possession:
The Meaning of Trance and Possession

The terms "trance" and "possession" are often used inconsistently and interchangeably. Bourguignon distinguishes between "trance" as a level of behavior and "possession" as native belief or theory about behavior or events. Trance is defined as "a state in which we observe a certain alteration of consciousness, an alteration which may bring about changes, in varying degree, of certain functions: changes in concepts of identity, in memory functions, in sensory modalities, and so forth." Trance is generally interpreted as some type of soul absence, and possession trance is interpreted as the taking over of the body and its functions by a spiritual entity.[57]

Our concern here is mainly with possession trance, but hallucinatory or visionary trance plays a role in some Caribbean cults. In the "mourning" ritual of the Spiritual Baptists (Shakers in St. Vincent, Shouters in Trinidad), the participants seem to experience phenomena "ranging from simple daydreams to complex hallucinations." Henney thinks it appropriate to call these experiences "pseudoperceptions" or "reported visual, or auditory, sensations."[58]

Important differences exist between spirit possession in many Caribbean cults and the seizures and possessions by the "spirit," presumably the Holy Spirit (only a few seem to have been possessed by the Devil), that occurred during the Scotch-Irish revival in Ulster in 1859 and in the camp meetings in Kentucky in the nineteenth century. In the latter situations, the minister condemned the wickedness of his hearers and portrayed Hell in vivid terms. Listeners felt guilty and were afraid; they wept, shouted, prayed, fell on the ground, shook in every joint, barked like dogs, and burst into a "holy laugh."[59] The leaders of Neo-African, ancestral, and revivalist cults in Haiti, Jamaica, Trinidad, Grenada, Belize, and St. Lucia do not frighten their followers into a state of possession. It is a mark of distinction to be possessed by a spirit, and one may receive important messages during this religious experience. In the absence of a remodeled African cult such as Shango or an ancestral cult such as Cumina on the island, the origins of possession trance in the Shakers church in St. Vincent may lie in the violent conversions and dramatic seizures of early Methodism.[60]

Features of Possession Trance

The literature on spirit possession reveals that certain features are associated with possession states throughout quite different cultures:

1. Induction of the state is frequently achieved through dancing to music that features a pronounced and rapid beat.
2. Induction frequently occurs following a period of starvation or a period of overbreathing.
3. The onset of possession is marked by a brief period of inhibition or collapse.
4. In the neophyte, collapse may be followed by a period of hyperactivity; once experience is acquired, a controlled deity-specific behavior pattern emerges.
5. During the state of possession there is frequently a fine tremor of head and limbs; sometimes grosser, convulsive jerks occur. A diminution of sensory acuity may be evident.

REVIVALIST AND OTHER CULTS

6. Return to normal consciousness is followed by a sleep of exhaustion from which the subject awakens in a state of mild euphoria.[61]

Varying degrees of dissociation, occur in spirit possession, ranging from "profound states of unconsciousness to dizziness to theatrical involvement to outright faking." Less than full dissociation has been observed in Xango African-derived cults in Brazil and Trinidad since 1940. Ribeiro finds that participants in Recife distinguish differences in depth of the state of dissociation attained by each possessee, lighter conditions being called "radiation states." Bastide says that a distinction is made in Brazilian candomblés between (1) possession by the gods and (2) possession by spirits of the ancestors and by Esu, and he reports a diversity in the types of "sojourns" of the gods. In São Paulo, umbandists place mediums into three categories: conscious, semiconscious, and unconscious. They estimate that only 15 to 35 percent of Umbanda mediums are unconscious during possession. Pressel estimates that not more than 5 percent of these mediums experience unconscious trance, characterized by glazed eyes for two or three hours; profuse perspiring for the same length of time; production of more saliva than usual; some difficulty with motor coordination, including difficulty with speech; unconsciousness; and the need to be supported for about thirty seconds after trance. In Trinidadian shango, every 'power' has a *réré* (*wéri*) or messenger-servant who may come to a ceremony after the deity leaves, or he may arrive before the *orisa* does. Some persons are possessed by a *réré* but never by a power; a *réré* does not manifest on a devotee as powerfully as does an *orisa*. One may be able to get a *réré* to come more quickly than a power. *Rérés* are mischievous, and they are afraid of the *orisa*. Abrahams found that some of the Zeckeeboom people (name given to the St. Vincent Shakers by nonbelievers in Richland Park because of the phrases they repeat in their trance-state) "walk around in semi-trance all of the time, go to market in Kingstown on Saturdays in their white robes, wandering through the crowds and touching people. It is as if, having received the power in the ring, they have been sent forth to demonstrate it with the non-believers."[62]

Henney identified three stages in possession trance in Shaker ritual in St. Vincent. In the first stage, a person may "jerk spasmodically, tremble and shake, and occasionally break into his own prayer or preaching with a yell. If possession develops to the second level, it may become a group phenomenon during which a rhythmic beat is established through the singing, humming, or chanting. Here the syllables "change to mere grunts and gasps—but these are emitted in unison. . . . Each individual, as if in a dance line, then produces much the same movements." At the third level, "the movements and sounds, having degenerated from the smooth rhythmic performance of the preceding level, are again random, patternless, and spasmodic. . . . However, the sounds are unlike those of the first level in that they are not occasional shouts and noises superimposed on a musical background. . . ." At this point, the possession trancers "gasp, sigh and shout in noisy confusion."[63]

Possession Behavior Is Learned Behavior

Possession behavior is culturally structured; the acts of possessed persons are so stylized that the initiated can identify the divinity possessing a devotee.[64] Ribeiro comments on "the awkwardness of new cult-affiliates" and says that their "weird" possessions are often pointed out and criticized by other members and priests as they call attention to and praise the "old hands" for their "composed and well-patterned" possessions.[65] To induce possession, Jamaican revivalists move counterclockwise around the altar "trumping" and "laboring in the spirit." As the body is bent forward from the waist, the breath is expelled and the maximum amount of air is breathed in on the upswing. Revivalists "groan" or "sound" as they forcefully exhale and inhale, and the hyperventilation produces dizziness and other effects in some persons.[66]

In Umbanda trance and possession in São Paulo, Brazil, polyrhythmic drumming, singing, handclapping, and sometimes the ringing of a bell, accompany the induction of trance. In most centers, the mediums dance and spin up to the point of spirit possession. In some centers, however, as well as in most private Umbanda sessions, the mediums rely on concentrating on the arrival of their spirit. Pressel saw only one case of hyperventilation being used to induce trance.[67] The dissociational states that the Shakers of St. Vincent experience during inside meetings are induced through prolonged preaching, testifying, and singing. They do not dance, and no musical instruments are used, "but a strong beat is marked by hand-clapping, foot-tapping, and beating a leather strap on a table serving as an altar."[68]

In addition to learning from their families the cultural concept of spirits that possess human beings, children learn the stereotyped motor patterns that are appropriate in trancing. Pressel reports that children in play imitate the jerking of the head and chest that is used in inducing and terminating spirit possession in Umbanda.[69] In São Paulo Umbanda, candidates for mediumship may be given special training, or instruction in trance and possession may be provided in public sessions. Techniques used to help an individual to dissociate include focusing his attention on a lighted candle; turning the person around several times, followed by the leader's passing his hand across the face of the novice and snapping his fingers; and holding the hands of a novice and rocking him back and forth on his heels. In the Apostolic Church in Mérida, Yucatan, Goodman found that "both men and women learn to speak in tongues."[70]

In possession trance in a number of Afro-Caribbean and Afro-Brazilian cults, there is some "choice" of the god that will possess the individual and, in many cases, a positive or negative correlation exists between the "character" of the divinity or divinities that possess him and that of the devotee.[71]

Before entering the "mourning room" in the Shaker church in St. Vincent, participants know what constitutes "appropriate" behavior in the mourning ritual. Some have "mourned" before and understand what is expected of them. All members of the sect have heard returning mourners recount their experiences during "spiritual travels," and all Shakers who have been baptized have gone through a briefer, but similar, ritual the night before baptism.[72] Dissociation during mourning is not regarded as spirit possession. Conditions during hallucinatory or visionary trance are similar to those used in sensory-deprivation experiments: "the mourner is confined, his visual perception is limited by a blindfold, his motility is restricted since he is required to lie on the ground in a specified position, he is fed a limited diet, he is isolated from his ordinary contacts and activities, and he is in a situation of dependency."[73]

REVIVALIST AND OTHER CULTS

Some trance experiences occur spontaneously outside ceremonies as protective devices. Hallucinating in a situation which is perceived as dangerous, a cult devotee may think that one of the deities he worships has driven away a threatening aggressor—supernatural or human.[74]

Bourguignon's trial formulation of a model of culturally patterned altered states of consciousness (Fig. 4.1) brings together in a parsimonious manner some of the evidence, as well as a number of assumptions, concerning ASCs, including possession trance.[75]

Spirit Possession and Mental Illness

Spirit possession cannot be equated with mental illness. Gardner Murphy pointed out nearly thirty years ago that dissociation is a normal

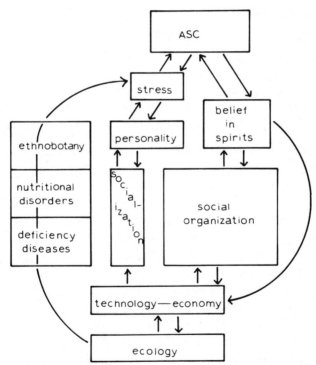

Figure 4.1. A Model of Culturally Patterned Altered States of Consciousness
Source: Erika Bourguignon, *Culture and the Varieties of Consciousness* (figure 1, p. 23), Copyright © 1974 by Cummings Publishing Co., Inc. Used by permission.

REVIVALIST AND OTHER CULTS

phenomenon in some cases and that it may be experimentally induced. About the same time, Herskovits wrote that spirit possession cannot be regarded as the equivalent of neurotic and psychotic manifestations of abnormality found in Western societies. Yinger's distinction between the atypical, or behavior "that departs from the statistically and culturally normal," and the abnormal, or behavior "that expresses intraindividual conflicts and malintegration" makes the point that needs to be stressed. It should be noted too that recent studies by psychiatrists and psychologists with anthropological training show that the majority of those actively involved in "peripheral" possession cults, and especially those who participate in main morality cults, "are only mildly or often temporarily neurotic in any valid sense."[76] According to Lewis, in possession cults, one finds

> some genuine schizophrenics and psychotics. But their number is small compared with the mass of ordinary "normally" neurotic people who find some relief from anxiety and some resolution of everyday conflicts and problems in such religious activity. Here the very marked lack of response to the cathartic therapies employed in possession cults in the case of seriously disturbed individuals . . . is itself a testimony to the robust mental health of the majority of participants. . . . The latter have no difficulty at all in communicating their problems. They operate within a culturally standardized medium of communication. Nor in contrast to the true self-insulated psychotic, do they miss their "cues." They respond in the expected way, and others react equally predictably.[77]

In Haiti, spirit possession is not used to explain or diagnose mental illness. Spirits may cause insanity by sending it, but one is not thought to be ill because a spirit is possessing him. Possession is a prerequisite for becoming an initiate of the vodun cult, but illness and cure are not required of the novitiate and the priest, as is the case in parts of Africa and in Asiatic shamanism.[78]

In vodun and other Afro-Catholic syncretic cults, as in the Fon and Yoruba spirit cults in West Africa, initiation is not prompted by illness thought to be due to possession. This is not the case in the Ndoep cult of Senegal or the Zar cult of Ethiopia. The Fon-Yoruba cults were not "marginal, therapeutic societies . . . . but cults of worship, linked to the power structure and the estabishment, whether of kinship and the

state or the kin group and the ancestors."[79] That no patterns of possession trance similar to those in vodun and related cults among other New
World Negroes are known for European societies is significant. Demonic
possession trance of earlier periods of European history was something to
be feared, a pathological phenomenon which called for exorcism.[80]

In Recife shango, Ribeiro found severe maladjustments in some
persons who become possessed, but he says that "their social and religious behavior was by no means appraised as abnormal by their relatives, employers, work partners, priests, and cult fellows." Priests of
this Afro-Brazilian cult themselves recognize the difference between normal and pathological cases because they occasionally bring followers to
Ribeiro with the explanation that their possessions are not proper ones,
and that they are "sick" and in need of help.[81]

After observing the behavior of candomblé members in Bahia,
Brazil, another psychiatrist wrote that a possessed individual must be
"in sufficient control of autistic and regressive behavior and of reality-
testing to be acceptable within the relatively rigid ritualistic group action"; and he added that no "frankly schizophrenic person would be able
to pass the probationary scrutiny." Stainbrook did find that some schizophrenic lower class patients acted out, on an individual basis, possessions
by African gods. In these psychotic cases, the major psychological goal
appeared to be similar to "the brief and transitory introjection and identification" achieved by participants in candomblé rituals.[82]

Although spirit possession and mental illness cannot be equated,
persons who use the ability to dissociate, along with other talents, to
become cult leaders, especially those who serve as full-time priests or
priestesses, seem to possess a "personality organization" significantly different from that of many of their confreres.[83]

Consequences of Spirit Possession

Ludwig uses the term "adaptive altered states of consciousness" to
refer to altered mental states which enable the individual "to acquire
new knowledge or experience, to express psychic tensions or relieve
conflict without danger to himself or others, and to function more adequately and constructively in society." Value judgments are required to
distinguish certain altered states of consciousness as adaptive or maladap-

tive; the latter are regarded as altered mental states "which serve no constructive purpose and which can, on occasion, endanger the individual or hamper his functioning in society."[84]

Lewis distinguishes between spirit possession in marginal possession cults and that in central morality cults. Peripheral possession, as seen in the *zar* cults of Ethiopia, for example, is regarded as an "oblique aggressive strategy" used by the weak and downtrodden to obtain attention and respect from privileged persons. Illness and misfortune are not the fault of the afflicted person, and the trouble that has been caused by amoral peripheral spirits must be treated by the patient's social superiors. When stress and conflict develop again, the compensatory strategy is repeated. On the other hand, main morality cults, consisting of ancestor cults and cults involving more autonomous divinities which are not simply deified human beings, use possession as a means of communication between men and the gods. Lewis found that peripheral cults appeal to those who are socially subordinate, especially to women, while central morality cults celebrate public morality and attract leaders from the upper strata of a society. In this view, peripheral and main morality possession cults may exist side by side in the same society, and, under changing social and political circumstances, a shift from one type to the other may occur. The boundaries between peripheral cults and separatist ecstatic religions are said to be "ill-defined and shifting." According to Lewis, in many respects Haitian vodun falls within the peripheral cult class, but in other respects, it could be called a separatist ecstatic religion.[85]

Bourguignon questions this characterization on two grounds: because most vodunists are unaware of the conflict of the world views between Catholicism and vodun, and because vodun appears to be a religion of the majority, and its supernatural coercion of the powerful is limited and partial.[86] On the basis of my observations in Haiti, I agree with her, and, for delimited groups, I would make the same point concerning *cumina* in the Morant Bay area of Jamaica, *santeria* in Cuba, the *candomblé* and *xango* in Brazil, and *shango* in Trinidad, especially if one goes back a generation or so. The possessing spirit among the Shakers of St. Vincent, the Jamaican revivalists, and the Trinidadian Shouters is the Holy Spirit. In these latter cults, possession trance is not used to

REVIVALIST AND OTHER CULTS

bring supernatural sanctions against those responsible for the deprivation of the downtrodden.[87] In Lewis's terms, they would be considered separatist ecstatic religions.

From the standpoint of the individual, spirit possession, as mentioned earlier, permits the socially sanctioned expression of actions which in other circumstances would be unacceptable or unavailable. Since it is the gods who are carrying out the actions, possessed persons may indulge in self-punishment, close physical interaction with others (rubbing, pushing, crushing, massaging, threatening, lashing, carrying, and so forth), reversal of sex roles, or in childish actions with no feelings of fear or guilt.[88] Dissociation, as Bourguignon points out, may divert the individual from a "realistic" solution to his problems, but in Haiti (and elsewhere) the self-serving nature of supposedly "dissociated" wishes is a notable feature of the phenomenon.[89]

Possession Trance and Sex Roles in the Cults

Bourguignon has proposed a hypothesis to account for the dominance of women who fall in possession trance in Afroamerican and African cults. Apart from the psychological functions of the cults, this view emphasizes a factor of social structure in the roles played by women and men inside the cult, as well as in the segment of the society in which the cult members live. The majority of the initiated, some of whom fall in trance, are women. Women who do not become possessed are present at the different functions in other roles, including the preparation of ritual meals. Some of the cult officials are men; others assume such responsibilities as coordinating ceremonies, sacrificing animals, maintaining the physical properties of the cult house, and acting as guardians and external protectors. The drummers are men and their part in the ritual is highly important. Male "outsiders" (sympathizers) attend the secular functions of the cult. As predominantly feminine institutions, the cults may serve as a balance to the predominantly masculine institutions in some societies where the latter exist.[90]

Healing, Including Mental Healing, in the Cults

Healing is another benefit that devotees obtain from cult affiliation. Private physicians are often too expensive, and public medical services

REVIVALIST AND OTHER CULTS

frequently require considerable time and are impersonal. At an Umbanda center, one receives personal attention—a very important psychological consideration. Also, the spiritualist religions stress the Brazilian belief in a spiritual self. Pressel points out that personal identity is symbolized as the spiritual self and that this self represents an individual's "inner worth, dignity, and integrity." [91]

Since the healing often associated with Caribbean cults includes mental healing, the question arises of the effectiveness of the procedures used in such curing. Representative of the general view of those who have given attention to the effects of community ceremonies when illness follows transgression of traditional rules is that of Kiev regarding the Haitian vodun cult. He asserts: "As in psychotherapy, the patient's favorable expectations are reinforced by the treatment setting and techniques and by the *hungan's* faith in his capacity to respond to the treatment. The *hungan's* initial pessimism, which introduces ambiguity into the situation, also increases the suggestibility and anxiety of the patient and promotes his desire to please the *hungan;* while the connection of treatment with dominant values, by enlisting the valuable support of the community, further reinforces the patient's faith in the *hungan* and his expectation of relief." [92]

Personalities of Cult Leaders: Norman Paul and Marcus Garvey

The career of Norman Paul, the originator of a shango cult in Grenada, exemplifies some of the personality factors which have contributed to the formation of syncretistic religious cults by New World Negroes. [93]

Born in 1898, Paul was the son of a small cocoa buyer who later worked on a large estate; his mother worked in the fields on the same estate. Earlier his father had lived in a closed community of post-emancipation immigrants from Nigeria at Munich, Grenada. Among the stories that Paul's father told him during his childhood were several about Egungun, a Yoruba ancestral deity. At the age of seven, one of his grandmothers, a field laborer, took Paul to live with her. This grandmother taught her grandchildren Big Drum songs and dances. They knew that she sat up late at night to fight *loupgarous* (werewolves) who dared to venture into the vicinity. At her house, Paul heard a woman who practiced witchcraft relate what she was doing or had done to persons living nearby. Paul's mother arranged Nation Dances (Big Drum ceremonies) for others, but she did not "make" *saracas* (sacrifices) at her own home.

While Paul was living with his grandmother, an aunt joined the Seventh Day Adventists. At that time, he and his cousins were taken from their school and sent to the Adventist school. At thirteen or fourteen, Norman Paul was taken out of school to begin work.

While praying at fourteen, Paul got a "shock." His body shook, and he thought he had an ague fever. The shock disappeared, but it left "a kind of gladness" in Paul, and he sang some hymns and repeated verses of Scripture. His mother knew that he had "started to make visions," but at this time Paul did not understand the meaning of these experiences. At 16, he and a sister, a brother, an aunt, and a cousin were baptized on the same day.

Recurring illness was one of Paul's personal problems. From the age of 18, he was troubled with abdominal pains, and he wore a truss until he had an operation for hernia in 1937. After the operation, the pain stopped for a while, but it came back occasionally. At times he "couldn't do anything, when they come and find me I cannot even talk." On the way to Aruba in 1929, Paul became ill in Trinidad with a "fever" which lasted a year. Later he became ill again and was treated unsuccessfully by a doctor. A healer cured him of this illness and attributed his suffering to the work of a spirit. This explanation fitted in with Paul's dream before leaving Grenada that a woman was sprinkling a powder on the ground in front of his house. He had realized then that the "two small things" (charms) he found by the door the next morning were "harmful" objects. At times Paul was unable to work regularly— once he did not work for more than a year.

In summary, Paul's personal problems included his relatively low occupational status as a baker, laborer, painter, and small trader; his intermittent unemployment; his physical illnesses (fever, hernia, hip trouble); his emotional disturbances (powerful guilt feelings when he did something wrong, including staying away from church for three months when he was 16 because he had gone to a Nation Dance on a Friday

REVIVALIST AND OTHER CULTS

night), fear caused by finding *ouangas* (harmful charms) placed in front of his door, disorientation following his hernia operation, worry about the spirit that he believed was troubling him, and resentment at being expelled by the Adventists in Carriacou in 1935 after he had been accused (falsely, he claimed) of buying and selling on the Sabbath.

Norman Paul was not responsible for his actions in the realms of religion, healing, and divination—this behavior, he believed, was sanctioned by powerful supernatural figures. Authorization for launching his own religious enterprise came from Oshun (St. Philomena), who told him to build a chapel, get an altar, acquire drums, and give a three-day feast. She told him also that when he placed fowl by the river as offerings he could ask for anything he wanted and he would receive it. Other "women powers" with whom Paul spoke later included St. Martha, St. Veronica, and St. Anne (Emanja), especially the latter spirit. Emanja's special work is the detection of evil spirits and the beating and casting out of these spirits, and, presumably, she assisted Paul in dealing with evil beings. Paul was also in touch with such male spirits as Ezekiel, Job, St. John, and St. Michael (Ogun).

The kinds of dissociation which are given support by cult members and their world view may, as mentioned earlier, divert leaders and followers from "realistic" solutions to their problems. Some of the dissociated behaviors are " 'split off' from the everyday roles of the self," but ritualized dissociation does provide the self with an alternate set of roles. The self-serving nature of some of the dissociated wishes is noteworthy.[94] In the case of Norman Paul, these desires were associated with taking the roles of doctor, evangelist, and prophet.

Although value judgments are always involved in assessing the consequences of altered states of consciousness, dissociation seems to have enabled Paul to acquire new experience, express psychic tensions without endangering himself or others, and function more adequately in society.[95] Though Smith refers to Paul's "development, [his] conversion, breakdown and extraordinary recovery," he does not comment on his subject's emotional stability over his lifetime. There is no indication in Paul's autobiography that he was not one of the majority of those actively involved in possession cults who "are only mildly or often temporarily neurotic in any valid sense."[96]

REVIVALIST AND OTHER CULTS

Another example of the personal qualities that have played an important role in the formation of religious and political cults in the Caribbean is provided by Marcus Garvey. Garvey, a black nationalist and the founder of the Universal Negro Improvement Association, was born in 1887 in St. Ann's Bay, Jamaica. Many of the early members of the Ras Tafari movement had belonged to this organization and regarded Garvey as the forerunner of their cult. In Jamaica in the 1950s, his slogans: "One Aim! One God! One Destiny!" and "Africa for the Africans At Home and Abroad" were repeated frequently in Ras Tafari meetings.

Marcus Garvey, Sr., was well-read and owned the only private library in St. Ann's Bay. As a skillful stonemason, his income was above average, but his "intractable nature" involved him in costly lawsuits and his fortunes dwindled.[97]

Garvey's education was piecemeal, and at fourteen he left school to become a printer's apprentice. By this time he was well aware of the social distinctions made in Jamaica on the basis of color—the rather clear-cut categories of white, colored, and black. After the death of his father, Garvey moved to Kingston and worked as a printer. Becoming interested in street-corner debates, where serious issues were discussed, he began to speak out during the heated arguments. City people resented the challenges of this jet-black interrogator, called him "country boy" and told him to "shut up." Despite such taunts, Garvey continued to practice public speaking, and he advanced to the position of foreman of a large Jamaican printing firm.

Blacklisted for leading a strike, Garvey found a job at the government printing office. The political publication, *Garvey's Watchman,* that he started about 1910 was financially unsuccessful. After helping to form a political organization, the National Club, he concluded that political work required full-time effort and more money than he could raise in Jamaica. His first step in a new direction was to take a job as timekeeper on a United Fruit Company banana plantation in Costa Rica. His work and his journalistic experiences there and later in Panama, were disappointing. In his further travels to Ecuador, Nicaragua, Honduras, Colombia, and Venezuela he was saddened by the exploitation of Negro laborers that he witnessed.

A journey to London in 1912 increased Garvey's knowledge of

REVIVALIST AND OTHER CULTS

Africa and stimulated his interest in African nationalism. While in London he read Booker T. Washington's *Up from Slavery,* a book that affected him greatly. In 1914 Garvey returned to Jamaica. Concerning this moment in his life he said later: "My brain was afire" with the thought of "uniting all the Negro peoples of the world into one great body to establish a country and Government absolutely their own." Almost immediately he founded the Universal Negro Improvement Association (U.N.I.A.) and in March, 1916, he came to the United States to promote his cause.[98]

By the time the U.N.I.A. convention adjourned in New York City in August 1920, Garvey's influence was at its height. Garveyism had become a movement of world significance, and Negroes throughout the world were developing a sense of pride in being black. When Garvey exclaimed: "Up you mighty race, you can accomplish what you will," black people responded enthusiastically "with a determination born of centuries of frustration and despair."[99]

A recent biographer, Elton C. Fax, provides insights concerning Garvey's personality. All who were closely associated with him found that his "pride and vanity had to be constantly catered to." He was suspicious of others and "insisted upon being 'the big-I-am.' " Fax refers frequently to Garvey's temper, his inflated ego, his stubbornness, and his impulsiveness, attributing these characteristics in part to the way that racial prejudice had brutalized him.[100] Naive and impractical in many ventures, Garvey was also tough in the stands that he took. On one occasion he warned European colonists in Africa: "We are going home after a long vacation and are giving notice to the tenant to get out. If he doesn't there is such a thing as forcible eviction."[101]

Garvey's greatest assets were his "personal magnetism" and "a genius for getting impressive projects underway."[102] W. E. B. DuBois found it difficult to characterize Garvey.

> He has been charged with dishonesty and graft, but he seems to me essentially an honest and sincere man with a tremendous vision, great dynamic force, stubborn determination, and unselfish desire to serve; but also he has very serious defects of temperament and training: he is dictatorial, domineering, inordinately vain and very suspicious.[103]

REVIVALIST AND OTHER CULTS

DuBois called Garvey "an extraordinary leader of men," and said that "he is able to stir them with singular eloquence and the general run of his thought is of a high plane."[104]

Garvey, "the bombastic nationalist leader," was also a religious man, and one of those who espoused the concept of a black deity.[105] After entering prison in Atlanta in 1925, he promised his followers that he would return after death. In this messianic message, he declared: "Look for me in the whirlwind or the storm, look for me all around you, for, with God's grace, I shall come and bring with me countless millions of black slaves who have died in America and the West Indies and the millions in Africa to aid you in the fight for Liberty, Freedom and Life."[106]

By 1937, Garvey expected black people throughout the world to attempt to overcome all obstacles in their struggle for equality. He had written the white man off as far as helping black men to acquire their rights was concerned. As Garvey saw it, *"black men and black men alone,* held the key to the gateway leading to their freedom."[107] His political and religious philosophy was, therefore, congenial to many black nationalist groups, including the Rastafarians, and he continued to provide inspiration for them, even after his death.

I agree with La Barre that uncritical belief in the mystical charisma of the shaman-messiah does not contribute to an understanding of the rise of crisis-cult phenomena. "Charisma," La Barre asserts, "is not a sacred or supernatural force but a secular sociopsychological phenomenon: the relationship of the culture hero to his communicants and the affinity of his message with their unconscious wishes."[108] There can be no doubt about the affinity of Garvey's message with the unconscious wishes of his followers—first in Jamaica, and then in the United States and in other parts of the world.

Proud, domineering, energetic and idealistic, Garvey was haunted by the discouraging life-situation of the majority of blacks and was driven by a consuming desire to elevate the condition of all persons of African descent. He worked tirelessly and eloquently toward that end until his death in 1940.

REVIVALIST AND OTHER CULTS

ᨔ᭰CHAPTER FIVE᭰ᨔ

South America:
Blacks in the Historical Churches, Pentecostalism, and Spiritualism

APPROXIMATELY half of the slave imports during the whole period of the Atlantic slave trade were brought to South America. Of the 4,700,000 slaves going to South America, 3,647,000 (38.1 percent of the total slave trade to the New World and 78 percent of the South American trade) went to Brazil. The Guianas accounted for 5.6 percent of the Atlantic slave trade (Surinam and Guyana received 5 percent and French Guiana .5 percent); and Spanish South America for 5.5 percent (Colombia, Panama, and Ecuador: 2.1 percent; Venezuela: 1.3 percent; Peru: 1 percent; and Argentina, Uruguay, Paraguay, and Bolivia: 1 percent).[1]

Blacks are unevenly distributed in South American countries. In Brazil, Negroes and mestizos constitute nearly half of the populations in the states of the northeast and east. They form 70 percent of the population in the state of Bahia, and approximately half in the states of Pernambuco, Ceara, Parahyba, and Maranhão. In the southern states of São Paulo, Paraná, and Rio Grande (S), they make up slightly more than 10 percent of the population, and approximately 5 percent at Santa Catarina. In the east and northeast blacks live mainly along the coastal littoral, formerly the plantation region which depended on slave labor. In

Venezuela, blacks are concentrated in those areas where formerly plantation slavery was extensive. In Colombia, Bolivia, and Ecuador, Negroes are found only in the coastal provinces or the valleys of the interior; in Peru, the small black population is found only along the coastal belt.[2]

As we shift attention from the Caribbean to South America, we discover many similarities of culture and social structure relevant to religion, but significant differences as well. In particular we note differences in size of population, ratios of whites to blacks, political systems, avenues of social ascension, the length of time connections with Africa were maintained by blacks, the policies of major Christian churches toward religious instruction for blacks during the slavery period, the integration of people of color into a single nationality in Brazil after abolition, and other differences mentioned in this chapter and the next.

In addition to Catholicism, the Protestant churches, and Pentecostal sects in South America, these chapters consider Neo-African cults in Brazil, Surinam, and French Guiana; spiritualist cults in Brazil (Umbanda) and Venezuela (María Lionza); and Batuque, an independent cult in Belém, Brazil.

Catholicism in Brazil

In tracing the development of Catholicism in Brazil, Bastide emphasized the importance of the Catholic familism of the large plantations during the regime of slavery. This familism centered in the cult of the saints-protectors of the patriarch and of the dead, and many of the beliefs of the Middle Ages were resuscitated. The Catholic priests on these plantations were, of course, under the control of the landowners. Two Catholicisms existed under these circumstances. The chapel was often divided into two parts, with the nave reserved for whites. Where this procedure was not followed, the priest gave two masses at different hours. Religious societies were organized by mulattoes, Creoles, and Africans, and even by specific ethnic groups. In the processions of festivals where all inhabitants marched, the order was based on pigmentation. In the *congadas* (popular theatrical plays which dealt with African subjects) put on by religious societies, the Catholicism of the blacks revealed a different aspect than that of the whites.[3]

The Jesuits adapted the dogma they taught to what they imagined the Negro mentality to be. It was felt necessary to attract Negroes by music, dance, and titles. In short, the priests did not believe that it was essential to break completely with the black's traditional customs, but to select those that would serve as a springboard to the true faith.[4]

During the colonial period, religion did not become "an opiate of the people" or the basis for messianic movements. The colored man (mulatto) did not seek a flight from reality or compensation for troubles on earth. For him religion was simply a channel of ascent, a means to improve his social status. Catholicism was conceived by him as more of a social activity than as a framework of doctrines and beliefs, more of an institution than a faith. Since the Catholic church was the official religion of the state, the lower social classes came to regard the ecclesiastical hierarchy as an agency that reinforced the power of the landholding aristocracy.[5]

At the end of the nineteenth century, when the clergy were recruited from foreigners or sons of immigrants rather than from old traditional families, attempts were made to eradicate the black Catholicism of the colonial period. Folk Catholicism, however, has not disappeared in Brazil. In the cities where priests and religious education are available, the descendants of Africans have the same Catholicism as whites. A large part of the working class, however, is of recent rural extraction and many rural traditions have been maintained. Among these people the cult of the saints lives on, as it does in rural areas, and patron saints are honored with fiestas whose form remains relatively unchanged.[6]

Unlike the situation elsewhere, in Latin America the largest proportions of "nonpracticing" Catholics are found among the peasantry. This element is neither irreligious nor antireligious; on the contrary, its culture is "saturated" with beliefs and practices concerning relationships to events and crises that the individual believes can only be controlled by reliance on supernatural agencies. Saints are approached through the "compact"—a promise to light a candle, dance in honor of the saint, make gifts to him, recite prayers, or make a pilgrimage to his shrine. In exchange the devotee hopes for a good crop, a marriage partner, protection against evil powers, or the curing of an illness. Devotees believe that failure to fulfill a promise will be punished by the saint. Folk Catholicism's belief in "liberating interventions" by supernatural powers has influenced the development of such groups as the Spiritualists, the Umbanda cult, and the Pentecostalists.[7]

The majority of Latin Americans classify themselves as Catholics, but the regular attendance at Sunday mass in Chile varies from place to place from 3.5 to 33 percent, and in Brazil it averages about 10 percent.[8] Hollenweger asserts that Catholicism has not yet succeeded in becoming a Brazilian church. The country has a chronic shortage of priests, and the majority of them are foreigners.[9] In 1966 there were only 7,748 priests in Brazil's 4,831 parishes, or less than one priest for every 10,000 people. Furthermore, the majority of these priests are stationed in the cities and many of them belong to teaching orders. According to Wagley,

> in the prosperous diocese of Ilhéus in Bahia, each priest was responsible for 23,000 people and several parishes. In some parts of northern Brazil, padres are in charge of two or three parishes, which include thirty or more communities. While in 1950 the United States had 44,000 priests for 30,000,000 Catholics, Brazil had little more than 6,000 priests for more than 90,000,000 Catholics. Even England and India have a higher ratio of priests.[10]

Although there are many forms of religious belief in Brazil, "Catholicism," as Wagley points out, "permeates Brazilian national culture, not so much as an active religious system but as a way of life—a fundamental national institution."[11] Recently the church has attempted to attract ordinary people through liturgical reform, but this is said to be "quite inadequate patchwork." (Hollenweger asserts that what is lacking in all the historical churches is a liturgy in which the people play a spontaneous part, as is the case with the Pentecostals.) In recent years many of the Catholic clergy have urged that attention be given to the problems of the Amazon region, the improvement of other rural areas, agrarian reform, and the problems of the urban slums.[12] In view of the number of "relaxed Catholics" in the upper classes, the traditional form of Catholicism of the middle classes, and the appeal of Pentecostalism to the lower classes, the effects of these changes seem problematical.

SOUTH AMERICA

Protestantism in South America

Protestantism came late to South America. From the early decades of the nineteenth century, European businessmen, mostly British, stationed in the major cities of Brazil and Chile were allowed to have their own religious services and chaplains. Only a few of these congregations eventually developed missionary programs among the local populations. In later decades, German Protestantism remained strictly a German concern with no interest in religious proselytism. After 1850, Protestant missionaries, mainly from the United States, began to extend their efforts to Latin America.[13]

Brazil's population of 100,000,000 is still overwhelmingly Catholic, but Protestantism has grown rapidly in recent decades. Protestantism has been nationalized in the sense that the ministers of most churches are Brazilians, and that many of the Protestant churches are separated from their mother churches abroad. Strong anti-Protestant feeling like that in parts of Mexico and Colombia does not exist in Brazil. The Episcopalians and the Methodists have attracted some persons among the conservative middle class of Brazil; Baptists and Pentecostals have had a greater appeal to people of mixed racial ancestry and lower-class origin. Regionally, Protestantism is strongest in the South with its large population of European immigrants, but it is also strong in Goiás and Mato Grasso in the frontier.[14]

With its emphasis on cooperation, personal responsibility, and self-help, Protestantism in Brazil and Chile since about 1930 has been one of the ways by which the rural migrant to the shantytowns of large cities has been able to find his lost identity. (Other alternatives include the various spiritualistic sects; Umbanda, a syncretistic cult combining aspects of African tribal religions and spiritualism; varieties of Neo-African religions known as *candomblé, macumba,* and *xango;* and political radicalism.)[15]

Social Class and Protestantism in Brazil and Chile

The historical Protestant churches in Brazil and Chile have not lost their lower-class membership. In forty congregations in Brazil, for example, lower-class members amounted to 56.3 percent of the total.[16] Nevertheless, the Pentecostal sects have had a tremendous appeal for the lower class, and a much higher proportion of new members had joined these groups rather than the historical churches. By attempting to reconcile class tensions and antagonisms in their own structures, the older Protestant churches seem to have become less attractive to those who seek redemption from a social order which is regarded as unjust. By stressing egalitarianism within the sect, Pentecostals in Brazil may be expressing a protest against the Catholic Church and the ruling class. Viewed in this way, Pentecostalism is a symbolic subversion of the traditional social order.[17]

If economic development and social mobility increase markedly, however, the class composition of the Pentecostal movement may change in South America and bring with it some degree of change from "other-worldliness" to "worldliness."[18] Some observers think that with the claimed 4 million adherents (70 percent of Brazilian Protestantism), the Brazilian Pentecostal movement not only occupies a key position in Latin American Protestantism, but in Brazilian politics as well.[19]

Willems points out two differences between the Pentecostal sects of Chile and Brazil. First, the secession in 1910 of the Pentecostals from the Methodist Church nearly paralyzed the historical churches in Chile. Little effort has been made recently to compete with the evangelizing techniques of the Pentecostal missionaries. In contrast, by evangelizing in public places, the historical churches in Brazil have continued to compete with the Pentecostals and have continued to grow slowly. Secondly, Brazilian Pentecostal leaders make greater use of the press and radio than do their Chilean counterparts.[20]

A group of Italians from Chicago brought Pentecostalism to Argentina in 1909. In 1921, Swedish and Canadian missionaries began to work in Buenos Aires and in other Argentine cities. Despite persecution, there were 50,000 Pentecostalists in the country by 1962, a ratio of 1 to 318. The Church of God (Cleveland, Tennessee) is the largest Pentecostal church in Argentina.[21] Since the Negro population of Argentina is exceedingly small, the majority of Argentinian Pentecostals are white.

Race and Latin American Protestantism

Notwithstanding the cultural origin of Latin American Protestantism, Willems found no evidence of racial prejudice and discrimination in the various denominations. Apparently, any efforts to establish separate "Negro churches" in Brazil would have meant complete failure for Protestant missionaries. The number of persons of some degree of African descent varies greatly by region and class composition of specific congregations. One study found that of a total of 142 members in a Methodist parish of a predominantly lower-class suburb of Rio de Janeiro, 47.9 percent were white, 29.6 percent mulattoes and 22.5 percent black. Willems believes that this is probably a typical distribution for communities of similar race and class composition. He found also that

> Even in predominantly middle-class congregations a sizeable percentage of the members is colored. For example, among the 125 attendants of an evening service in a middle-class Baptist church in São Paulo City we counted a total of 31 colored individuals. In two Methodist congregations with a similar constituency, the percentages of colored members were 21 percent and 25 percent. The churches seem willing to go to any length to prevent racial stratification within their congregations.[22]

In a study in the Federal District of Brazil, Saunders found that the members of a Protestant congregation distinguished or discriminated among, not against, racial backgrounds. Racial self-consciousness existed among the "definitely white" and the "definitely black" members of the congregation, and when a special church program was organized it was necessary to include an equal number of white and black persons. To prevent one of these groups from feeling discriminated against, it was necessary also to appoint equal proportions of Negroes and whites as Sunday School teachers. The choir, however, was assumed to be the province of *gente de côr* (people of color), and this element was predominant in it.[23]

Pentecostalism, especially in Brazil, is not divided racially as it is in the United States and in England.

The Pentecostal Movement

The Pentecostal creed was introduced in Brazil in 1910 by missionaries from abroad, but neither of the two largest sects, the Assembléia de Deus (Assembly of God) nor the Congregação Cristã do

Brasil (Christian Congregation of Brazil) was founded by an American. Both founders, however, had an American background. Luis Francescon, who started the Christian Congregation, was an Italian Catholic who had been converted in Chicago and joined the First Italian Presbyterian Church in that city. Several years later, after receiving a number of messages from the Lord, he embarked upon a missionary career. At first, his church in São Paulo, where services were conducted in the Italian language, was an Italian sect. The elders of the sect dropped Italian in 1935, and the church expanded rapidly outside the city and the state of São Paulo.[24] The Assembléia de Deus, established by the Swedish missionary Daniel Berg in Belém de Pará, caused a division in the local Baptist church. Swedish missionaries were still active in Brazil in the late 1960s.

Additional Pentecostal activities in Brazil began when two American missionaries of the Church of Christ were converted at a revival and joined the General Council of the Assemblies of God in the United States. The Assembléia de Deus Cruzada de Fé (Assembly of God, Crusade of Faith) is now related to Berg's organization through the National Convention of Assemblies of God. According to Willems, at least seven or eight other Pentecostal sects exist in Brazil, many of them continuously subdividing or changing their names. These new sects have adopted the techniques of the Crusade—the revival tent, the radio, and the Gospel of Immediate Salvation.[25]

Folk Catholicism, Migration to the Cities,
and Pentecostalism

With conversion to Pentecostalism, all of the subject's sins are forgiven, and he is at peace with the world. The convert rids himself of "disreputable" forms of behavior, behavior usually identified with the lower social classes. Thus the desire to become "respectable," to adopt middle-class norms and behavior, is an important factor in conversion. Utilitarian motives such as healing and becoming socially respectable are not alone, however, in determining conversion. Secularization has not proceeded far among the lower classes in Latin America, the members of which often feel a need for religion to help with problems that otherwise are difficult to solve. Willems asks why, if the Catholic church is ill-equipped to meet the religious needs of the masses, folk Catholicism with its cult of the saints can no longer meet these needs. He asserts that

> Folk-Catholicism is associated with crops and animals, with droughts and floods, with the evil spirits and demons of the jungle and the country crossroads. Life in an industrial city poses different problems believed to require a different approach to the supernatural. Basically unaltered are only the problems which accompany the life cycle of the individual, namely, birth, marriage, sickness, and death, and even these seem to gain a somewhat different significance in an urban setting. Secondly, the pantheon of saintly helpers is thought of, within the framework of folk Catholicism, as a local pantheon.

Migration, then, to a distant city tends to alienate the newcomer from the saints as well as from his relatives, friends, and neighbors who stayed behind. At the same time, folk Catholicism, with its belief in mystical experiences, in spirit possessions, and in charismatic leadership, facilitates the shift to Pentecostalism. The fact that the cult of the Holy Spirit is one of the most elaborate aspects of folk-Catholicism helps also to make the rural migrant feel at home in a Pentecostal sect.[26]

In the United States, the middle classes predominate; in Latin America, the lower classes predominate. It is for this reason that in the United States Pentecostalism, primarily a lower-class religion, consists typically of small sects, while in Brazil and Chile the major Pentecostal sects have more followers than all the historical Protestant churches together.[27] One of the reasons for the special affinity of Pentecostalism with the lower-class culture of Latin America was the relative ease with which the mystical tradition of folk Catholicism could be converted into institutions that have a direct relationship to the social changes affecting rural migrants. Pentecostal sects usually do not proclaim the second coming of Christ at some definite date in the future; their message concerning the immediate coming of the deity has a far greater appeal. Willems points out that the believer may expect the descent of the Holy Spirit here and now to the individual rather than to a group of people. The evidence for this conviction is seen in the everyday communion with or seizure by the Spirit of some members of the congregation. Another reason for the connection between folk Catholicism and Pentecostalism is the powerful tradition of the working of miracles in folk religion, a tradition that has been incorporated in the Pentecostal faith. A person who has been "seized" by the Spirit may find himself suddenly free of some "incurable" ailment. Or the pastor, when seized by the Spirit, may perform a miracle by touching a patient with his hands, or by praying over him. Or collective prayer offered by persons who have been baptized by the Spirit may produce the miracle of healing. A final reason for the congeniality of folk Catholicism and Pentecostalism lies in the substitution of possession by the Devil for beliefs in evil spirits, witches, and demons of European, Indian, or African origin. Prayer rather than exorcistic ritual is utilized to defend Pentecostals against the occasional seizure of a member of the congregation by the Devil.[28]

Spirit Possession, Prophesying, and Social Power

According to Bastide, a convert enters a Pentecostal congregation by a double baptism—the baptism of water in a river or pond and the baptism of the Holy Spirit—but these two baptisms cannot coincide. The second baptism is a mystic trance which manifests itself in the gift of prophecy or of speaking strange tongues. Frequently the Holy Spirit descends for the first time at the moment the believer is in the water up to his waist and as the leader quotes a verse from the Bible. Bastide likens this possession to the descent of the *orisha* in the *candomblé* at the beginning of a certain musical theme.[29] The nature of speaking in tongues, the respected power conferred by the Holy Spirit, is not agreed upon among Pentecostals. According to some believers, it is a foreign language unknown to the speaker except when possessed by the Spirit. Others believe that the "tongue" is a special idiom by means of which the Holy Spirit relays messages to the congregation or to some of its members.[30]

If one who speaks in another tongue cannot remember what he said or whether he said anything at all, a prophet who heard the message may translate it for the congregation. At times, the prophet may use tongues to reveal the inspiration he has received directly from God.[31]

The *tomada* (possession by the Holy Spirit) is a pleasurable experience in the Pentecostal groups of South America, offering as it does some relief from the drab existence of the lower classes. In addition, the first possession puts the stamp of divine approval on the individual, a step which is necessary before he can be elected or appointed to any office in the sect. Those who receive more than their share of power from the Spirit may find that professional careers within the sect are open to them, an interesting instance of a shift from religious power to social power within groups of people who stress their egalitarianism.[32]

Despite their lower-class origins and feelings of inadequacy, Pentecostal converts are quite aware of the importance of middle-class values in a class-conscious society. Thus Willems argues that the supernatural sanction inherent in the *tomada* and the powers received from the Holy Spirit are more than a temporary escape from the hardships of everyday life. They function to compensate the convert for his class-induced feelings of inferiority. In this puritanical religion, both the black and the white Brazilian seek the moral qualities that will permit them to ascend the social scale. Referring to the black Pentecostal, Bastide says it is "at the moment when he seems, trembling, speaking strange tongues, possessed by the Holy Spirit, to be nearest Africa that he is, in fact, farthest from it, that he occidentalizes the most."[33]

In utilizing the resources of every member in proselytizing activities, in making the convert feel that he is needed, and in addressing him as "brother," the Pentecostal sect provides security in a disorganized society. Willems' comment that the social function of the Protestant congregation in Chile and Brazil is both compensatory and substitutive seems particularly apt in the case of the Pentecostal movement. Pentecostalists feel that they have something to live for and something to live in.

In summary, this discussion of Pentecostalism in Latin America suggests (1) that persons of varying degrees of African descent do not belong to separate Pentecostal churches as they do in the United States and England; (2) that folk Catholicism has prevailed in the lower strata, but the cult of the saints no longer meets the religious needs of many lower-class persons; (3) that Pentecostalism includes a number of elements that are congenial with the mystical aspects of folk Catholicism; and (4) that Pentecostal sects seem to express a protest against what is believed to be the unjustness of the social order.[34]

SOUTH AMERICA

Religions of Blacks in Guyana

According to Smith, the structure of African religious doctrine became disorganized in British Guiana, but among the slaves funeral rituals were organized on the basis of tribal affiliation. Belief in witchcraft, sorcery, and divination persisted and played an important part in the daily life of the plantation. Drumming and dancing were prominent features of the lives of the slave population.[35]

Christianization in Guyana has never involved the development of new forms of liturgy, nor has it been accompanied by enthusiastic forms of worship. Not all ex-slaves were baptized, and not all who were baptized became church members. Elements of belief and practice which appear to be African have persisted to the present day, because, it is said, Christianity "remained both strong and orthodox so that instead of syncretism one got the parallel existence of two types of belief and practice." It is claimed that evidence on the nature of African forms of religious belief is scarce and difficult to evaluate, and that few, if any, blacks openly proclaimed adherence to a rival religion. In the 1860s, Duff, a Presbyterian clergyman, claimed he saw a revival of Obeahism. The ritual performances consisted mainly of drumming, dancing, and spirit possession. Smith observed similar dances in the early 1950s, and found "a powerful undercurrent of belief in magic, spirit intervention in everyday life and witchcraft."[36] Further studies of religion and magic in Guyana might produce additional information.

Spiritualism in Rio de Janeiro and São Paulo, Brazil, Including Umbanda

Spiritualism was introduced into Brazil about the middle of the nineteenth century. Unlike most areas of the world, where it was diffused from Europe and became something of a fad, it penetrated deeply in Brazil and by 1870 had acquired some of the aspects of an organized religion. The merging of spiritualism and elements of African religions has occurred in relatively recent years.[37]

Organized Spiritualism began with the formation of the Society for Spiritualist Studies of the Confucius Group in Rio de Janeiro. Accurate figures on the growth of Spiritualism in Brazil are not available. It did not become a mass movement until the 1920s, and its main growth came after World War II. The number of Spiritualists grew from approximately 400,000 in 1940 to nearly 700,000 in 1960, and to 750,000 in 1967.[38]

Statistics on the Spiritualists in Brazil are inaccurate. The State Department of Statistics in São Paulo lists only those Spiritualists who are members of a center. Since most Spiritualists meet in private homes, they are not covered by official statistics. The Umbanda religion is not recognized as a separate religion by the Census department, and the Kardecist Spiritualists do not allow the adherents of Umbanda to call themselves "Spiritualists." As a result, in official listings, a high percentage of Umbanda members and those who are inclined toward spiritualism appear under the rubric "Catholic."[39] A recent survey by J. P. Renshaw concluded that the number of Spiritists "runs into the millions and that their influence exceeds far beyond those included in the formal membership." Conservative estimates indicate that between two and three million persons are members of local centers.[40] The number of centers in São Paulo has been estimated at 4,000.[41]

Most of the members of Umbanda centers come from the upper-lower and middle classes. In the twelve groups Pressel observed in São Paulo, from 60 to 75 percent of the spirit mediums were women, but men participated in other ways—as drummers or as officers on the "board of directors" at the centers. The majority of Umbandists in these centers in São Paulo are between 20 and 40 years of age. Pressel points out the difficulty of classifying persons according to race because in Brazil racial categories are not based on physical characteristics alone, but include such criteria as wealth, education, and personal qualities. Reflecting the composition of the population in modern urban slums and in some middle-class areas, Umbanda encompasses, according to Pressel, "a wide range of physical types." Willems concludes that while "Negro membership looms disproportionately large," Umbanda "has attracted too many persons of non-African background to be classified as a 'Negro religion.'" Camargo found that in São Paulo whites attend Umbandist ceremonies "in large proportions" and that Japanese also sought the effectiveness of its magical procedures; Pressel states that half the membership of the centers she visited appeared to be "entirely of European origin."[42]

SOUTH AMERICA

Spiritualism's three phases since its introduction into Brazil include: the Spiritualism of the intellectuals, of the white lower class, and of the lower class of "colored" people. In the spiritualism of Alan Kardec, the second stratum of spiritualism, Negroes and mulattoes, were accepted on the condition that they receive only the spirits of whites. The spirits of caboclos and of Africans were regarded as inferior and as unfit to serve as protectors of mediums. In the third phase, the spiritualism of Umbanda ("bas spiritism"), the spirits of Indians and Africans were accepted. Umbanda "purified" the ancestral heritage of blacks by looking for roots in India or in Egypt. Blood sacrifices, long initiations, and sorcery were rejected, the orisha were redefined in "scientific" terms, and dead slaves were transformed into gods who descended into human beings to cure the sick.[43]

In the largest cities of Brazil, the racial unity of closed groups (candomblé, caboula, catimbo) was replaced by atomized interpersonal relations in the macoumba. That cult provided a minimum of intellectual or sentimental homogeneity.[44] When the spiritualism of Umbanda developed from the macoumba, some dogma began to appear.

> The spirits of the dead—in particular deceased Negro ancestors, and the *caboclos,* as spiritualized forces of nature—form great armies known as "phalanxes." At the head of each phalanx we find an *orisha,* either under his African name, or the Catholic saint's name corresponding to it. Thus *Oshossi* commands the "ranks of Urubatão," while *Ararigboia,* one of the "caboclos of the Seven Crossroads," commands the legions of the Redskins, the Tamoios, and the Jurema *caboclo.* Shangô (or St. Jerome) leads the forces of Intiaçan, the Sun and Moon, the White Stone, winds and waterfalls and poplars, and Kouenguelê Negroes now deceased; Omulá, operating in the black-magic counterpart to *Umbanda,* known as *Quimbanda,* leads a mixed bag of tribes, some real, some imaginary, souls, skulls, Nagos, Malis, Monurubis (Muslims), and *Quimbanda caboclos,* i.e., souls of local medicine men.[45]

In the belief system of Umbanda in São Paulo, five major types of spirits may be identified. First, the caboclo spirits are the spirits of dead Brazilian Indians. These stern spirits are valued for their advice concerning matters that require quick decisions. The second type of spirit is the *prêto velho,* the gentle and approachable spirits of dead Afro-Brazilian slaves. The *criança,* the third type of spirit, is the spirit of a dead child, usually a child three to five years of age. The fourth type of spirit is the *exu* (feminine counterpart is the *pomba-gira*). Such spirits are believed to be those of people who were evil. The *exus* are characterized by antisocial attributes and bad manners, ranging in their deeds from cursing to breaking up marriages and ruining business competitors. Some *exus,* thought to be more evolved spiritually, may be used to counteract the wicked ways of the evil *exus.* Some of the "bad" *exus* are said to be foreigners—French, Mexican, Japanese, German, Italian, and Portuguese. The fifth type of spirit, the orisha, represents a merging of West African beliefs and Catholicism. Both African deities and Catholic saints were intermediaries between man and a remote God (Olorun among the Yoruba), and the duties and functions of the two sets of supernatural beings were sometimes similar (for example, Ogun, god of iron and of war, and St. George). Pressel points out that some changes have occurred concerning the orisha in the shift from the earlier Afro-Catholic cults into Umbanda: first, in the candomblé, the membership was primarily female, while in Umbanda both men and women may be possessed by an orisha; and second, the Umbanda mediums are possessed by spiritual envoys sent by the orisha rather than by the orisha themselves. These envoys are the spirits of dead persons who are believed by the Umbandists to be more highly evolved spiritually than the other four spirit types.[46]

Umbandists organize their spirits into seven *linhas* (lines) headed in each case by an orisha and divided into seven *falanges* (phalanxes). Each phalanx is in turn divided into seven *legiões* (legions) of spirits. Considerable disagreement exists from one center to another concerning the position of certain spirits in the hierarchy, as well as which orisha heads each of the seven lines. The following organization of the lines is common in São Paulo:[47]

1. *Linha de Oxalá,* Jesus Cristo
2. *Linha de Iemanjá,* Virgem Maria
3. *Linha do Oriente,* São João Batista
4. *Linha de Oxóce,* São Sebastião

5. *Linha de Xangô*, São Jerônimo
6. *Linha de Ogum*, São Jorge
7. *Linha Africana*, São Cipriano

In addition to their beliefs about the spirits, Umbandists emphasize a theory concerning supernatural fluids. These spiritual emanations are thought to surround one's body and to come from three sources: "(1) from one's own innate spirit; (2) from spirits of the dead, which are freely floating about; and (3) from incarnate spirits of persons who are close by."[48] Some fluids exert a good influence on an individual; others affect one adversely. Umbandists combine illnesses and personal difficulties under the heading of "spiritual disorders." The generally recognized causes of these disorders are:

1. Religious negligence or ignorance. Medium has neglected to fulfill obligations due his orisha or lesser spirits who protect him.
2. Magic. Evil actions performed through black magic of *exus* in Quimbanda (centers specializing in black magic).
3. Unhappy spirits. A spirit may "agitate" the "fluids" in an individual and thus bring on "disorders."
4. Karmic forces. A new incarnation of a spirit may produce "disorders" in an individual. A medium may feel that her troubles have been sent as a result of her sins in the past.
5. Undeveloped mediumship. A catchall category overlapping others.
6. The "evil eye." Bad fluids may be passed along by this mechanism.[49]

Although the Umbandist ritual is complicated and uses practices derived from spiritualism and occultism, in some respects the traditional model developed in the cults of African origin persists.[50] In other respects, Umbanda deviates from that model. For example, a glass of water in which the "fluids" are reflected offers a simple alternative and constitutes a threat to the Nago divinatory system. Another difference is seen in the importance given to Eshu. There are many Eshu in Umbanda, some of them known only in Rio—Eshu Lalu, Eshu Tranca-Rua, and Eshu Caveira. The ritual songs sung to Eshu Caveira, who presides in a cemetery, approximate those of the vodun cult in Haiti. Any person can serve the Eshus as a "horse," a practice that is unknown elsewhere.[51]

In the Umbanda cult, mediums make spirits available to anyone for consultations concerning illness, occupational success or failure, the passing of examinations, and other personal problems. There are no séances, no calling up of the spirits of deceased relatives, no table turning, and for the most part activities are open and public. Umbanda is not a revitalization movement; its concern is in helping individuals to solve their personal problems. Participants engage in trance states and are not merely clients of practitioners.[52]

Bastide saw Negro syncretism in the cities of Brazil shifting from the old spontaneous syncretism of African and Indian practices to a controlled syncretism of a Brazilian religious ideology parallel to the development of political nationalism in the lower class. For example, some Umbanda priests now say that the "spiritualism" which brings Catholic saints, Indian spirits, and the orisha of slaves of earlier times together in a religious ritual is the equivalent on the mystical plane of the meeting and biological fusion of the three races of Brazil.[53]

The Cult of María Lionza in Venezuela

In the Spanish colonies no African culture was dominant. The Spaniards were seldom involved actively in the slave trade; for the most part their slaves were purchased from foreign traders. It was only during the final years of the slave trade in the nineteenth century that the majority of Negroes, obtained from Portuguese dealers, came from Nigeria and Dahomey. In Cuba, where slavery lasted until nearly 1900, Yoruba culture predominated and many priests and diviners in the *santeria* cult still know the Yoruba language. In Venezuela, where the slave trade was forbidden by the beginning of the nineteenth century and where slaves were liberated in 1864, Yoruban-Dahomean influences were not strong. One study shows that about half of the Negro peasants in Venezuela came from the Congo, the other half from the coastal area between Ghana and Nigeria. There are few Afroamerican cults, properly speaking, in Venezuela. African cultural characteristics are seen in the manner in which persons of African descent venerate the saints, and in oral literature, popular music, musical instruments, and folklore. Rather than an

African subculture, there exists in Venezuela a rural or peasent subculture. Persons of unmixed African descent are found only in remote regions of the country. Persons of mixed African, Indian, and European descent are found in nearly all of the other sections of Venezuela except the Andes.[54]

The cult of María Lionza is a popular religious movement still in the process of developing. In some respects, it resembles Umbanda in Brazil, and its success is attributed to the same reasons: concentration of uprooted masses in large urban centers, the lack of influence on the part of the Catholic Church, a search for a new and direct way of expressing religious feelings, disillusionment with existing social institutions, and distrust of modern medicine.[55]

This cult originated in the mountains of Sorte and in the state of Yaracuy during the colonial period in an area where African, American Indian, and European cultural elements were intermingled. In its original form, it was based on veneration of natural forces and on the spirits which inhabited rivers, caverns, and the forest. For centuries Venezuelan Creoles (persons of mixed Spanish and American Indian ancestry) have venerated the Virgin of Coromoto, perhaps as a replacement for an Indian female deity. Recently the cult has been influenced by modern spiritualism and by African-derived concepts. In this form it was introduced into the city where it expanded between the two World Wars. It has been transformed into a popular religion and diffused throughout the country, especially in the poorer sections of new urban centers. The devotees include many Spaniards, Colombians, Italians, and Portuguese, as well as persons of African descent from the former British Antillean islands. Nearly all of the leaders of the cult are Venezuelans, but some are of Antillean or Colombian origin.[56]

The most important sanctuary of the Queen (María Lionza) is located near the source of the Yaracuy river in the Sorte mountains. Altars are found near stones, in caverns, and on the banks of small streams, and María Lionza appears in a grotto at the top of the mountain for her followers. In the cities, devotees meet in the homes of the leaders of cult centers.

According to legend, María Lionza was an Indian princess who was kidnapped by a snake, governess of a lagoon. As punishment the snake swelled and burst, causing a flood which resulted in the death of the Jirajará Indians, the native tribe of the beautiful girl. The abducted virgin became the governess of the lagoon and of rivers, and, later, of all the wild animals and of plant life. She rode a tapir that lived in the Sorte mountains guarding treasures, punishing criminals, and helping the poor. María Lionza is also regarded as the Virgin of Coromoto, patroness of Venezuela.

María Lionza is surrounded by lesser spirits. A group of Venezuelan Indian leaders who fought against the Spanish, including Guaicaipuro, Tamanaco, Sorocaima, Chacao, Mara, and Yoroquí, behave ferociously when they come to a ceremony. Under Catholic influence, some Indian nature deities have been transformed into spirits who guard rivers and forests. In the cult of María Lionza, they are called Don Juans or St. Juans: St. John of the Four Winds; St. John of the Road (master of the crossroads who opens the road to other spirits and resembles Legba, the West African deity); Sr. Juan of Tobacco, who manifests himself in tobacco smoke; Sr. Juan of Hatred, protector of magicians; Sr. Juan of the River Yaracuy, master of the Yaracuy river; and so on. In recent years, the migration of Cubans and Trinidadians to Venezuela has introduced a number of African spirits—Obatalá, Orula, Yemanjá, Oshun, Ogun, Shango, and Elegua. Buddhist spirits have been added by some "semi-intellectuals" to the deities that are invoked and, at one time or another, the spirits of Simon Bolivar, General Gomez, Adolf Hitler, Pope John XXIII, Dr. José Hernández (a deceased medical benefactor who practiced for many years in Caracas), as well as priests of the cult who died some time ago have also joined the pantheon.

The concept of different "courts" or "lines" of spirits has taken shape in recent years. Every leader specializes in one or another of the categories, and the total number of "courts" varies among the devotees. The following is an incomplete list: [57]

Celestial court. Involves the saints; some say that María Lionza and her vassals form part of it.

Indian court. The great Venezuelan Indian leaders who fought the Spanish.

María Lionza court. María Lionza and her vassals; masters of the rivers and mountains; the "Don Juans."

African court (also called the *court of the Vikings*). Includes seven African deities received recently from Cuban *santeria*. A spirit called "Great Viking" is considered to be an African.

Simon Bolivar. Mentioned by some leaders and includes Simon Bolivar and El Negro Primero.

Astral court, cosmic fluids, stars.

Hindu court.

Persian court.

Greek court.

The leaders of the cult are totally ignorant of the true origin of the African "line" and of authentic *santeria* practices. They claim that it is dangerous to work with the powerful African spirits and say that they are hard to control when they manifest themselves in a violent manner. Although the African spirits are not yet well integrated into the cult, they are increasing in importance every year.[58]

In the towns, a room containing a large altar and the necessary paraphernalia is devoted to the cult; outside this room is a waiting room for clients. Objects on the altar include lighted candles, flowers, lithographs representing the Caciques ("chiefs"), María Lionza, and other spirits, as well as food, rum, tobacco, perfume, multicolored ribbons, and, sometimes, daggers, drums, or feathers. The three lithographs most frequently found on the altars represent María Lionza, portrayed as a beautiful white lady with long black hair; Guaicaipuro, an Indian chief; and Negro Felipe of Afrocuban origin. In the spirits of the Indian leaders who fought against the Spanish, some see an anti-European aspect of the cult directed against the white population of Venezuela, and this is said to be true also of the presence of the spirit of Negro Miguel, leader of a slave insurrection in the eighteenth century. The combination of Indian, black, and white spirits in the cult reflects the mixture of races and cultures that has taken place in Venezuela.

The ordinary devotees of the cult attend the rituals for the purpose of obtaining spiritual and material help, and they are ready to pay for the requests they make. Through the mediums they get in touch with spirits, receive advice, are cured of illnesses, and achieve other desired ends. They enter into agreements with the spirits and follow the orders they are given. To secure the most effective results, trips are organized by cult leaders to the Sorte caverns or to the forest sanctuaries in Mara-cuy. If a leader is unable to satisfy a devotee's wishes, the client may proceed to another spiritual center.

The beliefs and rituals in the María Lionza spiritualist centers are not uniform, due in part to the exterior influences from Cuba and Trinidad in recent years and in part to the fact that nearly all of the leaders are self-taught. Most of the mediums acquire their positions through visions following an intensive emotional experience, or after a miraculous cure, or because of contacts during childhood with family members who were devotees.

Although there is no formal initiation ceremony, sometimes a rit-ual called *Velacion* is performed to "uncover" someone who is attracted to the office of medium. Candles are placed around the candidate, and perfume and holy water are sprinkled while the priest prays. Tobacco smoke is blown above the novice and, finally, his head is washed. After the completion of this ritual, the medium presumably possesses the fac-ulty of receiving his spirits. Some spiritualists train neophytes in trance techniques, and there is a school in Caracas for instruction in healing.

Various spirits are invoked by the *Banco* (leader of the cult) and they manifest on him or the mediums, giving advice to the believers, curing infirmities, and performing magico-religious acts. In addition, those with mediumistic faculties predict future events and practice witchcraft. These persons never admit that their work is directed against an individual, but claim that what they do is advantageous to the com-munity. Formerly no sacrifices of blood or animals were made, but Cuban and Trinidadian influences in recent years have led some leaders occasionally to kill a cock or a pigeon to obtain blood for use in magical rites. In some centers, drums are used to summon the spirits of Indian chiefs.

At Quibayo, at the bottom of the sacred mountain of María Lionza, there are pilgrims' camps. Some devotees spend a month or more in the forest to fulfill their pledges to the spirits. Thousands of people come to Sorte, especially during Holy Week, to obtain cures for illnesses by bathing in the Yaracuy river and its tributaries, or to consult with healers who work in the region. A nationally famous healer performs magical operations there with the help of Dr. Hernández and the spirits of other doctors. For such an operation, the patient lies down on the floor surrounded by thirty candles and is hypnotized by the healer. Falling in a trance, the practitioner is possessed by the spirit of a physician. If the healer's diagnosis has been that of cancer of the stomach, he makes a slight incision in the patient's abdomen and pretends to extract a malignant object. Sick persons receive medicines prepared by the healer, and any improvement that occurs is due to these herbal remedies and to the psychological effects of the operations. A few years ago the pilgrims' camps at Quibayo were destroyed by the National Guard, and the leaders were imprisoned or expelled from the area. Since then devotees have returned in increased numbers and persecution has ceased.

Usually the healing rituals start with Catholic prayers and invocations to the saints and to the Virgin Mary. Purificatory rites involving the use of tobacco smoke, incense, and water follow. Libations of rum are thrown on the floor for the spirits. Then the medium falls in a trance and consults the powers. A spirit may ask a patient to return in a week or two and bring flowers, food, or alcohol. Mediums do not ask for money, but some of the services they render are known to be expensive. In general, the priests live well on the voluntary contributions of the believers.

Sometimes the medium induces trance by smoking cigars on an empty stomach, by hyperventilation, by rotating his head in a rhythmical manner, or by drinking a large quantity of alcohol. The cleverest adepts receive various spirits, sometimes speaking odd languages or talking amicably with the devotees. Sometimes a priest tries to transfer the spirit in his own head to the head of a neophyte. At times spirits manifest in a violent manner, and mediums, fighting among themselves, may cause physical harm to participants. These "spiritual fights" provide opportunities for the expression of repressed aggression. The *Banco* watches over the mediums and interprets the words of the spirit.

The María Lionza cult has no formal organization; every center is independent. Most mediums are women, but many leaders are men. Some leaders travel from one center to another exhorting devotees to make pilgrimages to Sorte. Later, they lead such trips and take charge of rituals in the mountains. There is considerable competition among leaders, and differences in rituals and opinions provoke frequent arguments. A woman in Caracas considers herself La Gran Chamana and claims that she alone has been appointed by the Queen to lead the cult throughout the country. Although she has published a book about her personal experiences, she has been unsuccessful in codifying the ritual or leading a national religious movement.

The cult of María Lionza has political and social aspects. Through the mouths of the mediums, the spirits make observations pertinent to the social order, laws, and the political system of the country. Leaders know how to influence their followers and are a force that has to be taken into consideration in elections.

This cult exemplifies the acculturative process in the realm of New World religions. The most notable Indian characteristics in this religion are the association of María Lionza and other spirits with nature deities and mythological figures of Amazonia, the Indian origin of some of the legends of the cult, the ritual use of tobacco, the extraction of malignant objects from the body of the patient in some of the curing rituals, and the availability of the spirits of famous Caciques. Among the Catholic elements are the derivation of María Lionza's name from the Virgin Mary, her association with the Virgin of Coromoto, the use of candles, the inclusion of lithographs and statues of the saints, prayer formulas and the use of rosaries, scapulars, incense, the cross as a symbol, and the acceptance of the Christian code of morality. Recent influences from Cuban *santeria* and Trinidadian *shango* are seen in the introduction of seven African divinities, emphasis on the mediums' ability to communicate directly with the powers, sacrifices of blood and animals, the formation of "lines" of spirits, the ritual importance of colors, and new medical and magical practices. The influence of spiritualism is found in concepts of reincarnation, contact with the dead, mediumistic practices, and trance. Magic, always important in the lives of Venezuelans, and especially in the lower socioeconomic classes, is an integral part of the cult.

The believers have no difficulty reconciling their affiliation with the cult of María Lionza with their status as practicing Catholics. They believe that the spirits, created by God, have been given the power necessary to help mankind. They think also that the leaders of the cult have received a gift to aid their fellow men, and the mediums believe that

they have been appointed by God. Devotees accept the Christian sacraments and they are required to confess and take communion before they
come to the center for important ceremonies. They say that they are
good Catholics even if they do not attend Mass regularly, claiming:
"When we believe in Almighty God and in Jesus Christ we must also
believe in the power of María Lionza."[59]

CHAPTER SIX

Neo-African and African-Derived Religions of South America

The Socio-Economic Context of Religious Cults of Blacks in South America

IN CHAPTER 3 I pointed out that most Neo-African religious movements among blacks in the Caribbean have arisen among peoples who were economically disadvantaged, socially subordinated, and politically powerless: slaves, peasants, or lower-class workers. To reiterate: the religious behavior of these persons of African descent in the Caribbean sector of the diaspora has been part of their attempt to identify with forces in the universe greater than themselves, to express themselves, to escape—at least temporarily and imaginatively—from rejection, discrimination, and exploitation, and, in some cases, to change their life-situations. In that discussion I held that the cults must be viewed in relation to the economic-social-political contexts within which they have existed. Likewise, the social structures within which Neo-African religions in South America have emerged must be considered.

Slavery separated African values from African social structures. Religion was forced to fit into another matrix. Among the niches in Brazilian social structure into which aspects of African traditions could be inserted were the *batuques* (dances performed by slaves), the fraternities of colored people, the organizations of *Negros de ganho* (slaves hired out to others by their owners or sent by them to sell merchandise in city streets), the "nations" (tribes or peoples) of the towns, and Sunday dances.[1]

Eventually Brazilian blacks transformed the *batuques* and the *caloundus* (African religious sects) into African associations, but since the followers of the divinities were not numerous enough in the new habitat to be reconstituted as separate organizations, they gathered in the same organization. The *caloundu* replaced the lineage, and the exogamous principle was applied to persons who served the same god rather than to clan members.

Since these African associations existed within a world dominated by whites, some of the "interpenetrations of civilizations" occurred independently of the pressures of social structures. For example, blacks saw in Catholicism the existence of a Supreme God so transcendent that he had to be approached through a series of intermediaries—Jesus Christ, the Virgin Mary, and a host of saints. This doctrine was congenial to the Africans because they too believed in a supreme God, Olorun or Zambi, who had withdrawn from the affairs of this world or who received human prayers only through the intercession of intermediaries—the orishas, the voduns, or the deified ancestors.

Unlike some interpreters of Neo-African religions in Brazil, Bastide attributed the syncretisms which occurred more to sociological factors and less to such psychological causes as their practice of borrowing efficacious divinities from other peoples in addition to the Catholic saints, or their seeking to elevate their religious life by transferring their beliefs and prayers from an uncivilized orisha to a civilized saint. He argued that secrecy was necessary to conceal from whites as much as possible of the African nature of the cult. This was done by covering the altar (where the stones of the gods devoured bloody offerings) with white tablecloths, paper flowers, and statues and lithographs of the saints. In this view, the saints originally were simply white masks placed over the black faces of ancestral divinities. Saints were chosen who most closely resembled the divinities worshipped in the cults, but petitions were actually addressed to Ogun rather than to St. George, or to Omolu rather than to St. Lazarus.

In Brazil, the Portuguese and Negroes never constituted rigidly closed castes. Instead, in the Brazilian patriarchal family the slaves were divided into categories: field workers, artisans, and house domestics. Channels of social ascension have always existed in Brazilian society, it being well understood, however, that the assimilation of the black to white values constituted the criterion of all social mobility.

The suppression of the slave trade destroyed the old social strcture, but it did not destroy African religions in Brazil. Neither the threats by religious officials of excommunication or of refusal of communion, nor the persecution of police, has ended the resistance of the Neo-African cults. These persecutions have succeeded only in transforming public ceremonies into secret rites, and they have not stopped recruitment.

Several social factors have furthered the maintenance of the African religions. The suppression of the slave trade did not stop all connections between Brazil and Africa. Some Brazilians traveled to Africa to increase their knowledge of the cults, and a prosperous trade in ritual objects has long existed. Some blacks who have not been able to afford a trip to Africa have kept a Bible in the Yoruba language, as well as Nigerian newspapers, as ways of maintaining a spiritual connection with the land of their ancestors.

Another reason for the failure of African religions to disappear has been the useful function they fulfilled when the social structure was being modified. Although slavery separated the races, it also united them by permitting some participation of blacks in the lives of whites. Abolition destroyed the patriarchal family, one of the few forms of social solidarity which had existed in Brazil. It aggravated the process of social separation that began with the early forms of urbanization, a process which had furthered the formation of the *candomblés*. Since the former slave was not prepared for the role of free citizen, he was unable to integrate himself into the new capitalist-industrial society.

Former slaves constituted an uprooted working class. In the economic competition of developing industrial capitalism, the mulatto got more opportunities than the darker black, and, in turn, the European or his descendants had an advantage over the mulatto. Similar developments occurred in rural areas. In the sugarcane region of the Northeast, the tutelary relationship between the mill owner and his slaves was replaced by the impersonal relations of factory manager and workers. In this situation, the candomblé provided the only center where blacks could associate fraternally. Cults offered mutual assistance to their members, and the spiritual leader acted as an intermediary between his followers and members of the dominant group.

To survive, however, the Neo-African religions had to adapt to the new social conditions. The *caloundus* had been associated with the "nations" and their gods and their rites varied according to the traditions of these "nations." The Bantu *caboula* was distinct from the Yoruba *candomblé* and the Dahomean *Tambor de Mina*. Ethnic recruitment stopped; marriages occurred between the representatives of different ethnic groups, and children born of these unions were "creoles" without any attachment to a definite tradition. Such marriages furthered syncretisms between the customs of African "nations" that had been rivals. In general, however, each cult preserved the tradition of its founders despite the fact that recruitment proceeded on the basis of the neighborhood, the prestige of cult leaders, or of friendship.

Although abolition disrupted the community of blacks, it also increased contacts with the white world. To some extent, blacks became involved in the battles between political parties and in the competition of the marketplace. In addition, because the Catholic Church opposed the formation of a black church distinct from the white church, blacks were included in festivals, processions, and congresses. This increase of contact with the Portuguese Brazilian world, which occurred at a time when contacts with Africa had decreased, seems not to have led to a decline of ancestral beliefs and norms. Bastide argued that a decline did not occur because the black who retained an interest in African traditions did not become a "marginal man" in the Stonequist sense.[2] Instead of becoming emotionally disturbed by feeling that he was a part of two traditions while belonging to neither, he kept the African and the Brazilian worlds separate within his personality and retained his composure. According to Bastide, this ability on the part of the black has enabled the candomblé to resist the attacks made on it by the environing society.

Perhaps the policy of national integration has been the greatest obstacle to the continuation of the Neo-African cults. With the replacement of the tutelary family by the state, the disorganized common people have been transformed into a conscious proletariat. Young blacks who attend integrated schools ridicule the candomblés, and most recruits now come from the economically disadvantaged and more or less illiterate masses. At the same time, some well-to-do artisans, merchants, and lawyers have joined the candomblés. Whether the candomblé will be able to adapt itself in the face of a policy of national integration remains to be seen. On the other hand, the new syncretistic cults which operate on a more individualistic basis, especially the Umbanda centers, are being augmented constantly.

Catholic Fraternities and African Religious Traditions in South America

Although slave-owners in South American societies allowed Negroes to be baptized, they paid little attention to their religious education. Often, Negro and white Catholicism were quite different. For one thing, the Negroes organized special fraternities under the protection of black saints such as St. Benedict the Moor, or Our Lady of the Rosary, and others. These societies were established along color or ethnic lines. For example, mulattos and dark-skinned Negroes usually had separate societies, and special fraternities were set up for those from the Congo. This division into "nations" helped to perpetuate African languages and African religious beliefs. When these societies were abolished, the cultural patterns associated with them declined.[3]

Colombian Negroes organized *cabildos* (associations) along ethnic lines. The Mandingos, the Caravali, the Congolese, and the Mina each had a king and princes. Banned by the governor because of quarrelsome brawls, they continued to operate secretly and thus perpetuated the cult of the dead. In Bolivia, a funeral society of San Brazilia is still called a *cabildo*. The free Negroes of Venezuela lived in a section called *Los Ranchos* and seem to have been divided ethnically. In Caracas during the middle of the eighteenth century forty societies existed within the fifteen churches of the city, some made up of slaves, who maintained the cult of their patron saint and were responsible for the burial of their members. In addition, some of the Negro fraternities cooperated in building houses for their members, gave assistance in agricultural tasks, and assisted econmically toward getting enfranchisement papers—practices in line with African traditions.[4]

NEO-AFRICAN AND AFRICAN-DERIVED RELIGIONS

Cabildos were formed also in Peru. The Angolas, Caravalis, Mozambiques, Congos, Chalas, and Terra-Novans established society houses in Lima. Festivals were celebrated in these centers under a king or a queen, and the members joined together to purchase the freedom of members. In Uruguay and Argentina, African "nations" founded centers which preserved African cults, including in Montevideo those from Congo, Benguela, Luanda, Mina, Bertoche, Magise, and Mozambique. The six divisions of the Congo "nation"—Gunga, Guanda, Angola, Munjolo, Basundi, and Boma—organized funeral ceremonies on St. Balthazar's Day in honor of their deceased. During this rite, the queen was possessed by the spirit of a deceased person, and all of the group's dead were invoked *en masse.* In 1807, Negro dances held in private homes without the supervision of a white person were forbidden, thus ending these African cults in Uruguay. In Buenos Aires, there were at least four "nations" (Congos, Mozambiques, Mandingos, and Benguelas) which met at mid-day for several hours every Sunday and feast day. Each had a king, a queen, a president, a treasurer, and a white auditor to verify the accounts. Meetings called "drums" were held on the special feast day of each society, with processions, dancing, and singing in their native tongue, accompanied by African musical instruments. In a cult named *bailar el santo,* members danced before an altar containing lithographs and statuettes of the saints, cocks' feet, food and drink. African deities were invoked in African languages, and the members entered into trances. In 1852, the slaves were enfranchised and allowed to emigrate to other parts of the continent if they wished. These developments led to the dissolution of the societies, and, eventually, to the absorption of the majority of Negroes into the general population of Argentina.[5]

In Bastide's view, African religions survived in most South American and Caribbean countries only because of the ethnic associations, and he believed that this is the reason why they are found today mainly in the cities where their "nations" were well organized. Likewise, "wherever the religious fraternities had their Negro dances banned on grounds of 'indecency' (as in Venezuela or Colombia), African religious traditions very soon withered away. They tended to become assimilated to folklore, and progressively acculturised."[6]

NEO-AFRICAN AND AFRICAN-DERIVED RELIGIONS

Neo-African Religions in the State of Maranhão, Brazil

Of two communities in the state of Maranhão studied by Octavio Da Costa Eduardo in 1943–44, the rural region of Santo Antônio dos Pretos had preserved fewer African religious beliefs and practices than had São Luiz, the capital, and those that had persisted there had been greatly diluted. For the most part, these traces of African traditions consisted of ritualistic dances during which the participants were possessed by certain spirits.

In the religion of blacks in Santo Antônio, African deities, in recognizable form, are almost entirely lacking. There are, however, African-like spirits called *encantados* [7] who possess devotees during ritualistic dances.

> The *encantados* are said by some in Santo Antônio to be spirits sent by Saint Barbara, their chief, and by others to constitute a special kind of angel created by Jesus. The *encantados* are held to be less powerful than the Catholic saints, but are believed to have the power to cure, to assure good bargains, to forecast the future, to aid in childbirth and in finding lost objects. [8]

Many of the spirits that possess their followers in Santo Antônio have Brazilian names: Pedro Angaço, Carrinho Doeiras, Maria Bárbara, Manesinho, Baíano, Moço Fina, Trovão (Thunder)—probably traceable to the Thunder deity of West Africa. The chief *encantado* is Kakamado (probably an African name); another is Kalunga, an Angolan name. Some *encantados* of African derivation who are honored with songs at the beginning of a ritualistic dance do not possess anyone. Among these *encantados* are Averekete (called Verekete in Santo Antônio) and Sobo, both from Dahomey, and Eowa, a Yoruban deity. Legba, a Dahomean god called Legua Bogi in Maranhão, is a highly esteemed *encantado*. Also, Lebara, the Yoruban god who corresponds to Legba in Dahomey, is found as part of the name of an *encantado*. Those who worship the *encantados* in Santo Antônio constitute an informal religious organization; monthly or bimonthly dances are the only occasions for formal worship. There are no initiation ceremonies, and the group lacks an acknowledged priest. Arrangements for a dance are made by two men, and these men play important roles during the ritual. [9]

Among the Catholic practices that are included in the religious syncretism of Santo Antônio is the rain ritual. If the rains do not come in December and January, the rural Negroes form processions and march around the village in the belief that they can prevail upon the saints and God to send rains. If rain still does not fall, a procession goes to a neighboring village, but the images of the saints carried in the previous march are left behind and an image from the other village is brought to Santo Antônio. The belief is that the saints will insist that God satisfy the wishes of the people so that they can be returned to their respective sanctuaries. The saints also help their devotees solve their economic problems, protect them from danger and sickness, and generally help them to find happiness. Each person makes a pledge of gifts and lighted candles, which amounts to a contract with his patron saint. It is noteworthy, however, that the African custom of redeeming pledges to supernatural figures only after the offerer has had his wish fulfilled is followed. The saints are believed to show their displeasure on those who do not keep their promises. In the village, many spend their nights during Easter week at the house where African-type dances are held. Story telling continues from Monday night through the night of Holy Thursday, as the participants say that they are attending the wake of "Our Lord." Mourning "Our Lord" on Good Friday, the women comb their hair only after twelve o'clock, and they give no greetings and ask no blessings before that time, all customs derived from the period of slavery.[10]

According to Eduardo, the beliefs and rituals just described are essentially Catholic, but the form and the underlying attitudes can be understood only by taking into consideration similar traditions of West Africans. As is the case with the African deities, the saints are treated in an intimate manner to persuade them to satisfy human wishes. Both the saints in Maranhão and the divinities in Africa act as intermediaries between man and the Creator. The pattern of story telling during the "wake" of Jesus during Easter Week can be traced back to the African custom of telling stories to amuse the dead.[11]

In the city of São Luiz, a considerable number of blacks—especially the women—attend church daily, and Sunday masses attract many more. Several times a year those who belong to cult houses pay the priests to recite mass to honor a saint and ask for his help, and the relatives of a dead person arrange for mass to be said for his soul. Many cult devotees go to confession and communion. Religious processions largely comprise blacks and persons of mixed descent, and many Negroes make the pilgrimage to a village thirty miles from the capital to honor São José de Ribamar. Blacks attend the same churches as whites, and both belong to the same church associations. There are, however, church societies which are exclusively "colored" in São Luiz as in other parts of Brazil; the most important of these is the *Irmandade* (sisterhood) of Our Lady of the Rosary.[12]

In São Luiz, African retentions have been carried on by groups of Dahomean and Yoruban descent under the names of the "Mina" or "Gege" house and the "Nago" house. The dances given by these cults, which are known as *terreiros* or *casas de mina*, are called *tambor de mina*. In these centers, African patterns of possession, dancing, and drumming have been continued.[13] African and Catholic beliefs have been integrated in the Dahomean and Yoruban houses. This is true also of the groups that Eduardo calls the African-derived houses, but these cults have added American Indian elements to the rituals, including the worship of Indian spirits and the use of magic called *pagelança* or *cura*.[14]

The initiation pattern followed in São Luiz resembles those carried on in Africa among the Dahomeans and the Yoruba, but some elements are absent and those which have been continued have been modified. The period of complete seclusion for several months has been reduced to eight days, and formal instruction is quite limited. The deities worshipped in the Dahomean house are African, and, as in Dahomey, they are grouped into three pantheons. The "families" in São Luiz include Da or Danbira, with the same attributes as the Dahomean Sagbata (Earth) pantheon; the Kevioso (Thunder) group, and Davise or Dahome that does not correspond to any of the pantheons in Dahomey (the Sky pantheon, headed by Mawu-Lisa of Dahomean belief, is missing).[15]

In the Dahomean house in São Luiz, the *vodun* (deities) are ranked according to age. The oldest gods have the greatest prestige, followed by a "mature" group, a younger group, and the youngest—the *tokhueni*. Some of the latter serve as messengers between the *vodun* and the cult initiates, acting as "guides" in "opening the way" for their elders when a ceremony or dance is held.[16]

NEO-AFRICAN AND AFRICAN-DERIVED RELIGIONS

In the Yoruban house in São Luiz, the Dahomean word *vodun* is often used, but the term *ôrixá* is heard frequently in songs. Although deities included in this house bear Dahomean, Yoruban, and Brazilian names, few are of Yoruban origin—Xangô, Yemanja, Shapana, Ogun, Eowa, Osain, and Aduda. The last two are mentioned infrequently and have no initiates. Three Dahomean gods—Lisa, Loko, and Bosa—have been incorporated into cult ritual and have devotees in the Yoruban group. *Encantados* with Brazilian names are thought of as nobles and bear such titles as prince, king, or *dom,* or are *caboclo* (Indian) spirits. Among the nobles who have devotees are King Kotelo, Servana, King Junko, Maria Alfa, Gama, Dom Luiz, Prince Viola, Rolo do Mar, and Menino Fama. Three Indian spirits have devotees: Caboclo Guerreiro, Caboclo Bahiano, and Caboclo Tabajara. The encantados—both nobles and caboclos—are said to live at the bottom of the sea,[17] and to be organized into three "lines": Nago (Yoruban), Taipa (Nupe of southern Nigeria), and the caboclo or forest line.[18]

Compared with the Dahomean cult group, the Yoruban house in São Luiz has retained a relatively small proportion of beliefs concerning the organization of gods of African origin. Shango is identified with Bade, the thunder deity of Dahomey, but the members of his "family" are Dahomeans: Loko, Verekete, Lisa, and Abe. Osain was said to belong to a different "family," and Ogun to still another "line," but neither of these could be specified.[19]

Although the Yoruban group has continued the trickster tradition of the Yoruba and the Dahomeans in modified form, the Yoruban name Eshu is seldom used. In Africa this trickster is believed to be able to perform good as well as evil deeds, but in the Yoruban group in São Luiz, Lebara or Elebara is entirely malignant. It is necessary to send him away before a dance begins in order to avoid trouble with him—for example, he might provoke a fight between dancers or observers, or ruin an offering for the gods.[20]

In a third type of cult center in São Luiz, the Yoruban-derived houses, most of the deities worshipped are encantados with Brazilian names: Indian tribes, including Tupi and Tupinambo; encantados called brancos (whites) or nobles, kings, princes, or doms. Very few spirits in these houses have African names: the most common are Ogun, Verekete,

Shapana, and Bade; the less common are Yemanjá, Eowa, and Shango. The decrease in the number of African elements and the acceptance of Indian and European spirits has gone farther in the Yoruban-derived houses than in the Yoruban group.[21]

The identification of African gods with Catholic saints in São Luiz, as in other parts of the New World, rests upon similarities in the powers or responsibilities of the two groups of supernaturals. In the Dahomean group, Sobo, mother of the Thunder god Kevioso, is equated with Saint Barbara because in Catholic belief the latter protects her followers from thunder. Sapata, Earth-god in Dahomey, who punishes with skin diseases, is equated with Saint Lazarus, the saint of smallpox. The equivalent of the Dahomean god Dosu is Saint George, the dragon-killer. Jesus Christ, God, and the Holy Ghost are called Evo-Vodun—they who are above all other vodun; Mae or Maedona is identified with Our Lady. Identification between African deities and Catholic saints is greater in the Yoruban cult than elsewhere in São Luiz. Among the identifications are the following:

Shango	St. Peter
Yemanja	Our Lady of Good Parturition
Shapana	St. Sebastian
Ogun	St. John
Osain	St. Francis
Eowa	Our Lady of Conception
Nana Buroko	St. Rita
Lisa	St. Paul[22]

Although it is believed that the American Indian deities assist and protect human beings, identification with the saints does not extend to them. Spirits regarded as nobles or whites, however, are equated with saints whose names they bear—Dom Sebastian is identified with St. Sebastian, Barbara with St. Barbara, and Dom John with St. John. In spirit possession by these new spirits, the Catholic pattern of the names of saints has been combined with the African pattern of possession.[23]

In São Luiz, worship of the deities closely parallels African patterns only in the "orthodox" Dahomean and Yoruban cult groups, and of these the Dahomean house adheres to purer forms of African ritual than the Yoruban. At the Dahomean cult center, the songs are sung in Fō, the language of Dahomey, and the dance rhythms are pure African. In the Yoruban house, however, the songs are sung either in Nago, in mixed Nago and Portuguese, or in Portuguese. In the Yoruban-derived groups only a few songs are sung in Nago, and according to the devotees of the Yoruban cult these are not sung correctly.[24]

Sacrifices are offered to the vodun in the sanctuary at daybreak, and the *vodunsi* ("daughters of the deity") who became possessed in the earlier part of the ceremony become possessed again. The blood of the animals is offered, the flesh is cooked, and the dishes then prepared are presented to the vodun. In the late afternoon, these dishes are removed and distributed to the members of the cult. That night and the following day, dances are held to honor the vodun to whom the sacrifices were offered.[25]

Spirit possession varies somewhat from one cult group to another in São Luiz. Seizures by the gods, especially in the Dahomean center, is restrained, but in the Yoruban-derived houses, possession is violent. While in most respects the cults in São Luiz are more African than in the rural community of Santo Antônio, no cult houses in the city reveal signs of motor behavior in the dances that are as characteristic of African possession as those found in the interior.[26]

In the Dahomean house, a special type of possession occurs. The *tobosa,* believed to be the spirit of a child, possesses a cult initiate for several hours a day for several days in succession. Such possessions take place only three times a year—at New Year's, Carnival time, and during the festivals for St. John in June. Should a dance (ceremony for the vodun) be held on one of these days, the initiate's behavior becomes entirely different after the *tobosa* has withdrawn and she becomes possessed by her vodun. As *tobosa,* the devotee speaks and acts like a child three or fours years old. As a vodun, she is grave and paternal or maternal. Psychologically, *tobosa* possession is similar to éré in Bahia and *weri* or *réré* possession in Trinidad. Various terms have been used to describe differences in the depth of the state of dissociation elsewhere: éré or "semi-possession" (Porto Alegre, Brazil—Herskovits, 1943, 505); "radiation states" (lighter degrees of possession in Recife, Brazil—Ribeiro, 1960, 2); "controlled" possession (Christ Army of Anang Ibibio of southeastern

NEO-AFRICAN AND AFRICAN-DERIVED RELIGIONS

Nigeria—Messenger, 1960, 272); an individual's "level of dissociation" on different occasions (Bourguignon, 1970, 90); *tokhoueni* (Bahia, Brazil—Bastide, 1960, 520); *weri* or *rêré* (Trinidad—Simpson, 1962, 1211–1212). In Bahia, these states follow full possession, but in Maranhão a *tobosa* possession precedes stronger possessions (Eduardo, 1948, 96), and in Trinidad the semipossession usually follows, but may precede, the arrival of an important power (Simpson, 1965, 31).

Beliefs about the soul in Maranhão illustrate the fusion of European and African cultural elements. The concepts of the guardian angel, the destination of the soul after death, prayers, and the help that souls can give those who pray to them are Catholic beliefs. Some of the ideas concerning souls, however, are similar to those held by the West African ancestors of Maranhão Negroes. The concept of multiple souls is found in Dahomey and among the Yoruba. The Bambara of Mali believe in two souls—one that provides life for the body, and another that leaves the body while the person sleeps. Multiple soul beliefs are found also in the Angola-Congo region. "Feeding" the guardian angel and the belief that a soul can be stolen by a conjurer are other West African beliefs that are part of the soul complex in Maranhão. The mixed attitudes of fear, respect, and piety with respect to the souls of the dead reveal ideas which have been derived from European and African sources.[27]

It is believed in Maranhão that the soul of a deceased person will linger near the house where he lived for seven nights after death. On the seventh, fifteenth, or thirtieth day after death, a rite known as the "visit of the grave" (*visita de cova*) is observed. At this time, some of the relatives and friends of the dead person recite Catholic prayers near the grave. In the rural community, few of the mortuary rites—including the wake, burial, and "visit of the grave"—show African characteristics. African elements that have persisted include the large expenditures made among rural people for the "mourners," and the resemblance of the "visit of the grave" to the definitive burial in Africa. Story-telling during the wake of a child is derived from Africa. Syncretization in death ceremonies is seen also in the intervention of the African-like spirits, the encantados, in the funeral ceremony.[28]

Negroes in São Luiz follow mortuary rites that are similar to those of whites in the city, but the anxiety and the great insistence among the blacks on proper burial is reminiscent of West Africa. In traditional African belief, only those who have been properly buried can enter the land of the ancestors and assume rightful places there.[29]

During the period of slavery, the Dahomean and Yoruban slaves in the city of São Luiz were exposed to Catholicism, but they seem to have had more freedom to retain the religious beliefs of their ancestors than plantation Negroes. The two cult houses established before the emancipation of slaves were led by freed slaves, but Yoruban and Dahomean slaves were permitted to join their free confreres when dances and ceremonies were held on Saints' days. In addition, the Dahomean and Yoruban slaves who were brought to the state of Maranhão were representatives of religions that were highly institutionalized and well-organized.[30] The religions of other African peoples, especially those of Senegal and of the Congo-Angola region, were less highly organized and had, therefore, less chance of being perpetuated in the New World. Although most of the Maranhão slaves came from Senegal and the Congo-Angola region, no religious elements of Senegalese origin and only a few Congo-Angolan religious traditions have persisted in this part of Brazil.[31]

Dahomean beliefs in São Luiz have been continued to a greater extent than Yoruban, in part because the descendants of the Dahomeans have always constituted a closed group. The Yoruban group is less unified, and its members seem to have weaker ties to their ancestors. In the groups that Eduardo calls "the Yoruban-derived centers," Yoruban traditions have been even more modified by the introduction of non-African elements. American Indian spirits play an important role in these cult houses, including having the duty of closing the ceremonies on the last night on which dances are held. In a special healing ceremony called the *pagelança,* the *pagé* or *curado* (healer), who is the counterpart of the Indian shaman, becomes possessed by an Indian spirit. He then removes from his client's body a needle, a thorn, a lizard, or some other object that has been injected by the evil magic of an enemy or his agent. Until recently, members of the other cult groups were not allowed to attend such healing dances.[32]

NEO-AFRICAN AND AFRICAN-DERIVED RELIGIONS

Candomblés in Bahia, Brazil

The candomblé, the name given to a Neo-African religion in Bahia, goes back at least 150 years, and one center is believed by some to be 200 years old.[33] At the middle of the twentieth century, there were approximately 100 cult centers in the state of Bahia, with an average of 300 persons in each. As Carneiro has said, the gods and the dead mingle with the living in the *terreiro* (cult center), listening to the complaints of the latter, giving advice, granting favors, resolving problems, and providing medicines for illnesses and consolation for misfortunes.[34]

Members of candomblés believe in a supreme god, usually called Olorun (a Yoruban term) or Zaniapombo (the word used in the Angolan, Congolese, and caboclo (Indian) candomblés). Devotees believe that the Supreme God created the universe, but that he has intermediaries who look after the affairs of human beings. There is no organized cult for Olorun nor any material representation of this deity. In some candomblés, he is mentioned in songs and myths. On the door of one candomblé these words were painted: *Kô si óbá afi Olorun* (There is only one god who is Olorun).[35]

Oshala (Obatala)—identified with the Church Nosso Senhor do Bonfim in Salvador, and, more rarely, with the Holy Spirit—receives as much homage as Olorun. Called Orisha Baba, Baba Oke, Lemba, and other terms, he is considered the father of all the other orisha and the grandfather of all mortals. In ceremonies, he appears in two forms—as an old man with a cane and as a young man, outspoken and outgoing.[36]

Below these divinities in rank are the *orisha* (Nago), *vodun* (Gege), *inkices* (Angola and Congo), and the encantados (Caboclos). Shango, god of storms, thunder, and lightning, appears in several forms, and is identified with St. Jerome, St. Barbara, St. Peter, or St. John the Younger. Oshossie, a hunter is equated with St. George. Due to his relationship as servant to Eshu, Ogun, god of iron and owner of all roads, is responsible for opening the crossroads so that other gods may come to ceremonies. He is identified with St. Anthony. Oshunmare, the rainbow, is equated with St. Bartholomew. This servant of Shango takes the form of a snake. Omolu, god of smallpox and, by extension, of all other contagious diseases, is the Doctor of the Blacks. Identified with St. Lazarus, St.

Bento, St. Sebastian, or St. Roque, he is very popular. He appears at ceremonies in two forms, as an old and a young man. Iroko (Loko) is sometimes identified with St. Francis of Assisi.[37]

Almost all of the female orishas are associated with water and are highly esteemed in the candomblés. Nanã, or St. Anne, is the "Mother" of water and the mother of all the orishas. Yemanjá, identified with Our Lady of the Conception, has diverse names because she symbolizes most of the African, European, and Amerindian myths about water. She is universally revered by blacks and by the populace in general in Bahia. Yansã, or St. Barbara, is a wife of Shango and, like Shango, controls storms. She is liked by the women in the candomblés because of her unpredictable and stubborn nature. Oshun, goddess of springs and creeks, is equated with Senhora Candeias. In one form she is said to live in the road with Ogun; in another form she appears with a fan and a sword. Two exceptions to the water as the province of female deities are Ossãe, an American Indian goddess who is owner of the leaves, and Oba, another wife of Shango, a warrior who is identified with Joan of Arc. It is believed to be very difficult to get Ossãe to come to a ceremony.[38]

Eshu controls all crossroads and dangerous places in the world. He acts as an intermediary between the orisha and human beings. For example, if Shango's help is desired, a devotee can get it more easily through Eshu. It is believed that Eshu will do any favor, good or evil, if he is given the things he likes—oil of dendé, a goat, alcoholic beverages, or tobacco. If neglected, he will unloose malevolent forces. According to Carneiro, only the Nagos (Eshu) and the Geges (Legba) really understand Eshu. The other "nations" who came to Bahia did not have a spirit similar to Eshu; therefore they associate him with the Christian Devil. Invariably, in a candomblé one shrine is dedicated to Eshu, and the door of that room is padlocked. The initial moments of every ceremony must be dedicated to him to prevent him from disturbing the ritual. Although Eshu is not regarded precisely as an orisha, he manifests on (takes possession of) human beings as an orisha does. In this case, it is not said that the person is a son or daughter of Eshu, but that he has a moral obligation with Eshu for the rest of his life. If Eshu manifests during a ceremony, he is permitted to dance in the candomblé, but not with the orisha. Carneiro knows of only one candomblé in Bahia where Eshu has appeared.[39]

NEO-AFRICAN AND AFRICAN-DERIVED RELIGIONS

Ibeji are known as inferior spirits; collectively they are called *érés* or *meninos* (little ones). They appear after the orisha in a period of transition to a normal state because the blacks believe that every person who has a *santo* also has an *éré*—Cosme and Damião, Crispim and Crispiniano, or Dôú and Alabá. A person possessed by an *éré* behaves like a child. The cult of the *meninos* is a traditional custom among the poor of Bahia, but it exists to a greater extent outside the candomblé than inside it. A mass must be given annually for the *meninos,* followed by a ceremony in the candomblé, in order for a devotee to avoid misfortune in the coming year.[40]

The *vodun* (Gege) are essentially the same as the orisha (Nago), but they are less well known by their real names because of the popularity of the Yoruba deities. Shango among the Geges is called Sobo (Soglo); Iroko is called Loko; Ogun is known as Gun (Gu); Oshunmare is Óbéssem; Ibeji are called Hôhô; Eshu is Lêba (Legba); and Nanā is called Nanā Burucu, as in Dahomey. Although the Geges resisted cultural absorption, they were almost completely absorbed by the Nagos. In Bahia, there are only three Gege candomblés, but these houses have maintained the Gege cult without change. A special feature of the Gege candomblé is the snake Dā. In Dahomey, every *vodun* has a snake.[41]

Although at times the Bantus were the dominant element of the slave population in the New World, few traces of their religion have persisted. Bastide's explanation of this phenomenon is that the Bantus were used mainly as agricultural laborers, while the Fon, Yoruba, and Mina (Dahomeans) were chosen as house slaves. The great majority of the Bantus were kept on the plantations, but many of the other Africans lived and worked in the towns, where it was easier to organize "nations." Moreover, the Bantus were more receptive to alien influences and more readily accepted westernization and conversion to Christianity than most groups. Their own less highly conceptualized religions were another factor in the earlier Christianization of the Bantus. Slavery's disruption of family groups made it difficult, if not impossible, to perpetuate the ancestor worship of the Bantus, and their localized nature-spirits did not fit into the scheme of things in the diaspora.[42]

For the most part, Angolan and Congolese candomblés have the same gods (*inkices*) as the Nago cult centers, but they have different names and they differ superficially in appearance. The equivalents are:

NEO-AFRICAN AND AFRICAN-DERIVED RELIGIONS

Nago	Angolan-Congolese	Nago	Angolan-Congolese
Ogun	Sumbo	Loko	Katendê
Nanã	Kêrê-Kêrê	Oxala	Lemba; Kassubéká
Yansã	Bamburucema	Oxunmare	Angôrô
Oxosse	Tauamin; Matalumbô;	Omolu	Burungunco
	Congombira	Exu	Alvaiá; Bombonjira[43]
Xango	Zaze; Kibuko		

Some aspects of the candomblés of the Angolan and Congo "nations" differ from the Yoruba-Fon rituals into which they have been absorbed. Hymns are sung in Portuguese. The music and musical instruments in the Bantu candomblés are quite different from those of the Yoruba-Dahomean groups. In the funeral ceremonies of the Bantu candomblés, the souls of the dead reside in the branches of certain trees rather than in pots.[44]

Candomblés of Amerindian origin are "degradations" of Gege-Nago candomblés, and, sometimes, of Islamic Negro (Nago, Hausa, and Tapa) and Bantu cults. The caboclo *encantados* are the same gods as the Nagos and Geges have, but they have undergone modification due to the influence of blacks from Angola and the Congo and, more recently, spiritualist influences. An example is Santo da Cobra or Cobra Caua, identified as St. Bento—a curious fusion of Omolu and Dã. Other adaptations include Bôrôcô (Nanã Burucu, of Dahomey) and Sereia Mukunã (Yemanja, a Yoruba deity). Ogun is multiplied in caboclo candomblés as Ogun Marinho, Ogun do Cariri, Ogun da Pedra Preta, Ogun da Pedra Branca, Ogun Menino, and still others.[45]

There are very few authentic indigenous gods—Tupã, the official god of Brazilians, and Tupinambá, who is the ideal representation of the Tupa tribe. Other Amerindian deities include Salavá (identified with St. Salvador), Peixe Marinho (identified with St. Joseph), Caipora (owner of the forest), Boiadeiro (cowboy)—similar to Oxosse (Nago). Spiritualist influence is seen in such encantados as Sete Serra, Pena Verde, Serra Negra, and Caboclos Jaci, Mata Verde, and Pedra Preta. A recent, unique contribution of the caboclo candomblés is Martim-Pescador, called Martim-Bangola among the blacks, a spirit of animals. This spirit functions as a messenger between mortals and encantados and so lacks the status of an encantado, but he is a guardian spirit. One who is possessed by Martim-Pescador acts like an intoxicated person and behaves mischievously. Another indigenous deity, Marujo, has the responsibility for guiding ships to harbor.[46]

At the beginning of this century one or two Muslim candomblés were still found in Bahia, but they are not in existence today. Another cult at Alagoâs, Brazil (Aunt Marceline) had syncretized with Yoruba religion. Among the many Muslims in Cuba were Mandingos, Wolofs, and Fulani, and the religion of Allah was established there. Eventually, as in Brazil, the Muslims joined the Yoruba cult, and Allah became identified with Olorun or with Obatala (Obbat Allah). At one time Muslim cults also existed at Surinam, but no traces of this religion are found today among either the Bush Negroes or the Creoles.[47]

Forty or fifty years ago, candomblés in Bahia were dedicated to the gods of only one "nation." Only a few are now so dedicated. One reason for this change is that the men of candomblés are no longer satisfied with attending only the feasts given in their own centers. By going to others, they are contributing to the mixture of African religions. Also, the assimilation of Catholicism has steadily increased and on a larger scale than heretofore. In some cases, initiates are required to attend mass before they are permitted to participate in cult rituals.[48]

A candomblé feast starts with the sacrifice of animals (dogs, cocks, and goats), and is followed by singing and dancing. The blood of the animals is used to wash the stones of the orishas in a secret propitiatory ceremony at the altar. For this part of the ritual, such offerings as a bottle of dendé oil, a plate of manioc flour, and a glass of water or of cheap rum are arranged on the floor. An animal sacrifice is presented to Eshu to prevent him from becoming angry and disturbing the ceremony. A high ranking "daughter" (*daga* or *sidaga*) dances around the sacred food and, later, throws some oil or manioc flour outside at the entrance of the house for the "man of the street," that is, for Eshu. For at least 25 years, some of the candomblés have omitted the traditional sacrifice of animals to Eshu. Instead, the daughters of the candomblé dance around the food and water that have been placed in the center of the room, and, at a certain point, throw out Eshu's food, saying "Eshu, here is your food; go away, this is not your place."[49]

The singing to all of the orishas is under the direction of the

NEO-AFRICAN AND AFRICAN-DERIVED RELIGIONS

"mother" who sits by the orchestra playing the *adja* (two pieces of metal which are struck together). Special dances are danced for each orisha. When the orchestra plays for her orisha, the "daughter" of the deity feels vibrations in her body, becomes dizzy, loses her balance, walks as if drunk, and taken over by the orisha, acquires another physiognomy and then recovers somewhat. She may take a sick person in her arms and cure her by lifting her into the air or blowing on her stomach or ears. If the possession is too extreme—that is, if the possessed person is "working" too hard, perspiring too much, or falling or beating herself—the *ekedes* (women assistants) restrain her. Meanwhile, other gods take possession of their daughters and stop the complete domination of the ceremony by, for example, Shango.[50]

After a deity manifests on a person, the devotee is taken into the house and dressed especially for the occasion. In caboclo candomblés, this custom is almost never followed. In those centers, the daughters dress in everyday dresses. Among the Nagos and the Geges, only Ossãe smokes and only Eshu drinks and smokes, but among the caboclos, Caipora and Boiadeiro smoke a pipe, Martim-Pescador drinks *cachaca* (rum), and the other encantados smoke cigars.[51]

Xangó in Recife, Brazil

According to Ribeiro, lower-class people in Recife prefer to attend sacrificial ceremonies for the orisha, listening to black oracles, or dancing in a candomblé instead of going exclusively to masses at a Catholic church, giving novenas to St. Teresa, or attending funeral services conducted by the Church.[52]

Throughout the first decade of the twentieth century cult groups in Recife were still distinguished according to their tribal origin: Egba, Bonina, Oyo, Igesha, and Ollorin, as well as Congolese or Angolan, or Islamic blacks. That is no longer the case.[53]

As in other parts of the New World, not every cult group has the same pantheon of gods, and the prestige of the divinities varies from group to group. Some gods, totally unknown in some houses, are the object of great reverence in other houses. The prominence of some of the deities is attributable to the fact that they are worshipped by major priests; in some cases, the ranking of the gods has changed over a period of time.[54]

In the Afrobrazilian cults of Recife, Olorun, the creator of the universe, who resides in heaven, does not wield power over earthly affairs and does not demand offerings. Oshala (Orishala) is believed to have charge of the other deities, but he shares his prerogatives and powers with two other gods—Oshaguiam and Oshalufan. Some devotees identify these three divinities with the Trinity, and some believers equate Oshala with Jesus through the use of the lithograph of Christ Sanctified.[55]

Opinion is divided on whether the next most important orisha is Yansan or Anamburuku. Yansan, also called Yamessan, Oya, or Oba (a deity of war), is identified with St. Barbara. She is the wife of Shango, the most popular of Afrobrazilian deities and the god whose name is used for all of the cults. Yansan exerts control over wind and lightning, but is also in charge of the souls of the dead. Anamburuku (Nanan), of the Dahomean pantheon, is considered to be the oldest, or the grandmother, of all the orisha. She is said to be the mother of Abaluwaye, the god of smallpox, and is intimately linked to the cult of the dead. Nanan, identified with St. Anne, has few followers in Recife. A ritual act of grinding corn in a mortar indicates her relationship with agriculture in the past.

Oshun, one of Shango's wives, is a goddess of wealth and is thought to bring prosperity to her devotees. Coquettish, voluptuous, and capricious, she controls springs, rivers, and lakes. Yemanja, another popular deity, is in charge of oceans and salt water; she is said to be the progenitor of many gods. Conceived as a mermaid, she is equated with the Virgin Mary. Ogun, Ode (a god of hunting, identified with St. Michael), Oshossi (another god of hunting, identified with St. Expedito), and Shango are her sons.

The position of Shango is more prestigious in Afrobrazilian cults than in Africa. Some of the more orthodox cult members in Recife, who consider themselves fervent Catholics, have identified Orishala with God and Shango with Christ.[56] Shango is believed to be temperamental—a fighter and an amorous adventurer. At ceremonies, this deity appears in at least three forms: as Dada (an old man), Ogodo, and Aganju. Ribeiro found no differences in the duties of these three aspects of this divinity, but it is said that during a storm their voices can be distinguished.[57] Abaluwaye, the next in rank in the hierarchy, is identified with St. Lazarus or St. Sebastian.

Ogun, god of war, and the hunters Oshossi and Ode, constitute a trio that is invoked immediately after Esu at the beginning of a ceremony. These three brothers are identified with St. George. Oshunmare, the rainbow, is the least well known of the Afrobrazilian deities in Recife; Ribeiro has never seen anyone possessed by this divinity in that city.

Eshu has a different kind of role, but one that is not less important than the parts played by the other deities. He is the master of the crossroads and the messenger of the orisha. He arrives first at a ceremony and "opens the way" for the other gods. None of the cult priests identify Eshu with any Catholic saint or with the Devil (the identification of Eshu with the Christian Devil was a mistake made by some missionaries in Africa and by certain observers of Afrobrazilian cults).[58] Eshu is known to everybody in the cult centers and is brought into every conversation about the cult. Every cult house has an Eshu—a figure on a little mound with seashells for his mouth and eyes. This figure is always saturated with oil of dendê and the blood of sacrificed animals.

In the organization of African cult groups in Recife, there was a time when diviners (specialists in consulting the oracle, Ifa) had the highest rank. Many of them had been slaves and claimed to have acquired their knowledge in their country of origin; others were descendants of those specialists who had been initiated in Brazil. The refusal of these specialists to initiate new people and their eventual disappearance has resulted in the transfer of their functions to the priests. With their limited knowledge of the *opele* (divination chain), the majority of priests in recent years have contented themselves with throwing shells (*dilogan*), a practice formerly limited to women.[59]

Neo-African Cults in Porto Alegre, Brazil

In the southern Brazilian city of Porto Alegre, the number of "houses" where African religions were practiced increased in the period

1920 to 1945. In 1942, there were 1,776 members of 52 houses in a city which then included approximately 50,000 persons of predominantly African ancestry.[60]

As in Bahia, few Gege cult-houses exist in Porto Alegre, but this "nation" is held in high esteem. The names of Mawu, the great god of the Dahomeans, and Aido Wedo, the rainbow serpent, are seldom heard in northern Brazil, but here they are well known. The well developed caboclo cult of the North seems to be absent in the South. Cult members used the word *pará* to designate the centers and their rituals, but *batuque* was employed by outsiders.

The African deities and the Catholic saints identified with them, as given by a priestess of the Oyo (Yoruba) "nation," were as follows:

Eshu (Leba, Elebara)	{ St. Peter (Eshu the elder) { St. Anthony (Eshu the younger)
Ogun	St. George
Oya (Iyansan)	St. Barbara
Aganju (Shango the younger)	St. Michael the Archangel
Ogodo (Shango the elder)	St. Jerome
Shango Dada	St. John
Ode	St. Onofré
Osain	St. Emmanuel
Shapana (Omolu)	Nosso Senhor de Bonfim (Christ)
Oba	St. Catherine
Oshun Panda	Nossa Senhora de Conceição
Beji	Sts. Comas and Damien
Oshun Doko	Our Lady of the Rosary
Yemanja	Nossa Senhora da Navegantes (Our Lady of the Navigators)
Oshala	The Holy Ghost ("Divino Espirito Santo")
Orunmila	St. Joseph

The absence of Oshossi from this list is noteworthy, but Ode, Oyo (Yoruba kingdom) name for the god of the hunt is included, and Oshossi's name is well known in Porto Alegre. The omission of two names, Oshunmare and Nana, that are prominent in Bahia occurs because they are Gêge (Dahomean) gods and the members of the group who provided these names were Oyo people.[61] Judging from the names of the cults, the most popular divinities in Porto Alegre were Oshun Panda (7 houses), Bara or Elegbara (5 houses), Shango (4), Oshala (4), Yemanja (3), Oya (3), Shango Dada and Orunmila (1 each). Others had the names of Catholic saints, or, in one case, a caboclo name, or they bore historical dates.[62]

In Bahia, Rio de Janeiro, and Recife, most of the initiates are women, but in Porto Alegre in 1942 there were nearly as many male as female members of the *parás*. A unique feature of the cults in southern Brazil was the principle of permitting priestesses to kill the animals sacrificed to most gods.[63]

Divination is an important function of the cult-head in Porto Alegre. The *kpele* (chain of shells) is thrown in the West African way to foretell fate and the wishes of the gods; other techniques of divination include the throwing of cowrie shells and water gazing. As in many other New World African societies, possession by the ancient deities is extremely important. As elsewhere, when his god "descends," the devotee dances, sings, prophesies, or manifests other characteristic behavior of the deity. As in northern Brazil, a possessed person returns to his normal state by passing through a kind of semi-possession called *éré*.[64]

The mythology and the structure of the public ceremonies have been preserved with much purity in Porto Alegre, but the organization of the African cults has declined. The hierarchy of the priesthood is less elaborate, and the number and variety of officials is smaller in the South. The rites of initiation are briefer, and the cult of the dead is less extensive. The solidarity which unites the members of a candomblé in Bahia, that of a family, does not exist in Porto Alegre. In Porto Alegre, the solidarity of an African cult is that of a neighborhood or comradeship. In Bahia, cult membership is inherited; orisha remain in the family but they can be transmitted either in the male or the female line. While there are no absolute marriage rules for believers in Bahia, the marriage of two persons who are followers of the same orisha is considered dangerous. In Porto Alegre, as in Recife, such marriages are permitted if the god of one of the marriage partners is replaced by another deity.[65]

The differences between the candomblés of the North and the African cults in Porto Alegre is attributed by Bastide to the economic and social situation in the South. In general, the social level of devotees in Porto Alegre is low; consequently the ceremonial aspects that are most expensive lose their richness and importance. In the South, the cult houses are the residences of the "fathers" and "mothers"—small houses indistinguishable from other homes of the proletariat. Because of the smallness of the houses, the Catholic altar tends to disappear, the exterior shrines are eliminated, and the *pegi* (altar) is much more modest than in the North. Sometimes, animal sacrifices cannot be afforded, and the descent of the gods is not accompanied by a change of symbolic clothing. Often the sacrifice given on one's initiation day has to be held every two or three years instead of annually.[66]

According to Bastide, that which remains in the African cults in the South is the essential activity of the descent of the gods, but as other elements have been lost, the ecstasy of possession has increased—it has more force and frenzy. Nevertheless, the believers in the African sects are strong Catholics. They retain their ancient traditions while respecting the festivals of the church. Catholicism here is simply added to African religion; it is no more mixed than it is in Bahia.[67]

An Independent Religious Cult in Belém, Brazil: The Batuque

Batuque is a highly syncretized Yoruban-derived cult that was brought to Belém from São Luiz in Maranhão around the turn of the century. It consists of a mixture of Yoruban and Dahomean beliefs and practices, as well as elements of Indian shamanism, folk Catholicism, and Iberian and local folklore. In Belém the American Indian and Catholic components have become more prominent through the addition of new spirits and new songs, more attention has been given to curing, and the cult has become more individualistic. During the past two or three decades, the major change in this religion has been the inclusion of spirits and rites from the Umbanda cult of Rio de Janeiro. Some of the concepts of Brazilian spiritualism have also been added, in part derived also from Umbanda.[68]

As is the case with Umbanda, Batuque is not a revitalization movement. Its appeal does not lie in a claim that it will change the world of devotees but in its offer of supernatural help to cope with life's problems. From a religion that comforted the slaves, the Batuque has become a religion that appeals to all those who are disadvantaged.[69]

In Belém, the most acceptable part of Umbanda is the emphasis on the demon spirits, the Exus. Formerly no one sought possession by the Exus and they were "dispatched," as they still are, by offerings of rum, gunpowder, and candles. Their permission was then sought to hold the ceremony by the singing of appropriate songs.[70]

Despite the influence of Maranhão on the Batuque cult, mediums from São Luiz who have come to Belém have objected recently to doctrines and songs of the local mediums, saying that they are taken from phonograph records and books instead of the old unwritten traditions. They disapprove also of the midnight ritual for the Exus and of the new encantados (spirits) from Umbanda. Such criticisms indicate that members of the *batuques* in Belém have accepted more ideas from Rio de Janeiro than have the devotees of cults in Maranhão.[71]

In many ways, the Batuque cult is a variety of folk Catholicism, a type of religion that is almost unrelated to the official Church.[72] Since the Christian saints are honored at the cult center, there is little or no need for devotees to visit churches. Prayers at the major *festas* are led by a cult leader or a neighborhood woman, and street processions in honor of a saint are organized without clerical assistance or consent. Despite their strong orientation toward the encantados rather than the Catholic saints, most of the Batuque cult members regard themselves as Roman Catholics. They see few, if any, basic contradictions between Catholicism and cult beliefs and practices. Batuque beliefs simply constitute ideological additions; they do not in any way replace Catholic beliefs.

Cult members are never heard to criticize Catholic doctrine, but hostility toward the clergy is occasionally expressed. The indifference of cult members to the sacraments of the Church has been attributed to the disinterest of devotees in the salvation of souls. Afro-Brazilian cults, including the Batuque, are not strongly other-worldly. Their main concerns have to do with the almost overwhelming problems of daily life.[73]

The origin of the term "encantado" is unknown. A literal translation as "enchanted one" is inadequate because encantado is a permanent status regardless of whether an encantado was born as such or was formerly a man or woman whose destiny was altered. Many of the ritual songs include the terms *vodun* and *orixá,* the Dahomean and Yoruban terms respectively for deity. In everyday speech, such terms as *guia* (guide), *santo* (saint), and *invisivel* (invisible one) are often used. Encantado is, however, by far the most common term. Cult members say that the encantados, like the Virgin Birth or the Holy Trinity, are a mystery that human beings cannot understand.[74] The two categories of saint and encantado are not equated or syncretized as they are in some Afroamerican religions. The term "santo" may be used as a synonym for encantado, but a more accurate translation in this context is "spirit" or "guardian spirit." Also, except in special cases, saints are not expected to possess people.[75]

The relationship between encantados and saints is of considerable interest. Each encantado "adores" a particular saint, and each devotee of the encantado is expected to revere the same saint by lighting candles to the saint's image, fasting, and saying special prayers on the saint's day. The saint's image represents both the saint itself and the encantado, and ceremonies for the encantado are often held on the day of the saint with which it is associated. In most cases, the believers are able to keep separate the identities of saint and encantado, the exceptions being St. Barbara, St. Sebastian, and the twin saints Cosmas and Damian.[76]

The contractual relationship between a Batuque member and an encantado resembles that between an individual and a saint. In return for performing certain ritual acts, the devotee expects that the encantado will provide protection and oversee his well-being. In addition to offering prayers, candles, and "adoration," the Batuque devotee often promises to perform some special act of devotion if his appeal in time of crisis is granted. In the latter case, however, his petition may be made to a saint who is reputed to specialize in certain kinds of problems and to be capable of working miracles rather than to the encantado with whom the supplicant has an intimate and long-term relationship.[77]

A few of the encantados are obviously of African origin. Averekete (or Verekete) is a Dahomean thunder deity, but in Belém he appears as an elderly, dignified *senhor* rather than as a young, fun-loving trickster. The deity of thunder and lightning in the Batuque is either Xangó or Badé—Xangó from Yoruba religion, Badé from Dahomean. Xangó (Badé) is thought to be a severe, dominating spirit who rarely possesses anyone. He is important to the devotees because it is believed that he provides the stones for the "seats" for the encantados. The favored stones for such places of residence are prehistoric stone axheads. Rainha Barba-Inhaçan (St. Barbara) is also associated with thunder and lightning. (According to Catholic hagiography, St. Barbara's pagan father was killed by lightning after he murdered his Christian daughter.) Much more approachable than Xangó-Badé, Oxalá, or Nana Buroco (female equivalent of Oxalá), she often descends to take possession of her followers. Most cult members believe that Rainha Barba rules over and sends the encantados to dance in the cult centers. Akossi-Sapata, Rei Toi Aduçu, Rei Noé, and Ben Bocu da Cana Verde have been borrowed from the Dahomean-derived Casa das Minas (Dahomean cult) in São Luiz. Because Akossi-Sapata, the deity of skin diseases, can be dangerous to a medium if not handled correctly, he is honored and invited to descend only once a year, during the festival for the saint he "adores," St. Lazarus, on February 11.[78]

Most of the encantados are not African, nor, according to the Leacocks, are any other features of an African tradition prominent parts of Batuque belief today. The largest number of encantados belong to the family of Rei Turquia (King of Turkey)—often called Seu Turquia (Seu is an abbreviation of *senhor,* Mr.). These encantados are called *turcos* (Turks), a term in Brazil applied to anyone from the Middle East (formerly a synonym for "Moor"). This family is said to have two hundred members, some with Portuguese names, some with Indian names, and some with the names of things (*goiabeira,* the guava tree, and so on).[79]

The encantados are grouped into families, a practice that is derived from the Casa das Minas (Dahomean cult) in Maranhão and, probably, ultimately from African tradition. Among the "lines" are those of Averekete, Rei Turquia (King Turkey), Rei Sebastião, Dom Pedro Angaço, Japetequara (Caboclo Velho), Falange de Bôtos (Phalanx of Dolphins), Dom José (Rei Floriano), Rainha Eowa, Principe de Espanha, Barão de Goré, and João de Mata (Rei da Bandeira). In addition to these families of spirits, four other lines frequently mentioned in Belém are Jurema, Ogun, Oxossi, and the Exus. This method of classification has been strengthened by this practice among the Umbanda cults of Rio de Janeiro and São Paulo, where the "guides" are divided into seven lines.[80]

NEO-AFRICAN AND AFRICAN-DERIVED RELIGIONS

A minority of the encantados belong to no "family." These unaffiliated encantados fall into two groups: those of high status are called *senhores, brancos,* or *orixás;* those of lower status are called *caboclos.*[81]

The Leacocks view the Batuque not as "some kind of imperfect copy of the candomblé, but as an independent, coherent religious system that deserved recognition in its own right." They acknowledge "its ultimate African origin," but emphasize the extent to which it has become "Brazilianized." This Brazilianization includes a membership that has been broadened to include people of all racial types, a pantheon that is composed mainly of spirits with Brazilian names, a hierarchy in the pantheon that reflects the social class system of Brazil, the singing of a majority of the songs in Portuguese, and the inclusion of many Catholic rituals in the ceremonies.[82]

Three traditions have contributed to the non-Christian Batuque spirits and lore: African, American Indian, and European or Luso-Brazilian. Among the Dahomean deities imported from Maranhão are Aduçu, Akossi-Sapata, Averkete, Badé, Ben Boçu, Legua Bogi, and Noé. Yoruban-derived *orixas* borrowed indirectly from or reemphasized because of Umbanda of Rio de Janeiro include Ogun, Oxossi Oxan, Inhaçan, Xangô, Imanjá, and Exu. The princes, nobles, and Turks, as well as Dom Carlos and João da Mata, are traceable to European or Brazilian history or folklore. The Indian encantados represent Brazilian idealizations of the aboriginies; they have nothing to do with persistences of Indian religions nor the actual history of Amazonian Indian groups. The principal genuine Indian contribution to the cult is the addition of animal spirits to the pantheon.

> The mysterious dolphins, the legendary Giant Snake, the alligator (Japetequara), the jaguar (Tapinaré), the hawk (Seu Gavião), the turtle (Tartaruga da Amazonas), the *tangaru-pará* (Tango do Pará), the shark (Barão de Goré), and the two macaw encantados (Mariana and Pena Verde) are derived from local shamanism and probably originated in the religions of the Tapí tribes.[83]

The small black people of the forest, the Carapiras, are also derived from Amerindian belief, and the tree spirits (Jarina, Jurema, and Goiabeira) may also have come from Indian tradition.[84]

The least influential of the supernaturals in the Batuque are the souls of the dead. It is believed that the proper place for the souls to appear is at a *mesa de espiritismo* (spiritualist séance). Such a séance is held in some centers every week with a view to giving the souls a chance to express themselves regularly instead of harassing the living from time to time, or trying to appear at other ceremonies. The souls called the "spirits of light" are said to be those of humanitarians: physicians, teachers, religious or political leaders, or slaves who were healers. One devotee explained the difference between the encantados and the souls of the dead by saying that the encantados are not dead. They have all the sensations that humans have, and their understanding of human nature is believed to be far greater than that of the saints or other supernaturals.[85]

For some time Afro-Brazilian cults have tended to become more individualistic, and the Batuque illustrates this trend. In the ritual, the medium is relatively free to establish a direct contact with an encantado, thus becoming independent of his *pai* or *mãe de santo* (male and female Batuque leader). This greater individualism has by no means eliminated the public ceremony. Batuque rituals, however, are less elaborate than those of the more conservative cults, and there are fewer of them. In the candomblés of Bahia, some of the Xangô groups in Recife, and the Dahomean Casa das Minas in São Luiz, the deities have African names and reside in Africa, songs are sung in modified African languages, leaders undergo long periods of training, initiation rites are elaborate, animals are sacrificed, and leadership is hierarchized. Batuque rituals echo these ultimate African derivations in the attempts that are made to call the encantados in a prescribed order, the divinatory rituals performed by some leaders, the sacrifice of chickens in some groups, and the relatively elaborate initiatory rites that some leaders sponsor. Batuque rituals, then, are still an important aspect of cult life, but they are not simply imperfect copies of those held in the more conservative groups.[86]

A batuque ceremony is preceded by a smoke purification of the cult center, a practice which is not common in the conservative cults. The ceremony itself opens with a short prayer by the *pai de santo* to the saints; in important ceremonies a *ladainha* (series of chanted prayers) may last half an hour or longer. After the Exus are dismissed by songs, Averekete is called, except on special occasions when Badé, Ogun, or another spirit may be summoned first. Usually Rainha Barba is called next and then the spirit in whose honor the batuque is being given. Otherwise there is no special order, except that ordinarily the *senhores* are called before the *caboclos*.[87]

Possession is the ultimate proof of the existence of the encantados. While some mediums seem to have had psychotic episodes in their past, the Leacocks argue that it is not necessary for a medium to be abnormal psychologically to achieve success. The behavior of the medium in trance is rational in the light of Batuque beliefs, and, for the most part, the medium communicates effectively with other people. For the Leacocks, "the essence of possession in the Batuque is enacting a role while in a psychological condition very similar to the hypnotic state." Learning is important in both hypnosis and trance, and in both cases individuals enact specific roles. For example, leaders, but not necessarily all mediums, are expected to give consultations while possessed by an encantado. Also, mediums of some standing, as well as male and female leaders, are expected to be able to enter trance on cue.[88]

Despite the trend toward individualism, Batuque rituals still have important social functions. They "certify to the larger society that the Batuque is in fact a religion and not simply a group of individuals who go into trance and carry on."[89]

The percentage of *pretos* (blacks) in the Batuque cult is higher than in the general population, in part because most Batuque members belong to the lower class and, in Belém, most dark-skinned individuals are in that class. The cult has twice as many white as black members. Leadership in the Batuque is not correlated with skin color. Of twenty-seven cult leaders among 180 devotees, three were *preto*, twelve were *moreno* (brown-skinned), and twelve were *branco* (white). This color distribution was approximately the same as that of the membership as a whole.[90]

The Leacocks cite Bastide's suggestion that the recent increase in nontraditional African-derived cults in Brazil is due largely to increased racial discrimination and exploitation accompanying industrialization. Bastide calls cults such as Umbanda "sects of imitation" and regards them as religions of a black proletariat, even though some of the groups

NEO-AFRICAN AND AFRICAN-DERIVED RELIGIONS

have white or mulatto leadership. In this view, such sects are outlets for racial protest on the part of blacks and *Caboclos* against white domination and serve as instrumentalities for the absorption of unassimilated blacks into the modern interracial society. According to the Leacocks, such an analysis is not relevant to the Batuque because the membership is not predominantly black, and they say that this would be true even if it were shown that dark-skinned individuals were predominant in the cult. Such individuals do not constitute a separate racial caste in Belém. Their dialect and their culture are indistinguishable from that of their lighter-skinned neighbors, and they are not separated spatially from them. Discrimination on the basis of color is slight compared with the problems of poverty faced daily by the lower socioeconomic class—long-term unemployment, illness (physical or mental), and marital difficulties.[91]

Unlike Camargo (1961, xii–xiii, 65–69, 96–97) and Willems (1966, 224–25), the Leacocks did not find that migration to the city is an important factor in the increase in mediumistic religions. Belém is neither so urban nor so impersonal as Rio de Janeiro and São Paulo, but its economic and health problems are similar. Mediumistic religions such as spiritualism and Pentecostalism, as well as Batuque, are prospering in Belém as in the southern cities. Possession religions in Belém, however, attract native-born, lower-class individuals to a greater extent than recent arrivals from the rural areas. The Leacocks argue that in a religion where trance is an important activity, it is impossible to account for membership strictly in terms of sociological variables. Psychological factors, particularly the aptitude (especially important for those who become mediums) to go into trance, must also be considered.[92]

In the ideology of the Batuque, few expressions of hostility have been found toward a racial or social elite, and there is no evidence of the "symbolic subversion of the traditional power structure" that Willems (1966, 226–30) mentioned for the Pentecostalists. On the contrary, the major encantados are identified with the upper classes. These spirits are called *senhores, brancos,* and *gente fina* (refined people) and are always treated with respect. Lower-class spirits (*caboclos*) are considered subservient to the *senhores.* They appear later at ceremonies, defer to the chief encantado of their medium, and retire quickly if they meet a *senhor.* [93] Batuque ideology, then, "seems to reflect not only a society divided into

NEO-AFRICAN AND AFRICAN-DERIVED RELIGIONS

two strata, but a society in which the lower class knows its place and keeps it."[94]

The Urban Macoumba in Brazil

In the early stages of industrialization in Brazil, blacks gained a means of earning a living and of social ascent, but they lagged far behind poor whites and recent immigrants in economic competition. In the largest cities, some African religions lost their traditional values. At first, the *macoumba* consisted of the introduction of certain orisha into the *caboula* (a Bantu cult). As the solidarity of class began to replace the solidarity of (African) "nations," it became a syncretism of elements from African and American Indian religions, popular Catholicism, and the spiritualism of Allan Kardec (a form of French spiritualism introduced into Brazil in the nineteenth century).[95] In the absence of a collective memory, each priest invented new forms of ritual and new spirits. The new forms were accepted by men and women who had nothing in common except their place at the bottom of society.

The devotees of *macoumba* became mediums, and the singing (in Portuguese) and dancing induce possession by the spirits of the dead rather than the orisha. Spiritualism has played an increasingly important role in the cult, but the spirits are now divided into such categories as suffering spirits, malevolent furies, and benevolent spirits. The African concept of reincarnation has been revised to refer to a return of the souls of the dead to atone for the sins of their previous existence.[96]

In the *macoumba* of Espirito Santo, the *eshu* are summoned to "open the way" for the orisha to come to the ceremony. Following this Yoruban-based part of the ritual, the "Ancient Negroes" and the "caboclos" are summoned—a rite that is both spiritualist and Indian. In the *macoumba* of Rio and the state of Guanabara, eshu, orisha, disembodied souls, and caboclos are invoked randomly by spontaneous trances. Dogma appears only in the "spiritualism of Umbanda."[97]

The transformation of the candomblé in Rio de Janeiro into the *macoumba* was characterized by violent possessions, advice given by spirits, animal sacrifices, use of incense, drumming, and chalking of designs on the ground (similar to making "verver" in Haitian *vondun*). It has passed increasingly from religion to magic, and the isolated sorcerer

NEO-AFRICAN AND AFRICAN-DERIVED RELIGIONS

has replaced the organized *macoumba*. Some whites, often foreigners (Portuguese and Spanish), and some Japanese have become *macoumberos*. *Macoumbas* in São Paulo show the same cultural mixture as in Rio except that the trance is limited to the *macoumbeiro* who receives the spirit of an African or a *caboclo* at a private ceremony or a magical consultation. Rural *macoumbas* are essentially individualistic and consist mainly of consultations with sick persons or those seeking revenge. According to Bastide: "The candomblé was and remains a means of social control, an instrument of solidarity and communion; the *macoumba* ends in social parasitism, or in the release of immoral tendencies, of rape, often of assassination."[98]

Religions of Blacks in Surinam

In Surinam, slave revolts began about the middle of the seventeenth century. Refugees who escaped to the surrounding jungle established villages in the interior of the country. Known as "Bush Negroes," these former slaves reconstituted much of their ancestral African culture. Their descendants are still called Bush Negroes in contrast to the more Europeanized "town Negroes" of Paramaribo. A group of blacks living in the Para region between Paramaribo and the hinterland is intermediate culturally between the town and the Bush Negroes.

The Winti Cult in Paramaribo. In 1928–29, the six principal groups of *winti* (gods) of Surinam town Negroes were of African origin. First, the *winti* dances to the seven Thunder gods (Kromanti gods of the Sky) include *Sofia Bada. Bade* is the most powerful member of the *So* (Thunder) pantheon in Dahomey. The second group, the Earth gods, are headed by the Earth-Mother whose "strong" (ritual) names included *Asase* (the Ghanian name for Earth Deity), *Aida, Waisa, Aisa,* or *Awanaisa* (in Fon, *Ai* means earth, and occurs in sacred names). In the third group, and among women the most prevalent types of *winti,* are those associated with snakes, but these gods overlap all of the categories of winti. Among these deities are Dagowe (the equivalent of *Dagbe,* an Ewe-Fon word for a sacred snake) and *Aninino* (the sacred python, *Onini,* of the Ashanti).

The fourth category of *winti* are associated with the river, but some of these gods enter into the group of snake deities, since the constrictor lives both in the water and on land. The Kromanti gods make up the fifth group, including *Opete* (a Twi word for vulture; in Ghana the vulture is the messenger who takes sacrifices to the gods). In the last main category are the gods of the bush, including the *Apuku,* little people of the bush, and the *kankantri,* the silk-cotton tree. The latter tree is sacred in West Africa; in Dahomey the souls of ancestors are believed to have resided in them. The *Apuku* correspond to the "little people" of the forest in West African belief—the *ijimere* of the Yoruba, the *mmoatia* of the Ashanti, and the *azizan* of Dahomey—and to similar supernatural beings in the New World—the *papa-bois* in Trinidad and the *'saci* in Brazil. In addition to these groups, the Herskovitses mentioned individual *winti* under the heading of "African spirits." Of outstanding importance among these spirits is *Leba,* the guardian of the crossroads (worshipped as the divine trickster in Dahomey).[99]

The Winti Cult in the Para Region. The Para region begins about 20 kilometers from Paramaribo and is intermediate between the capital and the hinterland, the territory of the Bush Negroes. Its villages are remnants of the former plantations that were cultivated by slaves.

In this polytheistic religion of the lower social strata of the Creole population in Surinam (persons of mixed Dutch and Negro ancestry), a god gives prosperity to those who worship him and punishes those who refuse to obey. Other names for this religion are *wenu, adjida, avodu* (from the Dahomean word *vodun*), *gado, jeje,* and *afkodré. Winti* means wind, and the gods are as invisible as the wind. Gods of the cosmos, the earth, the forest, and the water live in a stratified order that parallels the structure of human society. These gods were created by God or *Anana* (*Nanā* is the name of a Dahomean deity). Most of the *winti* are regarded as fallen angels who rose against God under the command of Lucifer (Mama Aisa) the supreme god on earth.

The geographical origin of most of the *winti* in Para cannot be determined. The Kromanti and Luango *winti,* however, are related to the Kromanti and Loango tribes. Legba, of the Fon, is called Leba. The *Apuku* are the equivalent of the *mmoatia* of the Ashanti. In Para, the *Apuku* and *Leba* have the lowest social positions, and Leba may not appear at a ceremony.[100]

In Paranegro belief, the soul has two parts: the *kra,* which is the source of a person's energy and corresponds to the concept of the *kra* among the Akan in Ghana, and the *jorka*. After death, the *jorka* leaves the body and leads an independent existence in the *dede kondre,* the realm of the dead. The *jorka* warns the living members of the family against harmful magic and evil influences in the world. This spirit is good or bad, depending on the character of the bearer.[101]

A *wisi-man* is a conjurer who becomes possessed by a malicious god and who has the power to order malicious spirits (*bakrus* and *papa-snekis*) to injure others. The opposite of the *wisi-man* is the *bonu-man* or *obia-man,* a person who can offset the former's evil deeds. A patient suffering from a serious disease consults a *luku-man* (seer), and, after the diagnosis, goes to the *bonu-man* for the healing ritual. After that ritual, the *kra* of the cured person must be made content with a dinner and a gold or silver necklace.[102]

The *winti* rites include some elements that are common to both Europe and Africa. Among these parallel traditions are the belief in and interpretation of dreams, and the concept of the werewolf, which is called *azema* in Surinam. Among the items of European origin are: the mirror used by the *bonu-man* in diagnosing; the story of the fall of the angels under Lucifer's leadership; the *switi watra,* the herb-bath containing such essences as rosewater, almond-spirit, and vanilla extract; Roman Catholic holy water; candles; alcoholic and nonalcoholic drinks; and cotton materials worn around the waist and the shawl. Wooding concludes, however, that the great majority of the elements of the *Winti* cult are reinterpreted Africanisms such as the multiple soul, the four realms of the *winti,* the death-rites, songs, and dances.[103]

The Winti Cult of the Djukas. The Djukas, one of the six Bush Negro tribes, live in the immense forest south of the savanna area of Surinam. These people are part of the descendants of the runaway slaves of the late seventeenth and the eighteenth centuries. The Djuka gods constitute a hierarchy under the Supreme God, Nana, or Nana Kediampon, or Nijankapon, the creator who remains remote from the human race. Nana has no special priests and very few offerings or prayers for protection are given to him. The principal Djuka gods are Grantata or Gran Gadu (also known as Sweli Gadu and Gwangwella), and Gedeunsu (Gede is a Dahomean deity). The first is served by the priests of the Oto clan, the second by the priests and priestesses of the Pedi clan. A number of minor gods, benevolent and malevolent, stand below the two major deities. This dichtomy is not clear-cut because the benevolent gods can be angered if neglected, and the malevolent deities may be appeased by the presentation of many offerings. These minor gods manifest themselves in human beings and one who is so possessed may be consulted while in a trance. The deity reveals through his medium the cause of illness, an accident, or other troubles, together with the appropriate cure (offerings, medicines, rites of purification). Thus the priests and *obiamans* (healers) are not the only ones who may be consulted about illnesses and misfortunes. The term for harmful magic is *wisi,* and the *obiaman's* opposing force is the witch, the *wisiman.* [104]

Another group that plays an important role among the Djukas as intermediary between living persons and the gods are the spirits of the deceased, the *jorkas.* The spirit retains the characteristics of the deceased. The *jorkas* fall into three categories: the Granjorkas, who performed great deeds during life and whose prayers are always heard by the gods; the *jorkas,* spirits who did not distinguish themselves while alive, but who were virtuous people; and the evil *jorkas* (*takru*) or wrongdoers in the community who continue to perform bad deeds and to bother the living. [105]

The religious duties of the High Priest and his staff are comprehensive, and they often take over tasks of civil government when religious aspects are involved. The priests give assistance to those who seek help from one of the gods, especially explanations of the causes of illness or death. Another duty of the priests is the administering of the "sacraments," rites performed for the purposes of healing and protecting. Such rituals include the exorcism of a witch or avenging spirit who is thought to have possessed a person, or a ceremony where one who is suspected of being a witch can swear that this is not true. A third duty of the priests is the staging of purification rites—rites related to the disposition of the estate left by one who has been put to death by the Great God because the deceased was a witch or committed some other offense against divine law, as well as rites concerned with the division of inheritances left by other deceased persons among the following: the Great God, the High Priest and his staff, and the next of kin. [106]

NEO-AFRICAN AND AFRICAN-DERIVED RELIGIONS

The Religion of the Boni in French Guiana

Three groups of people live in the basin of the Maroni River in western French Guiana: the Creoles—"persons of color" who lead individualistic lives and who have adopted some aspects of European life; the descendants of the rebellious slaves of the eighteenth century—Djukas, Saramaka, and Boni—whose customs and dialects (variations of *taki-taki*) are similar; and Amerindians. The exact origin of the "Black Refugees" is not known; most of their ancestors were brought from the Guinea coast of West Africa, but others were from further south, from the Congo and Angola.[107]

The religion of the Bush Negroes is a synthesis of elements of the religions of various West African peoples, especially the Ashanti, the Agni, the Mina, and the Fon, but also of the Congolese. This synthesis seems to have originated with the Saramaka, the first tribe constituted at the beginning of the eighteenth century, and to have been adopted with some modifications when the Djuka tribe was formed about 1760. The Boni, the last tribe to take shape, probably took over these beliefs during the period of servitude that they spent under the tutelage of the Djuka from 1815 to 1860. The Boni number approximately 1,000 persons in a population of 36,000.[108]

The supreme God of the Boni is Nana, more commonly called Masa Gadu (Kedi Amu and Kediampon in the Kumenti dialect), the creator of the lesser gods and all those who live on earth. According to the older people among the Boni, the first humans God created were a brother and a sister, Adam and Eve. This biblical myth, transposed by African thought, explains the beliefs of the Bush Negroes concerning twins.[109]

Through the ancestors of the living, Masa Gadu may intervene in human affairs, but for the most part he does not interfere with the actions of the lesser gods. The great gods of the Djukas—Gwangwéla and Gédéosu—are unknown to the Boni. There is no cult of Mada Gadu; there are no priests, no temples, and no ceremonies in his honor. Nevertheless, he is always present in the religious life of the Boni, associated especially with the cult of the ancestors. All ceremonies include an invocation to Masa Gadu, and, from time to time, he is invoked in cases of illness. One who believes that he is the victim of a malediction may petition Gadu.[110]

NEO-AFRICAN AND AFRICAN-DERIVED RELIGIONS

The cult of Odun is a basic feature of the social and religious life of the Bush Negroes. This secret cult, common among the Boni and the Saramaka, corresponds to the cult of Gwangwéla (Grantata) among the Djuka. Myths to explain the relationships between Nana and Odun are lacking, but it is clear that Odun was sent to mankind by Masa Gadu as law-giver and judge. The laws of Odun are negative; certain acts are forbidden to Bush Negroes who have taken a binding oath. Odun punishes violators by death or illness without the intervention of men.

Odun forbids: (1) sorcery (actions designed to kill); (2) vengeance (if one believes he is a victim of witchcraft, he must not invoke counter-witchcraft or invoke his ancestors against his enemy; one can only seek protection of *obia* (positive magic)—sooner or later Odun will kill the witch); (3) violence (it is a grave offense against Odun to make human blood flow); (4) restraint on the liberty of persons to reside in a particular place; and (5) all evocation of the spirits of the dead other than public ceremonies prescribed by custom; for example, no one can go to the cemetery to pray individually at the grave of his ancestors. Violence can be pardoned if the offender repents and makes an offering of tafia (rum) or leaves of tobacco in the chapel for Odun.[111]

Among the Boni, there are four categories of inferior divinities:

1. A series of gods who differ somewhat, but who have the same general nature—all speak the Kumenti dialect, and all are well disposed toward men and do not work *kunu* (witchcraft) against them.
    a. The *Kumeñti,* who have the appearance of jaguars and reside in the bush.
    b. The *Djadja,* who look like ocelots.
    c. The *Opete,* who look like vultures.
    d. The *Bũnsunki,* who look like Indian women and who reside in rivers.
2. *Ampuku.* Formidable gods of the bush capable of performing witchcraft (*kunu*) against humans. They speak a dialect that is well known among the Saramaka, but no one in Boni country speaks it. When they wish to be understood, they speak the ordinary Saramaka dialect. They appear at night in the bush dressed in a fashion that is unfamiliar to the Bush Negroes. They appear to be black men, but are unknown. Some are good,

some are bad; they can be conciliated by cult rituals developed mainly in Saramaka country. Possessions by these gods are rare.[112]

3. *Vodū* or *Papa gadu.* Still more formidable gods who incarnate themselves in the boa snake *dagowe.* They speak the Papa dialect.

4. The very formidable *Kāntamasu.* Gods of the *termitières* (termites' nests), who speak a language that no one understands and who use the *Kumēnti* dialect to make themselves understood.[113]

The *Kumēnti* gods, common to the Saramaka (Kromenti), Djuka, and Boni, are regarded as benevolent; their possession is much desired. In principle, only men can obtain *Kumēnti,* and only women can have *Būnsunki.* The *Kumēnti* are specialists in protection against fire and against sword and gun wounds. This cult is important in magic—even those who do not become possessed try to obtain from these gods an *obia* (charm) that will protect them against various dangers.[114]

The cult of *Kumēnti* has declined in recent years. Hurault found that as people try to earn money, they travel more, and that makes it difficult to hold ceremonies and dances. Because many who are ill are cared for in the hospital at Maripasoula, the Boni have less need for the cult of *Kumēnti.* Although the chapels dedicated to the *Kumēnti* were crumbling by 1956, great importance was still attached to *Kumēnti* charms, especially those protecting against swords and guns, and to the *Kumēnti bui,* the divination instrument.[115]

The *Būnsunki* possess only women, and possessions are infrequent. Men, however, may perceive *Būnsunki* in dreams and receive benefits. The *Vodū* are ill-natured and vindictive gods, highly respected but greatly feared. Taking the form of a boa, they reside in water and in certain trees. *Vodu* can possess either sex, and they often bring *kunu* (misfortune) to a lineage. They do not always represent an evil principle, nor do the *Kumēnti* always represent a good principle. The possession cult of *Papa gadu* is not declining, but the majority of the forty or fifty persons living on one river who had a *Papa gadu* in 1956 were old women. If a devotee respects the rules of the *Vodū,* he has nothing to fear. Possession by *Papa gadu* does not have the brutal character that possession by the *Kumēnti* has. *Papa gadu* are consulted especially to discover the causes of misfortune.[116]

NEO-AFRICAN AND AFRICAN-DERIVED RELIGIONS

Possession is the normal means of communication between the gods and men, and these incidents have a profound effect on the social life of the Bush Negroes. During possession a supernatural being (divinity, spirit of an ancestor) enters the body of a human being and speaks through him. The main reasons for desiring a *gadu* (spirit who possesses one) are to succeed in life, to be protected from enemies, to be respected, and to be helpful to one's lineage. In 1956, approximately one in six or seven adult men became possessed by a deity, and one in three or four adult women.[117] Hurault concludes that the possession cults in French Guiana differ from those of blacks in Brazil and in Haiti; they do not seem to be directly related to African religions.[118]

The Boni do not have religious fraternities properly speaking. There are only teachers (*bas*) who have been taught by other masters and who teach a small group of disciples (*kineki*), without regard to their villages or lineages, on their own responsibility. These teachers do not become possessed themselves, but they are thought to know the procedures which allow a neophyte to obtain possession with the minimum risk of getting an undesirable instead of a desirable *gadu* to come. The neophytes are taught the rudiments of the language of the divinity, the infusions of leaves to offer, and, in certain cults, formulas inviting the gods to come. The pupils are also taught individually or collectively to dance in the manner of the god. If a god is satisfied with a pupil, he will come into him. The idea of a spiritual death and resurrection of the possessed does not seem to have been retained by the Bush Negroes.[119]

The Bush Negroes understand the relationship between their beliefs and the Christian beliefs of the people among whom they live. They think they worship the same god as the Christians but in a different but also valid manner. They are not antagonistic to the Catholic or Protestant clergy, and most of them wear crosses or medallions. They see no contradiction between their beliefs and Christianity, and reportedly they do not intend to abandon their religion.[120]

North America:
Blacks in the Historical Churches of the United States and Canada

Religion and the Slaves in the Colonial Period

IN 1619 twenty Africans were sold as slaves to settlers in Jamestown, Virginia, by the captain of a Dutch man-of-war. In 1624, a Negro child was baptized, and from that time on Negroes were baptized in most of the oldest churches in the South.[1] As the number of Negro Christians in the colonies gradually increased, peculiar problems arose for the white church members. Clergymen were reproached for admitting Negroes into the church while they were held as slaves. Opposition to the christening of Negroes gradually disappeared when laws were enacted providing that slaves did not become free through accepting the Christian faith and baptism.

Although slaves were baptized and admitted to the Anglican church during the seventeenth century, the Church of England did not attempt to Christianize Negroes in America until the beginning of the eighteenth century. The Society for the Propagation of the Gospel in Foreign Parts was formed in London in 1701 to supply religious institutions among the inhabitants of the North American colonies: first, to the members of the established Church of England, and, second, to the Indians and Negroes. When the Indians in South Carolina reacted in a hostile way to the first missionary sent out by the Society, he turned his attention to the Negro slaves. Unfortunately, little is known about the religious behavior of blacks who were converted to Christianity through the efforts of this Society's missionaries.[2]

In colonial America the black church member was dealt with either by making him a subordinate member of a white church or as a member of a Negro church under the general supervision of whites. In the former case, where there were only a few Negroes in the churches, they were segregated in the gallery or certain pews, which they entered by a side door. If there were many Negroes and few whites in these congregations, usually separate buildings were used or the same churches were occupied at different hours.[3]

As the work of missionaries increased the number of black converts, the fears of the masters grew, and legislative acts such as one enacted by North Carolina in 1715 were passed. This law stated,

> That if any master or owner of Negroes or slaves, or any other person or persons whatsoever in the government, shall permit or suffer any Negro or Negroes to build on their, or either of their, lands, or any part thereof, any house under pretense of a meeting-house upon account of worship, or upon any pretense whatsoever, and shall not suppress and hinder them, he, she, or they so offending, shall, for every default, forfeit and pay fifty pounds, one-half toward defraying the contingent charges of the government, the other to him or them that shall sue for the same.[4]

This law made it necessary for white churches to admit Negro members, and other colonies enacted similar legislation.

Maryland passed a law in 1723 "to suppress tumultuous meetings of slaves on Sabbath and other holy days," an act intended to preserve good order but one which tended to check independent religious meetings among Negroes. In 1770 Georgia forbade slaves "to assemble on pretense of feasting," and any constable, on direction of a justice, was commanded to disperse any assembly or meeting of slaves "which may disturb the peace or endanger the safety of his Majesty's subjects; and every slave which may be found at such meeting, as aforesaid, shall and may, by order of such justice, immediately be corrected, without trial, by receiving on the bare back twenty-five stripes, with a whip, switch, or cowskin. . . ."[5] Whether such laws actually curbed the religious meetings of the slaves is uncertain, but it seems likely that they did even though some of the disorder and turmoil among slaves undoubtedly cloaked itself under the name of religion.[6]

In 1774, two members of the Brethren (Moravians), Lewis Muller and George Wagner, came from Europe to America, and the next year they were joined by Andrew Broesing, of North Carolina. Taking up residence on a Georgia plantation, they preached to whites and attempted to evangelize the Negro slaves. All three suffered from "the fevers" which prevailed in Georgia, and their preaching soon came to an end. Muller left after a few months; the two remaining Brethren, called upon to bear arms when the war of independence broke out, gave up their work by 1779. Apparently, the colonists nowhere assigned a missionary exclusively to the Africans, nor was a society established within the colonies for the purpose of promoting their religious instruction.[7]

One solution to the problem of what to do about the Negroes' participation in formal religion was to train teachers and preachers for the slaves from their own ranks. Among the first of these preachers was Harry Hosier, a man who traveled with the Methodist Bishop Asbury and often filled appointments for him. Another was George Leile (Lisle), sometimes called Sharp, after the surname of his master, who was born in Virginia about 1750. Before the Revolutionary War, his master moved to Burke County, Georgia, where he became a deacon in a Baptist church of which Rev. Matthew Moore was pastor. George Lisle was converted, baptized, and given the right to preach. He was manumitted and, migrating to Jamaica in 1783, organized a Baptist church in Kingston. Shortly after Leile left Georgia, a black man named Andrew Bryan began to preach to blacks and whites in Savannah. On January 20, 1788, he became minister of the First African Baptist Church in that city. He and his followers were forbidden to carry on religious services, but they persisted nevertheless. Their evening meetings were frequently disrupted and those present were whipped. Bryan and his brother, Sampson, were twice imprisoned. When being whipped publicly, Andrew Bryan declared that he would continue to preach about Christ. In the end, his critics were silenced by his forbearance and influential white patrons came to his support. The civil authority gave him liberty to hold his religious gatherings under certain regulations, and his master provided the use of his barn where he preached for two years with little interference.[8]

Though the Anglican church carried on some missionary work among the slaves, they were not concerned with changing the Negroes' status as bondsmen. The Quakers opposed the system of slavery, advocated religious training of the slaves as preparation for freedom, and, in many cases, freed their slaves and worked to remove the legal restrictions against private manumission.[9] This opposition to slavery on the part of the Quakers alone was relatively ineffective, but after 1750 Methodists and Baptists included the cause as a part of their religion.[10] According to Frazier, the relation of the free Negroes to whites became a real issue only when the Negroes were evangelized by the latter two denominations.[11]

All students of the religious life of black Americans agree that the evangelicals had a great advantage over the Anglicans and other early missionaries. Evangelical religion was straightforward, personal, and not highly ritualistic. It appealed to the untutored masses, white and black, of the colonial frontier. To become a Methodist or a Baptist it was not necessary to know the creed, the catechism and other articles of faith, and to be able to follow the ritual of the service. It was necessary only to repent and to accept Christ as a personal Savior. During the Great Awakenings (1720–1740 and 1790–1815) enthusiasm ran high for reaching blacks with the gospel, and large numbers of Negroes were converted. The emotionalism of the early evangelical faith helped to set the nature of black worship. In the religion to which the Negro masses were exposed, shouting, dancing, weeping, jerking, and speaking in tongues played prominent parts. These aspects of worship were believed to be proof that the Spirit was "at work in the heart of man, and they were also taken as evidence of the depth and sincerity of the conversion."[12]

By the nineteenth century, few American Negro slaves had failed to come under the influence of some type of Christian religious instruction.[13] Nevertheless, only a minority of the blacks regularly attended church at the opening of the century, and, as a group, their religious instruction was greatly neglected.[14]

The Absorption of African Traditions into Black Folk Religion

Genovese asserts that the power of the whites, the existence of small plantation and farm units, and the early closing of the slave trade crushed much of the memory that blacks had of African religions.[15] Nevertheless, certain features of African tradition were absorbed into black folk religion. Since dancing was sinful, black Methodists "shouted." The "shouting," however, "could not have been more clearly African." It included clapping hands, beating time with feet, walking in a ring in single file, shouting, dancing in the manner of the Charleston, and singing in the call-and-response pattern. Spirit possession appeared much less frequently among the slaves in the United States than among those who participated in *vodun* in Haiti or in the African-derived cults in Brazil, but ecstatic seizures did occur.[16]

Among the slaves, beliefs about the Devil were closer to the character of Legba of the Dahomeans or the Yoruban Eshu than to the whites' Satan. These West African trickster-gods can be beneficent as well as malevolent; much depends upon the way they are treated by human beings. The tradition which holds nothing to be entirely good or entirely bad, deeply embedded in African thought, was reflected in the belief of the slaves that the Devil could be a friend in need.[17]

The conversion experience is common to fundamentalist Christianity in the southern United States, but one element has "an unmistakeable African flavor." The "little man" in the conversion stories told by black rural Southerners in the late 1920s bears a strong resemblance to Legba, the West African divinity who intervenes in the lives of men, acts as a messenger of the other gods, and announces death. Rawick comments that this kind of personal relationship with the deities was natural to the African slave in the New World. The "little man" who "announces death and is associated with tricks and mischief appears before the sinner as the symbol of his misdeeds, as the announcer of death and as the bringer of good fortune—the spiritual rebirth of conversion."[18]

NORTH AMERICA

Another belief of African origin that was prevalent during the slavery period and has persisted in parts of the rural South and in urban areas is the conviction that the dead can return to earth in spiritual visitations that are helpful or dangerous to the living.[19] During the 1920s Puckett found folk beliefs about the soul among southern blacks that resemble traditional African ideas.[20]

In many of the clandestine prayer meetings held in a cabin in slave quarters or in a grove of trees that was believed to be sacred, an upturned iron kettle or pot was used in an attempt to deaden the sounds of the singing and shouting. It is doubtful if the pots were effective for that purpose, but they may have been a continuation of certain West African traditions. Among the Yoruba, pots are symbols of the gods who provide protection to their followers. In Dahomey, there is a ceremonial pot for each ancestor. In the New World, a reinterpretation of the African belief that certain ceremonial pots were associated with supernatural protection may have given the slaves courage to hold prayer meetings in places where such meetings were prohibited.[21]

Many of the elements in the initiations that Zora Hurston underwent in various cult groups in the southern states in the 1930s corresponded with practices in West Africa, and in Catholic countries in the New World where traditional African beliefs have persisted. Among these were seclusion of the novitiate, fasting, wearing of special clothing, dancing, spirit possession, sacrifices, acquiring a new name, and references to running streams of water and to thunder and lightning.[22]

During slavery and later, a fervent commitment to Christianity among blacks was widely accompanied with belief in witchcraft. Abundant evidence exists of hoodoo's syncretism of African, European, and American Indian beliefs and practices.[23] In the antebellum period, voodoo was never a major force outside New Orleans. For the most part, the hoodoo of the plantation slaves was unorganized conjuring and healing, but as its reputation spread, it "strengthened the slaves' commitment to the folk aspect of their religion and their sense of being in the hands of powers other than those of the whites."[24]

Genovese makes the important point that if the slaves and free Negroes of the cities had not gained some degree of control of the churches from the whites, folk beliefs might not have been incorporated so easily into black Christianity. According to this view: "Without that degree of autonomy within the structure of formal religion folk belief might have remained an antithesis, and the slaves might have had to make the hard choice between Christianity and an anti-Christianity."[25]

Religion and the Institution of Slavery in the Nineteenth Century in the United States

The Haitian revolution of the 1790s soon had an effect on the master class of the southern United States. New state laws were passed as safeguards against rebellion. In 1800 South Carolina enacted a law stating that,

> It shall not be lawful for any number of slaves, free Negroes, mulattoes, or mestizoes, even in company with white persons, to meet together and asssemble for the purpose of mental instruction or religious worship, either before the rising of the sun or after the going down of the same. And all magistrates, sheriffs, militia officers, etc., etc., are hereby vested with power, etc., for dispersing such assemblies.[26]

When the white churches petitioned, the rigor of this law was slightly modified in 1803. A similar law in Virginia in 1804 forbidding all evening meetings of slaves was modified in 1805 to permit a slave, accompanied by a white person, to listen to a white minister. In addition, a master was "allowed" to employ a religious teacher for his slaves. Similar laws were passed by Mississippi.

In 1831, Virginia forbade slaves and free Negroes alike to preach or to attend religious services at night without permission. In North Carolina slaves and free Negroes were forbidden by law to preach, exhort, or teach "in any prayer-meeting or other association for worship where slaves of different families are collected together." Maryland and Georgia enacted similar laws. In Mississippi a law of 1831 declared that it was "unlawful for any slave, free Negro, or mulatto to preach the gospel" on penalty of thirty-nine lashes upon the naked back. A Negro who received written permission from his master might preach to the Negroes in his immediate neighborhood, providing six respectable white slave-owners were present. In 1832 Alabama forbade the assembling of more than five male slaves off the plantation to which they belonged, but attendance at public worship held by white persons was not forbidden.[27] It should be remembered that legislators, fearing insurrection, grew panicky during the early nineteenth century and passed a variety of laws that were harsher than the treatment often given to slaves.

Because of the antislavery views of southern Baptists and Methodists in the eighteenth and early nineteenth centuries, many slaveholders looked with disfavor upon the work of these denominations among their slaves. Later, southern clergymen became supporters of slavery and the master class came to regard organized religion as an ally, as "the best instrument to preserve peace and good conduct among the negroes."[28]

In a well-known work published in 1842, Jones set forth the objections often given at that time to providing religious instruction for Negroes in the slave states, gave replies to those objections, and explained the benefits to masters and slaves of such instruction. To the objection that "If we suffer our Negroes to be instructed the tendency will be to change the civil relations of society as now constituted," he replied that "we separate entirely their *religious* and their *civil* condition, and contend that the one may be attended to without interfering with the other. . . ." To the second objection: "If we suffer our Negroes to be religiously instructed, the way will be opened for men from abroad to enter in and inculcate doctrines subversive of our interests and safety," he replied that "the *Gospel* is not feared, but *the agents* by whom it is preached. . . . the most effectual method to preclude the introduction of improper teachers, is for us to *take the religious instruction of our Negroes into our own hands, and to superintend it ourselves.*" To the objection that "the religious instruction will lead to neglect of duty and insubordination," Jones replied in part: "The Gospel recognizes the condition in which the Negroes are, and inculcates the duties appropriate to it." To a fourth objection: "The Negroes will embrace seasons of religious worship, for originating and executing plans of insubordination and villany," he replied that "a proper regulation of the times and places of meeting, and the faithful supervision of religious teachers, assisted by deacons and elders, or planters, would preclude all serious disorders." Finally, to the objection that "religious instruction will do no good; it will only make the Negroes worse men and worse hypocrites," he asked:

"Why should the Gospel produce an effect on Negroes, contrary to that which it is designed to produce, and which it actually produces on all other men, and on some whose condition is worse than theirs?" The benefits to be derived from the religious instruction of the slaves were given as: (1) Better understanding of the relations of master and servant: and of their reciprocal duties; (2) the pecuniary interests of masters will be advanced; (3) increased safety; (4) the promotion of morality and religion of the masters; (5) much unpleasant discipline will be saved the churches; (6) the souls of our servants will be saved.[29]

As the slaveholders themselves gave more attention to religion in the late antebellum period, they increasingly paid white ministers to preach to their slaves. Moreover, "if preachers could not come, or even if they could, the slaveholders would preach to the slaves themselves, and their wives would conduct Sunday school for the children or Bible readings for the adults."[30] The dominant whites were careful to provide a censored version of Christianity for the slaves. Special catechisms and sermons were prepared for them, and special instructions were given to their religious teachers. In *Suggestions on the Religious Instruction of the Negroes in the Southern States,* issued by the Presbyterian Board of Publications in 1847, missionaries were advised to ignore the civil condition "of the slave and to listen to no complaints against masters or overseers." In preaching to the bondsmen missionaries should condemn "every vice and evil custom," advocate the "discharge of every duty," and support the "peace and order of society." They were asked to teach the slaves to give "respect and obedience [to] all those whom God in his providence has placed in authority over them."[31]

Parts of the Bible, such as the Lord's Prayer and the Ten Commandments, were favored by the master class for the religious instruction of the slaves. Bible stories were dramatized for the bondsmen and incidents and characters were related to the experiences of Negroes. Many passages of the Old Testament reinforced the religious sentiments of the slaves, but the book of Exodus was preeminently appropriate. Black religionists told and retold the story of the deliverance of the Jews from slavery in Egypt and the possession of the land promised to their fathers.[32]

NORTH AMERICA

Religion and the Slave Revolts in the United States

Much has been written about the role of religion in making the antebellum southern Negroes submissive and obedient. Benjamin Mays called this religion "otherworldly" and "compensatory," and E. Franklin Frazier advanced the same thesis. Harding does not deny the sedative quality of much of the religion of the slaves, but he suggests that there were black responses to religion which went beyond submissiveness to defiance.[33]

Black religionists were neither reckless nor ultraconservative men; they realized the risks involved in insurrection on the part of inexperienced and unarmed slaves and they acted with caution and constraint.[34] Most of the slave preachers did not advocate insurrection. They pictured the delights and the glories of a more just world to come, but for many of them the "otherworldliness" of their preaching was an interim strategy to provide emotional relief from the hardships of slavery. Wilmore calls this kind of otherworldliness "otherworldliness-disruptive" and asserts that the black Christian's hope for a better world in the future was accompanied in his daily intercourse with whites by subterfuge, sabotage, the slowdown, pretended stupidity, obsequiousness, and other types of resistance used as tactics of survival.[35]

Religion was one of the factors that contributed to some of the major slave insurrections, but the religious influence in the conspiracies cannot be attributed to the white churches in the North or the South, the Christian antislavery societies of the North, or the Methodist circuit riders. Inspiration for the revolts came from slaves themselves or from former slaves who had become ministers of or who had attended the new independent black churches in Baltimore, New York, Philadelphia, or other northern cities.[36]

The best-known of the slave revolts of the nineteenth century were those led by Gabriel Prosser, Denmark Vesey, and Nat Turner. Gabriel Prosser, a slave of Thomas Prosser, was a student of the Bible whose favorite hero was Samson. Believing that God had designated him as a deliverer of the Negro people, Prosser explained to his followers the parts of the Scripture which he believed referred to the condition of the black slaves and the necessity of attacking the Philistines, especially Judges 15. Thousands of slaves were involved in the plot to seize control of Henrico County, Virginia. About one thousand slaves gathered outside Richmond on the evening of August 30, 1800, for the attack, but a great storm caused them to disband in confusion. Even before the storm broke, two slaves revealed the plot to their master and the conspirators began to be arrested by the militia. Within a few days, 35 slaves were hanged, and on October 7 Prosser was executed.[37]

Denmark Vesey, leader of a revolt in South Carolina in 1822, was a member of a black congregation which broke away from the white Methodist church in 1817. The religious class system of the independent African Methodist Association of Charleston was used to recruit participants and to disseminate messages during the five-year period before the insurrection.[38] Vesey searched the Bible for texts to support his dreams of destroying the enemies of the blacks. Despite his careful planning, the conspirators were betrayed, and Vesey and his associates were hanged.

Nine years later the Nat Turner insurrection took place in Virginia. Born a slave in Southhampton County, Virginia in 1800, Nat Turner read the Bible avidly. Eventually he became convinced that he had been ordained to some "good purpose in the hands of the Almighty" and fled into the forests of Virginia as a runaway. After a month "a spirit" drove him from the forest, and in 1825 Turner had his first major vision foretelling his future. "White and black spirits were battling in the air. Thunder rang out, the sun was darkened, and he watched in awe as blood flowed through the land. The same spirit promised him the wisdom and strength needed for the task [ahead]."[39] After a number of visions, the main revelation came in May 1828. According to Turner: "I heard a loud noise in the heavens and the Spirit instantly appeared to me and said the Serpent was loosened, and Christ had laid down the Yoke he had bourne for the sins of men, and that I should take it on and fight against the Serpent; for the time was fast approaching when the first should be last and the last should be first."[40]

The Spirit had told him also that natural signs would appear to inform him when to start his messianic work. In an eclipse of the sun, Turner found that sign. Turner was not a formally ordained preacher; he was a religious charismatic. He exhorted his fellow slaves and convinced them that he had been chosen by God to deliver them.[41]

In the rebellion Turner led on August 21, 1831, about sixty white persons were killed, but seventy Negroes were surrounded and overcome by soldiers of the United States Army. Thirteen slaves and three free Negroes were immediately hanged; Turner was captured on October 20, tried, sentenced to death, and was hanged on November 11.[42]

Slave revolts anywhere in the Americas had poor prospects, but in the United States in the nineteenth century those prospects were practically zero. Although they were rare, the revolts served a purpose by combatting, among both whites and blacks, the myth of black docility.[43]

Racial Policies of Baptists and Methodists in the United States

Originally, most Negroes were either Baptists or Methodists. The First Baptist church in the North American colonies was established in Providence, Rhode Island, by Roger Williams in 1639. In 1690, the Baptist church in Charleston, South Carolina, was founded. By 1790 the denomination had churches throughout the middle and southern states. Revivals were common, and one which began in 1785 continued for six or seven years. According to Du Bois: "Thousands were converted and baptized, besides many who joined the Methodists and Presbyterians. A large number of Negroes were admitted to the Baptist churches during the seasons of revival, as well as on ordinary occasions. They were, however, not gathered into churches distinct from the whites south of Pennsylvania, except in Georgia."[44]

Under the supervision of whites, the Baptists permitted some Negroes to preach to Negro members as early as 1773, but these preachers had no voice in general church affairs. Nearly one-fourth of the 73,471 Baptists in the United States in 1793 were Negroes. Until the middle of the nineteenth century most Negro Baptists were affiliated with white churches, and in churches of mixed membership the blacks were often in the majority. In the latter churches, Negro members had no voice in decision-making except in the reception and discipline of members of their race.[45]

The early Baptists held few slaves; the Philadelphia Association approved abolition in 1789, and a Virginia Association advocated emancipation about the same time. Associations in Kentucky and Ohio were divided on the question. The Baptists took stands against the slave trade in 1818 and in 1835, and missionary Baptists actively proselyted among the slaves.[46]

Methodism was introduced in New York in 1766, and John Wesley sent forth the first Methodist missionaries from New York in 1769. The first conference of the church was held in Philadelphia in 1773, and from that year until 1776 there was a great revival of religion in Virginia. In 1780, the General Conference in America declared slavery "contrary to the laws of God, man and nature and hurtful to society." The Methodist church soon retreated from that stand by saying that it only sought the destruction of slavery "by all wise and prudent means," and ministers were allowed to hold slaves in slave states. In 1787, preachers were urged by the General Conference to work among slaves and receive worthy ones into full church membership. In parts of the South, the Methodists had so many members that their churches were often called Negro churches. In 1797, the 12,215 Negro Methodists constituted one-fourth of all Methodists in this country. According to Du Bois, the Methodists yielded further ground in 1816 to those who favored slavery, and in 1844 the censure of a bishop who married a slaveholder split the Methodist church on the question. By 1859, there were reportedly 468,000 Negro church members in the South, of whom 215,000 were Methodists and 175,000 Baptists. These sizeable memberships were attained despite the fact that many restrictions on the worship of blacks remained. In Maryland there were numerous local laws restricting worship—camp-meetings were forbidden, as were all meetings except those held in regular churches with the consent of white pastors. In other states the restrictive laws of the 1830s were still in effect or had been strengthened. In 1866, the General Conference of the Methodist Episcopal Church authorized the organization of separate congregations and annual conferences, and in 1870 two bishops were appointed to organize the black conferences into a separate and independent church. Later that year the Colored Methodist Episcopal Church (now the Christian Methodist Episcopal Church) was formed.[47]

After the Civil War, the largest body of Negroes was attracted to the Baptist church. The greater freedom which had characterized this church prior to emancipation continued and was a major factor in its expansion. Every man was said to be the equal of every other among the Negro Baptists, and it was easier for one to become a prominent figure in that church than in the Methodist church. Because of the whites' fear of insurrection, not many African Baptist churches were permitted in the South before the War. When the pressure was removed, many groups of Negroes formed Baptist churches.[48]

Racial Policies of the Episcopalians, Presbyterians, and Congregationalists in the United States

Although the Anglicans were first in evangelizing the slaves, the Protestant Episcopal Church bowed to its southern membership to preserve unity within the denomination and limited itself mainly to urging slaveholders to provide religious instruction for their slaves. The "Negro work" of the church was administered separately. Throughout the period of slavery, Negro clergymen or deputies were not permitted to attend the Protestant Episcopal convention or to participate in the general government of the church. Partly for this reason, the development of Episcopal churches among Negroes was difficult.[49]

Direct efforts on the part of Presbyterians for the religious instruction of Negroes began with the Reverend Samuel Davies and the Reverend John Todd in Virginia in the middle of the eighteenth century. In 1787, the Presbyterian Synod recommended that steps be taken toward gradual emancipation, and in 1795 the question of excluding slaveholders was discussed, but the outcome was an injunction of "brotherly love" for them. The question was discussed again in 1815 and in 1818; in 1835 further discussion was postponed, and in 1846 the question was dropped on the ground that Christ and the Apostles did not condemn slavery.[50] In 1833 the Presbyterian Synod of South Carolina and Georgia declared that the Negroes in the slave-holding states had no regular and efficient ministry and almost no churches and it also said that there was insufficient room in the white churches for their accommodation. At that time the Synod knew of only five churches in the South built expressly for the use of Negroes. In 1834, the same Synod said: "The gospel, as things are, can never be preached to the two classes (whites and blacks) successfully in conjunction. The galleries or back seats on the lower floor of white churches are generally appropriated to the Negroes, when it can be done without inconvenience to the whites. When it cannot be done conveniently, the Negroes must catch the gospel as it escapes through the doors and windows. If the master is pious, the house servants alone attend family worship, and frequently few of them, while the field hands have no attention at all. So far as masters are engaged in the work (of religious instruction of slaves), an almost unbroken silence reigns on this vast field."[51]

Also in 1834, the following declaration was made by the Presbyterian Synod of Kentucky: "Slavery deprives its subjects, in great measure, of the privileges of the gospel. The law, as it is here, does not prevent free access to the scriptures, but ignorance, the natural result of their condition, does. The Bible is before them. But it is to them a sealed book. Very few of them enjoy the advantages of a regular gospel ministry."[52]

In 1861 the General Assembly of the Presbyterian Church declared that "the slave system had generally proven 'kindly and benevolent' and had provided 'real effective discipline' to a people who could not be elevated in any other way. Slavery, it concluded, was the black man's 'normal condition.' "[53]

Proselyting by the Presbyterians resulted in fewer than 20,000 Negro members prior to the Civil War. Unlike the Methodists, the Presbyterians did not use a system of itinerant leaders to gather recruits, and the appeal of Presbyterianism was too intellectual to attract large numbers of Negroes. Woodson quotes Bishop Tanner as saying: "It strove to lift up without coming down and while the good Presbyterian parson was writing his discourses, rounding off the sentences, the Methodist itinerant had traveled forty miles with his horse and saddle bags; while the parson was adjusting his spectacles to read his manuscript, the itinerant had given hell and damnation to his repentant hearers; while the disciple of Calvin was waiting to have his church completed, the disciple of Wesley took to the woods and made them reecho with the voice of free grace, believing with Bryant, 'The groves were God's first temples.' "[54]

Although the leaders of the Congregational church "sympathized with the slave, aided the fugitive, and preached to the unfortunate the principles of religion so dear to the hearts of their communicants," the

Congregationalists reached very few Negroes. The hold of the evangelical sects on the Negroes was so great that about the only successful effort to establish a working black body in the denomination was the forming of the Dixwell Avenue Congregational Church in New Haven in 1829.[55]

Unlike the Baptists and the Methodists, the Episcopalians, Presbyterians, and Congregationalists did not split along racial lines. Since there were fewer Negroes in those churches, the crisis over seating a large number of former slaves and freemen that was precipitated in the Baptist and Methodist churches of New York and Philadelphia did not arise. Also, the blacks who were attracted to the Presbyterian and Episcopal churches tended to be closer in class affiliation and complexion with the whites than was the case among the black Baptists and Methodists. The emphasis, moreover, upon a highly educated ministry in the Episcopal and Presbyterian churches kept the number of black ministers who might have created a mass church to a minimum, and gave these pastors greater confidence in their ability to take their place in the church councils. Nevertheless, as Wilmore points out, the black pastors were not able to develop "truly integrated churches."[56]

The Racial Policies of Catholics in the United States

With the exception of Maryland and Louisiana, extensive contacts did not exist between Negroes and the Catholic church in the antebellum South. Most slaveholders were Protestant, and most of the missionary efforts among the slaves were carried out by Baptists and Methodists. However, according to a Jesuit report to Rome, there were 3,000 black Catholics in Maryland in 1785. In 1724 Bienville, the founder of New Orleans, issued his Black Code, requiring all slaves to be instructed in Catholicism and baptized. During the next few decades, thousands of Louisiana slaves were baptized as Catholics. In the period 1790 to 1810 outmigration from Louisiana, Maryland, and the Caribbean increased the number of black Catholics in other states.[57]

The number of black Catholics in Louisiana in 1865 was around 63,000, in Maryland approximately 16,000, and for the United States, about 100,000. The first comprehensive census of Negro Catholics, taken in 1928, reported 200,000 black Catholics. The 1939 diocesan census found 297,000 black Catholics in the United States, an increase of 50 percent in eleven years, but part of this increase may have been due to more careful diocesan reporting. By 1967, the number of black Catholics had grown to 808,332 (table 7. 1).

TABLE 7.1

NEGRO CATHOLICS IN THE UNITED STATES BY REGION:
1947, 1957, 1967

Region	1947		1957		1967	
	N	Percent	N	Percent	N	Percent
Southern states	160,758	46.8	236,146	41.0	275,366	34.1
Border states and D.C.	58,892	17.1	106,606	18.5	135,185	16.7
Northern states	70,121	20.4	122,835	21.3	160,232	19.8
Midwestern states	42,121	12.3	76,039	13.2	152,868	18.9
Western states	11,775	3.4	34,299	6.0	84,681	10.5
Totals	343,667	100.0	575,925	100.0	808,332	100.0

SOURCE: Commission for the Catholic Missions Among the Colored People and the Indians, *Annual Reports* 1948, 1958, 1968. Quoted in H. M. Nelsen, R. L. Yokley, A. E. Nelsen, eds., *The Black Church* (New York, 1971), 249.

One factor in the dramatic rise in the number of black Catholics between 1939 and 1967 may have been status pressure on middle-class Negroes rising on the social scale. Affiliation with Catholicism, as well as with Baptist and Methodist churches of higher status, and Episcopal and Presbyterian churches, may have afforded some middle-class Negroes a way of escaping from social ties with fellow members of the lower class.[58] In some cases, the first connection with the church has been through a parochial school to which they have sent their children. A related factor in the appeal of Catholicism to middle-class Negroes is the emphasis in religious services on traditional ritual in contrast to the emotionalism of many Protestant Negro churches. In addition, since World War II, the Catholic church in the South has been active in trying to desegregate schools and colleges. As Feagin points out, the Catholic church may not in fact have been more helpful in Negro rights causes, but the fact is that Negroes perceive it this way.[59] Still another factor in the increase in the number of black Catholics in the United

NORTH AMERICA

States, especially in the period 1945–1960, was the migration of Puerto Ricans to the mainland. Although the majority of Puerto Ricans are classified in the Census as white, those who are classified as Negro constitute a sizeable group.

The Growth of the Independent Negro Church After 1815

Under the stimulus of the Black Power movement of the late 1960s and the early 1970s, some writers called the founding of the independent Negro church the beginning of the Black Revolution. This position traces the black rebellion back to the petitioning of black people for the independence of their churches from white control in the 1770s and 1780s.[60] Many white churches and church bodies were reluctant to permit separate congregations, and where they were formed, white ministers presided over many of them, and black congregations were supervised by civil officials and white church organizations.

Perhaps the first regular Negro church organization in the United States was a Baptist church started at Williamsburg, Virginia, in 1776. Two years later three Baptist churches were founded, one in Augusta and two in Savannah, Georgia. The first black Episcopal church in the United States, St. Thomas' in Philadelphia, grew out of the group which left St. George's Methodist Church when two Negro leaders, Richard Allen and Absalom Jones, entered the front section of the gallery and were ordered to leave. St. Thomas' was received into the communion of the Episcopal Church on October 12, 1784, and Jones was ordained as its first deacon.[61]

Richard Allen organized the Free African Society, a mutual aid organization, in Philadelphia in 1787, and in 1794 he organized the Bethel African Methodist Episcopal Church. For several years he retained affiliation with the white Methodists, and in 1799 they ordained him a deacon. Other African Methodist Episcopal churches were founded in other cities, and in 1816 the representatives of these groups met in Philadelphia to establish the African Methodist Episcopal Church. Allen was elected bishop and the articles of religion and rules of the Methodists were adopted. Other early black Methodist and Baptist churches included the Zion Methodist Church, New York City (1796), Joy Street Baptist Church, Boston (1807), Abyssinian Baptist Church, New York

(1808), and First Baptist Church, St. Louis (1830). The first black Presbyterian church, known as the First African Presbyterian Church of Philadelphia, was formed in 1807 with twenty-two members.[62]

The denominational separation of blacks and whites began, then, toward the end of the eighteenth century, but it was not immediate or complete. It was preceded by separation in seating and entrances by side doors. Black preachers were sometimes called upon to speak in the predominantly white denominations, but blacks did not participate in decision-making.[63]

Out of the vigorous protests that Negroes made in Philadelphia and other northern cities against segregation in church buildings and against other forms of racial discrimination, together with the attitudes produced by the controversy over slavery in the South and the inclination of many Negroes to form independent organizations, came the Negro church of today. By 1825 the large Negro denominations—the African Methodist Episcopal, the African Methodist Episcopal Zion, and the Negro Baptist church, together with smaller denominations—had been formed.[64]

In the South, the "invisible institution" of the Negro church spread among the slaves. Concerning this institution an ex-slave wrote:

> Our preachers were usually plantation folks just like the rest of us. Some man who had a little education and had been taught something about the Bible would be our preacher. The colored folks had their code of religion, not nearly so complicated as the white man's religion, but more closely observed. . . . When we had our meetings of this kind, we held them in our own way and were not interfered with by the white folks.[65]

The African Methodist Episcopal (A.M.E.) Church was founded in Baltimore in 1816 by blacks who had withdrawn from the Methodist Episcopal (M.E.) Church in order to gain greater freedom of action among themselves than they believed they could achieve in the parent church. The first bishop of the new church was the Reverend Richard Allen, a man who had led a "class" of forty Negroes within the M.E. Church in 1787. In basic doctrine, organization, and ritual, the new A.M.E. church differed very little from the M.E. Church. During its first fifty years, the growth of this church was slow and mainly in the

North. Membership increased from about 8,000 in 1826 to 20,000 in 1856 and to 75,000 in 1866. By 1890, the eight southern states reported 315,169 members, more than two-thirds of the entire membership of the church.[66]

The African Methodist Episcopal Zion (A.M.E.Z.) Church was formed in 1820 from a union of Negro churches in New York, New Haven, Long Island, and Philadelphia. The formal establishment of this church had been preceded by a congregation of blacks who organized in New York City in 1796. Members of that congregation had been members of the M.E. Church, but they embarked upon separate meetings for the purpose of developing their abilities and being of greater usefulness to one another. From its inception until the close of the civil war, the A.M.E.Z. Church expanded in the North, but little organizing was done in the South until after 1865. This church's policy of lay representation is of long standing, as is the lack of a bar to the ordination of women.[67]

The early independent black churches were known by both blacks and whites to be strongly opposed to slavery. Benjamin Quarles asserts that the Negro church was not squeamish "about bearing witness against slavery (as compared to the white churches)."[68]

After the Civil War, the opening of the South to Northern churches gave Negroes the opportunity to join the A.M.E. Church, the A.M.E.Z. Church, and other Methodist bodies. In the decade 1860–1870, the A.M.E.Z. Church grew from 20,746 members to 200,000. By 1880, the A.M.E. Church claimed 400,000 members. Most of the members of these two churches were the freedmen of the rural South.[69]

By 1866, only 78,742 of the 207,742 black members of predominantly white churches in the South in 1860 remained in those denominations. The general conference of the M.E. Church in 1866 authorized the organization of the Negro members, with their ministers, into separate congregations and annual conferences, and in 1870 two bishops were appointed to organize the black conferences into a separate and independent church. In December 1870, the Colored Methodist Episcopal Church (now the Christian Methodists) was formed. This new church adopted the same articles of faith, the same form of government, and the same disciplinary rules as the parent body.[70]

For many years, the separate black Baptist churches, unlike the Methodists, continued their affiliation with the white Baptist conferences. The first independent Negro Baptist conferences were the Providence Baptist Association in Ohio, organized in 1836, and the Wood River Baptist Association in Illinois, formed in 1838. A larger regional body, the Western Colored Baptist Convention, was established in 1853.[71]

Following the emancipation of the slaves, most of the Negro Baptists in the South who had belonged to white churches formed separate churches. The two largest black Baptist churches, the National Baptist Convention of America and the National Baptist Convention, U.S.A., were both formed in 1880. The number of black Baptists grew from 150,000 in 1850 to 1,604,310 in 1894, and in the latter year there were 13,138 Negro Baptist churches and 10,119 ordained black preachers.[72]

A notable study of the Negro church attributes its origins to five characteristic forces: growing racial consciousness, individual initiative, splits and withdrawals, the migration of Negroes from rural areas in the South to southern and northern cities, and the missions started by other churches. Mays and Nicholson say that the Negro church began "as a means of separating an unwanted racial group from common public worship" and that it has survived "because of the economic, sociological, and psychological forces in the church and in its environment."[73]

Churches originating from discrimination and increasing racial consciousness seem to have appeared principally in the period 1750 to 1865, while those attributable to individuals and groups desirous of having the Negro direct his own religious activities originated from 1866 to 1899. Churches resulting from schisms increased especially from 1900 to 1914, and from 1915 to the early 1930s the most influential factor in the development of new churches was the migratory movement of Negroes. From the pre-Revolutionary period until the years of the Great Depression a few black churches have originated as missions of other churches.[74]

The Presbyterians and Episcopalians administered their "Negro Work" or "Colored Work" separately. Technically, these black churches have always been an organic part of the white denominations, but they have been less independent and less black-oriented than the black Baptists and Methodists. According to Meier and Rudwick, in the antebellum period Presbyterian officials tried to avoid conflicts in ecclesiastical government by giving equal rights and privileges to Negro delegates when presbyteries and synods were held, but the Episcopalians "maintained the attitude of a colonial power dealing with natives." [75]

During the nineteenth century blacks in the United States entered upon missionary programs in Africa and the West Indies. The Reverend Lott Carey, a slave preacher of Richmond, Virginia, organized the African Missionary Society in 1815, and in 1821 sailed for Liberia with the second load of colonists from the United States to that country. The A.M.E. Church sent missionaries to Haiti in 1824, and branches of African Methodism were established there and in Santo Domingo a few years later. By the end of the century, additional A.M.E. missions had been started in Cuba, Jamaica, Antigua, the Virgin Islands, Tobago, Barbados, Trinidad, Bermuda, the Bahamas, and at Paramaribo (Dutch Guiana), and at Georgetown, British Guiana. The money and the personnel that the black denominations could provide were insufficient, however, to maintain an extensive missionary enterprise outside the United States, and the predominantly white denominations were disinclined to give any assistance. [76]

The Census of 1906 showed that there were 36,770 Negro church organizations with a membership of 3,685,097. In 1906, the distinctly Negro denomination having the largest number of communicants was the National Baptist Convention, followed by the A.M.E. Church, the A.M.E.Z. Church, and the Colored Methodist Episcopal Church. Taken together, the Baptists and the Methodists had 96 percent of the total number of Negro communicants, and of the Negro church members in that year, 86 percent belonged to denominations organized and controlled exclusively by Negroes. [77]

Although the memberships and the facilities of Negro churches increased considerably during the 1890s, the conservative and progressive elements of these churches continued to drift apart. The cleavage

NORTH AMERICA

was no longer between old and young, but rather one caused by a difference in ideas. These groups differed, among other matters, in their interpretation of religion, in their views concerning the importance of the church in community life, and in attitudes toward the relation of the church to the individual. These differences led Woodson to remark in 1921: "As poverty is jealous of opulence, so is ignorance jealous of intelligence; and in this case the jealousy all but developed into caste hate." The progressive (educated) element could not accept the biblical interpretation nor the vision of the hereafter portrayed by the illiterate ministers of the church. The conservative Negro churchmen regarded the educated communicants as a menace to the church. It was said that the educated class had information but lacked judgment, and that the principles of religion must be accepted unconditionally. The progressive Negroes insisted that the plaintive plantation hymns and the tiresome minister who covered the universe in his discourse should give way to music of a refined order and to a minister who could preach to the point. When the other group refused to have in their churches the musical instruments used in theaters and dance halls, would not listen to an attack on the ministers they preferred, and dismissed the proposal to replace time-honored customs with innovations borrowed from the white churches, many intelligent people left the church. Some of those who left were received by the Congregationalists, the Presbyterians, the Episcopalians, and the Catholics.[78]

A northern observer in a rural town in Mississippi in the middle 1930s found that

> the Negro ministers, usually preachers rather than pastors, are remarkably well fitted in their jobs; on the platform they are graceful, secure, and have the highest histrionic talents. They hit their stride easily in talking, and preach smiling, occasionally sizing up the audience and varying the attack at will. The object, of course, is to master the crowd and bring it to a high pitch of emotional participation in the service.[79]

The members of the congregation in Southern Town listened intently as the preacher repeated himself and uttered stereotyped phrases while collecting his thoughts. In many cases his sermons were memorized and acted out.[80]

In the early 1940s, Myrdal's staff found that the spiritual singing, especially in the rural Southern and the smaller Northern churches, was different from anything found in the white churches. But the ordinary hymns sung in the various white Protestant churches were also in common use. The responses given by the audience to the preacher's words were different, but the contrast was less if made with lower-class white churches. The custom of "testifying" before the church was an important part of rural and small town religious services. Members of the congregation spoke of mystical experiences as evidence of a valid conversion. Some asserted that they had asked the Lord to put a song in their mouths and that he had done so. Some testified they had asked that they be allowed to see a star fall and that this had happened. Some had had a vision involving a white man; others had heard a voice giving a special message.[81]

In the mid-1940s, there were approximately 500 churches in the Black Belt of Chicago, and the thirty or more denominations claimed a total membership of more than 200,000. About 10 percent of the churches in "Bronzeville," but less than 10 percent of the blacks attending church, were affiliated with predominantly white denominations, including the Methodist Episcopal Church, the Episcopal, Presbyterian, Congregational, Catholic, Lutheran, Christian Scientist, Seventh-Day Adventist, and Disciples of Christ. Nearly half of the churches and more than two-thirds of the church members in Chicago's black population at that time were affiliated with the National Baptist Convention, U.S.A., Inc., or the National Baptist Convention of America. Black congregations had "virtually no face-to-face relationships with any of their white co-religionists." The Baptists especially thought of their organization as a "Race church." Their leaders combined "serving the Lord" with fighting the "Job Ceiling" and demanding equal economic opportunity.[82]

Although every large city has had several large community-conscious churches, most black churches have been small, inefficient, and financially troubled. Rivalries between denominations and congregations, and the struggle among prominent preachers for the most desirable pulpits and for national offices, have greatly reduced the impact of black religion in community life. Another factor that contributed to reducing the influence of the black church in the second quarter of the twentieth century was the rising competition from secular organizations. "Social clubs"; fraternal orders such as the Masons, Odd Fellows, and Elks; and Greek-letter fraternities increasingly met needs formerly provided for by the church.[83]

In 1970, the Baptist and Methodist denominations remained largest in numbers of churches, church members, and pastors. Approximately 9,668,000 blacks belonged to the three national Baptist organizations: National Baptist Convention, U.S.A., Inc. (5 million), National Baptist Convention of America, Inc. (2,668,000), and Progressive National Baptist Convention, Inc. (2,000,000). The number of churches given by the three groups were 26,000, 11,398, and 1,450; the number of ministers were approximately 27,500, 7,598, and 1,000 respectively. In the A.M.E. Church there were 5,878 churches, 5,878 pastors and 1,500,000 members. The A.M.E. Zion Church had 4,083 churches, 2,400 ministers and 770,000 members. The Christian Methodist Episcopal Church had 2,523 churches, 1,792 ministers and 444,493 members.[84]

From its inception, the Negro church has not differed markedly from the lower-class white Protestant church. No major innovations have been made in theology or in the general character of the church service. Choir singing, hymn singing by the congregation, organ music, prayer, collection, and sermons have been much the same in the average black and white Protestant churches. For more than a century, only a slight emphasis on "race" in the sermons distinguished the Negro church from the white.[85]

Joseph Washington maintains that the black independent religious bodies are not sectarian movements seeking to satisfy "individual needs by religious means" because religion alone cannot solve the personal problems of black people, and because they are not churches in a universalist sense. Instead, in his view, they are established sects that exist for the purpose of trying to bring established churches into line with the criterion of inclusiveness.[86] One difficulty in accepting this interpretation of the purpose of black churches unqualifiedly is that the leaders and many members of Negro churches, especially in the older, well-established denominations, have acquired a vested interest in perpetuating separate institutions.

NORTH AMERICA

In recent decades, several trends have developed in the religious affiliations of blacks in the United States. One development, going back to the beginning of the twentieth century, is the appearance of new types of churches. Many of these represented doctrinal splits within established churches. These secessions adopted names like "Holiness," "Church of God," "Apostolic," and "Pentecostal." Other religious, or quasi-religious, groups emphasizing "nationalistic" or radical qualities, including the Black Muslims, have appeared. These sects and cults are considered in chapter 8. A second development within the black religious community has been the severing by many middle-class Negroes of their affiliations with the Baptist and Methodist churches and the joining of the Episcopal, Presbyterian, and Congregational churches.[87] A third trend is the tendency of the black intellectual to reject the church as irrelevant to the difficult realities of race.[88] A fourth trend is some increase in participation in interracial churches.[89]

Secular Achievements of the Negro Church, 1910–1960

Although less true in recent decades than in earlier years, the Negro church has served as a community center. Especially in the South, there were few public buildings available for recreational use. Only the large cities had private enterprises which provided halls for Negro meetings and entertainment. Formerly, nearly every public man had to rely, at least in part, on the churches to reach the black community. As Woodson remarked in 1921: "The lecturer on 'men, women, children and things in general' asks for a hearing there; the phrenologist holds his seances in this sanctuary; the spurious 'foreigner' in quest of a collection seeks there the opportunity to tell a credulous people about wonders of other lands; and the race leader demands this rostrum from which he, like the watchman on the wall, sounds the alarm for an advance against the bold enemy who, if not checked, will fix upon the race disabilities and burdens until all the hopes of liberty will be lost."[90]

In addition to serving as a clearing house and meeting place for innumerable activities, the Negro church has been a mutual aid center. For example, in the 1920s the Olivet Baptist Church in Chicago utilized a pastor, five assistant pastors, 42 departments and auxiliaries with 512 officers, including 24 paid workers, in carrying out its community program. More recently many black churches, including a number of storefront churches, have established day-care centers for children and have provided various kinds of assistance to those in need.[91]

Blacks have found gratification through the expressive patterns provided by the church—singing together, praying together, engaging in the formal expression of religious fellowship, and celebrating special occasions. A related psychological function of the black church has been its provision of release from the frustrations which have accompanied economic and political restrictions. In the social and moral isolation of the black masses, the church has been "a nation within a nation."[92]

One of the main attractions of the black church has been the opportunity it has given its adherents to participate in an organized group, to compete for prestige and offices, and to win acclaim.[93]

Protest against the racial system of the United States has not been a noteworthy characteristic of the Negro church. White and black scholars may have gone too far, however, in expatiating on the emphasis the black church put on "otherworldliness" in the nineteenth century. In telling his followers what to expect in the next world, the black preacher is said to have been "whetting appetites for what everyone knew white people were undeservedly enjoying in the here and now, and . . . he was talking about a just God from whom everyone gets his due—including black folks."[94]

Woodson and other scholars have pointed out that there were Negro ministers in the early decades of this century who spoke out on racial questions despite strong criticism and even sanctions from some members of the white community and from some blacks. Most black churchmen, however, have been more conservative than other black leaders. According to one view, this conservatism was fortunate because at the end of the nineteenth century and the beginning of the twentieth, the church acted as a kind of balance wheel. "The Negro church has known how far it can safely instruct its people to go in righting their own wrongs, and this conservatism has no doubt saved the Negro from the fate of other oppressed groups who have suffered extermination because of the failure to handle their case more diplomatically."[95]

In the early 1930s, Mays and Nicholson argued that the Negro minister had an opportunity and freedom in his church life to condemn injustices from the pulpit that pastors of other racial groups might well envy; no doubt some pastors did have such freedom of speech. At the same time, the concept of the nonviolent, patiently suffering white Christ enunciated by conservative evangelicals and revivalists had become a prominent feature of Christian imagery. In fact, in nearly all rural areas and in many urban communities, the preacher was recognized until the middle 1940s as the local leader of Negroes. Often he transmitted the wishes of whites to the black group and sought favors from them for his people.[96]

The Negro church, then, did not lead the opposition to the racial system during the period 1910–1960, but in some cases it was able to modify its harshness, and it contributed to the maintenance of solidarity of blacks in their pressure to improve their position. In many cases, churches helped to support schools, and funds were raised continuously in Negro churches to fight discrimination. At times, the National Association for the Advancement of Colored People, and other organizations devoted to the cause of racial justice, would have been unable to carry out their programs without the aid of the black church.[97] If the black church did not give much lead to reform, it did not differ greatly in this respect from Christian churches in general in the United States or elsewhere.

The Black Church and the Struggle for Civil and Human Rights Since 1960

Although the black church did not generally take the lead in reform during the nineteenth century, a number of black religionists were advocates of protest and revolt. In addition to those mentioned earlier as leaders of slave revolts of the 1820s and 1830s, the names of Lott Carey, Daniel Coker, Martin R. Delany, Henry Highland Garnet, Alexander Crummell, Edward W. Blyden, Henry McNeal Turner, and James T. Holly should be added for the latter part of the century. Of these clergymen, Blyden and Turner were especially noteworthy for their advocacy of black emigration to Africa and black self-determination. In addition to the leadership provided by these well-known churchmen, many less well-known black persons obtained in their churches the organizational experience necessary to question discriminatory practices.[98]

Adam Clayton Powell, posing as a champion of blacks and Puerto

Ricans, used his considerable persuasive powers and his church to promote his own political career as well as to advance black causes. Using the Abyssinian Baptist Church as his base, Powell picketed in the 1930s to get jobs for Negro women as clerks at Woolworth's in Harlem, and in the 1940s he asked why no Negroes were members of the faculties of city colleges. In 1945, he was elected to Congress, and in the 1950s, his name was appended to every antisegregation amendment proposed for federal appropriation bills. His church became a political party with its own patronage system, and Powell rose to be one of the most powerful politicians in the country.[99] Although the chairmanship of the House Committee on Education and Labor is not a position directly related to civil rights issues, for years Powell used his occupancy of that post to bolster his declining influence with his constituents.

The principal religious figure in the civil rights movement of the late 1950s and until his death in 1968 was Martin Luther King, Jr. The drama of the Montgomery bus boycott which he led in 1957, together with his ability and charismatic personality, brought him to the forefront of the Negro community.

> King's contribution to the Black revolution gave the lie . . .
> to the allegation that Black preachers were nothing but Uncle
> Toms and that Black Christianity was hopelessly out of step with
> the temper of the times. Despite the fact that he was never able to
> muster the full resources of the Black church and received only
> token support from many of the most prestigious Black ministers,
> King nevertheless projected upon the nation a new image of the
> Black church and a new awareness of the radical possibilities inher-
> ent in Black religion.[100]

For a time Dr. King served as the main person linking black and white protesters. Despite the rising sentiment among many younger blacks in the middle 1960s in favor of separate black and white organizations, he was planning, at the time of his death on April 4, 1968, a mass march on Washington which would have included blacks, Puerto Ricans, American Indians, Chicanos, and poor whites. Other ministers, including James Bevel, Hosea Williams, and Jesse Jackson, also used religion effectively during this period to bring the civil rights struggle to the black masses and to the nation at large.[101]

Still other ministers addressed themselves to community problems:

Milton Galamison, who was active in the instigation of the New York City school boycotts; Gardner Taylor, who served as a member of the New York City Board of Education; Obadiah Dempsey, a leader in the fight against narcotic addiction and drug traffic in the New York City; Eugene Callender, who was active in Harlem Neighborhoods Association; and Leon Sullivan, leader of boycotts against businesses that had employed few or no Negroes and organizer of the Opportunities Industrialization Centers to train and place unemployed blacks in Philadelphia and other cities. In the late 1960s, many Negro ministers emerged as leaders of the growing Negro rebellion.

Despite the campaigns of black ministers and laymen against segregation in housing, education, industry, and other areas, the protest by blacks against segregation in religion itself has never been strong. Given the reasons for the formation of the Negro church, it seems likely that religion will by the last of the social institutions to be integrated. For many blacks, the church remains almost the only place where they can find self-esteem. Until such self-esteem can be obtained elsewhere, many blacks will not be willing to give up this sanctuary.[102]

Black Power and Black Theology

Thirty years ago Myrdal and his associates pointed out that the Negro church is undoubtedly a power institution in the sense that it has the Negro masses organized and, if the church groups decided to do so, they could enlist the blacks behind a program. The fact is that historically the black church has been relatively ineffectual in improving·the Negro's position in American society. Most churches are small, with intense competition between the preachers and congregations, and with a weak economic basis.[103]

A considerable number of black ministers, professors of theology, and theological students became disillusioned with the civil rights movement in the late 1960s and the early 1970s. Many of these religionists tried to formulate a theological position that would be in accord with the black power movement. No single definition is adequate to describe the black power movement, but it is said to be concerned with "organizing the rage of black people and with putting new, hard questions and demands to white America."[104] According to Hamilton, black power must "(1) deal with the obviously growing alienation of black people and their distrust of the institutions of this society; (2) work to create new values and to build a new sense of community and of belonging; and (3) work to establish legitimate new institutions that make participants, not recipients, out of people traditionally excluded from the fundamentally racist processes of this country."[105]

In analyzing the black church in recent years, black theologians have (1) delineated the roles played by black religionists in the slave revolts and by the nineteenth-century leaders who advocated emigration to Africa and black self-determination; (2) explained what many black ministers have "really meant" when they have preached on otherworldly themes; and (3) reinterpreted the messages of such leaders as Father Divine, Daddy Grace, and Prophet Cherry as opposition to sin and immorality because such acts were seen as obstacles to power.[106] The purpose of new cults such as the Black Jews and the Black Muslims has been regarded as the union of black people for self-determination.

In 1968, discussions occurred within the traditional Negro churches (the A.M.E. Church; the A.M.E.Z. Church; the Christian Methodist Church; the National Baptist Convention of America; the National Baptist Convention, U.S.A., Inc.; the Progressive Baptist Convention of America) on the question of how these denominations could best identify with the black struggle. Three main points of view arose within the black Protestant denominations: (1) advocacy of the continuation of traditional theology and liturgical expression and continued support of integration and nonviolence; (2) the formulation of a black theology and the support of radical tactics of bringing about social change; or (3) some combination of these two strategies. Dr. King's death served to increase the doubts and uncertainties of a great many members of the black church. Questions were raised about the function and the ethos of black religion, but fear also existed that questioning of traditional black religion would lead to "the complete radicalization of the church and the rejection of time-honored practices."[107]

The situation was somewhat different among the black communicants of predominantly white churches in 1967 and 1968. The concept of black power was widely hailed, and black caucuses were formed in a number of denominations. In October 1968, a meeting of the Second Annual Committee of Black Churchmen in St. Louis included representatives of all of the traditional Negro churches as well as the various black caucuses: the Black Catholic Clergy Caucus; Black Churchmen of the American Baptist Convention; the Coordinating Committee of Black Lutheran Clergymen; the Black Caucus of the Unitarian-Universalist Association; Black Methodists for Church Renewal; members of the United Presbyterian Church; and the interdenominational Association for Black Seminarians.[108]

The black membership of the "white" churches, and particularly the clergy, provided the most vocal element of black religion in 1968. Although the black caucuses represented only 2 million of the 22 million black church members in the nation, they constituted the core of the black power advocates in religion. Because this minority lacked a broad power base, and also because the caucuses themselves were often in disagreement, it was unable to play a strong leadership role in black religion.[109]

Among those who have written extensively about black theology and the relationship between black power and black theology are Albert B. Cleage, James H. Cone, Joseph R. Washington, Jr., and Gayraud S. Wilmore. Cleage argues that the illusion that Jesus was white dominated the world for nearly 500 years only because white Europeans dominated the world for that length of time. According to Cleage, the historic truth is emerging—

> Jesus was the non-white leader of a non-white people struggling for national liberation against the rule of a white nation, Rome. The intermingling of the races in Africa and the Mediterranean area is an established fact. The Nation Israel was a mixture of Chaldeans, Egyptians, Midianites, Ethiopians, Kushites, Babylonians and other black peoples, all of whom were already mixed with the black people of Central Africa.[110]

Cleage's church in Detroit, the Shrine of the Black Madonna, is dedicated to a Black Messiah. This congregation believes that the purpose of Christianity is to free black people, and that in the Black Revolution any means necessary should be used toward that end. In his efforts to stimulate black consciousness, Cleage claims that all religions— Islam, Buddhism, Judaism, and Christianity—stem from black people.

White religion was "the primitive religion of the pagans with a pantheon of gods throwing thunderbolts and cavorting about heaven and
earth, filled with lust and violence. . . . The white man had never
created a genuine religion. He has only borrowed religions from non-
white peoples."[111]

Cleage attempted to take the initiative from the black nationalists
who have questioned the power of blacks as Christians and sought to
make them Muslims. According to Washington, however, in emphasizing the black tradition of Christianity, Cleage "goes overboard." For example, Cleage asserts: "We now understand that Christianity is our
religion, that Israel was a Black Nation. . . . All the people in that
part of the world were black. There wasn't any way in the world Israel of
Biblical times could have been a white nation. We have made our dis-
covery and we symbolize our new faith with the Black Madonna."[112]
Washington calls Cleage "a tragic figure" who allows rhetoric to outdis-
tance logic and therefore to limit his potential among blacks.[113]

In *Black Theology and Black Power,* Cone defines black power as "an
affirmation of the humanity of blacks in spite of white racism." He asserts that "only Blacks know the extent of white oppression, and that
only Blacks are prepared to risk all to be free." Black power, then, seeks
conflict rather than understanding, and black support but not white
good will.[114]

Cone asks if it is possible for men to be black and to identify with
the biblical tradition expressed in the Old and the New Testaments. He
asks also if the message of the gospel has any meaning for the advocates
of black consciousness. His position is that for the Christian, the goal of
black power is consistent with the gospel of Jesus Christ and that "black
rebellion is a manifestation of God himself actively involved in the
present day affairs of men for the purpose of liberating a people."[115] In
his theology, "being black in America has very little to do with skin
color. To be black means that your heart, your soul, your mind, and
your body are where the dispossessed are. . . . Therefore, being recon-
ciled to God does not mean that one's skin is physically black. It essentially depends on the color of your heart, soul, and mind."[116]

Further developing the theme that blackness is a symbol of what
oppression means in America, Cone asserts that "the focus on blackness

does not mean that *only* blacks suffer as victims in a racist society, but that blackness is an ontological symbol and a visible reality which best describes what oppression means in America. . . . Blackness, then stands for all victims of oppression who realize that their humanity is inseparable from man's liberation from whiteness."[117] In this view, then, whiteness is equated with evil, or at least, the white structure of American society must be considered as "part of what the New Testament meant by the demonic forces."[118]

Washington asserts that black church leaders and black power advocates have reached a new rapprochement; their common ground is the attribution of personal failures and the failure of the black churches to the same set of educational, economic, and social conditions. In many cases, black power leaders have returned to black churches. According to Washington, however, black theologians are not providing American blacks with the leadership required for the creation of a new social order. In relation to Christianity, black power should be seen as

> the embracing of Black identity; it is a return to and a search for roots; it is unity of blacks; it is the renouncing of the "American Christ" insofar as his followers are paternalistic, condescending, engaged in keeping blacks separate, poor, illiterate, intimidated, and restricted. The call to humility by white Christians and their attempts to put down the responsive rage of black youth in the name of love, as well as sending them off to war without providing them with equal employment at home leads to a rejection of Jesus by these black youth.[119]

Although Washington expressed the hope in 1969 that a holocaust would be prevented by the new respect black people have for themselves and through the use of black power, responded to by whites through radical social changes, he saw no real basis for a new society without racial war.[120] In a later work, his position was that what black church, sect, and cult types have in common is the "primary goal of acquiring power or life to live strongly for themselves and black people."[121] He argues that a theology of black religious folk would transcend Christian dogma; spiritual power would increase secular power. According to Washington, this goal can only be achieved through black sectarian thought and action. It cannot be achieved "from within white Christian theology seeking to include the black experience."[122] He sees the task of black theology as that of integrating the black community, of bringing the different sects and cults to realize that the one thing they all have in common is their blackness. "Blackness as the fact of disinheritance and the drive to overcome it means the differences between black sects and cults are not to be eliminated, but the underlying reality of blackness is to be revealed as transcending. The theme of blackness is reconciliation of all black people for power in this society."[123]

Wilmore's examination of black religion and black radicalism begins with the religion of the slave. He asserts that "the folk religion of the Negro, suffused with the yearning for social justice, and bearing the role of protest and relief, was betrayed by moralistic and dictatorial Black preachers" in the early decades of the twentieth century. He traces the development of the black Holiness and Pentecostal churches during this period as they challenged the established black denominations and the color prejudice of the white churches. He holds that the contribution of the black church to black nationalism in the United States, Africa, and the Caribbean "is considerably more profound than simply providing the pride, sense of independence, and the organizational and social skills requisite for the development of nationalistic movements in the twentieth century. The Black church . . . erected the politico-theological foundation for Black nationalism . . . and pan-Africanism as it developed from the early Du Bois to Malcolm X."[124] Substantiation of the latter claim would be difficult.

In sociological terms, crises in the life of a group are often accompanied by explanations that attempt to place the new experience within a systematic religious framework. For minority group members, theology may interpret disadvantage "as a peculiar sign of God's grace, of the special mission of the group, of its unique insight based on its unique experiences." Thus theology may claim that the oppressed group has been chosen to bring a message to all mankind, and it may tell the unjustly treated group that in the end it will prevail in a holy war.[125] The domestic and international events of the two decades following World War II brought about a reordering of the relations between blacks and whites in the United States. During that period, black theology and black theologians played a role in stimulating black consciousness, black pride, and black nationalism, and in increasing black power.

Blacks in the Historical Churches of Canada

Most of the descendants of African slaves brought to North America are found in the Caribbean, parts of South America, and the United States, but approximately 125,000 blacks reside in Canada. A young slave was brought to New France in 1628, and by the middle of the eighteenth century there were about 4,000 black slaves there. After the slaves were freed in British North America in 1833, blacks continued to enter Canada in small numbers. The major source of black migration to Canada has been the West Indies, and the majority of these migrants have arrived in recent years: *1946–1955,* 5,169; *1956–1968,* 43,795; *1969,* 13,803; *1970,* 13,286; *1971,* 11,202—a total of 87,255.[126]

The economic situation in Nova Scotia in the eighteenth century set the black loyalists apart from the white society as an exploited class, and the social conditions of the 1780s hastened their development as a distinct and separate community. Most important among these influences was a fundamentalist religious revival then sweeping the province. Religious gatherings of any kind attracted free blacks by the hundreds.[127]

Blacks were confined to special galleries in some Methodist churches; those who were nominally members of the Church of England in Halifax were segregated into their own congregations. According to Winks, most congregations seemed to prefer that Negroes worship elsewhere, but not necessarily for racial reasons. Newly arrived Negroes seemed to many whites to be less tutored socially, more vigorous in sermon and singing, and less sound doctrinally.[128]

In the separate all-black settlements, such complications did not arise. After establishing black congregations, Anglican priests visited them once or twice a year. Most of the time black lay readers were in charge, and a similar pattern was followed by the Methodist evangelists. Other Christian sects which gained large black followings in the 1780s were the Huntingdonians (an evangelical group that had broken with the Anglicans) and the Baptists. Despite differences in liturgy and doctrine, members of the black chapels retained the fervor that had characterized their conversion during the revivalist crusade. As Walker observes, "they saw that God did not give the white worshipers the same attention he gave the blacks. In the white churches there were no visions, convulsions, or voices, no visible proof that God had made a personal call." [129]

Another factor which contributed to an increase in the number of black church organizations in the 1780s was the rapid decline in the social mobility of free Negroes. Because blacks were denied access to the pulpit, those who wished to be preachers sought high religious office through segregated religious organizations. [130]

In January, 1792, during the Sierre Leone exodus, 1,196 blacks left Nova Scotia. The emigrants had been recruited from the free labor reserve and so were relatively more prosperous than those who were left behind. The exodus resulted in a shattering of the black settlements. [131]

The position of free blacks improved during the first part of the second decade of the nineteenth century, but the economic condition of most blacks declined in 1815–1816. In the cities and in the new all-black settlements, the descendants of loyalist and refugee blacks merged. The separate schools, churches, and residential neighborhoods—forced upon the blacks by white society—had acquired a positive meaning by 1840. In this peripheral society, blacks developed their own leadership and their own religious style. [132]

Although the early Negro churches in Canada did not generally support social activism, there was one issue which gained universal support: the condemnation of slavery as a moral evil. Winks contends, however, that intellectually and financially, the Negro church, at least in the maritime provinces, retrogressed during the nineteenth century. [133]

By 1900 the Baptist church predominated among Negroes in Canada. The first Negro-sponsored Baptist churches in Upper Canada (now the southern part of Ontario province) were interracial, but few remained so after the early 1840s. In October 1841, delegates from Baptist churches in Amherstburg, Sandwich, and Detroit organized an international association, declaring that they were unable to "enjoy the Privileges we Wish as Christians with the White Churches in Canada."

250

Within twenty years, the Amherstburg Association had grown from 47 founding members and seven churches to more than one thousand members in nearly twenty churches. The same development occurred in Nova Scotia and New Brunswick. In 1840 the seven Negro Baptist churches in Nova Scotia had 273 members; in 1879, twenty-two congregations had 2,440 adherents; and in 1953, a "constituency" of 10,000 was claimed.[134]

One historian concludes that in Nova Scotia a few families created a religious aristocracy with the result that the church was held to "more than ordinary frozen and conservative theological and social positions." Unlike the situation in Ontario and the West, the ministry long remained the only means of gaining access to the Negro aristocracy in the province. In 1964–65 the leadership of the Baptist church in Nova Scotia favored activism of the Martin Luther King type, and by the end of the 1960s some churches were receiving visitations from Black Panther leaders. This greater interest in the secular world resulted in a divided Negro community.[135]

Not all Canadian Negroes have been affiliated with the Baptist church; a few have belonged to the Christian Union and to Colored Zion churches, and there have been a few black Roman Catholics. There have been a few "nonpracticing Mormons," as well as a number of Pentecostalists. A former slave was a Quaker minister to several communities in Ontario in the 1890s. The Christian Science movement has had few followers among Negroes in Canada, but the Presbyterian, Congregational, and Anglican churches have retained "substantial smatterings" of black members.[136]

The more orthodox Methodists were the only serious competitors of the Baptists. Going farther than the Baptists in self-segregation, they eventually founded the African Methodist Episcopal (A.M.E.) Church, the British Methodist Episcopal (B.M.E.) Church, and the African Methodist Episcopal Zion Church. As a result of the formation of these churches, relatively few Negroes remained with the parent Methodist Episcopal Church in British North America. When the Methodist churches in Canada merged with the Congregational and most of the Presbyterian churches, the B.M.E. and the A.M.E. remained separate. In 1926, the United Church agreed to "recognize them as our brothers in Christ" without absorbing them. No significant changes occurred in the point of view of black B.M.E. leaders between the 1880s and the early 1950s. Activist ideologies were opposed, as were efforts at union with the A.M.E. Church and the United Church.[137]

A recent study of blacks in Nova Scotia points out that until the migration of West Indians in the 1960s, Canada's largest black population (about 25,000) lived in Nova Scotia. In this province most of the blacks were found in poor, isolated, nonagricultural areas. Racial discrimination began in the early period of black settlement as whites and blacks competed for land and jobs. Discrimination in education was marked and only a few blacks received any education at all.[138]

Although the black Baptists of the early nineteenth century are reported to have been fundamentalists, at the present time the greatest difference between the religious patterns among Nova Scotian blacks and those in other parts of the New World is in the virtual absence of fundamentalism. Even the Baptist church at Africville, which was well known for its spiritual singing, hand clapping, and dancing thirty or so years ago, has lost some of its expressiveness. During this time it has declined in membership and influence in the community. Henry hypothesizes that a change occurred within the black church somewhere in the middle of the nineteenth century which caused the Baptist churches to shift from fundamentalism toward a standard denominational Baptism. One of the most important influences in bringing about this change may have been the general decline of fundamentalist evangelism throughout the province, which affected blacks as well as whites.[139]

There is a Baptist church in all of the larger black communities of Nova Scotia, but one minister often serves three or four different church groups. Except in the larger churches in Dartmouth, Halifax, and one or two other places, church attendance is low. Ladies' church groups and youth organizations exist in name only. The relatively brief church service follows the standard Baptist order of worship, the hymnal is printed in Great Britain, and there is no shouting, public confession, speaking in tongues, or other features of fundamentalism. Henry concludes that Nova Scotian blacks have a strong religious faith but that the organized Baptist church seems to play a less important role in their lives than it does in other New World black communities.[140]

NORTH AMERICA

In the 1970s, two historians came to different conclusions concerning the significance of separate black institutions in Canada. Winks emphasizes their contribution to segregation. In summarizing the condition of the Negro church he asserts:

> Begging ministers, poverty-stricken churches, and a narrow anti-intellectualism contributed to a sense of separation from the Christian community as a whole; Negro associations and separate Negro sects heightened the sense of distance on both sides of the color barrier; illiterate preachers who . . . indulged in 'religious burlesque'—all these hurt the Negro in his slow climb toward acceptance. But Christian resignation, misunderstood, did more harm. Too often did the Sandwich Baptist Church choose Matthew 18:4 as the text with which to open its business meetings; too many had fallen asleep in Christ.[141]

Walker stresses the protection provided by separate black institutions to an evolving black identity. He holds that the victory of the black community hitherto has been in its endurance, an endurance which makes possible "a united attack on the racism of the present."[142]

CHAPTER EIGHT

Sect and Cult Among Blacks in North America and Britain

BLACK PENTECOSTALISM IN THE UNITED STATES[1]

Early History

NEW RELIGIOUS SECTS came into existence in North America before the American Revolution. The "Great Awakening" of the 1740s (Protestant revivals, especially in the New England colonies) established the model for the periodic revivals which have continued for more than two hundred years. At times, these were interdenominational; for example, the Great Western Revival of the early 1800s included Presbyterians, Methodists, and Baptists.[2] Although there was no direct connection between the Quakers and the Shakers, and later the Mormons, and the Pentecostals, American revivalism was accompanied from the beginning by involuntary screaming, glossolalia, convulsions, falling, and fainting. Ecstatic "Spirit baptism" manifested by speaking in tongues occurred sporadically in the U.S.A. in the late 1800s.[3]

Shortly after 1900, a large number of new sects appeared in the mountainous regions of North Carolina and Tennessee and spread rapidly through the growing mill towns. A correspondent from one of the mill villages in Gaston County complained in the *Gastonian Gazette* in 1910 of " 'tongue exhorting' in his village by persons 'claiming that they are possessed of gifts of the Holy Ghost,' and thereby helping to 'lead men's wives astray.' " Later that year he denounced the "holy dance," attributing such manifestations to "hypnotism" and, therefore to "demonism." Subsequently, the Pentecostal Holiness Church, the Church of God (Cleveland, Tennessee branch), the Free-Will Baptist Church, and the Free-Will Baptist Holiness Church each established a number of churches in the county.[4] These were white churches.

Although there were Pentecostal outpourings prior to 1906, the actual Pentecoastal movement originated in a revival among American blacks. W. J. Seymour, a Negro Holiness preacher who had studied in Parham's Bible school in Houston was invited to come to Los Angeles by the woman pastor of a black Holiness church. After a theological disagreement, Pastor Neeley Terry ejected Seymour. In the meetings that Seymour then conducted in the homes of members of the congregation, many who were members of Holiness churches experienced the baptism of the Spirit. Soon, Seymour rented an old Methodist church at 312 Azusa Street, the site regarded by many Pentecostals as the birthplace of the world-wide Pentecostal movement. People came from all over the country, among them white pastors from the South, to receive the blessings of the Spirit. That meeting continued, day and night, for three years. In 1908, however, the whites withdrew from the Azusa Street revival.[5]

Although the Azusa Street Mission lasted until 1923, the Pentecostal movement did not depend upon it for leadership.[6] Pentecostalism expanded rapidly, and by 1972 there were approximately two hundred Pentecostal denominations in the United States. The largest white Pentecostal organization is the Assemblies of God, which proclaims the two-stage way of salvation. A significant number of organizations preaches the original, three-stage way. The leading groups in the latter category are the thirty or more Churches of God, among them a number of the largest black denominations.[7]

Pentecostalists have often claimed that their movement emerged and grew largely because many of the major denominations neglected the lower strata of American society. A historian reared in the Pentecostal faith states that

SECT AND CULT

these groups had accumulated wealth, built enormous churches, appointed them handsomely, eliminated the "prayer and praise" service from the program of worship, and in some instances even provided little or no room for the people of the laboring class in the sanctuary itself. The result was that multitudes severed their affiliation with the so-called "middle-class" denominations like the Methodist and the Baptist.[8]

Former Holiness groups such as the Church of God (Cleveland, Tennessee), the Fire-Baptized Holiness Church, and the Church of God in Christ became Pentecostal churches in the early 1900s. This association occurred because the Pentecostals represented everything the nineteenth-century Holiness movement had advocated. They were revivalistic fundamentalists, who acknowledged the role of the Holy Spirit in the believer's life and were puritanical in their rejection of tobacco, alcohol, the theater, and cosmetics.[9]

During the first decades of the twentieth century, the Pentecostal movement spread in North and South America, Europe, Africa, and Asia. Thousands were converted in Pentecostal Missions, Assemblies of God, Gospel Hall Tabernacles, Glad Tidings Halls, Churches of God, or Full Gospel Assemblies. By 1970, Pentecostalism across the world may have had between 25 and 35 million adherents.[10]

According to some specialists, by the year 2000 the Christians of Latin America and Africa may outnumber those of the other three continents because a considerable proportion of them will belong to the "spontaneous non-literary Pentecostals."[11] The European theologian Hollenweger maintains that the growth of the Pentecostal movement throughout the Third World thus far has depended more upon its ability to use the American Negro's capacities of understanding and communicating by means of enthusiastic spiritual manifestations—hymns, speaking in tongues, and spontaneous forms of worship—than upon the "baptism of the Spirit."

Pentecostal Belief and Ritual

Fundamentalism, millennialism, baptism by total immersion, and the "baptism of the Spirit" evidenced by talking in tongues characterize the Pentecostal churches.[12] Almost all Pentecostal denominations teach that the Bible is (1) "the inspired word of God and its content is infallible divine revelation," and (2) "the infallible rule of faith and conduct, and is superior to conscience and reason, but not contrary to reason."[13] According to the Doctrine of Justification, the fundamental experience, essential to salvation, for the Pentecostal is conversion or regeneration. Pentecostals take the apostolic church as their model, attribute the degeneration of the church to the disobedience of Christians, and seek the gifts of the Holy Spirit. Healing through prayer is sought by those who cannot or will not be treated medically and is related to the doctrine of miracles. Pentecostals believe in "the personal existence of the Devil and his angels, the evil spirits," and that many are possessed by such spirits. The eschatological element is of great importance in Pentecostal preaching, including the second coming of Christ, the Judgement, the resurrection, and the millennium.[14] In the language of Pentecostals, "the early rain at Pentecost" was followed by a long period of drought, but the "latter rain" (the final age of revival) has now come to the earth in the days before the end.[15]

The salient points in the ethics of Pentecostal groups are: (1) Tithing; (2) observance of Sunday; (3) refusal of military service; (4) taboos on pleasure and food, including the prohibition of smoking and alcohol (except on the continent of Europe); (5) sex taboos (make-up, jewelry, short dresses and low necks, short hair, divorce only for adultery and remarriage of the innocent party [in some groups this applies only to officials]), theater and movies, marriage with unbelievers, dancing, emancipation of women; (6) ethical rigorism—the function of the church is to get as many people as possible to heaven.[16]

A major difference between Pentecostalism and other types of Protestantism is found in the levels of communication. The principal means of communication in the Ecumenical movement is through verbal agreement. Among Pentecostals it is through a correspondence of sentiments.[17] In the Apostolic Overcoming Holy Church of God, for example, services are quite emotional affairs, with the participants speaking in tongues and engaging in ecstatic dancing. In this church, no hymnals are used; the songs are spirituals; and rhythm is emphasized in

SECT AND CULT

the singing through the use of drums and tambourines, as well as the stamping of feet and the clapping of hands.[18] The spiritual and the related contemporary Gospel music have long communicated Biblical themes in black American communities. Also, they have been adapted in hymns of white Pentecostals and they have been taken to Latin America, Africa, Italy, Indonesia, Russia, and other countries. According to Hollenweger:

> Where Pentecostals work in a pre- or post-literary society they do not think along systematic and logical lines but in parables and associations. Their main medium of communication is not the book or the newspaper but the proverb, the chorus, the joke, the testimony, the miracle story, the television and radio program. If in a given culture dancing and singing are the forms of communication, the embodying of the message is in dancing and singing. If eating and walking together on a pilgrimage are the forms of communication in the respective culture, then this will be the embodying of the message.[19]

The Separation of Black and White Pentecostals in the United States

The Pentecostal Revival has been called a contribution from the black community to the white one. Contrary to a declaration at the beginning of the revival, the movement divided between 1908 and 1914 into a black part and a white part. Most black denominations, however, included some white members and some of the white groups retained a few black members. The reasons for this separation have never been clearly identified, but Hollenweger attributes the segregation largely to the criticism by the traditional white denominations of Pentecostalism's humble black beginnings rather than merely to prejudice on the part of the white Pentecostals.[20]

Among the black Pentecostal churches that were at one time integrated with white Pentecostals are the Pentecostal Assemblies of the World and the Fire Baptized Holiness Church of God of the Americas. The former church was merged with the Apostolic Assemblies by 1918–19, but by 1924 the white members withdrew and formed the Pentecostal Church, Inc. In 1908, the Fire Baptized Holiness Church of

God of the Americas separated from the predominantly white Fire Baptized Holiness Association of America after ten years of association because of "the growing prejudice that began to arise."[21]

By 1936, of the 353,000 Pentecostals in the United States 51,500 were Negroes—14.5 percent of the movement compared with 9.7 percent of the total population. In 1970 Hollenweger estimated that the world's black Pentecostals numbered at least 1.5 million and up to 5 million, depending on whether the Church of God in Christ was counted at 1 or 3 million members and whether the statistics of the House of Prayer of All People were accepted.[22]

Variations of Black Pentecostalism

The following varieties of churches are found among black Pentecostals in the United States:

Three Crises or Three-Stage Way of Salvation [23]

Christ's Sanctified Holy Church (Colored)
Church of Christ (Holiness) USA
Church of God (Holiness)
Church of God (Holiness) USA
Church of God (Mother Horn)
Church of God (Mother Robinson)
Church of God in Christ
Church of the Living God (Christian Workers for Fellowship)
Church of the Living God (The Pillar and Ground of Truth)
Churches of God (Holiness)
Fire Baptized Holiness Church of God of the Americas
Free Christian Zion Church of Christ
Free Church of God in Christ
Holiness Church of God, Inc.
Holstein Church of God
House of Faith
House of God, Holy Church of the Living God, The Pillar and Ground of the Truth, House of Prayer for All People
House of Prayer for All People
House of the Lord
Interracial Church of God

Triumph the Church and Kingdom of God in Christ
United Holy Church of America, Inc.

Two Crises or Two-Stage Way of Salvation

National David Spiritual Temple of Christ Church Union, Inc.,
USA

Oneness or Jesus Only Groups

Apostolic Church of Jesus Christ
Apostolic Overcoming Holy Church of God
Church of Our Lord Jesus Christ of the Apostolic Faith, Inc.
Church of the Lord Jesus Christ of the Apostolic Faith, Inc.
The House of the Lord
Pentecostal Assemblies of the World, Inc.

Father Only Organizations

School of the Prophets

Groups Which Cannot Be Identified

Latter House of the Lord for All People and the Church on the
Mountain, Apostolic Faith
Pentecostal Church
Sought Out Church of God in Christ and Spiritual House of
Prayer, Inc.

Five of these sects—three of the three-stage way of salvation variety, one Oneness or Jesus Only group, and an independent church led by a Negro who follows the Assembly of God model—illustrate the range of these black Pentecostal churches.

With twice the membership of the white Assemblies of God, the largest Pentecostal denomination in the United States is the Church of God in Christ. The founder, Charles H. Mason, received his early ministerial training in the Missionary Baptist Church in Tennessee, but he joined the Holiness church in the 1890s. A few years later he established the Church of God in Memphis. In 1906, Mason spent five weeks at the Azusa Street revival in Los Angeles, where he received the Spirit baptism and spoke in tongues. In 1907, an Assembly called by Mason declared that the Church of God in Christ was henceforth a part of the Pentecostal rather than the Holiness movement. In doctrine, the Church of God in Christ differs little from that of Pentecostal denominations like the

Church of God (Cleveland, Tennessee) and the Pentecostal Holiness Church. This church maintains a widespread missionary program in South Africa, Thailand, Jamaica, Haiti, Liberia, and West Africa. Its constituency is predominantly southern Negro. In 1963, the Church of God in Christ claimed to have 4,100 churches, "an inclusive membership" of 413,000, 3,850 ordained ministers, and more than "two million adherents" around the world.[24]

The Church of the Living God (Christian Workers for Fellowship) was founded by William Christian, a former slave. Without education, Christian joined the Baptist Missionary Church and soon began to preach. He claimed to have received a revelation from the Lord in 1888, and in April 1889 he organized the Church of the Living God (Christian Workers for Fellowship) in Wrightsville, Arkansas, a place where there had been numerous church secessions and mergers. From the beginning, the doctrine of this church has tried to combat certain racist teachings, and particularly the claims of some Baptist preachers in the latter part of the nineteenth century that Negroes were not men, but the outcome of a human father and a bestial mother. Opposing this teaching, the Church of the Living God asserts that the saints of the Bible belonged to the black race.[25] Since Jesus has no earthly father, He is considered to belong to all people and to be "colorless." With headquarters in Oklahoma City, Chief Bishop F. C. Scott claims that the church has 72,000 members in 276 congregations.[26]

Founded by Bishop Marcelino Manoel da Graca in 1919 in West Wareham, Massachusetts, the House of Prayer for All People was formerly one of the largest "deviant" groups of Negro Pentecostals in the United States. At the time of Graca's death in 1960, the group claimed to have 300 churches in 60 cities and an estimated 3 million followers.[27] "Daddy Grace"—or "Sweet Daddy" as he was often called—was born in 1881 on Brava, Cape Verde Islands off the coast of West Africa and was a former railroad cook and migrant cranberry picker. Although the official doctrine of the House of Prayer for All People resembled that of Pentecostalism, some observers stated that "the beliefs boil down to a worship of 'Daddy Grace.'" Grace is quoted as saying: "Never mind about God. Salvation is by Grace only. . . . Grace has given God a vacation, and since God is on His vacation, don't worry Him. . . . If you sin against God, Grace can save you, but if you sin against Grace, God cannot save you." Soap sold in Grace's name was said to heal sicknesses and it was believed that his stationery enabled those who purchased it to compose good letters. Grace dominated the organization for forty years, but the church experienced a period of turbulence following his death. According to Nichol: "Services begin with congregational singing, accompanied by piano or band and interlarded with shrieks, handclapping and stamping. As the tempo and volume increase, members advance to the front of the auditorium to dance on the sawdust-covered floor; others flit about the aisles and passageways. Some collapse and fall prostrate to the floor; some speak in tongues. Many raise their arms and cry."[28]

The Pentecostal Assemblies of the World, a Jesus Only or Oneness sect, is said to be "the continuation of the great revival that began at Jerusalem on the Day of Pentecost, A.D. 33."[29] Reliable information is lacking on the beginnings of the church; probably it came out of the Assemblies of God on the basis of additional revelation. Organized about 1915, a black evangelist, G. Y. Haywood, is regarded as the founder. By 1960 the church reported 550 congregations and 45,000 members. It maintains missions in Nigeria, the Bahamas, Jamaica, Haiti, China, India, Israel, and Jordan.[30]

The House of Revelation and Salvation, an independent Pentecostal sect, was established about 1955 by a black minister who was trained in an Assemblies of God Bible College. The authoritarian leader directs two churches in one metropolitan area in the United States and maintains an extensive mission school and orphanage complex in three Caribbean countries. Ninety percent of the working membership of 75 people in the home church are lower- and middle-class blacks; the other tenth are lower- and middle-class whites. Followers receive healing, counseling, and "a faith-enhancing dynamism," while the leader gains "extremely rewarding financial support." Gerlach and Hine compare the home church with the work that is carried on in the Caribbean mission program.

> Growth rates and religious fervor, unimpressive in the home church, are noticeably higher on the 'growing edge' in the Caribbean mission field. . . . As the home center becomes more rou-

tinized and financially more secure, the leader can delegate more authority, thereby allowing himself more time in which to promote conditions favorable to the rapid growth, religious excitement, and flexible organization that are characteristic of the early stages in movement growth. Role conflict is not one of the leader's problems, for he swings back and forth between bureaucratic and charismatic leadership with great versatility.[31]

Social and Political Aspects of Black Pentecostalism in the United States

A survey of Pentecostalism in the United States—largely white Pentecostalism—in the late 1960s found that participants tend to be politically conservative. Social change through social action is not encouraged by the Pentecostal ethic. Instead, Pentecostalists expect radical changes to come about through supernatural means. Nevertheless, Gerlach and Hine suggest that the movement is conceptually revolutionary because "it encourages an experience through which an individual believes himself to be radically changed and many converts behave accordingly in social situations."[32]

The members of many of the black Pentecostal groups have helped each other spontaneously, but the social and political aspects of life have come into the programs of most of these churches rather indirectly. For example, in the sanitation workers' strike in Memphis under the leadership of Dr. Martin Luther King, the Church of God in Christ provided headquarters for the strikers in its Mason Hall. The participation recently of some Pentecostal denominations in international and national ecumenical bodies, such as the World Council of Churches and the National Council of Churches, is evidence that the social aspect of their religion may assume a more prominent place in the future. The job training program established in Brooklyn by Bishop F. D. Washington is another instance of greater interest in the social aspects of community life in the same Pentecostal church. According to Bishop Washington, many unbelievers will not come into a church no matter how attractive the building nor how eloquent the minister. To reach such persons he purchased a large house across the street from his church and established a center for persons qualified to receive job training regardless of their religious background or beliefs. Bishop Washington also became the head of a low-income housing project.[33] Under the direction of Arthur Brazier and other black Pentecostals a program of black self-determination has been established by the Woodlawn Organization in Chicago. This group has set up control stations for consumers, publicized overcharging on rents and the lack of repairs in slum housing, organized rent strikes, attempted to improve the schools, and formed youth organizations to assist in maintaining order.[34]

While eschatology does not characterize the Pentecostal movement to the same extent that it does the Adventists and Jehovah's Witnesses, Pentecostalists are interested in Judgment Day and interpret contemporary political events as signs of the imminent second coming of Christ. Greater emphasis, however, has been placed on the millennium. Some observers see this escapist tendency as stemming from the social conditions of the majority of Pentecostal followers.[35] What seems to be decisive here is not some type of deprivation in itself, but the feeling of deprivation. Sects function to overcome feelings of deprivation associated with poverty, sickness, racial discrimination, speech and language difficulties, handicaps of character, loneliness, status contradictions, and so forth.[36] Pentecostalism thus far has been mainly a class religion, one that is almost ideally adapted to the needs of the lower socioeconomic classes.

Willems' comment that the social function of the Protestant congregation in Chile and Brazil is both compensatory and substitutive applies to Pentecostal denominations in general and to black Pentecostal churches in particular. They give fellow members something to live for and something to live in, that is, "a kind of miniature community rather than the usual church congregation, limited to scheduled performances of rather peripheral interest to the individual member."[37] I pointed out earlier that the Pentecostal revivals in the United States have attracted some persons other than the poor and the intellectually deprived. Further economic development and increased social mobility in the United States and elsewhere may produce significant changes in the class composition of the Pentecostal movement. Such a change would shift the emphasis from "otherworldliness" to a "worldier" value orientation.[38]

As Gerlach and Hine point out, once a social movement is well under way, it may spread into groups where the conditions of disorganization, deprivation, or oppression (or, in the case of Pentecostalism, the failure of the church to be alive and "relevant") associated with its rise do not and never did exist. In this analysis, when a movement begins to grow, "it can be plucked up and transplanted to social soil where the generating conditions do not exist." Both the Pentecostal and the Black Power movements in the United States were found to bear out this conclusion.[39]

A Black Pentecostal Church in Pittsburgh

A recent study focuses on the distinctive quality of social relations, ideology, and behavior in an urban black Pentecostal church. Zion Holiness Church is one of about twenty such churches in metropolitan Pittsburgh and one of thousands of small Pentecostal churches located in black urban ghettos throughout the United States. Zion belongs to a Pentecostal sect which began in the South in 1895 when a group of black ministers were ousted from the black Baptist church organization in Jackson, Mississippi. The leading founder soon broke from the new group and established his own sect. When purged from that organization for introducing a new doctrine of baptism of the Holy Ghost accompanied by speaking with tongues, he founded a new organization under the same name, Church of Holy Christ (a pseudonym).[40]

Six ministers other than the pastor and his helper are recognized as leaders, prophesiers, and prophets. These men are addressed as elders and frequently have an opportunity to preach at Zion and at other churches. In addition to these officials, Zion has a deacon board, a trustee board, a choir, a chorus, a young people's choir, an usher board, a church secretary, a church treasurer, a church announcer, church nurses, a pianist, an organist, a pastor's aide group whose members provide personal assistance to the pastor and his wife, a group of financial captains who lead drives for funds, an official church reader, and women missionaries who "teach" rather than "preach".[41]

The typical Sunday morning church service begins with a selection by the choir and one by the chorus, and these are often followed by a solo sung by a prominent woman member of Zion. After these musical numbers, the bishop (pastor) talks for about fifteen minutes on events of the week, incorporating in his remarks praise and reprimands for members of the congregation who have "found favor in [his] and God's sight." The bishop preaches through "parables" filled with references to his boyhood experiences on the farm and in the city as a laborer. Drama is constantly enacted as the service proceeds.

 A member is "happy" (possessed of the spirit), speaking in tongues, or prophesying. A financial report is given. An announcement is made. A visitor is asked to say a word. The minister is preaching, the congregation is singing. One, two or fifteen members are "shouting." Sister Roach, dressed in an attractive outfit, is walking back and forth in front of the pulpit waving her handkerchief as she reacts to the spirit. Sister Dankins is running around the entire auditorium. Two or three sisters are walking around in the front of the auditorium in the spirit. A brother is shaking violently in his seat, and several other brothers are holding him so he does not hurt himself.

Members clap, sing, and dance as the "spirit hits them." During the emotional portion of the minister's sermon ("coming home"), the pianist plays moving chords at the end of every phrase and the audience responds by repeating the pastor's words or other praise words. The demonstrative part of the service culminates in a "shout" (dance).[42]

Interaction among the members of Zion, characterized by intimacy, fission, competition, mobility, and political alignment, is expressed in a system of symbolic expression. Prominent among the images of this church community are the rural landscape, the farm, human anatomy, animals, death, the physical world, and the supernatural. These symbols serve to validate and identify these southern black Baptist rural migrants apart from the larger society.[43]

Zion Holiness Church is a part of the religious subculture of Pittsburgh's black ghettos. Other subcultures available to residents of these areas include drug, "hustler," and street-corner. The ideological themes stressed in Zion's symbolic system differ from the major values of mainstream America, but many mainstream ideals (marriage, stability, achievement, mobility, work, and so forth) are shared.[44] One effect of participation in this Pentecostal church is the promotion of individual social mobility.[45]

SECT AND CULT

The members of Zion perceive themselves as "the despised few," yet they invite others to join their "way of carrying on." Their in-group feeling protects them from out-group disdain and reinforces their solidarity. In their view, hardship is to be expected and suffering legitimates the position of the majority of Zion's members who are poor, uneducated, and economically immobile. Solutions for their plight are believed to lie in the supernatural future.[46]

Some of the psychological requirements of Zion's members are met through prophecies, testimonies, and spiritual possession, but other needs are satisfied through the numerous activities sponsored by the church. Special events range from choir rehearsals through bus trips, prayer meetings, conventions, church dinners, picnics, and auxiliary group meetings. When a member is sick, an offering is collected. When legal problems arise, the pastor goes to court. When one must move, his furnishings are transferred by volunteers. When there are special needs, food baskets are delivered. When members die, funeral arrangements are made according to their wishes.[47]

Zion has been a community as well as a church for more than fifty years. In its patterned interactions a group of individuals who consider themselves as "outcasts," but who also describe themselves as "sanctified folks" in contrast to "worldly folks," seek security and identity from fellow members. Each member has a role to play, and only in such a community as this can life have meaning and dignity. Few of its original members are still living. Competition from other subcultures and the gradual disappearance of one of its most important original needs—an intimate association for southern rural black migrants, have made the problem of recruitment increasingly difficult. Unless new ways of attracting the new types of ghetto dwellers are created, Zion may not survive many more years, at least not in its present form.[48]

BLACK CULTS IN THE UNITED STATES

In the disorder and discrimination which characterized most urban settings in the United States in the 1920s and 1930s, large numbers of lower-income blacks were neglected by both the traditional white and black churches. At the same time, many of these individuals found unsatisfying the emphasis which the Holiness and Pentecostal churches placed on withdrawing into a spiritual world with separate standards. In this period, innumerable black cults emerged which placed more emphasis upon the community of blacks than upon individual conversion. These cults combined belief in God with attempts to construct more satisfying life conditions for their adherents. Often, magical procedures were involved in the special healing powers claimed by cult leaders, and some of these groups were headed by a prophet who assumed the role of a black Christ or black God or both.[49]

Father Divine's Peace Mission Movement

Father Divine established dozens of missions or "heavens" in the United States, Europe, Africa, and Australia. The public followers (angels), as well as persons who subscribed to the beliefs and practices of the cult but otherwise lived as ordinary citizens in the community, regarded this charismatic leader as a supernatural being. The Father Divine Peace Mission Movement maintained a strict code of ethics and enforced a discipline so effectively that a member was seldom involved with the police. The regulation of an angel's life was almost complete. A member

> renounced the things of this world completely. He no longer plans his own life, but lives it completely in accordance with the instruction of Father Divine. If he is the possessor of worldly goods, he disposes of them in a manner agreed upon between him and the leader. He does not choose his own vocation or business, but places himself at the disposition of the Father, making himself completely subject to Father Divine's suggestion, instruction, or command. Literally everything which such a member receives, the bread he eats, the raiment he wears, his lodging and work, whatever personal remuneration he may receive, comes through the direction of Father Divine.[50]

The Peace Mission Movement has been called "a massive cooperative, based on the biblical Last Supper."[51] There were no ministers, no reading of the Scriptures, and no formal services. There was little that was otherwordly about the ministry of Father Divine. He established blacks in small businesses and urged his followers to patronize these enterprises. He prohibited race prejudice and discrimination among those in the movement. Addiction to alcohol, narcotics, and tobacco was reduced to the vanishing point. Physical and mental illness decreased among his disciples, as did the death rate. He fed, clothed, and housed black and white people at minimal or no expense. Father Divine's followers supported civil rights and the social welfare of the poor and were constantly urged to put into effect "a plan for a 'righteous government' in which there will be equality for all mankind, with the abolition of such evils as lynching and Jim Crow practices."[52] In addition to its economic and political aspects, the movement met many of the emotional needs of persons who were overwhelmed by the anonymity of city life and by racial oppression. The "cost" of the benefits received from Father Divine was complete submission of the self to his will.

Other cults that played a prominent role among Negroes in the eastern United States in the post-World War I period included Bishop Ida Robinson's Mount Sinai Holy Church of America, Inc., founded in Philadelphia in 1924, and the United House of Prayer for All People, founded by Bishop Marcelino Manoel da Graça (Daddy Grace) in West Wareham, Massachusetts, in 1919. Both groups grew out of Pentecostal revivalism, and both practiced faith healing, foot washing, and extensive female participation. To Christian fundamentalism these cults added shouting, dancing religious services.[53]

The Black Jews

The Prophet F. S. Cherry was the first of the leaders of the Black Jews. He regarded white Jews as frauds and interlopers and maintained that his followers were the true Israelites of the Bible. According to Cherry, Jesus was black and during his services he often shouted: "Jesus Christ was a black man and I'm offering fifteen hundred dollars cash to anyone who can produce an authentic likeness of Jesus Christ and show I'm wrong." Then he would wave a picture of the white Christ and ask, "Who the hell is this? Nobody knows! They say it's Jesus! That's a damned lie! Jesus was black."[54]

In the period 1919–1931, at least eight Black Jewish cults arose in Harlem—groups that were given to splitting, disappearing, and reorganizing. The "rabbis" differentiated themselves from one another largely by their interpretations of orthodox Jewish law and custom. Arnold Ford, a black Jew from Barbados who became musical director of Marcus Garvey's Universal Negro Improvement Association (UNIA), was one of the most important of the early Black Jewish figures. He disagreed with Garvey on many points, but the UNIA's militancy, its glorification of blackness, and its elevation of Africa to a place of great civilizational importance appealed to him and to many of his followers. When Garveyism collapsed, its black nationalism persisted in the cults of the Black Jews and Black Muslims.

The Black Jews claim that they are Ethiopian Hebrews or Falashas whose names and religion were taken away during slavery. They reject the term Negro, and they repudiate Christianity as an alien religion. In addition, Christianity is held to be the religion of a group which is doomed to apocalyptic destruction. Hebrew is believed to be the sacred language, the language spoken by Adam and Eve in the Garden of Eden. Black Jews maintain that they are strictly kosher, and the eating of pork, crabs, catfish, lobster, duck, frankfurters, and bear are forbidden.[55] In brief, they invented a history, a culture, and a religion in an attempt to escape from the stigma of being black and from being rejected by whites.

Worship by Black Jews is characterized by restraint and sobriety. There is no screaming, fainting, running about, or spirit possession during services, and one important "rabbi" attacked Christianity by ridiculing and imitating the religious behavior of a Southern country Negro. The Black Jews hold their regular services on Friday nights and Saturdays, and they celebrate all Jewish holidays, as well as bar-mitzvahs and weddings, in somewhat modified ways.[56]

Unlike the Black Muslims, the early Black Jews were uninterested in withdrawing from the outside world by setting up communal enterprises. Their educational programs were supplementary to those of the public schools, and at least some of the "rabbis" valued the few contacts they had with Jewish educational and religious institutions. Within these Black Jewish groups there was a great deal of informal cooperation. At the time of Brotz's study in 1964, the Black Jews in New York City were almost entirely nonpolitical. Their interests centered in their rituals and in their belief that they had recovered their true name, identity, and language. The only practical activity in which they were interested was their housing development in Long Island. Rejecting what they called the white man's religion, and asserting their independence of his moral principles, gave the Black Jews a feeling of superiority in a world where black people had long been subjected to scorn and discriminatory treatment by whites. Although Black Jews repudiated the way of life of the demoralized Negro lower class, they blamed white society for the despised habits of this group. They felt that they had emancipated themselves.[57]

In 1971, the Black Jews of New York, Philadelphia, Boston, Chicago, and Los Angeles numbered approximately 44,000. Most of the members of the Ethiopian Hebrew congregations in the United States are natives of the West Indies or the American South. Although the younger members of these congregations increasingly feel pressures to identify with the contemporary black movement, most of them have continued to give cultural concerns priority over those of race.[58]

Moorish American or Islamic Cults

During the 1920s and 1930s various Moorish American or Islamic cults grew up around the theme of the "Moorish" or "Asiatic" origin of black Americans. Such names as "Negro," "colored people," and even "black people" were repudiated. Their god was non-Christian. Perhaps the most influential of these groups was the Moorish Science Temple of America founded in Newark, New Jersey, about 1913 by Timothy Drew, a North Carolinian who was later called Noble Drew Ali, the prophet. The movement spread quickly to New York, Philadelphia, Chicago, Detroit, and to a number of southern cities.[59]

Members of the first Moorish Science Temples never failed to emphasize the racial aspect of the movement, and most devotees remarked that through the prophet he, or some member of his family, had been healed of mental, physical, or financial difficulties. The Temples declined after Noble Drew Ali allowed some charlatans to join the movement and to sell charms and herbs as a part of religious devotion. Drew's death led to the splitting of the cult into many smaller groups, but such practices as changing the names of believers, food taboos, abstention from cosmetics, asceticism, and the study of esoteric literature, as well as continued disaffection with the Christian church, proliferated in the ghetto.[60]

In Detroit in 1930, Allah's incarnation was a stranger who said he came from the Holy City of Mecca in Arabia. He used the name Wallace D. Fard or Wallace Fard Muhammad, but he was also known as Mr. Farrad Mohammad, F. Mohammad Ali, Professor Ford, and Wali Farrad. Calling himself "the Supreme Ruler of the Universe," Fard denounced the iniquitous white man and exalted black Afro-Asians. Within three years he had developed an effective organization called The Nation of Islam, one of the earliest officers of which was Elijah Muhammad, who was born Elijah Poole in Georgia. The Prophet, W. D. Fard, disappeared about June 1934, shortly after Elijah Muhammad had been made Minister of Islam. Fard became identified with the god Allah, and Muhammad assumed the title of "Prophet."[61]

Between 1934 and 1946 Elijah Muhammad organized branches in Chicago, Milwaukee, and Washington, D.C. By 1962 the membership of the Nation of Islam was variously estimated from 10,000 to a quarter of a million, and groups had been organized in 22 cities.[62]

To combat the forces that had weakened the Negro community, Muhammad denounced the matriarchal type of family, the failure to save money and to accumulate capital, the folk belief that "white is right," and personal indolence and laziness. A study of the Black Power movement in the late 1960s concluded that the puritanical ethics of Black Muslims and the pressure of black coalition leaders in many cities of the United States constituted a far more successful attack on the problems of prostitution and drugs than had been effected through sermons in Negro churches or by white service organizations.[63]

Essien-Udom points out that Muhammad's eschatology of the Black Nation would not meet the usual tests of knowledge, logically or empirically. According to his teachings, Mahdi or Saviour, is the God of the Black Nation and is a black man. Originally, the black man inhabited the moon, but several trillions of years ago a black scientist caused a tremendous explosion on the moon. The earth, which had been attached to the moon, fell 36,000 miles from the original orbit. The first people to inhabit the Earth were black people—members of the Tribe of Shabazz. Blacks in the United States are the chosen of the Black Nation

SECT AND CULT

(black, brown, red, and yellow peoples). Caucasians were grafted from black people and are inferior physically and mentally. Black people founded civilization before whites were created. The Resurrection means only that the time has come for the Negro to receive justice. The destruction of the world will mean only the destruction of Caucasians and Christianity. In the Redemption of the Black Nation after the final judgment, the blacks who have been oppressed by the white race will inherit power over the earth. The eschatology seeks to reverse the myth of white supremacy and to develop a different self-image in the black masses that is equally false but definitely functional.[64]

Because its objective is said to be the establishment of a Black Nation, the Nation of Islam's ideology is political. In practice, however, the movement is apolitical. Muhammad distrusted all political action, except in a Negro-controlled state, as a means of attaining anything other than civil rights in American society. The alternative to a Black Nation in the Western Hemisphere is a return to "our native land," but the location of that native land has never been specified.[65]

Minister Malcolm X Shebazz, who was converted to the Muslim movement in 1947 while confined in a maximum security prison in Concord, Massachusetts, found a large audience among northern blacks who were looking for tactics other than the marches, rallies and picketing which were being used to desegregate lunch counters in the South. After having risen to the position of chief aide to the Prophet, he was suspended by Muhammad in December 1963, ostensibily for making an unauthorized remark about the assassination of President John F. Kennedy. Actually, differences in point of view between Muhammad and Malcolm X had been developing for some time. In March 1964, Malcolm X left the Nation of Islam and organized a new movement consisting of a religious group, the Muslim Mosque, Inc., and a secular Organization of Afro-American Unity. By this time he had discontinued advocacy of a separate nation, saying that he thought blacks should stay in the United States and fight for good education, housing, and jobs. During April and May 1964, Malcolm X visited Egypt, Lebanon, Saudi Arabia, Nigeria, Ghana, Morocco, and Algeria. As a result of his pilgrimage to the Holy City of Mecca, he underwent a "spiritual rebirth" and no longer subscribed to "sweeping indictments of one race."[66] Malcolm X was assassinated in February 1965, but through his books—*The Autobiography of Malcolm X* and *Malcolm X Speaks*—his influence continued after his death.

The Black Muslims have sought neither to restore the traditional culture of Africa nor to reinstate the Southern American rural subculture. They have devised a history and a belief system which combine a political ideology with certain elements of Christian and Muslim teachings. Although the movement has the appearance of a wholly anti-white movement, Essien-Udom concluded that "properly conceived it is uncompromisingly anti-lower-class Negro values, anti-Negro middle-class complacency and opportunism, and anti-white paternalism and injustice."[67]

In the late 1960s and the early 1970s, the Nation of Islam was the most consistent critic of black churches, a stand widely appreciated by large numbers of black people who continued to attend church but who secretly admired Elijah Muhammad's denunciation of the transgression of Christianity.[68]

Black Storefront Churches

A myriad of small black religious cults located in storefronts and houses exists in northern urban areas. Frequently led by one man or woman, most of their regular followings consist of twenty to forty persons—or even fewer. These groups represent deviations within the Christian tradition, and, for the most part, they have been apolitical. Many of these black groups are "Spiritualist," a sect that seems to have originated in New Orleans and to have been transplanted to the North. These churches have offered healing, advice, and charms intended to bring good luck or to ward off evil forces. Equally important, the Spiritualist church in the black community has not condemned card-playing, dancing, policy (numbers), or the "sporting world." Basically, then, the attraction of the black Spiritualisms has been "their straightforward utilitarian use of religion."[69]

Sect and Cult Among Blacks of Canada

At one time Father Divine's movement was fairly active in Canada. The Peace Mission Movement gained a following of whites as well as of

Negroes during the depression of the 1930s, a period when there were eleven "heavens" in Canada—most of them in British Columbia. The movement received some impetus in 1946 when Father Divine took as his second wife a white woman from Vancouver. The most militant Negro religious organization ever established in Canada was a branch of the African Orthodox Church formed in Sidney (British Columbia) in 1921. A representative of Archbishop George A. McGuire, the church's founder, ministered to the religious needs of West Indians who worked in the steel mills. Few Canadian-born blacks joined the church. Another militant quasi-Methodist group, organized in 1906, lasted less than three decades.[70]

West Indian Pentecostals in England

West Indians migrating to England seldom join English churches. Migrants who were members of some sect in the Caribbean may not join the same sect in England, but they are likely to join some religious group. Many of these Negro churches have Church of God as part of their official names. Some of the black churches are almost identical in beliefs and ritual with the white Churches of God; others differ from them in ways that their members consider important. Calley classifies Pentecostal sects in England in two ways—according to whether they baptize in the name of the Father, Son, and Holy Ghost or in the name of Jesus only, and whether they are, in the United States, white or black sects.[71]

Father, Son, and Holy Ghost	Jesus Name
Church of God	Pentecostal Church of the World
Church of God of Prophecy	Church of the Lord Jesus Christ
New Covenant Church of God	of the Apostolic Faith
Church of God in Christ	

Negro Churches	White Churches
Pentecostal Churches of the World	Church of God of Prophecy
Church of the Lord Jesus Christ	Church of God
of the Apostolic Faith	
New Covenant Church of God	
Church of God in Christ	

Two-thirds of all West Indian migrants in England come from Jamaica, and practically all of the members of the Pentecostal sects studied by Calley in 1960–62 were from that island. Pentecostals are typical of the West Indian population in England; most are unskilled workers, a few are skilled workers, and fewer still have white-collar jobs. Women predominate among the 5 percent of the West Indians in Britain who are closely enough attached to Pentecostal sects to be considered members and the 10 percent who are sufficiently interested to attend services, at least infrequently.[72]

Like Pentecostals everywhere, West Indian Pentecostals in England are biblical fundamentalists. Members prefer one another's company rather than the company of other West Indians, and they cooperate by looking after each other's children, helping one another to find housing accommodations and work, and sometimes lend or give one another money. Like other Pentecostals, the West Indian sectarian thinks ill of the world and follows the biblical teaching to withdraw from it. In the early 1960s, Calley found that morals and ethics have little to do with the relationship of the West Indian Pentecostal to his fellow men; he is much more concerned with his relationship to God. The sins of special concern to the Pentecostal, those that should be avoided by all "saints" include: smoking, drinking, attending movies and dances, straightening the hair, wearing certain kinds of clothes, and "fornication."[73]

The ordinary ritual of the West Indian Pentecostals consists of testimony, glossolalia, dancing, ritual twitching, prayer, preaching, hymns, invocation of the Holy Ghost, and Bible readings. Intermittently, the rituals of communion, foot-washing, and baptism are performed.[74]

The testimony of a West Indian Pentecostal can be spoken or sung. If sung, it consists of a hymn, with the congregation joining in after the first verse or so. Spoken testimony ranges from a patterned recitation of thanks to Jesus to a long exhortation about being faithful to God. Calley found that most of the talking with tongues is conscious and intentional, often providing "fill-in" during testimony or prayer when the "saint" runs out of words. He observed also that involuntary glossolalia is quite rare. Like speaking in tongues, "dancing in the Spirit" is

SECT AND CULT

regarded as a "blessing." Some members remain seated and stamp rhyth-mically, others dance in one spot, and still others twirl and prance. For the most part, sermons are intended to stimulate members to have ec-static experiences rather than to be informative.[75]

A West Indian Pentecostal service in England may end with an "altar call" ("coming to the throne of grace") to any persons present who may need healing or "deliverance" (from sin or trouble). Healing rites consist of prayer, the laying on of hands, and anointing with oil, singly or together. Sect members believe that at least some illnesses are caused by the possession of evil spirits. Because they are often pregnant and concerned about their health, and because of the ailments that their young children have, women are involved in healing rites about three times as frequently as men.[76]

Unlike the Seventh Day Adventists, who proselytize vigorously, the West Indian Pentecostals proselytize only sporadically. The latter congregations alternate between months of waiting for Christ to arrive, and praying for revival and holding meetings on street corners in an at-tempt to find new converts.[77]

Calley concludes that the existence of the Pentecostal sects in En-gland cannot be accounted for in terms of economic deprivation. Some of the members of these groups are relatively prosperous, some are unem-ployed. The emergence and continuation of these sects are attributed more to the general difficulties experienced in settling down in Britain than to poverty. Migrants find prejudice and discrimination in what they consider to be a lack of courtesy on the part of many Englishmen to difficulties in obtaining housing and employment. Such negative factors are not the only ones behind sect activity; the Pentecostal church affords opportunities for meaningful participation in a collectivity. I point out in connection with my discussion of black Pentecostalism in the United States that the sect gives an adherent "something to live for and some-thing to live in." Among other roles offered by the sect are those of evangelist, convert, religious teacher, deacon, youth leader, and so on.[78] According to Calley's interpretation, most migrants do not participate in church services (if they participate at all) out of a desire to identify with English society, but rather for the purpose of emphasizing their sepa-rateness from it. Nevertheless, he holds that the sects play a positive role

SECT AND CULT

in the assimilatory process by cushioning the impact on the individual of life in a new type of society. Initially impeding assimilation, eventually they facilitate it.

In 1972, the adult membership of the independent black churches in Birmingham was estimated at 4,565, but regular attendance was two or three times as large because of the number of adults and children attending Sunday school. These persons constituted approximately one-fifth of the 50,000 to 60,000 West Indians and Africans residing in Birmingham. Taken together, they form one of the largest Christian denominations in the city. Many, but not all, of these churches are varieties of Pentecostalism.[79]

Segementation and proliferation of groups has promoted the growth of these churches. Taking into consideration different cultural elements: West African, West Indian, North American (black and/or white), and British, Gerloff has devised a classification of the black churches in Britain based on degrees of cultural alienation.[80] Cherabim and Seraphim, a fundamentalist church founded in Nigeria, is the only black church in Birmingham that is termed "single alienation." Thus West Africans are said to be less alienated from their cultural heritage than are the descendants of West Indian slaves.

West Indian churches whose forms and beliefs are a blend of West African cultural elements and Western-British missionary teachings reveal a "double alienation." Churches which typify the reaction of some West Indian immigrants to the "spiritual deadness" and the failure of British established Christianity to accept newcomers include the Church of the First Born, the Assembly of the First Born, and the International City Mission.

"Triple alienation" is seen in the Holiness and Pentecostal movements which arose in the United States and spread to the West Indies and then to England. These bodies—which were originally affiliated organizationally, doctrinally, and economically with North American headquarters—are by far the largest black churches in England and include the New Testament Church of God, the Church of God of Prophesy, and, much smaller in size, the Pilgrim Wesleyan Holiness Church. Similar to the first two churches are a few smaller Church of God bodies—the Church of God (Holiness) and the Bible Church of

God. Also in this group of churches transplanted from the West Indies is the Seventh Day Adventist Church, a multiracial sect which has the highest percentage of West Indians in its membership outside the all-black churches. According to Gerloff, only those churches succeeded in establishing branches in Britain which "were already fairly indigenized in the West Indies and competent to become the church of West Indians for West Indians, not of British or American leaders catering to the needs of West Indian immigrants."[81] (The one exception to this statement is the Church of God of Prophesy, a church which still has an American supervisor.)

In the expansion of black Christian communities in Britain, some bodies eventually broke away from white North American organizations, the United Church of God, for example. Independent movements such as the Life and Light Fellowship arose; also, affiliations with black headquarters in the United States took place: Triumphant Church of God, African Methodist Episcopal Zion Church, and Apostolic Church of God. The Church of God in Christ, the largest Pentecostal body, as well as the largest black church in the United States, has never been very significant in Jamaica, but it has two flourishing branches in Britain. All of these groups state that they belong to the "same Church of God" all over the world.[82]

The small groups which represent "fourfold alienation" have attempted to meet and enter into religious fellowship with British Christians (Pentecostals, Evangelicals, and Nonconformists). The Seventh Day Adventist church is the only functioning multiracial community with a well-established organization. Others in this category are three small organizations: Church of God Fellowship; the Shilo Pentecostal Fellowship; and the Baptist Church of God in London, a fellowship of West Indian Pentecostals and Free British Baptists.[83]

Although fissions over doctrinal and behavioral issues, and the segmentation and proliferation of groups, may seem to contradict the possibility of cooperation both between the various black churches and with other groups, Gerloff holds that this is not necessarily true. For the black Christian communities, two kinds of involvement are distinguished. "Internal" involvement, or "conscientization" within the religious community, means becoming conscious "of one's own dignity and creating meaning in a deprived situation through appropriate ideologies," while "external" involvement refers to "rediscovering interrelations in society and acting freely on them." From this viewpoint, two conclusions emerge: (1) without basic recognition from the larger community there is no impetus to engage in social and political action, and (2) West Indian churches will contribute to social change if changes occur in British society as a whole. Because of their spiritual belief that "salvation is the salvation of God's people all over the world regardless of name, colour, or nationality," Gerloff asserts that the black independent churches in Britain have already made an outstanding contribution in the field of race relations.[84]

Writing about the contribution of Pentecostalism to theological study, Hollenweger notes that Pentecostal theological books are "mostly boring and old-fashioned." Actually, he asserts, their theology is not in their books. In Brazil, Chile, Mexico, and Africa—but not in the United States or Great Britain—the Pentecostal mode of communication transcends the barriers of education, color, social class, and nationality.

> Taken seriously this offers a real possibility of discovering a methodology of theology in an oral culture where the medium of communication is—just as in biblical times—not the doctrine, but the song; not the treatise but the TV programme . . . . The ecumenical problem of the future . . . will take place between the oral and the literary Christians and theologians.[85]

In similar vein, Tinney asserts that "the ecumenical and interracial factors inherent in Pentecostalism may offer mainstream Christianity, both Catholic and Protestant, some direction in building a truly integrated church."[86]

Gerloff lists three theological issues that must be considered in connection with the Pentecostal movement.[87] The first of these is "the tragic marriage between fundamentalism as a notional rational language and Pentecostalism as a living liturgy and spiritual witness within an oral-associative tradition." The second issue is the preoccupation with speaking in tongues. Because glossolalia, defined by Hollenweger (*Pentecost*, 225), as "a meditative, non-rational form of prayer," was rejected by established Christianity, some Pentecostals have made a narrow doctrine out of this phenomenon. In other Pentecostal groups, "speaking in tongues is still regarded highly, greatly appreciated as a spiritual gift, but not as the essential sign of the outpouring of the Spirit."[88] The third issue involves pneumatology, or the doctrine concerning the Holy Spirit. Instead of limiting the doctrine of the "charismata" of the Spirit to seven or nine spiritual gifts, one interpretation holds that for Paul "receiving the Spirit" and "becoming a Christian" are identical, and that he used the term charismata for "so-called supernatural gifts as for so-called natural gifts" (being married, teaching, etc.).[89] This view of "charismatic" means that each human being has something to contribute, and that different gifts, conditions, and vocations must be taken seriously. Thus interpreted, the doctrine of the Holy Spirit has a powerful appeal to the oppressed, the isolated, the disadvantaged, and those who feel that they are disadvantaged.

CHAPTER NINE

Conclusion

AT THE OUTSET I stated that this book is concerned with the religions of persons of African descent in the New World, but that it is not a study of black religions in the sense that all of the religions considered were originated by blacks or that the memberships of all the groups are made up entirely of black persons or even of a black majority. It is, rather, a study of the religions that have played an important role in the culture history of blacks in the Caribbean, North and South America, and Britain.

The African Diaspora in the New World, Slavery, and the Religions of Blacks

This book is concerned with the African diaspora in North America, the West Indies, and Latin America, and, to a much lesser extent, in Britain, during the past four hundred years. It should be pointed out, however, that there have been successive dispersals of population out of sub-Saharan Africa to other parts of the world for 10,000 years.

In the Atlantic slave trade, blacks were shipped from eight coastal regions in Africa: Senegambia, Sierre Leone, the present Ivory Coast and Liberia, the Gold Coast (present-day Ghana), the Bight of Benin region from the Volta to the Benin River, the Bight of Biafra, Central Africa (Angola), and southeastern Africa from the Cape of Good Hope to Cape Delgado and including Madagascar. But the actual origins in the interior are often uncertain. It is estimated that slave imports into the New World totalled nine or ten million.[1]

The main center of the Atlantic slave trade was tropical America. Forty-two percent of the slaves were brought to the Caribbean islands, approximately half to South America, 2 percent to Middle America, and 7 percent to North America. Probably the Atlantic fringe from Brazil through the Guianas to the Caribbean coast and islands received 90 percent of the trade.[2]

The question of whether slaves received better treatment in the Latin than in the English and Dutch colonies is still controversial. The "Black Code" of the seventeenth century in the French and Spanish possessions prescribed baptism and instruction in the Catholic religion for all slaves, but in some areas this obligation was widely disregarded. Many Catholic priests encouraged matrimony between slaves and advocated their manumission. Genovese attributes a part of the difference between Brazilian and United States' rates of intermarriage, access of blacks to positions of respect and power, and integration of people of color into a single nationality to Catholicism. Recent evidence, however, seems to indicate that slaves were better off materially in the United States. In nineteenth-century Brazil, some slaveowners considered it more profitable to purchase new slaves than to raise slave children. In the United States the prohibition of the importation of slaves from Africa in 1807 meant that slavery could survive only so long as it could replenish itself, and that necessitated some interest in the physical care of the slaves. In the highly capitalistic slavery of the United States, slave owners generally used force optimally, not maximally. The ability to survive and multiply is shown in the pattern of Afro-American populations at the middle of the twentieth century. Although the United States imported less than 5 percent of the slaves, it had nearly one-third of the black population in 1950. The Caribbean islands imported more than 40 percent of the slaves during the Atlantic slave trade but had approximately 20 percent of the Afro-American population in 1950. Regional and temporal differences within countries themselves make it difficult to judge the relative severity of slave systems.[3]

Slavery, a vital fact of the experience of Afro-Americans, was an important force in shaping their religions. On plantations, many of the slaves were isolated physically and socially from persons of European de-

CONCLUSION

scent. Often in poor health, slaves were economically and politically dependent. In some parts of the New World, they were excluded for long periods of time from the established religions, or they were only partially instructed in religion. At other times, the historical churches discriminated against blacks in various ways. In the Catholic countries, permission to organize religious fraternities along ethnic lines furthered the continuation of African religious traditions. Varying combinations of socioeconomic and religious circumstances have strongly influenced the degree and the direction of religious participation and innovation by Afro-Americans.

Race, Class, and Religion in the Caribbean and South America

Among the religious groups discussed in chapters 2–6 the following relationships between race and religion may be discerned.

Religious Groups in the Caribbean and South America Whose Membership Is Limited to Blacks or to Blacks and Amerindians

Vodun (Haiti)
Vodu (Dominican Republic)
Shango (Trinidad, Grenada, Venezuela)
Xangó (Recife, Brazil)
Pará (Porto Alegre, Brazil)
Encantado cults (Santo Antônio dos Pretos, Brazil)
Mina or Gégé and Nago (São Luiz, Brazil)
Santeria (Cuba)
Winti (Surinam)
Boni (French Guiana)
Cumina (Jamaica)
Convince (Jamaica)
Big Drum (Grenada, Carriacou)
Kele (St. Lucia)
Ancestral cult of the Black Carib of British Honduras (Belize)
Revivalist (Jamaica)
Shakers (St. Vincent)
Streams of Power (St. Vincent)
Ras Tafari (Jamaica)
The Dreads (Dominica)
Candomblé (Brazil)

Religious Groups in the Caribbean and South America Whose Membership Is Not Limited to Blacks or to Blacks and Amerindians

Catholic Church
Historical Protestant Churches
Pentecostal Churches
Macoumba (Brazil)
Batuque (Belém, Brazil)
Umbanda (Brazil)
María Lionza (Venezuela)
Spiritualists (Puerto Rico)

In the Caribbean and in South America, policies of admission to the historical Christian denominations have varied with respect to blacks and Amerindians since the beginning of colonization, but most churches have been open to blacks at least since Emancipation.[4] Unlike their counterparts in the United States, Pentecostal groups in South America have never been organized along racial lines. Some candomblés in Bahia, Brazil, are of Amerindian origin. In the evolution of the macoumba in the urban centers of southern Brazil, some whites, often foreigners (Portuguese, Spanish) and a few Japanese have become cult leaders. The membership of Umbanda groups in São Paulo, Brazil, includes many persons of European origin and some Japanese. Although the Batuque of Belém, Brazil, is derived ultimately from African religions, its members include individuals from a variety of racial backgrounds, and mediums are not chosen by their color. The devotees of the cult of María Lionza in Venezuela include Venezuelan Creoles, Spaniards, Colombians, Italians, Portuguese, and persons of African descent.[5]

Religions that are limited mainly to persons of lower-class status and those which are not as restricted by class lines are listed below.

Religious Groups Whose Membership Is Limited Mainly to Persons of Lower Class Status

Vodun (Haiti)
Vodu (Dominican Republic)
Shango (Trinidad, Grenada, Venezuela)
Xangó (Recife, Brazil)

CONCLUSION

Pará (Porto Alegre, Brazil)
Encantado cults (Santo Antônio dos Pretos, Brazil)
Mina or Gégé and Nago (São Luis, Brazil)
Candomblé (Brazil)
Santeria (Cuba)
Batuque (Belém, Brazil)
María Lionza (Venezuela)
Winti (Surinam)
Boni (French Guiana)
Macoumba (Brazil)
Cumina (Jamaica)
Convince (Jamaica)
Big Drum (Grenada and Carriacou)
Kele (St. Lucia)
Ancestral cult of the Black Carib of British Honduras (Belize)
Revivalist (Jamaica)
Shouters (Trinidad)
Shakers (St. Vincent)
Streams of Power (St. Vincent)
Spiritualists (Puerto Rico)
The Dreads (Dominica)

*Religious Groups Whose Membership Is Not Limited to Persons of Lower
Class Status*

Catholic Church
Historical Protestant Churches
Pentecostal Churches
Umbanda (Brazil)
Ras Tafari (Jamaica)

Why Religious Cults Have Arisen and Flourished in the Caribbean and South America

I have stressed the point that a religious cult cannot be attributed to any one factor—economic, ecological, sociological, psychological, or cultural. In the Caribbean and South America, the presence of two or more major religious traditions, or types of traditions—notably African, American Indian, and Christian—existed side by side during slavery. For many reasons, large numbers of blacks could not participate fully either in Christianity or in a traditional African religion. These two religious sources did provide, however, elements which could be combined into syncretistic, or hybrid religions, which were emotionally satisfying.

From West African religions the cultists drew the names of prominent deities and their temperamental tendencies, the concept of multiple "souls," sacred objects, musical and dance patterns, possession by spirits, initiation rites of seclusion and indoctrination, death rituals, proper types of offerings to divinities and spirits, magical charms, methods of divination, and concern for the goodwill of the ancestors. Depending upon whether they had had some exposure to Catholicism or to Protestantism, these religionists borrowed and modified numerous Christian theological doctrines, hymns and chants, prayers, passages from the Bible, and symbols.

The rapidly growing cult of Umbanda in Brazil includes some remodeled European spiritualistic doctrines, and a belief in the availability and helpfulness of several categories of spirits: dead Brazilian Indians, dead Afro-Brazilian slaves, dead children, people who were evil, and spirits who represent a merging of African deities and Catholic saints. The belief system of the spiritualistic cult of María Lionza in Venezuela brings together the spirits of American Indian nature deities, modern Venezuelan heroes, Buddhist spirits, and the spirits of several European notables of recent times, as well as a number of African divinities.

Two other major variables have interacted with the cultural factor in the development of Caribbean and South American religious cults: the socioeconomic conditions of segments of the population, and the personality tendencies of cultists, especially of cult leaders. For the most part, the members of the cults considered here have had little or no economic standing and have been politically powerless. Through their religious behavior devotees have attempted to reduce their suffering, combat the "meaninglessness" of their lives, or overcome injustice. In Haiti, for example, 85 to 90 percent of the population constitutes a poverty-stricken rural and urban proletariat. For the majority of Haitians, educational and medical services have been meager or nonexistent, and the government has been a democracy in name only. Christian doctrine has not been combined to any extent with educational and health programs or other activities that would serve as alternatives to vodun. Or to take a less extreme example, in the relatively immobile society of Trinidad the Shouter and Shango cults have provided satisfactions that thousands of lower-class persons have not been able to obtain in the historical churches (Catholic, Anglican, Presbyterian, and Methodist), or in the newer sects (Pilgrim Holiness, Gospel Hall, Seventh Day Adventist, and Jehovah's Witnesses).

In this book the emergence and continuation of religious cults and sects in the Caribbean and South America is attributed largely to the interaction of these three major variables—cultural, socioeconomic, and psychological. Among the contingent factors which have affected the development of these religions are the degree to which a group of people has been physically isolated from other segments of the population, the extent of the group's continuing contact with Africa, the quality and continuity of leadership, cohesiveness within the group, and whether the group has been stimulated and challenged by the presence of rival cults and sects. The amount of influence exerted by these contingent factors has varied from place to place, a point which I have attempted to document in chapters 2–6 and to which I make reference in the following sections of this chapter.

SOME COMPARISONS OF RELIGIOUS CULTS WITHIN COUNTRIES: TRINIDAD, JAMAICA AND BRAZIL[6]

Trinidad: Shango and Shouters

The present participants in the Shango cult of Trinidad in the Port of Spain region refer to themselves as "Yoruba people" and to their ceremonies and procedures as "Yoruba work." One of the important traditional Yoruba religions in Nigeria honors Shango, the god of thunder. Shango is not the only African deity followed by devotees of the cult in Trinidad that bears his name. It seems likely that the newly imported Africans of Yoruba origin and the blacks of Yoruba descent who were brought to Trinidad from the French islands of the West Indies early formed an ethnic association similar to those organized elsewhere in the Caribbean and South America. In 1858, de Verteuil wrote:

CONCLUSION

They are besides guided, in a mixed degree, by the sense of association; and the principle of combination for the common weal has been fully sustained wherever they have settled in any number; in fact, the whole Yarraba race of the colony may be said to form a sort of social league for mutual support and protection.[7]

In such a setting segments of old Yoruba ceremonies could be performed, and, in time, blended with elements of Catholicism.[8]

Henney traces the origins of the Spiritual Baptists (the Shakers of St. Vincent and the Shouters of Trinidad) to the early years of the twentieth century in St. Vincent. About a decade later the cult spread to Trinidad.[9]

Shangoists in the Port of Spain region have combined a number of West African beliefs and practices, in pure or reinterpreted form, with elements of Catholicism. Such Yoruba gods as Shango, Ogun, Obatala, Oya, Aja, Osain, and Oshun are among the leading "powers" of the cult. The polytheism of West African religions has been reinterpreted by equating certain of the old Yoruba gods with selected Catholic saints. Presumably the fundamentalist Shouters believe only in the Trinity, but at times offerings are given to the saints.[10]

Among the similar or identical ritual objects used by both Shangoists and Shouters are crosses and crucifixes, swords, lighted candles at the four corners (of the *palais* and of the church), and ceremonial robes and dresses (white and of other colors); pictures and lithographs of God, Christ, and the Saints; bowls and vases of flowers and of leaves; the Bible, accessories used in healing (goblets and plates, parchment paper, chalk, leaves, grasses, roots, incense, oils and perfumes), pots of water, and altars. Shango objects which are conspicuously absent from a Spiritual Baptist church include drums, thunder-stones, daggers, hatchets, knives, (wooden) guns, rattles, whips, shayshays (ceremonial brooms), anchors and oars, large wooden keys, stools (earthen or concrete shrines for the gods), and statues of saints. Ordinarily one would not find in a Shango chapelle a large brass handbell, religious mottoes and placards, a "chariot wheel" (a bicycle wheel, suspended from a center post, which is spun from time to time during the service), or a pulpit.[11]

Ritual acts which the two cults have in common consist of pouring water at the four corners, anointing the heads of devotees with olive oil,

CONCLUSION

throwing food to the spirits, writing symbols and messages with chalk, handclapping, dancing during ceremonies (the "rejoicing" and the shaking of the Shouters often involve some dance steps, and dancing is an important part of a Shango ceremony), spirit possession, certain prayers (Hail Mary, the Lord's Prayer, and the Apostles' Creed), animal sacrifices (only pigeons in the case of the Shouters, and only in certain churches), baptism (a Spiritual Baptist rite required of both Shangoists and Shouters), and mourning (an optional rite conducted by Spiritual Baptists but observed by some members of both cults).

The meanings of these acts vary somewhat from one group to another within the same cult, and they also vary between the two cults. A Shango leader gives orders and makes announcements during a ceremony but, unlike a Shouters pastor, he does not preach and he makes less use of the Bible. There is no "groaning" or "grunting" (hyperventilating or overbreathing) at Shango ceremonies, but this method of facilitating spirit possession, called "adoption" in Trinidad, is followed by some devotees in some Shouters groups. Although rum is always offered to Ogun, and perhaps to one or two other powers at a Shango ceremony, it is never used during a Shouters ceremony. A variety of powers, a number of them with African names, are expected to "manifest" on the participants during a Shango rite.[12]

The Spiritual Baptists meet with much greater regularity than do the shangoists. The big ceremonies at a Shango center occur once a year, and "prayer" meetings may or may not be held from time to time. Shouters meet every Sunday evening, and occasionally have special ceremonies. A Shouters group has more officers, is more highly organized, and is more democratic than a band of shangoists.[13]

The healing procedures used by some leaders among the Shouters are virtually the same as those followed by Shango practitioners. Officials of a Shouters church who try to exclude all Shango elements from their operations use no drums and kill no animals during healing sessions. Usually they employ relatively simple healing techniques, emphasizing especially prayer and Bible reading. They may or may not anoint a sick person with olive oil. If they use bush teas in healing, they claim that the Holy Spirit tells them which leaves, roots, and barks to include. Some of these leaders use no water, no candles, and no special garments during healing periods. If a Shouters leader undertakes the driving out of an evil spirit, his procedures include some of the same elements utilized by Shango practitioners on similar occasions. Although differing in content, dreams and visions serve about the same purposes in the two cults. Divining the future is of importance both to shangoists and to Shouters, but the methods of forecasting differ somewhat; for example, the casting of obi seeds is not used by the Spiritual Baptists—at least not by those who do not mix Shango and Shouters rituals.[14]

Thousands of persons in Trinidad who are recorded by the Census as Christians—Roman Catholics or Protestant—are regular or occasional participants in the two Afro-Christian cults. Some shangoists attend services in one of the principal Christian denominations with some regularity. For some, the principal attractions of a Shango *chapelle* or a Shouters church are the healing and conjuring which are available through cult leaders. In addition to mixing Shango and Shouters elements in the same ceremony, some cult leaders carry on *orisha* or Spiritual Baptist rites separately, either at the same location or at different places.[15]

Jamaica: Cumina, Convince, Revivalism, and Ras Tafari

The most likely source of both the Cumina and Convince ancestral cults is the religion of the Blue Mountain Maroons of the nineteenth century.[16] The Revivalists are descended from the Native Baptists and the Afro-Christian cults of the period 1780 to 1820 and of those who were caught up in the Great Revival of 1861.[17] Ras Tafari, an anti-white religio-political movement, is an offshoot of the Universal Negro Improvement Association founded by Marcus Garvey about 1915. Cumina and Convince are more African than Revivalism, and the latter is more African than Ras Tafari.

Cumina is primarily a family religion, but a Convince group revolves around a single leader (Bongo Man). A Revivalist group has numerous officers under the control of a Shepherd, Father, Mother, or other leader. The long discussions and debates, often followed by votes of those present, make Ras Tafari more democratic than the other popular religious groups in Jamaica.

Cumina spirits (zombies) are divided into three ranks: sky gods, earthbound gods, and ancestral zombies. Cumina theology resembles

CONCLUSION

West African and Congo religions. The names of the gods are different (among the 39 sky gods listed by Moore, only one—Shango—clearly has the name of a West African deity).[18] Bongo spirits in a Convince group are ghosts of persons who are believed to have belonged to the cult during their lifetime. The most powerful ghosts come from Africa, supposedly the home of Bongo. The next most important ghosts are those of Jamaican slaves and the Maroons who participated in the cult until recent times. Finally, and least useful, are ghosts of Jamaicans whose deaths have occurred most recently.[19] The divinities of Revivalism include such Old Testament prophets as Solomon, Joshua, and Jeremiah; Matthew, Peter and other Apostles and Evangelists of the New Testament; the Trinity; Michael, Gabriel, and other archangels; Moses; Satan and his chief assistants; Ariel, Uriel and other beings from Hebrew magical tradition; other supernatural figures of unknown origin; and the spirits of the dead. Although denied by some Ras Tafarians in recent years, originally one of the basic beliefs of the cult was the divinity of Haile Selassie, the late Emperor of Ethopia. Unlike Cumina, Convince, and Revivalist rituals, spirit possession is not a part of Ras Tafarian meetings.[20]

Brazil: Batuque and Umbanda

Earlier in this century, the beliefs and ceremonies of Batuque, a contemporary spiritualist cult found in Belém, Brazil, included Yoruban and Dahomean traditions, elements of Indian shamanism, folk Catholicism, as well as Iberian and local folklore. In recent decades, a major change has occurred through the inclusion of spirits and rites from the Umbanda cult of Rio de Janeiro.[21]

The spirits worshipped by devotees of Batuque are the *encantados,* but these spirits are not equated or syncretized with the Catholic saints as they are in Cuban santeria, Brazilian candomblés, Haitian vodun, or Trinidadian, Grenadian, or Recife (Brazil) shango. Most Batuque members regard themselves as Roman Catholics, and the beliefs of their cult are additional beliefs which do not in any way replace Catholic beliefs. Each encantado "adores" a particular saint, and each devotee of the encantado is expected to revere the same saint by offering special prayers on the saint's day. The contractual relationship between a member of Batuque and an encantado resembles that between an individual and a saint.[22]

The cult's immediate predecessor seems to have been the Yoruban and Dahomean cults of São Luiz in the state of Maranhão, but the Leacocks emphasize the extent to which it has become Brazilianized and call it an independent religious system. Most of the encantados in Batuque are not African, nor are other features of African tradition prominent features of the cult. Three traditions have contributed to the Batuque pantheon and lore: African, American Indian, and European or Luso-Brazilian. The major encantados, called *senhores, brancos,* and *gente fina,* are identified with the upper classes. Some of the deities have been imported from Dahomey, some from Nigeria, and some Yoruban-derived *orixas* have been borrowed indirectly from or reemphasized because of Umbanda of Rio de Janeiro. The Indian encantados represent Brazilian idealizations of the aborigines and have nothing to do with continuations of Indian religions. The principal Indian contributions to the cult are the addition of animal spirits to the pantheon, the small black people of the forest, and, possibly, the tree spirits. Since members of Batuque believe that the proper place for souls to appear is at a *meso de espiritismo* (spiritualist séance), the souls of the dead are the least influential of the supernaturals.

Umbanda, the rapidly growing spiritualist cult in Brazil, does not constitute a single religion. In São Paulo, Pressel found that "the more African forms of Umbanda, heavily influenced by Candomblé and Macumba" were at one end of Camargo's continuum of spiritualism and the European spiritualism of Allen Kardec was at the other end.[23] Members of a typical Umbanda cult center in São Paulo believe in five major types of spirits: the caboclo spirits of dead Brazilian Indians; the *prêto velho* (gentle spirits of dead Afro-Brazilian slaves); the *criança* (spirit of a dead child); the *exu* (spirits of people who were evil); and *orixas* (spirits who represent a merging of West African deities and Catholic saints.[24] Umbandists organize their spirits into seven *linhas* (lines), each headed by an *orixa* and divided into seven *falanges* (phalanxes). Each phalanx is in turn divided into seven *legiões* (legions) of spirits. A common organization of lines in São Paulo includes those headed by Oxalá (Jesus Cristo), Iemanjá

CONCLUSION

(Virgem Maria), Oxóce (São Sebastiao), Xangô (São Jeronimo), and Ogum (São Jorge).

Although the Umbandist ritual uses practices derived from spiritualism and occultism, in some respects the traditional model developed in the cults of African origin persists. In 1970, Bastide pointed out that two opposing tendencies create an ambiguity in the umbandist world; a) innovations contribute to the progressive deafricanization of the cult, and b) reafricanization due to the urging of some leaders that umbandists be initiated in the candomblés so that they can bring knowledge more authentically African to their followers.[25]

Like Batuque, Umbanda is not a revitalization movement. The main concerns of both cults are the almost overwhelming personal problems of daily life.[26] Pressel found that Umbanda is linked with modernization and that the "conceptualization of what constitutes a personal problem that spirits can deal with has changed somewhat from traditional concerns to those related to an industrial society."[27]

The Leacocks "found no evidence . . . that the Batuque is a protest movement of any kind. . . . the appeal of the Batuque is not that it promises to change the world in which the members live, but that it will help them to survive in that world."[28] They argue that Bastide overstresses the racial aspect of newer religions like Umbanda and Batuque when he says (Les Religions Africaines au Brésil, 522–26) that they represent "a protest by 'Negroes' or a 'colored class' against their lower-class status."[29] In a later discussion of Umbanda, Bastide asserts that this type of spiritualism, like the Black Muslim churches in the United States and the Ras Tafari movement in Jamaica

is at heart a protest-movement directed against white prejudices. That is why it supports a number of those African beliefs or customs which are widespread among the coloured masses. The existence of the Orisha is admitted. There is a priesthood of the babalaõ. Against Allan Kardec, the possibility of a special Negro spiritualism is envisaged, in which contact is made with the spirits of former slaves, who return to earth, via their mediums, to do good, in spite of the past, to the descendants of those who enslaved them. But since, at the same time, Africa is conceived of very much in the same ways as the whites saw it, i.e., as a land of "barbarism,"

CONCLUSION

such people are liable to invent a whole mass of myths and ideologies which, while pretending to revivify the African heritage, in fact tend to betray it . . . . The African continent becomes a mere way-station for an esoteric science which supposedly originated in India, and made its way thence to the coloured population of Brazil. The African theory of reincarnation is identified with the Indian theory of *karma;* the cult of the *orishas* is based on certain passages in Annie Besant; and so on. Thus for these people the 'return to Africa' is really a *rejection* of Africa as their mother-country (the contemptuous image created by the whites still lingers on) in order the better to claim affinity with Asia, cradle of world civilisation, and already at the top of the cultural ladder while Europeans were still a mass of savages.[30]

Although the Negro membership of Umbanda is large, it is by no means limited to persons of African descent. In view of this fact, Bastide's claim that Umbanda represents a protest against white prejudice should not be given much weight.

SOME COMPARISONS OF RELIGIOUS CULTS BETWEEN COUNTRIES IN THE CARIBBEAN AND SOUTH AMERICA

Trinidad, Jamaica, Grenada, and St. Vincent

Among the lower-class black populations of these four countries, the widest range of religious cult-types is found in Jamaica. However, Cumina and Convince, the most African of the Jamaican cults, are less African than the Shango cults of Trinidad and Grenada. Despite its orientation to Africa, the Ras Tafari movement in Jamaica actually includes only a small number of Africanisms.[31] Numerous African and European cultural elements have been combined in the several varieties of Jamaican revivalism. Unlike the Shouters cult in Trinidad, Shakerism in St. Vincent has not been directly influenced by a cult of the Shango type.[32]

Jamaican revivalists believe in the Trinity and in possession by the Holy Spirit. In Jamaica, possession of revivalists is more violent, and, unlike the Shakers and Shouters, they have ways of inducing possession. During certain rituals the revivalists offer sacrifices, including bloody of-

CONCLUSION

ferings to the spirits, and an occasional animal sacrifice (pigeons only) is made by the Shouters in Trinidad. The Shakers of St. Vincent offer no sacrifices.[33]

The Shango cults in Trinidad and Grenada are quite similar. The major powers are the same in both cults, and in both they are associated with certain Catholic saints. All of the gods are invited in succession to each annual ceremony, and the methods of summoning and worshipping the gods are almost identical. Shangoists and Shouters in Trinidad maintain interesting connections because adherents of both groups must submit to Shouters leaders in baptismal, "mourning," and "building" ceremonies (the second and third rites are intended to enhance an individual's spiritual understanding), and because some Shouters attend, and sometimes participate in, Shango ceremonies, or they consult a Shango leader about healing, divining, or conjuring. The Shango cult in Grenada has been influenced by the Nation Dance in honor of African ancestors and by the Grenadian Shouters church. Norman Paul's "African Feast" cult in Grenada closely resembles Shangoism, but its founder combined African traditions with elements of Seventh Day Adventism, the Nation Dance, Shakerism, and magic from such books as Albertus Magnus and the Sixth and Seventh Books of Moses.[34]

Brazil, Cuba, and Haiti

Many similarities exist in the Neo-African religious cults of Brazil, Cuba, and Haiti. In São Luiz, Brazil, religious rituals closely parallel African patterns only in the "orthodox" Dahomean and Yoruban cult groups, with the Dahomean house adhering to purer forms of African ritual than the Yoruban.[35] In a third type of cult center in São Luiz, the Yoruban-derived houses, most of the deities are of European or South American Indian derivation and have Brazilian names. At the Dahomean house, the songs are sung in Fō, and the dance rhythms are pure African. At the Yoruban center, the songs are sung either in Nago, in mixed Nago and Portuguese, or in Portuguese. In the Yoruban-derived groups, only a few songs are sung in Nago. Identification between African deities and Catholic saints is greater in the Yoruban cult than elsewhere in São Luiz.

At the middle of the twentieth century, there were only three cult houses in Bahia that had maintained the Gege (Dahomey) cult without change. In other Bahian candomblés Gege traditions have been almost completely absorbed in the Nago (Yoruba) rituals.[36] Members of Bahian candomblés believe in a supreme god—Olorun (a Yoruba term), or Zaniapombo (a word used in the Angolan, Congolese, and caboclo candomblés). Oshala (Obatala) is often ranked second among the gods. Below these divinities are the *orisha* (Nago), *vodun* (Gege), *inkices* (Angola and Congo), and the *encantados* (Caboclos). Among the most popular and powerful deities are Shango, Ogun, Oshossie, Omolu, Nanā, Yemanja, and Oshun, all equated with one or another of the Catholic saints. For the most part, Angolan and Congolese candomblés have the same gods (*inkices*) as the Nago cult centers, but their names are different and they differ superficially in appearance. The music and musical instruments in the Bantu candomblés are, however, quite different, and hymns are sung in Portuguese. Candomblés of Amerindian origin are said to be "degradations" of Gege-Nago candomblés, and sometimes of Islamic Negro (Nago, Hausa, and Tapa) and Bantu cults.[37] Most of the caboclo encantados are the same gods as the Nagos and Geges have, but they have been modified by Angolan-Congo influences and, more recently, spiritualist influences. These candomblés include a few authentic indigenous gods and a number of encantados from spiritualist cults. In short, whereas forty or fifty years ago candomblés in Bahia were dedicated to the gods of only one "nation," only a few are still so dedicated.

In Bahian candomblés, as well as in Cuban santeria and Trinidadian shango, Eshu must be the first deity invited to a ceremony. In all three cults, rites are performed to prevent him from becoming angry and disturbing the ceremony. In Bahia, a feast starts with the sacrifice of animals, followed by singing and dancing. Later in a secret propitiatory rite the stones of the orishas are washed in the blood of the animals, and an animal sacrifice is presented to Eshu. Where this traditional sacrifice of animals is omitted, the daughters of the candomblé throw out Eshu's food and dismiss him in the same way that shangoists perform this rite in Trinidad. As in candomblé ceremonies in other parts of Brazil—São Luiz, Recife, Rio de Janeiro, Porto Alegre, and São Paulo, as well as in Cuban santeria, Haitian vodun, and Trinidadian shango, special songs are sung and special dances are danced for each orisha who comes to the ceremony.

Most of the non-European elements in Cuban santeria are derived from Yoruba beliefs and rituals. Among the deities, many of them identified in the minds of believers with Catholic saints, are Echú, Changó, Shapana, Elegba (Gege), Oya, Obatala, Yemajá, Ochun, Ochosí, Oko, Osanyin, the Ibeji, Ogun, Egungun, and Orunmila or Ifá. African components in the ritual include the pattern of possession, the retention of animal sacrifices, drumming, singing, and dancing. Thirty years ago Bascom found that the sacred stones, blood, and herbs were of great importance in santeria's form of worship. Devotees believe, as Haitian vodunists and Trinidadian shangoists do, that the power of the stones is increased by allowing the blood of sacrificial animals to flow onto them. As in Nigeria, the special herbs, mixed with water, serve to cleanse, refresh, and prepare devotees and ritual objects for contact with the orisha. Striking similarities exist between two forms of Afro-Cuban divination—Ifa, which uses an *opele* (divination chain), and *dilogun* (sixteen cowrie shells), and Yoruba divination. Ortiz's detailed accounts of *lucumi* (*santeria*) dances demonstrate the African authenticity of the rituals.[38]

Most of the *loa* (vodun deities) in Haiti belong to two groups—Rada (Dahomean or Yoruban) and Petro (other parts of Africa). In recent decades, cult groups and ceremonies other than these two groups have been rare. Such Dahomean gods as Legba, Damballa, Erzilie, and Gédé, along with the Yoruban deities Ogun and Shango, play prominent roles in vodun. All of these *loa* and many others are equated with Catholic saints, but dozens of divinities—some of which are known only in one locality or by one extended family—seem to be of Haitian origin. The dead rank second only to the loa, and in the North, neither the dead in general nor the dead twins specifically may be overlooked in any vodun service. As in the candomblés of Brazil, Cuban santeria, and Trinidadian shango, each god is summoned by the playing of his drum rhythm.

In Métraux's view, in comparison with Bahian candomblés and Cuban santeria, the vodun cults of Port-au-Prince "cut a sorry figure." Because vodun has retained many fewer theological and mythological concepts of African religions than the candomblés and santeria, it

CONCLUSION

seemed to him a "decadent and bastardized African religion."[39] The differences between vodun and the other religions are attributed to the inability of the Haitian peasant to devote as much money to his cult as his confreres in Brazil and Cuba, and to the importation of slaves to the latter countries up to the second half of the nineteenth century compared with the bringing of the last Africans to Haiti more than 170 years ago. Legba and Damballa illustrate the changes that have occurred in the personalities and attributes of African gods who are included in vodun. According to Métraux:

> In Fon mythology Legba, as interpreter to the gods, fulfills a function of primordial importance in the whole system of religion. He alone can deliver the messages of the gods in human language and interpret their will. He is also the god of destiny, he who presides over divination with palm-nuts or shells. . . . He is also a phallic god, represented in front of every house by a little mound of earth out of which sprouts a phallus made of iron or wood. Out of this most potent of gods the Voodooists have made an impotent old man who walks on crutches. Recalling vaguely his role as divine messenger they have made a sort of doorman out of him, the supernatural guardian of the "barriers" who must be invoked first of all loa. He has also remained the guardian of houses and to an even greater extent of roads, paths and crossroads. Legba-carrefour has become an important magician and presides over the ceremonies of sorcerers. Legba has lost much of his majesty but in exchange he has acquired new functions.
>
> In Haiti, Damballah-wèdo is a benovolent snake spirit who haunts the springs and climbs on trees, whereas in Dahomey he is described by the clergy as one of the many manifestations of Dā, who is less a divine person than a force. Dā 'controls all life and motion.' While Mawu, the supreme god, is Thought, Dā is Life. He manifests himself "in the world in a number of ways; it is said that there are many Dā, or rather manifestations of Dā, but the chief of them is Dā Ayido Hwedo (in Haiti Damballah-aido-wèdo), most commonly seen as the rainbow." He is a being with a dual nature, both male and female. Coiled in a spiral round the earth, he sustains the world and prevents its distintegration. As he revolves around the earth, he sets in motion the heavenly bodies. Because his nature is motion, he is also water. . . . Dā is the creator of mountains and also the excreter of metals. In the latter capacity, he partakes of the nature of the sun.[40]

CONCLUSION

The candomblés and santeria represent purer forms of African religion than vodun, but the parallelism of cultural development in religious groups in Brazil, Cuba, and Haiti that have a common origin but have been separated in space and time is remarkable. Haitian peasants have retained many of the beliefs from the religions of the Fon, the Yoruba, the Congo, and other ethnic groups, and they have combined these elements with as much Catholic doctrine as they have been able to acquire, and have added magical beliefs imported from the provinces of France and some of their invention. At the same time, the ritual of vodun, as Métraux observes, has been remodeled less than its system of beliefs.[41]

What the Cults Have Accomplished:
Gains and Costs

Religiously, the cults provide supernatural explanations of human existence, and the closely related magical rituals furnish the means of alleviating human problems. Some devotees experience "religious thrills" through speaking in unknown tongues and by becoming possessed by an African deity, an ancestor, or the Holy Spirit. In the realm of art, a well-staged *santeria, candomblé, vodun,* or *shango* ceremony includes drumming and dancing of excellent quality. In the Neo-African cults in various places in the Caribbean and Brazil, and in some of the revivalist ceremonies in Jamaica, the colorful and dramatic performances afford highly valued recreation for both participants and spectators.

For many devotees, cult membership compensates for their lowly social positions in the larger society. Group cohesiveness gives fellow believers a sense of belonging and of identity. Religious offices and important roles in ceremonies provide opportunities to exercise leadership and gain social recognition. The most sophisticated members of a cult derive intellectual satisfactions from discussing and elaborating the many points of the belief system. They share with the rank-and-file adherents the satisfactions that come from joint participation in the familiar routines of the rituals.[42]

Religious cults offer strong leaders upon whom adherents can rely for emotional support. Healing is an attraction for cultists who distrust modern physicians and find them too expensive, and for those who find public medical services too time-consuming and impersonal. Moreover, in time of great need, one can count on one's confreres for material aid.

Spirit possession permits the socially sanctioned expression of actions which in other circumstances would be unacceptable. The gods, rather than the possessed person, are responsible for actions performed during the ceremony. Also, ritual dissociation provides the self with an alternate set of roles, thus allowing the individual an enlarged field of action. From society's standpoint, some of its needs are met by possessed individuals who act out ritualized group conflicts and aspirations, including important cultural taboos.[43]

Cult participation may involve costs as well as rewards: heavy economic expense, and, in some cases, a heightening of emotional disturbances. From the standpoint of those who are concerned about social change, preoccupation with cult rituals reduces the time, thought, and energy that members can devote to political activity and thus tends to give support to the status quo. Given the life situation of the lower class and the slow rate of social change in Caribbean and South American countries, the gains derived from cult participation seem to most believers to outweigh the costs.[44]

Haitian vodun exemplifies, perhaps in extreme form, what a Caribbean syncretistic cult can and cannot accomplish. It has changed little in a half century, and it makes heavy demands on its believers. At the same time, it offers a sense of community, social diversion, protection against unseen dangers, and it enhances family solidarity. But vodun has stagnated; it does not have the capability of formulating new policies for the benefit of the rural people. Bastien comments that, to his knowledge, "no houngan has ever sponsored the building of a school, promoted a program of community development, sought to introduce new crops or innovated an agricultural technique. . . . The type of change needed today is beyond the comprehension of Vodun and contrary to its interests."[45] One might speculate, however, that reactionary political regimes of the sort that have perennially afflicted Haiti would oppose activism on the part of religious leaders, either in the Catholic church or among practitioners of vodun.

An assessment of the accomplishments of the Rastafarians, the cult at the other end of the Caribbean religious continuum, is more difficult.

CONCLUSION

They are neither an anachronism nor the wave of the future in Jamaica. There is no Rastafarian political party, and no member of the group has been elected to political office. Some of the Rastafarian beliefs and their fight for the recognition of the black Jamaican are seen in the Black Power movement of the late 1960s and the early 1970s. As Nettleford points out, the question which has not yet been answered is whether black nationalism in Jamaica is a form of strategy, the substance of recent protests, or a mixture of the two. If it is political strategy, this movement has much in common with the agitation of 1938 against foreign exploitation of the country's resources and control of its economic and intellectual life. As substance, that is, a forced and sudden black control of the country, it would reverse Jamaica's commitment of the early 1940's to evolutionary development.[46]

Eventually, the religions of the whites in the Caribbean—Catholicism or one form or another of Protestantism—became the religions of millions of descendants of slaves, but only in the last two or three decades has the majority of the ministers in the largest denominations come from the West Indies. Tens of thousands of persons of African descent in the region have become involved, to a greater or lesser degree, in the beliefs and rituals of a wide variety of syncretistic cults. For more than a century these groups have met the needs of the most disadvantaged sections of West Indian populations—needs that have not been met by the conventional churches or by secular organizations. The future of each cult will depend upon a number of factors, including changes in the general economic situation where it is located, and upon the nature of the competition it encounters from alternative modes of adjustment.

The Relative Decline of Neo-African Religions, Ancestor Cults, Revivalism, and the Historical Churches in the Caribbean and South America

In the Caribbean and South America, most of the Neo-African cults, the ancestral cults, and revivalist cults that we have considered, as well as the historical churches, are declining in size and influence, while the Pentecostal and spiritualist groups are increasing—in some cases, quite rapidly.

CONCLUSION

The campaigns against vodun launched from time to time by the Catholic church in Haiti from 1896 to 1939 were ineffective. In the latter year, the "movement of the *rejectés*" (rejectors) was started and resulted in thousands of peasants bringing their sacred objects to the priests for destruction. In 1941, the church secured the aid of the government and the army cooperated with the priests in locating and destroying vodun temples and ritual objects. Following a reaction on the part of the peasants, a massive return to "superstition" began. Later, François Duvalier, President of Haiti from 1957 to 1971, used vodun as one means of retaining power.[47] Nevertheless, most observers agree that the vodun cult in Haiti has been weakened in recent decades.

An important factor in the decline of vodun has been the decay of the large extended family. The small family is now autonomous, and the vodun cult has been divorced from the former familial structure. According to Bastide, the large cult-centers have split up into many minor sects "under priests whose training is not adequate to keep the ancestral traditions alive."[48] A deepening poverty in the countryside has impoverished the ritual there, and the expansion of urbanization and the further proletarianization of the population have modified the nature of the cult.[49]

Métraux made the interesting point that although the religion of Haitian peasants is still, to a considerable extent, African, the institutions and political ideals of Haiti are those of a Western state.

> Voodoo gods, in spite of their African names and lore are under the influence of their environment. . . . the *loa* have the tastes of modern man, his morality and his ambitions. They are no longer the gods of an African tribe, exotic and remote, but deities who act and think in the industrialized world of today.[50]

Tourism is another factor which has had a powerful effect on the cult.

> Sanctuaries have become neon-lighted theatres. Great sums may have been made by the *hungan* and *mambo,* but they have driven away true believers from their temples. It is true that this shameless prostitution of religion, at the hands of its own priests, flourishes only in Port-au-Prince, but it will end by shaking the faith of the country people who are under the influence of the capital.[51]

CONCLUSION

Finally, although Protestants constitute little more than a tenth of the population in Haiti, they are inimical to vodun by virtue of their uncompromising opposition to the cult.[52]

Among the recent changes in the candomblé is the spread of these cults up and down the east coast of Brazil. In Bahia, a change has occurred in the dedication of temples. Today only a few candomblés are dedicated to the gods of only one "nation." Male devotees do not wish to be limited to the feasts given in their own centers; their attendance at other ceremonies contributes to the mixture of African religions.[53]

In earlier years Ifá diviners held the highest rank in African cult groups in Recife. The refusal of these specialists to initiate new people resulted in the disappearance of their kind and the transference of their functions to the priests. Because their knowledge of the *opele* (divination chain) is limited, most priests in recent years have relied on throwing shells (*dilogan*), a practice formerly limited to women.[54]

The policy of national integration in Brazil has hindered the continuation of African sects. According to Bastide, the replacement of the tutelary family by the state has resulted in the transformation of the disorganized common people into a conscious proletariat. Young blacks who attend integrated schools reject the candomblés, and new recruits have come mainly from the economically disadvantaged and more or less illiterate masses. In the 1950s, numbers of well-to-do artisans, merchants, and lawyers joined candomblés, but the future of the religion is uncertain.[55]

The Convince ancestral cult of eastern Jamaica has been declining in strength and popularity for two decades or more. Hogg attributes this to several causes: competition among Bongo men; improvements in economic and social conditions due to governmental programs in agriculture and education; the availability of other forms of recreation such as movies, dances, and cricket; greater conflict between the cult and Christian attitudes and values; and the rise of Ras Tafari as a protest movement. Cumina, another ancestral cult found in eastern Jamaica, has declined in rural areas. These rituals have disappeared in the anomic urban environment, but Cumina drumming occurs on special occasions in West Kingston. Although some minor ceremonial changes have been introduced recently, the Kele ancestral cult in St. Lucia has not basically changed for many decades. Since most of those who take the cult

CONCLUSION

seriously are older persons, it seems doubtful if Kele rituals will be per-petuated for other than recreational purposes.[56]

It has always been difficult to estimate the number of adherents to revivalism in Jamaica. The Census of 1943 listed 4,230 members of "Pocomania," but the census officials did not believe that figure showed the extent of revivalism's following.[57] Later Censuses did not include this category at all. Undoubtedly many revivalists and persons who are influenced in one way or another by revivalism are included in the Census reports under the category of "Baptist," the second largest de-nomination in the island, or under "Other Religions" or "Not Speci-fied."[58]

After 1953, Revival in Kingston steadily lost ground. Some former devotees moved away, others lost faith, and still others joined the Church of God or became attached to the Ras Tafari movement. Poco-mania in rural Jamaica has also fought a losing battle. In St. Mary, many agree with the traditional beliefs and premises of Pocomania, but being Christian is a stronger value. Some leaders have moved toward Christian orthodoxy, others have carried on a delaying action by devel-oping a set of reciprocal obligations and privileges among the bands and independent members of wide areas. Hogg found that the more success-ful leaders of Pocomania bands in Spanish Town and Kingston try to bolster their position by elaborating the pageantry and theatrics of cere-monies. Such tactics have led to continual innovation both in the cere-monial and the structural aspects of the cult.[59]

A law prohibiting the practice of Shakerism was enacted in St. Vin-cent in 1912, and an ordinance against the Shouters was passed in Trinidad in 1917. The Shakers went underground after 1912, but they were persecuted by the police until the early 1930s. The law was re-pealed in 1965. The law prohibiting the Shouters in Trinidad had not been enforced for years before its repeal in 1961. In recent years, both Shakerism and the Shouters cult have flourished in a modest way, and today, the pastor of a Shaker church may christen babies, conduct fu-neral rites, and perform marriages—provided that he has obtained the proper license. We have referred earlier to the modifications that have been made in ritual practices of the Shouters in previous years as a result of the juxtaposition of this cult and shangoism. Since Shango is not

CONCLUSION

practiced in St. Vincent, the Shakers have not been subject to its direct influence.[60]

Although the number of Protestants in the Caribbean increased more rapidly during the second quarter of the twentieth century than in preceding periods of similar length, the historical Protestant churches have declined since the end of World War II. In Jamaica, for example, between 1943 and 1970, the proportion of Baptists on the island dropped from 26 percent to 18 percent, Anglicans from 28 to 15 percent, Methodists from 9 to 6 percent, and Presbyterian/Congregationalists from 9 to 5 percent. In those years, however, the Roman Catholic Church increased its membership from 5 to 8 percent.

In Brazil, both Catholicism and the historical Protestant churches have lost ground in recent decades to Pentecostalism. The Roman Catholic Church in Brazil has a chronic shortage of priests, and regular Sunday attendance at mass averages approximately 10 percent. Liturgical reform and advocacy of economic reforms by many of the Catholic clergy in recent years have not greatly increased the Church's appeal to the masses. Many newcomers to the city regard it as an agency for the benefit of the rich and powerful. Protestantism came late in Brazil and expanded slowly after missionaries arrived during the second half of the nineteenth century. The growth of Protestantism in the first half of the twentieth century coincided with the emergence of an industrial and urbanized society. With its emphasis on cooperation, personal responsibility, and self-help, the historical Protestant churches in Brazil, particularly the Baptists, have had an appeal to lower-class persons, as well as to about an equal number of members of the middle class.[61]

The Present Status of Religio-Political Cults in the Caribbean

The Ras Tafari movement in Jamaica has never presented a united front. Cleavages have existed between those who have emphasized its spiritual aspects and those who have stressed racial-political matters. There have also been differences over the use of violence, the wearing of beards, the value of a Marxist framework of ideas, and the use of ganja (marijuana).[62] Dancing and drumming became important features of the meetings of some groups in the 1960s. The belief in the divinity of

Haile Selassie, originally a central feature in Rastafarian ideology, was beginning to receive less emphasis before Selassie's dethronement in 1974, followed by his death in 1975.[63] Nettleford has expressed doubt that the Jamaican people as a whole would ever accept Rastafarianism as a legitimate form of religious worship, and that possibility now seems more unlikely than ever.[64]

Beginning in the late 1950s, some groups in the movement began to place more emphasis on the need to change the social system of Jamaica than on a return to Africa.[65] In the mid-1960s the verbal attacks against the "anti-Christ Babylonian enslavers" were transformed into calls for " 'peace and love' not only for the black man but for all humanity." Some of the "Brethren" were even willing to work for "Babylon" (the rich and powerful, especially in Kingston) whenever work was available. Then and later, the emphasis which some groups placed on black power and "the Africanization of Jamaica" (jobs, education, and the use of the country's resources for the benefit of persons of African descent) introduced further complexity into Rasta ideology.[66]

It is difficult to estimate the strength or the potentiality of the Ras Tafari movement. In its early days, virtually all of its members and sympathizers were poor people, but in recent years "a good number of comfortable middle class" persons have been attracted to the movement.[67] As yet there is no Ras Tafarian political party, and no member of the movement has been elected to political office. Rastafarians no longer have a monopoloy on social protest. A whole subculture of protest has developed in Jamaica. In the 1960s the "rude boys" (a radical political movement) made use of the doctrine of Babylonian captivity but wanted redemption for the poor blacks to occur in Jamaica. Black Power advocates extended this position by arguing for "native (i.e., black) ownership and control of the country's economic and intellectual resources."[68]

Another aspect of this new subculture is pop protest music. Most of the performers of reggae are black, and some of them are Rastas. This music has profited the sound system operators and manufacturers, many of whom are Chinese. In 1975, the singers were attempting to unionize in the hope of gaining a share of the profits. Some of the Rasta style of singing has been adopted by youth arms of the political parties, particu-

CONCLUSION

larly the youth movement of the Peoples National Party. The commercial element in the pop music in this group fits rather oddly with its Marxist-populist outlook and its original renunciation of any involvement with "Babylon" (the Jamaican political-economic establishment).[69]

Although Black Power groups have been formed in Trinidad and in other places in the Caribbean, the Ras Tafari movement itself has not spread widely. In 1974, Rastafarian-like youths in Dominica started a group known as the "Dreads." In November 1974, this group and similar associations were prohibited by an Act of the House of Assembly from wearing any special mode of dress or other distinguishing mark. Several youths were arrested and imprisoned under this law in 1974–75; ostensibly, by the middle of 1975 the Dread movement no longer existed. In the following months, a committee was appointed by the government to meet with the Dreads and to make recommendations concerning social and economic reforms.[70]

The Rise of Spiritualism and Pentecostalism in the Caribbean and South America

Bastide hypothesized that increased interest in nontraditional African-derived cults in Brazil in the post-World War II period was due to increased racial discrimination and exploitation accompanying industrialization. He regarded cults such as *umbanda* as outlets for racial protest on the part of blacks and Amerindians and as instrumentalities for the absorption of unassimilated members of these groups into modern interracial society. As noted earlier, the Negro membership of umbanda is large, but the cult is by no means limited to persons of African, or of African and Amerindian, descent.[71]

A more convincing explanation of the rapid growth of umbanda is found in the list of contributing factors given by Pressel. First, industrialization, together with improved communication and transportation, has reduced the isolation of Brazil's regional groupings. Second, medical services and facilities have not increased to any great extent. Third, the Catholic church has changed relatively little and has not attracted the intensive involvement of large numbers of ordinary people. Fourth, the concept of possessing spirits, found among the indigenous Indians, and in Kardecismo, has a strong historical and contemporary base in Brazil.

CONCLUSION

Fifth, in a changing sociocultural environment, the emphasis on consultation concerning personal problems has given umbanda an advantage over religions like candomblé. Sixth, umbanda's link with Kardecismo makes it more prestigious and acceptable than the lower-class possession religions. Seventh, umbanda's emphasis on the "heart" has had a strong mass appeal. Eighth, in umbanda, the syncretism of orishas with the saints provides an appeal lacking in Kardecismo and Pentecostalism in a country where people think of themselves as Catholic. It is Pressel's impression, therefore, that umbanda "has become something of a 'national folk religion,' in the sense of being the religious part of modern mass culture associated with a technical world."[72]

The Leacocks found that Bastide's attribution of the growing popularity of such cults as umbanda to an increase in racial discrimination accompanying the stresses of industrialization was not relevant to the Batuque in Belém. Membership in the Batuque is not predominantly black, and Bastide's hypothesis would not apply to it even if dark-skinned individuals were predominant in the cult. Such individuals do not constitute a separate racial caste in Belém. Their dialect and their culture are the same as those of their neighbors, and they are not separated from them residentially. Whatever discrimination there is on the basis of color is minor compared with the problems of poverty. The Leacocks found that Batuque has gained followers because it offers lower-class persons, especially women, help in solving their personal problems.[73]

The cult of María Lionza, an old syncretistic religion which originated in the mountains of Sorte in Venezuela, expanded when it was introduced into urban centers between the two World Wars. During that period it was influenced by modern spiritualism and by African-derived concepts. Among its devotees this popular religion now includes Venezuelans, Spaniards, Colombians, Italians, Portuguese, and persons of African descent from the former British West Indies. In many ways this spiritualist cult resembles umbanda in Brazil, and it has succeeded for about the same reasons: the presence of large numbers of poor people in overcrowded urban slums, the lack of influence on the part of the Catholic church, a search for new ways of expressing religious feelings, distrust of modern medicine, and disillusionment with existing social and

CONCLUSION

religious institutions. In Pollak-Eltz's view, this cult is "the most conspicuous expression of a new nationalism based on the total integration of all the diverse races and cultures of the Venezuelan people."[74]

The Pentecostal movement in Brazil has grown rapidly since the end of World War II. This movement did not simply take over the lower-class membership of the historical Protestant churches; but the Pentecostal sects did begin to compete with them for such members. According to one report, one thousand people a day were being converted to Protestantism (almost exclusively to Pentecostalism) in Brazil in the early 1970s, and Pentecostalists now constitute 70 percent of the country's Protestants.[75]

Since secularization has not proceeded far among lower-class persons in Brazil, the need for a religion to help with the difficult problems of everyday life is strongly felt. Those who have migrated to the cities no longer have to worry about crops, livestock, and the evil spirits of the jungle, but they still have to face the problems associated with birth, sickness, family life, employment, and death. The rural migrant can no longer rely on the saintly helpers of folk Catholicism, because he regards them as belonging to a local pantheon. However, the mystical experiences, spirit possessions, and charismatic leadership of folk Catholicism facilitate the shift to Pentecostalism.[76]

Jamaica offers a striking example of the spectacular growth of Pentecostalism in the Caribbean. From 1943 to 1970 the Church of God increased from 3.5 percent of the population to 17 percent, and the Pentecostal Church increased from .5 percent to 3 percent. In Haiti, the Pentecostal movement has expanded rapidly through the segmentation of religious cells as members move from one city to another. The number of Pentecostals in Puerto Rico increased from 7,600, or 8.5 percent of the Protestants on the island in 1942, to an estimated 75,000 or 80,000 in 1969—or 30 percent of the Protestant group.[77]

In these and other countries in the Caribbean and South America, Pentecostalism offers hope of redemption from a social order which is regarded as unjust. In its proselytizing activities, it utilizes the resources of every member. In making the convert feel that he is needed, and in addressing him as "brother," the sect provides security in a disorganized society. In addition, becoming a Pentecostalist makes a convert "respect-

CONCLUSION

able" and enables him to adopt middle-class norms and behavior. Among the business and professional people who have been attracted to Pentecostalism in recent years are many individuals who suffer from real or imaginary disadvantages.[78]

Pentecostalism and spiritualism, the two fastest growing religions in the Caribbean and Brazil, differ in several respects, but one difference is especially striking. In the macoumba and umbanda of Rio de Janeiro, the batuque of Belém, the María Lionza cult of Venezuela, and the spiritualist cults in Puerto Rico, control by the group is minimal. These cults have become more and more individualistic as devotees seek aid from the spirits in the solution of their personal problems—mainly those associated with poverty. This trend is seen clearly in the macoumba in Rio de Janeiro and São Paulo, a cult which has passed increasingly from religion to magic as the isolated sorcerer has replaced the organized macoumba.[79] In contrast to the individualistic emphasis of spiritualism, Pentecostalism is characterized by strong group cohesion. As noted previously, the Pentecostal sect makes use of every member in its religious activities, thus making the convert feel that he is wanted and that his contributions are appreciated. Like all sects, Pentecostalism functions to overcome feelings of deprivation associated with poverty, loneliness, and handicaps of all kinds.[80]

Racial Attitudes and Policies of the Historical Protestant Churches in the United States Through 1870

In the eighteenth and early nineteenth centuries, many slaveholders, fearing that religious instruction would promote rebellion, looked with disfavor upon the work of Baptists and Methodists among their slaves. When southern clergymen became supporters of slavery, the master class came to regard organized religion as an ally. Special catechisms and sermons were prepared for slaves, and special instructions were given to religious teachers. Missionaries were asked to teach the slaves to give "respect and obedience [to] all those whom God in his providence has placed in authority over them."

Much of the slaves' religion had a sedative quality, but there were defiant responses to it. Some of the "otherworldly" preaching of the slave preachers was accompanied by such survival tactics as subterfuge, sabotage, the slowdown, pretended stupidity, and obsequiousness.

A large number of Negroes were admitted to the Baptist church during the frequent emotional revivals that were held during the eighteenth century, but separate churches for blacks and whites were not formed south of Pennsylvania, except in Georgia. Under the supervision of whites, the Baptists permitted some Negroes to preach as early as 1773, but these preachers had no voice in general church affairs. The Negro Baptist Church was formed about 1825, but most Negro Baptists continued to be affiliated with white churches until the formation of the large Baptist denominations in 1880.

Although the Methodists soon retreated from their 1780 stand that slavery is "contrary to the laws of God, man and nature and hurtful to society," preachers were urged in 1787 to work among slaves and to admit worthy ones into full church membership. By 1797, Negro Methodists constituted one-fourth of all Methodists in the United States. In the years just before the Civil War, Negro Methodists outnumbered Negro Baptists in the South. Afterward, a larger number of blacks were attracted to the Baptist church.

Because of the influence of its southern membership, "Negro Work" of the Episcopal Church was administered separately. During the period of slavery, Negro clergymen and deputies could not attend the Protestant Episcopal convention nor participate in the general government of the church. The church did not take a stand against slavery, limiting itself mainly to urging slaveholders to provide religious instruction for their slaves.

Although the Presbyterian Synod recommended in 1787 that steps be taken toward gradual emancipation, Synods in later years failed to act on the question of excluding slaveholders from the church. In 1861, the General Assembly of the church concluded that slavery was the black man's normal condition. Like the Episcopalians, the Presbyterians administered their "Negro Work" separately. Unlike the Baptists and the Methodists, however, the Presbyterians, as well as the Episcopalians and the Congregationalists (who sympathized with the slaves but made few black converts), did not split along racial lines. Where blacks and whites

CONCLUSION

worshipped together in these three denominations, the crisis over seating that arose in the Baptist and Methodist churches of such cities as New York and Philadelphia did not occur, owing to the small number of Negroes. Where there were black Episcopalian and Presbyterian pastors, "truly integrated" churches did not develop.

Why the Independent Negro Church Arose

Although some black people petitioned for the independence of their churches from white control in the 1770s and 1780s, many white churches and church bodies were reluctant to permit separate congregations. In many cases where they were formed, white ministers presided over them and they were supervised by civil officials and white church organizations. At least four regular Negro Baptist churches were established between 1776 and 1778 (Williamsburg, Virginia, 1776; and Augusta and Savannah, Georgia, 1778), and a black Episcopal church was organized in Philadelphia in 1784. Black Methodist and Baptist churches were also started in New York City and Boston between 1796 and 1808.

The denominational separation of blacks and whites was preceded during the last quarter of the eighteenth century by separation in seating and entrances. Occasionally black preachers were called upon to speak in the predominantly white churches, but blacks played no part in decision-making. Dissatisfaction with these arrangements and other forms of discrimination, together with the differences in the attitudes of blacks and many whites over slavery and the desire of many Negroes to have independent organizations where they could develop their own abilities, led to the founding of the independent black denominations.

The representatives of several black Methodist Episcopal churches that had been affiliated with the white Methodists met in 1816 and founded the African Methodist Episcopal Church. The African Methodist Episcopal Zion Church was formed in 1820 and the Negro Baptist Church by 1825. In 1866, the General Conference of the Methodist Episcopal Church authorized the organization of separate congregations and annual conferences, and in 1870 two bishops were appointed to organize the black conferences into a separate and independent church. Later that year the Colored Methodist Episcopal Church (now the Christian Methodist Episcopal Church) was formed. For many years, most of the separate black Baptist churches, unlike the black Methodists, continued their affiliation with white Baptist conferences. When greater freedom of action was possible following emancipation, most of the Negro Baptists in the South who had belonged to white churches formed separate ones. The two largest black Baptist churches, the National Baptist Convention of America and the National Baptist Convention, U.S.A., were both organized in 1880.

The Continuing Interest of Blacks in the United States and Canada in the Historical Churches

The great majority of blacks in the United States who are affiliated with religious bodies belong to the historical churches, particularly to the independent Baptist and Methodist denominations. Ninety percent of the Negro Protestants are in separate denominational organizations. Perhaps 10 to 15 percent of northern and western Protestant churches are interracial to some degree, but probably no more than 1 or 2 percent of the blacks of the United States belong to interracial churches.[81] Rivalries between denominations and congregations, as well as increasing competition from secular organizations, have reduced the influence of the black church. During the late 1950s and the 1960s, however, black ministers and church leaders became considerably more active in civil and human rights movements than they had been earlier. Kenneth Clark makes the important point that "the Negro has managed to salvage some personal self-esteem from his church, and until he achieves such self-esteem elsewhere he will not give up this, his last and only sanctuary."[82]

The number of black Catholics in the United States increased from approximately 100,000 in 1865 to 343,000 in 1947, and to 800,000 in 1967. This increase has been attributed to several factors: a way of escaping from social ties with fellow members of the lower-class, the establishment of a connection with the church through parochial schools to which black families have sent their children, the appeal of traditional ritual in contrast to the emotionalism of many black churches, and the belief, correct or not, that the Catholic church has been more helpful than Protestant churches in Negro rights causes.[83]

CONCLUSION

Black churches in Canada have almost always been conservative theologically, socially, and politically. The majority of Canadian Negroes have belonged to the Baptist church, and few cults have appeared. Never outstanding, the Negro church in Canada in the 1970s was moribund.

The Rise of Interest in Cultism in the United States, and in Pentecostalism in the United States and England

A multitude of sects and cults evolved among black people, particularly among the recent migrants to urban centers in the United States, during the early decades of the twentieth century. The Holiness and Pentecostal sects attracted the largest number of black followers. The Pentecostal movement grew rapidly after 1906 because of the neglect of many of the major denominations of the lower socioeconomic strata, but Pentecostalism was not limited to these groups. Regardless of race or class, many persons who suffered a real or imaginary disadvantage because of education, sex, temperament, appearance, or a status inconsistency compensated for such a handicap by affiliating with this movement. Pentecostalism is fundamentalist and millennialist, and, like sects in general, repudiates the compromises of the church. Literal obedience to the Synoptic Gospels is stressed, as is individual perfection and asceticism. In some Pentecostal groups, economic development and increased social mobility have shifted the emphasis to some extent from "otherworldliness" to a "worldlier" value orientation. Although the Pentecostal Revival has been termed a contribution from the black community to the white one, the movements divided in the United States approximately sixty years ago into black and white parts.

West Indians who migrate to England seldom join the historical churches there, but those who were members of a religious sect in the Caribbean are likely to seek out and join some religious group in Britain. Pentecostal churches are the most popular. Segmentation and proliferation of groups have promoted the growth of these black churches.

The early twentieth century also saw the emergence of numerous black cults in the United States which stressed the community of blacks more than individual conversion and perfection. Among these, Father Divine's Peace Mission movement was one of the largest and best known. Father Divine, regarded as a supernatural being, regulated completely the lives of his followers. He conducted informal quasi-religious meetings, provided the necessities of life for his "angels," supported civil rights causes, and met the emotional needs of lonely and rejected people, black and white. Other prominent black religious cult leaders included Daddy Grace and Bishop Ida Robinson.

Black Jewish groups flourished in Harlem in the post-World War I period. Claiming to be Ethiopian Hebrews or Falashas, they repudiated Christianity and held Jewish religious services in somewhat modified ways. For the most part, the Black Jews were nonpolitical and they did not withdraw from the outside world by setting up communal enterprises.

From the 1920s on, various Moorish or Islamic cults grew up in American cities. These groups repudiated the terms "Negro" and "colored" and emphasized that their god was non-Christian. Elijah Muhammad, the leader of the largest Black Muslim group—the Nation of Islam, repeatedly denounced the weaknesses of Negro society and sought ways and means of combating white paternalism and injustice.

Although the Black Muslim movement has contributed to an increase in pride and dignity in the black community, it has had some dysfunctions. Attacks on the white man have promoted mutual mistrust and endorsed segregation.[84]

Four months after the death of Elijah Muhammad, his son and successor as Supreme Minister of the Black Muslims, Wallace D. Muhammad, announced (June 15, 1975) that membership was open to Caucasians. Abdul Karim Hasan, the Supreme Minister's representative for seventeen western states, asserted that Muslims "are now able to associate with non-blacks and maintain their own self-esteem." The effects of this change in policy are not yet known.[85]

Thousands of small storefront cults have appealed to the black underclass by combining deviations from the Christian tradition with healing, personal advice, and magical charms designed to bring luck or to divert evil forces. These black "Spiritualist" churches attract members also by not condemning card-playing, dancing, and policy.

In addition to answers to the ultimate questions of life that are provided by any religious belief system, and to the secular benefits of-

CONCLUSION

fered by the black churches—historical, Holiness, and Pentecostal—
black religious cults have yielded other advantages. Father Divine,
Daddy Grace, Bishop Ida Robinson, and other prophets were semi-
deified leaders with whom their followers could identify. Pentecostalists
derive feelings of superiority from challenging sin and injustice, withdrawing from the world, and looking forward to the millennium. Some
black religious cults have enabled their adherents to get out from under
the stigma of color by denying that they are Negroes. Unlike the black
nationalists of more recent years who emphasize their blackness, Black
Jews and Black Muslims stress their Jewishness or their identity as
members of the Nation of Islam. Among the disadvantaged the search
for identity and validity takes many forms and never ends. Among
blacks, sects and cults have been important agencies in that quest.

The Attempt in the United States to Combine Black Power and Black Theology

In the late 1960s and the early 1970s a considerable number of
black ministers, professors of theology, and theological students, who
had become disillusioned with the civil rights movement, attempted to
formulate a theological position that would be consistent with and
would support the Black Power movement. The Black Power movement
is concerned with "organizing the rage of black people and with putting
new, hard questions and demands to white America." Discussions occurred within the traditional Negro churches concerning how these denominations could best identify with the black struggle. Also, black
communicants of predominantly white churches formed black caucuses.
Although these caucuses represented only 2 million of the 22 million
black church members of the United States, they constituted the core of
the black power advocates in religious organizations. Although this minority has been vocal, thus far it has been unable to play a strong leadership role in black religion.

The most extreme advocates of "black theology" are Albert B.
Cleage and James H. Cone. According to Cleage, the white man has
never created a genuine religion; Jesus was the non-white leader of a
non-white people, and the purpose of Christianity is to free black people. Cone holds that being black in America has little to do with skin

color. Instead, it means "that your heart, your soul, and your body are where the dispossessed are," and he regards the "white structure of America society" as "part of what the New Testament meant by the demonic forces." Joseph R. Washington Jr. sees the task of black theology as that of integrating the black community, of bringing the different sects and cults to realize that the one thing they have in common is their blackness. Gayraud S. Wilmore asserts that the black church provided the politico-theological foundation for black nationalism and pan-Africanism as it developed from the early Du Bois to Malcolm X.

Differences in the Religions of Blacks in the United States and in the Caribbean and South America

More Africanisms are found in the religions of blacks in the Caribbean and South America than in the United States. The development of slavery in various parts of the New World was affected by the presence or absence of sugar culture. This industry made a great difference in the rate at which the slave labor force grew. A large majority of the slaves brought into the British, French, and Dutch Caribbean colonies were involved in the cultivation of sugar. In Brazil, the proportion of slave imports engaged in this industry was approximately 40 percent, and the estimate for Spanish America is between 30 and 50 percent. In the United States, however, the sugar industry played a minor role in the growth of slavery. At its peak, sugar was never more than a minor southern crop, and just before the Civil War it utilized less than 10 percent of the slave labor force.[86]

The differences in the ratios of black to total population among the colonies in the New World are striking. By 1770, the ratio of Negro to total population in the British Caribbean was 91 percent, and the proportion in the French Caribbean was similar. In the North American colonies the ratio was 22 percent in 1770, and in the southern colonies it reached 40 percent. The absence of a sugar industry in the North American colonies also affected the size of plantations. The average size of the work force on a sugar plantation in Jamaica at the end of the eighteenth century was approximately 180 slaves. At that time the average number of slaves on a holding in Virginia and Maryland was less than thirteen.[87] Because of the small percentage of whites who lived on the sugar islands of the Caribbean and because of the size of the typical plantation, blacks had little contact with European culture. In the North American colonies, blacks were usually a minority of the population and lived in small units where they had frequent contacts with the European master class. In addition, into the nineteenth century the great majority of the persons in the slave populations in the British and French Caribbean were born in Africa. By contrast, the African-born component of the black population in the United States had shrunk to about one-fifth by 1810 and then decreased rapidly.[88]

One of the consequences of these demographic differences was a considerably greater amount of contact with African traditions on the part of slave populations in the Caribbean and South America than was the case with those living in North America. By 1860, 99 percent of the slaves in the United States were native-born, and some of them were fourth- and fifth-generation Americans.[89] I mentioned in chapter 3 that more than 1,000 post-emancipation immigrants arrived in Grenada from Nigeria in 1849, and that immigrants came to Trinidad from Dahomey about 1855. Slavery was not abolished in Brazil until 1888, and contacts between African cult leaders in Brazil and their counterparts in traditional religions in Africa have continued until the present time.

For the demographic and ecological reasons just mentioned—the ratios of blacks to total population, the size of plantations, the frequency of contacts between blacks and Europeans, and the proportion of African-born slaves—the likelihood that traditional African religious beliefs and rituals, in more or less pure or reinterpreted form, would be perpetuated was considerably greater in the Caribbean and South America than in North America. These differentials are important in explaining why Neo-African cults and ancestral cults (attenuated Neo-African cults that may have had more African characteristics at one time) did not develop in North America.

The Catholic Church began missionary work in the Caribbean in the middle of the seventeenth century. In some South American countries, notably in Brazil, two Catholicisms developed on the large plantations, where one part of the chapel was reserved for whites or masses were given at different hours for whites and blacks. The folk Catholicism centered in the cult of the saints-protectors of the patriarch and of the dead.[90]

CONCLUSION

In Haiti, Cuba, Brazil, and a number of other South American countries, slaves were allowed to form religious fraternities along ethnic lines where African languages, dances, and religious reliefs could be perpetuated. The presence of numerous saints in Catholicism may have appealed to Africans who were acquainted with dozens of divinities in tribal religions. Borrowing divinities from other religions was not a new idea to Africans living in the New World; this practice is of frequent occurrence in Africa.

The development of independent Negro churches in the United States early in the nineteenth century seems to have been due partly to the resentment felt by a number of black leaders in northern cities toward separate arrangements in Protestant churches for the entrance and seating of blacks. In part, the interest in forming separate religious bodies arose from the exclusion of blacks from participation in decision-making in the predominantly white churches. Differences between whites and blacks in attitudes toward slavery, and the desire on the part of blacks to develop their own abilities and skills furthered the formation of the independent Negro church. White Protestant denominations both in England and the United States devoted considerable effort and substantial financial outlays to missionary programs in the Caribbean, often to congregations that were largely or entirely made up of blacks. Somewhat later, many of the independent Negro churches in the United States established branches in the Caribbean and South America.

The revivalist cults in the Caribbean and the storefront cults in the United States have much in common. In both cases, they are small, more or less temporary, dominated by a charismatic leader, and emotional. In addition to providing Christian fundamentalism in diluted form, these cults offer healing services, counsel, and magical charms. Although leaders of revivalist cults and storefront churches often denounce wrongdoing, they are decidedly sympathetic with minor (and sometimes major) transgressions of prevailing moral codes.

Spiritualism has never had the following in the United States that it has enjoyed in Brazil and Puerto Rico. Introduced into Brazil more than a century ago, it had acquired some aspects of an organized religion by 1870. Umbanda, a cult which merges spiritualism and elements of African religions, is, however, a relatively recent development. Most of the members of this cult come from the upper-lower and the middle classes, and in some centers in São Paulo about half the membership is entirely of European origin.[91] In Umbanda, there is no calling up of dead relatives, but mediums make the spirits of the cult available to anyone for consultations concerning illness, employment, or other personal problems.

In Puerto Rico, two-thirds of the Catholics and one half of the Protestants included in a survey taken in the 1960s believed in spiritualism. To the poor ("the darker ones"), it offers supernatural help in coping with life's problems.[92] The spiritualist medium attempts to deal with these problems by summoning, interrogating, and manipulating spirits of the dead.

Forty years ago there were 51 "Spiritualist" cult centers among the array of storefront churches in Chicago's Black Belt. In many respects this cult resembles the Revivalists of Jamaica, the Shouters of Trinidad, and the Shakers of St. Vincent. Hymns have been borrowed from the Baptists and Methodists, and altar, candles, and statues have been appropriated from the Catholics. Despite its name, this cult rarely offers messages from the dead.[93]

Pentecostalism has grown rapidly in the Caribbean, Brazil, the United States, and Britain since the end of World War II. In Brazil and Chile, but not in the United States and Britain, Pentecostalists have transcended racial barriers. In Jamaica, the Pentecostal movement has increased spectacularly in recent decades but the question of race has not arisen in a population that is listed as more than 90 percent African or Afro-European.

Ras Tafari, the black religio-political movement in Jamaica, includes segments that are much more militant than the Black Muslims of the United States. Both movements have relatively small memberships, but many sympathizers. Both have denounced the white man and have sought to better the position of blacks. A major difference between these cults is the denunciation of "lower-class Negro values" and the sponsoring of puritanical ethics by the Black Muslims."[94]

CONCLUSION

Notes

1. Slavery, Freedom, and the Religions of Blacks in the New World

1. Fernandez has proposed a typology of African religious movements in relation to two continua, one phrased in instrumental-expressive terms, the other involving the two poles of a traditional or acculturated symbolism. The four quadrants in his analysis are Messianic, Nativist, Reformative, and Separatist. James W. Fernandez, "African Religious Movements—Types and Dynamics," *The Journal of Modern African Studies*, 2, no. 4 (1964): 531–49.

2. The concept of the "Diaspora" usually has referred to Jewish settlements outside Palestine which became the modern state of Israel. In recent years it has come to be used also with reference to peoples of African descent living outside Africa. See Arnold Ages, *The Diaspora Dimension* (The Hague, 1973), 3–19; St. Clair Drake, "The African Diaspora in Pan-African Perspective," *The Black Scholar*, 7, no. 1 (September 1975): 2; George Shepperson, Introduction to Martin L. Kilson and Robert I. Rotberg, eds., *The African Diaspora: Interpretive Essays* (Cambridge: Harvard University Press, 1976), 1–10.

3. Drake, "The African Diaspora," 5–6; Bernard Lewis, "The African Diaspora and the Civilization of Islam," in Kilson and Rotberg, *The African Diaspora*, 37–56.

4. Joseph E. Harris, *The African Presence in Asia: Consequences of the East African Slave Trade*. (Evanston: Northwestern University Press, 1971): 118–19.

5. Frank M. Snowden, *Blacks in Antiquity: Ethiopians in the Greco-Roman Experience*. Cambridge: the Belknap Press of Harvard University Press, 1970.

6. Paul Edwards and James Walvin, "Africans in Britain, 1500–1800," in Kilson and Rotberg, *The African Diaspora*, 172–204.

7. Michael Banton, *Racial Minorities* (London, 1972), 69–72.

8. Philip D. Curtin, *The Atlantic Slave Trade: A Census* (Madison, 1969), 128–30.

9. A recent study suggests a need for a substantial upward revision of the estimates of slave imports. See J. E. Inikori, "Measuring the Atlantic Slave Trade: An Assessment of Curtin and Anstey," *Journal of African History*. 17 (1976): 197–223.

10. Curtin, *The Atlantic Slave Trade,* 89.

11. The literature on slavery is vast, and the subject has attracted new interest on the part of historians and social scientists in recent years. Representative of these works are the following:

Cohen, David W. and Jack P. Greene, *Neither Slave Nor Free: The Freedman of African Descent in the Slave Societies of the New World* (Baltimore, 1972).

Curtin, Philip D. *The Atlantic Slave Trade: A Census* (Madison, 1969).

Davis, David Brion. *The Problem of Slavery in Western Culture* (Ithaca, 1966).

Degler, Carl N. *Neither Black Nor White: Slavery and Race Relations in Brazil and the United States* (New York, 1971).

Fogel, Robert W. and Stanley Engerman, *Time on the Cross: The Economics of Slavery in the Antebellum South.* (2 vols., Boston, 1974).

Foner, Laura and Eugene D. Genovese, eds. *Slavery in the New World: A Reader in Comparative History* (Englewood Cliffs, N.J., 1969).

Genovese, Eugene D. *Roll, Jordan, Roll: The World the Slaves Made* (New York, 1972).

Goveia, Elsa. *Slave Society in the British Leeward Islands* (New Haven, 1965).

Gutman, Herbert G. *Slavery and the Numbers Game: A Critique of Time on the Cross* (Urbana, 1975).

——. *The Black Family in Slavery and Freedom. 1759–1925* (New York, 1976).

Hoetink, H. *The Two Variants in Caribbean Race Relations: a Contribution to the Sociology of Segmented Societies* (London, 1967).

Jordon, Winthrop. *White Over Black: American Attitudes Toward the Negro, 1550–1812* (Chapel Hill, 1968).

Kilson, Martin L. and Robert I. Rotberg, *The African Diaspora: Interpretative Essays* (Cambridge, Mass., 1976).

Klein, Herbert. *Slavery in the Americas: A Comparative Study of Virginia and Cuba* (Chicago, 1967).

Patterson, Orlando. *The Sociology of Slavery: An Analysis of the Origins, Development and Structure of a Negro Slave Society in Jamaica* (London, 1967).

Rawick, George P. *From Sundown to Sunup: The Making of the Black Community* (Westport, Conn., 1972).

To these titles five earlier works of great importance should be added:

Elkins, Stanley M. *Slavery: A Problem in American Institutional and Intellectual Life* (Chicago, 1959).

Franklin, John Hope. *From Slavery to Freedom: A History of American Negroes* (New York, 1947).

Phillips, Ulrich B. *American Negro Slavery* (New York, 1918; 1967).

Stampp, Kenneth M. *The Peculiar Institution* (New York, 1956).

Tannenbaum, Frank. *Slave and Citizen: The Negro in the Americas* (New York, 1947).

1. SLAVERY, FREEDOM, AND BLACK RELIGIONS

For an illuminating evaluation of the various points of view in the interpretation of the nature and significance of the institution of slavery among the Post-World War II historians, see David Brion Davis, "Slavery and the Post-World War II Historians," *Daedalus,* 103, no. 2 (Spring 1974): 1–16.

12. See Tannenbaum, *Slave and Citizen,* 52–107; and Elkins, *Slavery,* 63–80.

13. Eugene D. Genovese. *Roll, Jordan, Roll: The World the Slaves Made.* (New York, 1972), 179.

14. Quoted in Degler, *Neither Black Nor White,* 65.

15. Fogel and Engerman, *Time on the Cross,* 128, 148–150, 232, 237; Gutman, *Slavery and the Numbers Game,* 18–41.

16. Fogel and Engerman, *Time on the Cross.*

17. Thomas L. Haskell, "Were Slaves More Efficient? Some Doubts About 'Time on the Cross,' " *The New York Review of Books,* September 19, 1974, 40.

18. Gutman, *Slavery and the Numbers Game,* 1–2, 166–167, 170–171. Gutman criticizes Fogel and Engerman's argument and evidence that enslaved Afro-Americans worked hard and diligently because they wanted to and because profit-maximizing owners skillfully mixed a few punishments with many rewards to encourage productive slave labor (Gutman, *Slavery,* 16). The field hand is seen neither as Sambo (a reference to the passive personality type portrayed in Elkins, *Slavery, passim*) nor as Horatio Alger with a black skin (Fogel and Engerman, *Time on the Cross, passim*).

19. Degler, *Neither Black Nor White,* 75.

20. Curtin, *The Atlantic Slave Trade,* 28–30.

21. *Ibid.,* 92.

22. Davis, *The Problem of Slavery,* 232–33.

23. Curtin, *The Atlantic Slave Trade,* 89–92.

24. *Ibid.,* 88–91.

25. Davis, *The Problem of Slavery,* 229. See also Genovese's contention that a comparative analysis of the treatment of slaves in different countries must proceed on at least two different levels simultaneously: first, conditions must be evaluated for a certain year or decade according to the exigencies of the world market at a given moment; and second, conditions must be assessed according to the technological level of each section of the slave economy. Eugene D. Genovese, "The Treatment of Slaves in Different Countries: Problems in the Applications of the Comparative Method," in Foner and Genovese, eds., *Slavery in the New World* 202–10. Hoetink (*The Two Variants,* 178–188) provides an interesting comparison of the conditions of slavery in two Dutch regions—a relatively mild form in Curaçao and the more severe treatment of slaves in Surinam.

26. J. Milton Yinger, *The Scientific Study of Religion* (New York, 1970), 255. The definitions of cult, sect, established sect, and church given here are based on Yinger's book, 252–80.

27. *Ibid.,* 253. 257.

28. See James W. Fernandez, "Symbolic Consensus in a Fang Syncretist Cult," *American Anthropologist,* 67 (1965): 902–9.

29. Fogel and Engerman, *Time on the Cross,* 22–24.

1. SLAVERY, FREEDOM, AND BLACK RELIGIONS

2. The Caribbean:
Blacks in the Historical Churches

1. Parts of chapters 2–4 were included in G. E. Simpson, "Religions of the Caribbean," in *The African Diaspora: Interpretive Essays* (Cambridge, Mass., 1976), edited by Martin Kilson and Robert I Rotberg, 280–311. Used by permission and copyright 1976 by the President and Fellows of Harvard College.

2. J. B. Ellis, *The Diocese of Jamaica: A Short Account of Its Growth and Organization* (London, 1913), 41.

3. Philip D. Curtin, *Two Jamaicas: The Role of Ideas in a Tropical Colony, 1830–1865* (Cambridge, Mass., 1955), 34.

4. Pere Jean-Baptiste du Tertre, *Histoire Generale des Antilles Habitees par les Français* (1667). Quoted in Rev. C. Jesse, "Du Tertre and Labat on 17th Century Slave Life in the French Antilles," *Caribbean Quarterly*, 7 (1961): 153–55.

5. James G. Leyburn, *The Haitian People* (New Haven, 1941), 116, 117.

6. *Ibid.*, 119–20, 126.

7. *Ibid.*, 127, 128–29.

8. Raymund Devas, *Conception Island: The Troubled Story of the Catholic Church in Grenada, B.W.I.* (London, 1932), 57; A. W. Singham, *The Hero and the Crowd in a Colonial Polity* (New Haven, 1968), 36, 38. Devas discusses at length the quarrels and conflicts over religion between the French and the English and between Catholics and Protestants. Reports on insurrections and schisms, the persecution of the Catholic church, church finances, schools sponsored by the Church, the assignment of priests to parishes, and the commands of governors, chief justices, attorney generals, archbishops and bishops occupy most of the book.

9. Devas, *Conception Island*, 117.

10. *Ibid.*, 136–38, 248, 263.

11. *Ibid.*, 397–99, 399–404.

12. *Ibid.*, 222.

13. Francis X. Delany, *A History of the Catholic Church in Jamaica, B.W.I., 1494 to 1929* (New York, 1930), 26–27.

14. *Ibid.*, 43.

15. The Population Council, *Jamaica* (New York, 1971), 2. The history of the Catholic church in the former British colonies of Jamaica and Grenada differs considerably from the situation in the Dutch colony of Curaçao. The Dutch took Curaçao from the Spanish in 1634 and imported the first slaves into the island in 1648. Rather than encourage the incorporation of large numbers of blacks into the Dutch Reformed faith, the Protestant aristocracy allowed Catholic missionaries to come to the colony with the implicit responsibility of "Christianizing" the blacks. In 1960, approximately 83 percent of the population of Curaçao was Catholic, about 10 percent was Protestant, and less than 1 percent was Jewish. In recent years, new Protestant groups have come to the island, and the Seventh Day Adventists have made a special effort to attract the black population. William A. Anderson and Russell R. Dynes, *Social Movements, Violence, and Change: The May Movement in Curaçao* (Columbus, 1975), 26, 29, 31, 47.

2. BLACKS IN HISTORICAL CHURCHES

16. Henry H. Breen, *St. Lucia: Historical, Statistical, Descriptive* (London, 1844), 248–49.

17. Jesse, "Du Tertre and Labat," 153.

18. Wilfred Easton, *West Indies: What of the Church?* (London, 1956), 5–6.

19. Elsa Goveia, *Slave Society in the British Leeward Islands at the End of the Eighteenth Century* (New Haven, 1965), 263.

20. Lowell J. Ragatz, *The Fall of the Planter Class in the British Caribbean, 1763–1833* (New York, 1928), 18.

21. Ellis, *The Diocese of Jamaica*, 40–41.

22. *Ibid.*, 41–42.

23. Ragatz, *The Fall of the Planter Class*, 28.

24. *Ibid.*, 284–85.

25. Robert W. Smith, "Slavery and Christianity in the West Indies," *Church History*, 19 (1950): 173.

26. *Ibid.*, 177. In Jamaica such an Act was passed in 1797 (Ellis, *Diocese of Jamaica*), 55.

27. Ellis, *Diocese of Jamaica*, 42–43, 52–53.

28. *Ibid.*, 42–43.

29. Goveia, *Slave Society*, 284.

30. Smith, "Slavery and Christianity," 177–78.

31. *Ibid.*, 178–79.

32. Ellis, *The Diocese of Jamaica*, 69.

33. *Ibid.*, 67–68.

34. *Ibid.*, 70.

35. Sir Alan Burns, *History of the West Indies* (London, 2nd ed., 1969), 667.

36. Alfred Caldecott, *The Church in the West Indies* (New York, 1898), 258–259.

37. J. E. Hutton, *A History of Moravian Missions* (London, 1922), 22, 28.

38. *Ibid.*, 29, 33–34.

39. *Ibid.*, 44–45. For an excellent analysis of the basic principles of Moravian missionary churches, see Goveia, *Slave Society*, 272–84.

40. Larsen, Jens P. M., *Virgin Islands Story* (Philadelphia, 1950), 66, 67–69.

41. Hutton, *A History*, 49.

42. *Ibid.*, 49.

43. *Ibid.*, 50–51.

44. Goveia, *Slave Society*, 271–72.

45. Smith, "Slavery and Christianity," 173.

46. Hutton, *A History*, 52–53.

47. *Ibid.*, 214–15.

48. *Ibid.*, 228–29.

49. Goveia, *Slave Society*, 272.

50. G. G. Findlay and W. W. Holdsworth, *The History of the Wesleyan Methodist Missionary Society* (London, 1921), vol. 2: 31–32.

51. Goveia, *Slave Society*, 281, 282.

2. BLACKS IN HISTORICAL CHURCHES

52. Bryan Edwards, *History, Civil and Commercial, of the British Colonies in the West Indies* (London, 1801), vol. 1: 492.

53. Hutton, *A History,* 253–54.

54. *Ibid.,* 256–57.

55. *Ibid.,* 259–61.

56. Larsen, *Virgin Islands Story,* viii.

57. *Ibid.,* 7–8, 19, 21, 24.

58. *Ibid.,* 61, 75.

59. *Ibid.,* 64, 75, 91–92.

60. *Ibid.,* 94–95, 99.

61. *Ibid.,* 24–25, 112, 127–28.

62. *Ibid.,* 138.

63. *Ibid.,* 186.

64. *Ibid.,* 237–38.

65. Findlay and Holdsworth, *The History* 2: 29–30.

66. *Ibid.,* 2: 29–32.

67. *Ibid.,* 2: 35.

68. Smith, "Slavery and Christianity," 174.

69. Goveia, *Slave Society,* 294–95.

70. Findlay and Holdsworth, *The History,* 2: 25–26; Ragatz, *The Fall of the Planter Class,* 284.

71. Findlay and Holdsworth, *The History,* 2: 26.

72. Goveia, *Slave Society,* 288–89.

73. Findlay and Holdsworth, *The History,* 2: 45.

74. *Ibid.,* 2: 52, 72.

75. *Ibid.,* 2: 73–78.

76. *Ibid.,* 2: 83–84, 89, 92.

77. Frederick Pilkington, *Daybreak in Jamaica* (London, 1950), 67.

78. Ernest A. Payne, *Freedom in Jamaica: Some Chapters in the Story of the Baptist Missionary Society* (London, 1933), 30–31.

79. Findlay and Holdsworth, *The History,* 2: 321, 326–27, 341.

80. *Ibid.,* 2: 355–58.

81. Pilkington, *Daybreak in Jamaica,* 107.

82. Findlay and Holdsworth, *The History,* 2: 391.

83. Payne, *Freedom in Jamaica,* 19–20, 26.

84. Pilkington, *Daybreak,* 103.

85. Payne, *Freedom in Jamaica,* 61–62.

86. *Ibid.,* 65; 68–70, 80–81.

87. Reverend George McNeill, *The Story of Our Missions in the West Indies* (Edinburgh, 1911), 21, 32, 34–36.

88. *Ibid.,* 37, 40–41, 44, 46, 55, 57.

89. *Ibid.,* 85–88.

2. BLACKS IN HISTORICAL CHURCHES

90. Lewis Davidson, *First Things First: A Study of the Presbyterian Church in Jamaica* (Edinburgh, 1945), 5.

91. Caldecott, *The Church in the West Indies,* 63; Goveia, *Slave Society,* 302; 305; 324.

92. Devas, *Conception Island,* 255.

93. Easton, *West Indies,* 7–8.

94. W. Stanley Rycroft, "The Contribution of Protestantism in the Caribbean," in *The Caribbean: Its Culture,* ed. A. Curtis Wilgus (Gainesville, Florida, 1955), 159. Table reprinted by permission of the University Presses of Florida.

95. J. Merle Davis, *The Church in the New Jamaica* (New York, 1942), 40–41, 43.

96. Easton, *West Indies,* 17.

97. *Ibid.,* 16–17.

98. Gérard R. Latortue, "The European Lands," in *The United States and the Caribbean,* edited by Tad Szulc (New York, 1971), 178.

99. Easton, *West Indies,* 10–12.

100. *The Christian Century,* 90 (November 1973): 1166–67.

101. Henry P. Van Dusen, "Caribbean Holiday," *The Christian Century,* 72 (August 17, 1955): 946.

102. *Ibid.,* 947.

103. *Ibid.,* 947–948.

104. *1943* data from *Eighth Census of Jamaica and Its Dependencies* (Kingston, 1943), 140; *1960* data from Population Council, *Country Profiles: Jamaica* (New York, 1971), 2; *1970* data provided by George Cumper of Kingston, Jamaica. The doctrinal difference between the two Pentecostal groups (Church of God and Pentecostal) in Jamaica is that the former baptize in the name of Father, Son and Holy Ghost, the latter in the name of Jesus Christ.

105. Roswith Gerloff, "Black Christian Communities in Birmingham," in Alan Bryman, ed., *Religion in Birmingham,* Institute for the study of Religious Architecture and Worship, University of Birmingham, 1975, 75.

106. Van Dusen, "Caribbean Holiday," 947; Peter Kami, "Revolutionary Cuban Pentecostals," *Pentecost and Politics* (Bristol, 1955), 15.

107. Luther P. Gerlach and Virginia H. Hine, *People, Power, Change: Movements of Social Transformation* (Indianapolis, 1970), 46, 65–66.

3. Neo-African Religions
and Ancestral Cults of the Caribbean

1. Concerning particularist explanations—political, military, economic, psychological, or anthropological—of "crisis cults" La Barre asserts: "The most that one can concede is that, in some cults, certain components seem relatively more salient; in other cults, other components appear to be; but all components are likely, in some degree, to be implicated in any cult." Weston La Barre, "Materials for a History of Studies of Crisis Cults: A Bibliographic Essay," *Current Anthropology,* 12 (1971): 26–27.

3. NEO-AFRICAN RELIGIONS

2. Roger Bastide, *Les Religiones Africaines au Brazil* (Paris, 1960), 219–21.

3. Roger Bastide, *African Civilizations in the New World* (New York, 1971), 93–112; Bastide, *Les Religiones,* 160, 165–66.

4. George E. Simpson, "The Belief System of Haitain Vodun," *American Anthropologist,* 47 (January 1945): 37–38.

5. Donald Hogg, "The Convince Cult in Jamaica," *Yale University Publications in Anthropology,* no. 58 (1960): 19–20.

6. Philip Sherlock, *Shout for Freedom,* Macmillan Caribbean, 1976, vii–x.

7. J. Milton Yinger, *The Scientific Study of Religion* (New York, 1970), 388.

8. J. D. Y. Peel, *Aladura: A Religious Movement Among the Yoruba* (London, 1968), 15.

9. Melville J. Herskovits, *The Myth of the Negro Past* (New York, 1941; Boston, 1958), 121; M. G. Smith, *The Plural Society in the British West Indies* (Berkeley, 1965), 33–34; Andrew T. Carr, "A Rada Community in Trinidad," *Caribbean Quarterly,* 3 (1953): 35–41; Hogg, "The Convince Cult," 16–17.

10. Herskovits, *The Myth,* 137–38.

11. Melville and Frances Herskovits, "The Negroes of Brazil," *Yale Review,* 32 (1942): 256.

12. Carr, "A Rada Community," 38; Smith, *The Plural Society,* 33–34.

13. George E. Simpson, "Four Vodun Ceremonies," *Journal of American Folklore,* 59 (1946): 154–67.

14. George E. Simpson, *The Shango Cult in Trinidad* (Rio Piedras, Puerto Rico, 1965), 93–94.

15. G. E. Simpson, "Jamaican Revivalist Cults," *Social and Economic Studies,* 5 (December, 1956): 404–5.

16. M. G. Smith, *Dark Puritan,* (Kingston, Jamaica, 1963), 34.

17. Hogg, "The Convince Cult," 20.

18. Such associations were found also in Martinique, St. Lucia, Colombia, Venezuela, Peru, Bolivia, Uruguay, and Argentine (Roger Bastide, *African Civilisations in the New World,* New York, 1972, 91–99). In addition, such "nations" are known to have existed in Trinidad (Andrew T. Carr, "A Rada Community in Trinidad," *Caribbean Quarterly,* 3 [1953]: 35–54), and in Grenada (M. G. Smith, *The Plural Society in the British West Indies* [Berkeley, 1965], 33–34.

19. Herskovits, *The Myth,* 220.

20. Bastide, *Les Religions,* 225.

21. In response to the question of whether the "Voodoo" cult originally existed only on Haiti or whether it flourished throughout the French Antilles, Bastide cites Maurice Satineau's assertion (*Histoire de la Guadeloupe sous l'Ancien Régime, 1635–1789,* Paris, 1928) "that it was to be found in Gudadeloupe, linked with the worship of reptiles and other animals, in the form of secret societies that plotted against the whites. According to him, it was about 1720 that the "Don Pedro" ritual was introduced.

3. NEO-AFRICAN RELIGIONS

Adepts of the latter were made to drink rum mixed with gunpowder, and went into ecstatic trances of a peculiarly violent sort. However, these wild dances were banned, and at some time after 1750 they disappeared from the cities, surviving only in the remote countryside. Only a few traces of this phenomenon survive among the modern peasant population, perhaps more noticeably on Martinique than on Guadeloupe." Bastide, *African Civilisations*, 148.

22. Bastide, *African Civilisations*, 11.

23. *Ibid.*, 11, 139–45.

24. *Ibid.*, 11, 115–22.

25. *Ibid.*, 12.

26. Alfred Métraux, *Voodoo in Haiti* (Paris, 1959), 28; M. J. Herskovits, *Life in a Haitian Valley* (New York, 1937), 267; William R. Bascom, *Shango in the New World* (Austin, Texas, 1972), 12.

27. Harold Courlander, *The Drum and the Hoe: Life and Lore of the Haitian People* (Berkeley, 1960), 16, 18; Simpson, "The Belief System," 38–40.

28. W. R. Bascom, "The Focus of Cuban Santeria," *Southwestern Journal of Anthropology*, 6 (Spring, 1950): 64; W. R. Bascom, "The Yourba in Cuba," *Nigeria*, no. 37 (1951): 14.

29. Fernando Ortiz, *Los Bailes y el Teatro de los Negros en el Folklore de Cuba* (Habana, 1951), 199–253; Harold Courlander, "Abakwa Meeting in Guanabacoa," *The Journal of Negro History*, 29 (1944): 464–69; Isaac Barreal, "Tendencias Sincreticas de los Cultos Populares en Cuba," *Etnologia Y Folklore*, no. 1 (1966): 22–23.

30. Octavio Da Costa Eduardo, *The Negro in Northern Brazil: A Study in Acculturation* (New York, 1948), 81–86.

31. Bascom, *Shango*, 7; Edison Carneiro, *Candomblés da Bahia* (Rio de Janeiro, 1948), 44–46.

32. M. J. and Frances S. Herskovits, *Trinidad Village*, (New York, 1947), 22; Frances Mischel, "African 'Powers' in Trinidad: The Shango Cult," *Anthropological Quarterly*, 30 (April 1957): 45; G. E. Simpson, "The Shango Cult in Nigeria and in Trinidad," *American Anthropologist*, 64 (December 1962): 1204, 1217; J. D. Elder, "The Yoruba Ancestor Cult in Gasparillo," *Caribbean Quarterly*, 16 (September 1970): 9, 12.

33. Carr, "A Rada Community in Trinidad," 36, 42.

34. On Haiti's colonial origins, the drawing of "caste" lines, and the rigidifying of these lines, see James G. Leyburn, *The Haitian People* (New Haven, 1941), 14–31, 79–98. On the sociology of the plantation system and modern Caribbean society and culture, see Sidney W. Mintz, "Caribbean Society," in *International Encyclopedia of the Social Sciences* (New York 1968), 2: 311–14.

35. G. E. Simpson, "Haiti's Social Structure," *American Sociological Review*, 6 (1941): 640–49.

36. Alfred Métraux, *Voodoo*, 60.

37. Robert I. Rotberg, *Haiti: The Politics of Squalor* (Boston, 1971), 9–24.

3. NEO-AFRICAN RELIGIONS

38. Simpson, "Haiti's Social Structure," 645–46. A comprehensive recent analysis of Haitian politics is presented in Rotberg, *Haiti,* especially in chapters 4–6. See also Leyburn, *The Haitian People,* 211–49.

39. Harold Courlander, "Vodoun in Haitian Culture," in H. Courlander and Rémy Bastien, *Religion and Politics in Haiti* (Washington, D.C., 1966), 22.

40. This account of vodun is based mainly on G. E. Simpson, "The Vodun Cult in Haiti," *African Notes,* 3 (1966): 11–21; Alfred Métraux, *Voodoo;* Simpson, "The Belief System of Haitian Vodun," 35–59; M. J. Herskovits, *Life in a Haitian Valley* chaps. 8–11; and Harold Courlander, *The Drum and the Hoe* (Berkeley, 1960), chaps. 2–4. See also: Lorimer Denis and François Duvalier, "L'Evolution stadiale du vodou," *Bulletin du Bureau d'Ethnologie* (Port au Prince, 1955), 2nd ser., no. 12, 1–29; Maya Deren, *Divine Horsemen, The Living Gods of Haiti* (London, 1953); Jean Price-Mars, *Ainsi Parla L'Oncle* (Paris, 1928); Odette Mennesson-Rigaud, "The Feasting of Gods in Haitian Vodu," *Primitive Man,* 19 (1946): 1–58; Milo Marcelin, "Les Grands Dieux du Vodou Haitien," *Journal de la Société des Américanistes de Paris,* n. ser., Vol. 36 (1947): 51–135.

41. Rotberg, *Haiti,* 25–26.

42. Leyburn, *The Haitian People,* 141.

43. Métraux (1959, 323–29) wrote that one cannot speak of "a true assimilation of loa to Catholic saints." However, I did not find that the two groups of divinities "stand apart and belong to two entirely different religious systems" as he claimed. In Plaisance, the names of the saints and the loa were alternated in vodun songs, both categories were included in prayers, offerings were given to both, and, in some cases, a devotee became possessed by both. Many symbols of Catholicism are displayed on vodun altars, and the use of holy water has been borrowed from the church. While most of the Catholic songs and prayers come at the beginning and the end of a vodun service, they seem to me to be integral parts of the ceremony. Feasts for the loa tend to come on the days of the festivals of the saints with whom they correspond. During Lent many vodun altars are covered with sheets following the Catholic practice of covering images in the church. Pilgrimages to the shrines of patron-saints are attended by more vodunists than pure Catholics, and on All-Souls' night Gédé spirits of the dead run through the country areas and the towns.

44. Herskovits, *Life in a Haitian Valley,* 156, 267–68, 310–14; Métraux, *Voodoo,* 86–90; Courlander, *The Drum,* 317–31; Simpson, "The Belief System," 39.

45. Herskovits, *Life in a Haitian Valley,* ch. 11. In many parts of West Africa, as well as in the African diaspora, twins are highly regarded and are given special treatment. If the spirits of twins are not placated with proper rituals, they may cause illness and other misfortune. On the cult of the twins in Haiti, see *ibid.,* 202–4; Courlander, *The Drum,* 31–32; and Métraux, *Voodoo,* 146–53.

46. M. J. Herskovits, *Dahomey,* vol. 2 (New York, 1938), 238.

47. Alfred Métraux, "The Concept of Soul in Haitian Vodou," *Southwestern Journal of Anthropology,* 2 (Spring 1946): 92.

48. G. E. Simpson, "The Vodun Service in Northern Haiti," *American Anthropol-*

3. NEO-AFRICAN RELIGIONS

ogist, 42 (1940): 236–54. See also, Métraux, *Voodoo*, 157–92; and Herskovits, *Life in a Haitian Valley*, 159–76.

49. Courlander, *The Drum*, 41–74; G. E. Simpson, "Four Vodun Ceremonies," 154–67. For a remarkable collection of songs related to vodun deities, see Courlander, *The Drum*, 75–94.

50. Herskovits, *Life in a Haitian Valley*, chap. 12; Courlander, *The Drum* chap. 7; Métraux, *Voodoo*, chap. 5; G. E. Simpson, "Haitian Magic," *Social Forces*, 19 (1940): 95–100; and G. E. Simpson, "Magical Practices in Northern Haiti," *Journal of American Folklore*, 67 (1954): 395–403.

51. Carlos Esteban Deive, *Vodu y Magia en Santo Domingo* (Santo Domingo, 1975), 161–62.

52. *Ibid.*, 189.

53. Deive (1975, 171–74) lists 139 Dominican lua, including severals Baróns (del Cementerio, Lacuá, Sandí and Samedí, Zumbi); Guedés (Carfú, Limbó, Ba, Luí, Liá, Luis Guedé, Papa Guedé); Ogúns (Balendyó, Badagrí, Batalá, Fegai, Negué, Panamá, Onsú); and Legbás (Atibón, Carfú, Manosé, Macuté, Gramisí). A table by Deive (1975, 175–178) compares the main Dominican lua with the corresponding Haitian loa, with the variations in names according to the personalities of some of the latter deities. Correspondences between thirty male and sixteen female lua and Catholic saints are given by Deive (1975, 226–227).

54. *Ibid.*, 162.

55. *Ibid.*, 202–4.

56. M. J. Herskovits and F. S. Herskovits, *Trinidad Village* (New York, 1947), 17–22.

57. G. E. Simpson, *The Shango Cult*, 9–10; Lloyd Braithwaite, "Social Stratification in Trinidad: A Preliminary Analysis," *Social and Economic Studies*, 2 (1953): 7.

58. Braithwaite, "Social Stratification," 73–144.

59. *Ibid.*, 92–93.

60. *Ibid.*, 122–126.

61. For an excellent discussion of racial identity in the West Indies, see David L. Lowenthal, *West Indian Societies*, (London, 1972), 250–264.

62. Braithwaite, "Social Stratification," 49–50.

63. *Ibid.*, 130.

64. Simpson, *The Shango Cult*, 98.

65. This account of Trinidadian shango is based on G. E. Simpson, *The Shango Cult in Trinidad*; G. E. Simpson, "Shango Cult in Trinidad," *African Notes*, 3 (1965): 11–21; G. E. Simpson, "The Shango Cult in Nigeria and in Trinidad," 1204–19; and G. E. Simpson, "The Acculturative Process in Trinidadian Shango," *Anthropological Quarterly*, 37 (1964): 16–27. See also: M. J. and F. S. Herskovits, *Trinidad Village*, 321–39; Mischel, "African 'Powers' in Trinidad" 45–59; and Elder, "The Yoruba Ancestor Cult," 5–20. In his article on "A Rada Community in Trinidad," Andrew T. Carr (1953, 36) reports that groups of Rada, Ibo, Congo, and Mandingo peoples lived at the

3. NEO-AFRICAN RELIGIONS

northeastern corner of Port of Spain around 1870. The founder of the Rada compound is said to have arrived from Dahomey about 1855 at approximately 55 years of age. Ceremonies for the Rada gods, thanksgiving rites, sacrificial rituals in times of trouble, rites for the dead, and initiation ceremonies were still being given in the late 1940s and early 1950s. Carr found that the Rada community at Belmont had "succeeded in preserving a remarkable purity of strain" of Dahomean customs and beliefs. *Ibid.,* 36–54.

66. Bastide remarks that during the period of slavery in Brazil, black gods had to hide behind the statues of Catholic saints or the Virgin. As syncretism proceeded, the altar with statues of the saints was made highly visible to convince occasional white visitors that the members of the candomblé were good Catholics. According to Bastide, the Catholic altar has no functional role in ceremonies where the orisha are honored. Bastide, *Les Religions Africaines,* 380.

67. William Bascom, "Yoruba Concepts of the Soul," in A. F. C. Wallace, ed., *Selected Papers of the Fifth International Congress of Anthropological and Ethnological Sciences* (Philadelphia, 1960), 401. In his discussions with informants about "soul" concepts, Bascom encountered a certain amount of confusion. In talking with Yoruba people in Africa now, it is clear that the views of many concerning what happens after death have been influenced by Christian doctrines which have been preached among them for more than a century and by Muslim beliefs to which they have been exposed for much longer (*ibid.,* 401). In 1964, I found that village and urban informants in the Ibadan area of Nigeria regarded *ori* and *ojiji,* as well as *ipin* and *enikeji,* as synonymous (Simpson, *Yoruba Religion*).

68. P. A. Talbot, *The Peoples of Southern Nigeria,* vol. 2 (London, 1926), 191–92; Daryll Forde, *The Yoruba-speaking Peoples of South-western Nigeria* (London, 1951), 30.

69. Talbot, *The Peoples,* 305.

70. Simpson, *The Shango Cult,* 102. A similar belief is found in Jamaican revivalism in the case of skilled operators who can summon and utilize the duppy, a kind of second soul, of a deceased person (Simpson, 1960, 334).

71. Smith, *Dark Puritan,* 139. Smith comments: "In Cuba, where divination persists, acculturation contexts are rather different."

72. Among others, Frobenius reported that prescriptions of herbs and medicines, mixed with ghee, palm oil and nut oil, given by Shango to the priest were used widely among the Yoruba. Leo Frobenius, *The Voice of Africa,* London (1913), vol 2: 217.

73. Smith, *Dark Puritan,* 3–6.

74. Elsa Goveia, *Slave Society in the British Leeward Islands* (New Haven, 1965), 251, 262, 338. For an analysis of social structure throughout the West Indies, see Lowenthal, *West Indian Societies,* especially 81–100, and 162–212 (East Indians, Creoles, Amerindians, Bush Negroes, Javanese, Portuguese, Chinese, Syrians).

75. Smith, *The Plural Society,* 33–34.

76. Angelina Pollak-Eltz, "The Shango Cult in Grenada, British Westindies," *Proceedings, VIIIth International Congress of Anthropological and Ethnological Sciences,* 3 (1968): 59–60.

3. NEO-AFRICAN RELIGIONS

77. Smith, *Dark Puritan*, 8. This summary of Paul's cult is based on *ibid.*, 74–78, 101–102, 109, 132–39.

78. For an account of Paul's personality characteristics, see chapter 4 of the present work.

79. Smith, *Dark Puritan*, 98.

80. Simpson, *The Shango Cult in Trinidad*, chapter 1.

81. Smith, *Dark Puritan*, 136.

82. *Ibid.*, 136–37.

83. *Ibid.*, 137–38.

84. *Ibid.*, 133–34. The divinatory procedure described here is exactly the same as it is in Trinidadian shango and similar to one type of divination among the Yoruba. See Simpson, *The Shango Cult*, 111–12.

85. Smith, *Dark Puritan*, 134.

86. Bascom, "The Yoruba in Cuba," 14. For an excellent recent description of santeria temples, including altars and ritual equipment, see Lydia González Huguet, "La Casa-Templo en la Regla de Ocha," *Etnologia Folklore*, Núm. 5 (Enero-Junio 1968), 33–57.

87. Bascom, "The Yoruba, in Cuba," 14–17, and Bascom, *Shango in the New World*, 14–15. Courlander points out that it is hard to know how many of the Yoruba tales about the orisha were actually created in Cuba, and, also, that personalities of the orisha, their relationships to one another, and on occasion their sex have been altered. Harold Courlander, *Tales of Yoruba Gods and Heroes* (New York, 1973), 213.

88. Bascom, "The Focus of Cuban Santeria," 64–68.

89. William Bascom, "Two Forms of Afro-Cuban Divination," in Sol Tax, ed., *Acculturation in the Americas* (Chicago, 1952), 169–79.

90. *Ibid.*, 176.

91. This summary of a number of Afro-Cuban religious dances is based on Ortiz, *Los Bailes*, 199–253. Verses (with African words) that accompany the dances, as well as musical notations, are given in this volume. In another work (*Hampa Afro-Cubana: Los Negros Esclavos*, Havana, 1916), Ortiz provided information on the diversions of slaves on holidays and on Saturday nights. Dancing was preferred as a form of recreation for the slaves and was regarded as harmless by their masters (*ibid.*, 235). For an account of various dances, see *ibid.*, 230–34. There were some opportunities to dance on workdays (*ibid.*, 228), and singing was permitted during working hours (*ibid.*, 235). At times drumming was prohibited because it was regarded as too noisy or because it was feared the slaves would use the sounds of drums to send messages when they were conspiring (*ibid.*, 230).

92. Ortiz, *Los Bailes*, 202–209. Copular pantomime is seen, however, in the Abakwa ritual in Cuba (Courlander, 1944, 467).

93. Ortiz, *Los Bailes*, 209.

94. *Ibid.*, 209–13, 223.

95. *Ibid.*, 235.

3. NEO-AFRICAN RELIGIONS

96. *Ibid.*, 246–47.

97. *Ibid.*, 247–51.

98. *Ibid.*, 251–53, 348–49.

99. Because Oro is also the name given to a "buzzer" (ritual object) that is used in some funeral rites, some people do not regard Oro as a pantomimical figure of death similar to Egungun (Ortiz, 1951, 355). In the Ibadan area of Nigeria, a priest who serves the orisha called Oro uses an *oro* stick to prevent witches from causing havoc. The *oro*, a piece of iron or wood, preferably *obo* wood, five or six inches long with a hole punched in one end of it, is carefully prepared with roots and leaves. It is tied to a string and the string is fastened to a stick. When whirled it makes a whistling noise. Since witchbirds must not see, smell, or eat *obo* wood, the witchbirds inside the witches die when *oro* is used, and the witches also die. Or Oro may be asked to destroy the trees which harbor witchbirds. Other evildoers may be driven mad by the sound of *oro* (G. E. Simpson, *Yoruba Religion and Medicine in Ibadan*). In Nigeria, Gelede spirits protect members of the all-male Gelede cult from witchcraft. During the annual festival, "the men masquerade as women, wearing women's clothes and flaunting prominent bullet-like breasts. Some look grossly pregnant, and others carry wood carvings of children on their backs. All wear grotesquely carved masks." Raymond Prince, "Indigenous Yoruba Psychiatry," in Ari Kiev, ed., *Magic, Faith, and Healing* (New York, 1964), 109.

100. P. Amaury Talbot, *In the Shadow of the Bush* (London, 1912), 44. Reprinted in Harold Courlander, *A Treasury of African Folklore* (New York, 1975), 270–74.

101. Courlander, *A Treasury*, 275.

102. *Ibid.*, 276.

103. Courlander, "Abakwa Meeting in Guanabacoa," 464–65.

104. *Ibid.*, 466. The costume of an *iremé* photographed by Courlander in 1941 is similar, but simpler, than the one pictured in Ortiz (*Los Bailes*, 358), and the one shown in Talbot *In the Shadow of the Bush* (London, 1912).

105. The two figures reproduced here are from Courlander, "Abakwa Meeting," p. 467, by permission of the Association for the study of Afro-American Life and History, Inc. According to Talbot, when a man joined *Nkanda*, the highest and final grade of the Egbo secret society on the Calabar Coast, "he is rubbed on head and chest with yellow powder (*ogokk*). Five rings are made on front and back. Two yellow, one round each breast, a white one in the center some few inches below, and, beneath this again, two more yellow ones, forming a square with those on the breasts. On the back the rings are arranged in the same way, but the central one is yellow and the four outer ones white. The arms are ornamented with alternate stripes of white and yellow, and till the last rite is finished, the man goes bare save for a long loincloth which reaches from waist to feet." Talbot, *In the Shadow*, (reprinted in Courlander, *A Treasury of African Folklore*, 273–74).

106. The bull-roarer, called *Eboku* by the Bakundu, is used by secret societies and is greatly feared, especially by non-members, who believe it to be the voice of the *juju* [evil spirit]. Courlander, "Abakwa Meeting," 469.

107. *Ibid.*, 467–68.

3. NEO-AFRICAN RELIGIONS

108. Ortiz, *Los Bailes,* 357–76.

109. Barreal, "Tendencias Sincreticas," 22–23. See also Lydia Cabrera, *El Monte* (Miami, 1971), 195–220.

110. Bascom, "Shango in the New World," 20.

111. Erika Bourguignon, "Ritual Dissociation and Possession Belief in Caribbean Negro Religion," in Norman E. Whitten and John F. Szwed, eds., *Afro-American Anthropology: Contemporary Perspectives* (New York, 1970), 94. Bourguignon cites Goveia, *Slave Society,* 24 on "the persistence of the African traditions in the religious and magical beliefs and rituals of the Negro slaves in the Leeward Islands." Goevia's comment is based on Clement Caines' report of 1804 (*The History of the General Assembly of the Leeward Islands which were convened for the purpose of investigation and ameliorating the condition of the slaves throughout those settlements and effecting a gradual abolition of the slave trade,* vol. 1, St. Christopher: Basseterre [1804], 130–35) concerning "the use of dancing in their religious ceremonial, and the high place accorded to spirit possession—'the most envied condition at which a Confuist can arrive'—as a form of religious experience" (Goveia, *Slave Society,* 247–48). Concerning religious syncretisms in Dominica, Taylor writes: "Although some religious syncretism is found here (especially since there is now a movement in favor of obia, seen as the 'true African religion'), Dominica is not as rich in this respect as the larger islands (Trinidad, Jamaica, etc.)." Personal communication from Douglas Taylor, December 28, 1973.

112. Angelina Pollak-Eltz, *Cultos Afroamericanos,* (Caracas, 1972), 170; Michael M. Horowitz, *Morne-Paysan: Peasant Village in Martinique* (New York, 1967), 82. These magical packages are similar to *ouangas* in Haiti. Kembois (sorcery) was widely practiced in St. Lucia in the 1840s (Henry H. Breen, *St. Lucia: Historical, Statistical, and Descriptive,* London (1844), 249–50. In 1972, in the Babonneau section of St. Lucia, informants reported that consultations with *chembwatès* (sorcerers) still occur. See G. E. Simpson, "The Kele (Chango) Cult in St. Lucia," *Caribbean Studies,* 13 (1973): 110–16.

113. Herskovits, *The Myth,* 197–198; M. J. Herskovits, *The Human Factor in Changing Africa* (New York, 1962), 101–2.

114. For an excellent analysis of Jamaica's social system, see M. G. Smith, "The Plural Framework of Jamaican Society," *The British Journal of Sociology,* 12 (1961): 249–62. On the political aspects of Jamaica's social structure from the 1930s to 1968, see Gordon K. Lewis, *The Growth of the Modern West Indies* (New York, 1968), chapter 7.

115. The 1960 Census of Jamaica classified the population as 76 percent African; 15 percent Afro-European; 1 percent Chinese and Afro-Chinese; 3 percent East Indian; and 3 percent "other." The Population Council, *Country Profiles: Jamaica* (New York, 1971), 2.

116. In 1960 agriculture accounted for about 38 percent of the labor force, but this proportion is declining steadily. Manufacturing accounted for 15 percent of the labor force, personal services accounted for about 30 percent of the female labor force, and construction employed about 13 percent of the employed males. *Ibid.,* 3.

117. *Ibid.,* 3; Simpson, "Jamaican Revivalist Cults," 322–27.

3. NEO-AFRICAN RELIGIONS

118. Wendell Bell, "Equality and Attitudes of Elites in Jamaica," *Social and Economic Studies*, 11 (1962): 409.

119. Leonard Broom, "Urbanization and the Plural Society," *Annals of the New York Academy of Sciences*, 82 (1960): 882–84.

120. Leonard Broom, "The Social Differentiation of Jamaica," *American Sociological Review*, 19 (1954): 123–24.

121. Philip C. Curtin, *Two Jamaicas*, (Cambridge, Mass., 1955), 32–34, 168; G. E. Simpson "Jamaican Revivalist Cults," 411 ff; Donald Hogg, "The Convince Cult," 21; J. G. Moore and G. E. Simpson, "A Comparative Study of Acculturation in Morant Bay and West Kingston, Jamaica," *Zaire* (1958) no. 1, 82–83.

122. For a discussion of the dissatisfactions underlying the Ras Tafari movement in the 1960s, see Rex M. Nettleford, *Mirror Mirror: Identity, Race and Protest in Jamaica* (Kingston, Jamaica, 1970), 47–52. On Negritude and the Black Power Movement, see Lowenthal, *West Indian Societies*, 280–92. Of special interest is Lowenthal's comment that "black power in the West Indies is not only anti-white, it is anti-coloured." *Ibid.*, 286.

123. Bell, "Equality and Attitudes," 415.

124. The Population Council, *Jamaica*, 6.

125. This account of the Cumina religion is based entirely on the work of Joseph G. Moore, *Religion of Jamaican Negroes: A Study of Afro-Jamaican Acculturation* (Ann Arbor: University Microfilms; Doctoral Dissertation Series, Publication 7053, 1954). See also, J. G. Moore and G. E. Simpson, "A Comparative Study of Acculturation in Morant Bay and West Kingston, Jamaica," *Zaire*, nos. 9–10 (1957), 979–1019, and no. 1 (1958), 65–87 (reprinted in G. E. Simpson, *Religious Cults of the Caribbean: Trinidad, Jamaica, and Haiti*, Rio Piedras, Puerto Rico, 1970, 157–200). The names of some of these "nations" are actual African tribal names: Ga, Ibo, and Yoruba. The African-sounding names may refer to the Mandingo, Moyo, Machonde, and Mumbake tribes. See G. P. Murdock, "Index of Tribal Names," *Africa: Its Peoples and Their Culture History* (New York, 1959), 425–456.

126. Moore and Simpson, "A Comparative Study," 1958, 74.

127. There are a number of names of gods in this list which may have been derived from the names of African gods, but in their present form this is almost impossible to determine. For a comment on the probable African origin of Cumina, see Orlando Patterson, *The Sociology of Slavery: An Analysis of the Origin, Development and Structure of Negro Slave Society in Jamaica* (London, 1967), 198–202.

128. Moore and Simpson, "A Comparative Study," 1957, 984–86.

129. Moore, *Religion of Jamaican Negroes*, 149ff. In Cumina, the personal spirit (soul) goes directly to Oto, King Zombie, never to return to earth, if, in life, the person had never been possessed by a zombie. If a person has been possessed by a zombie, his soul takes on a new quality and, at death, joins all ancestral zombie spirits and can return to "duties" of various kinds on earth, including attending cult ceremonies and possessing living individuals. See Moore and Simpson, "A Comparative Study," 1957, 991.

3. NEO-AFRICAN RELIGIONS

130. For details on Cumina drums and drumming see Moore and Simpson, "A Comparative Study," 1957, 1000–1002.

131. *Ibid.*, 1957, 1004. For details on the dances performed by Cumina devotees during possession, see *Ibid.*, 1957, 1004–7.

132. *Ibid.*, 1958, 77–78.

133. This summary of the Convince cult is based on Hogg, "The Convince Cult in Jamaica," 3–24.

134. *Ibid.*, 16.

135. *Ibid.*, 20–23.

136. Smith, *The Plural Society*, 33–34.

137. This account of the Nation Dance in Carriacou is based on Andrew C. Pearse, *The Big Drum Dance of Carriacou* (Ethnic Folkways Library Album No. P 1011, New York, 1956), 1–6.

138. The Free Ring is a space that is left open for the spirits of the ancestors to dance in. Pearse says: "In the old days people used to see them. You know of their arrival because the music becomes 'brisk'. Misfortune is said to have come on those who carelessly or presumptuously danced in a free ring. Sometimes a Spirit may take non-human form, such as a crab or a bird." *Ibid.*, 3.

139. Pearse comments: "This does not of course imply that the Congo or Temné or Arada items are necessarily a pure survival of the music of those nations, but undoubtedly at some stage in the history of the festival Africans of these different nations or collections of nations connoted by these names have attempted to pass on to the mixed groups of singers and dancers in Carriacou some items of their own music, and have danced as these strangers played it for them." *Ibid.*, 2.

140. The material in this section appeared first in a research commentary of this title in *Caribbean Studies*, 13 (October 1973): 110–16. I collected the data in and near Babonneau, St. Lucia, in October 1972. For assistance in this study I am indebted to Father Charles Jesse, Eric Branford, Peter Joseph, Noah Delaire, and Simon Joseph.

141. According to Bascom (1972, 5), Shango worshippers among the Yoruba of Nigeria "wear strings of alternating small red and opaque white beads, imported from Europe and known as kele, as their insignia." M. J. Herskovits reported that in Bahia, Brazil, the wearing of a necklace, the kélé symbolized the subjugation of the candomblé initiate for three months after the ceremony called *panan*. Cited in Bastide, *African Civilisations*, 121.

142. See Daniel J. Crowley, "Supernatural Beings in St. Lucia," *The Caribbean*, 8 (1955): 241–44, 264–65.

143. Harold F. C. Simmons ("Notes on Folklore in St. Lucia," in Edward Brathwate, ed., *Iouanaloa: Recent Writing from St. Lucia*, Department of Extra Mural Studies, St. Lucia, June 1963, 46) found that the heart, liver and genitals are cooked separately, and that "pots of meat, rice, and yam, cooked separately without any salt or seasoning" are used for a food-offering. Frobenius (*The Voice of Africa*, 191), reported that the Yoruba in Nigeria sprinkled the blood of sacrificial animals on the altar, drained the

3. NEO-AFRICAN RELIGIONS

rest of the blood into a pot, and cooked the kidneys and liver of these animals in the blood. In Trinidadian shango, some of the blood of animal sacrficies is sprinkled on the stools (shrines) of the principal powers (deities), some is collected in vessels, and some is mixed with "sweet" (olive) oil and served on the final night of the ceremony. Also, the liver, part of a hind leg, and part of a front leg of a goat are cooked separately without salt, as are the liver, kidneys, head, and one leg of a fowl, as an offering to St. Michael (Ogun). See Simpson, *The Shango Cult in Trinidad,* 104.

144. M. G. Smith, "A Note on Truth, Fact, and Tradition in Carriacou," *Caribbean Quarterly,* 17 (1971): 134–35.

145. Douglas M. Taylor, *The Black Carib of British Honduras* (New York, 1951), 37.

146. *Ibid.,* 102.

147. M. J. Herskovits, *Cultural Anthropology* (New York, 1955), 214; Bascom, "Yoruba Concepts of the Soul," 401–410.

148. Taylor, *The Black Carib,* 104–5.

149. Herskovits, *Life in a Haitian Valley* 239–242.

150. Taylor, *The Black Carib,* 107–8.

151. *Ibid.,* 115–22.

152. *Ibid.,* 124.

153. *Ibid.,* 126. For an account of the ceremony in Trinidad, see Simpson, *The Shango Cult,* 50–51.

154. Taylor, *The Black Carib,* 128.

155. *Ibid.,* 130–31.

156. *Ibid.,* 133.

4. Revivalist and Other Cults of the Caribbean

1. G. E. Simpson, "The Acculturative Process in Jamaican Revivalism" in A. F. C. Wallace, ed., *Selected Papers of the Fifth International Congress of Anthropological and Ethnological Sciences* (Philadelphia, 1960), 332. Hogg (*Jamaican Religions,* 296) found that rural Pocomanians in the Highgate-Richmond area in St. Mary's concerned themselves "mainly with ghosts, water spirits, and to a lesser extent with angels." For an account of Revivalists and Pukkumerians in Jamaica in the early 1920s, see Martha W. Beckwith, *Black Roadways: A Study of Jamaican Folk Life* (Chapel Hill, N.C., 1929), chs. 10–11.

2. J. G. Moore and G. E. Simpson, "A Comparative Study of Acculturation in Morant Bay and West Kingston, Jamaica," *Zaire,* nos. 9–10 (1957): 980–82 (reprinted in Simpson, *Religious Cults of the Caribbean,* 157–200).

3. Philip D. Curtin, *Two Jamaicas* (Cambridge, Mass., 1955), 32–34; 168.

4. *Ibid.,* 171. *Obeah* (witchcraft) practices were offset by *myalism* (counterwitchcraft).

5. Anthony F. C. Wallace, "Revitalization Movements," *American Anthropologist,* 58 (1956): 267, 276.

3. NEO-AFRICAN RELIGIONS

6. These five spirits are described in *The Sixth and Seventh Books of Moses,* (Chicago, 1916), 9, 122, 139.

7. Moore and Simpson, "A Comparative Study," 986–89; Simpson, "The Acculturative Process in Jamaican Revivalism," 333–34; G. E. Simpson, "Jamaican Revivalist Cults," *Social and Economic Studies,* 5 (1956): 344–45.

8. One shepherd possessed a short staff with a knob on one end, which he referred to as a "conjurer's rod."

9. Simpson, "Jamaican Revivalist Cults," 366–76; Moore and Simpson, "A Comparative Study," 1011–16. For an account of a nine-night ceremony, see G. E. Simpson, "The Nine Night Ceremony in Jamaica," *Journal of American Folklore,* 70 (1957): 329–35. The Pocomania ritual in Morant Bay is described in J. G. Moore and G. E. Simpson, "A Comparative Study of Acculturation in Morant Bay and West Kingston, Jamaica," *Zaire,* no. 1 (1958): 65–69. For an account of a major Table of a rural Pocomania band in St. Mary's, see Hogg (*Jamaican Religions,* 311–26). Hogg also gives descriptions of urban Pocomania Tables in Spanish Town (*Ibid.,* 367–75).

10. In addition to a soul, which returns to God for judgment, each person is said to have a shadow or "duppy" which remains behind after death. See Beckwith, *Black Roadways* (Chapel Hill, 1929), 104. For a comment on the African background of obeah, see Orlando Patterson, *The Sociology of Slavery,* London, 1967, 182–95.

11. For details on healing and conjuring procedures, see Simpson, "Jamaican Revivalist Cults," 383–99.

12. M. J. Herskovits, *The Myth of the Negro Past* (New York, 1941), 253.

13. This and the following paragraphs dealing with the acculturative process in Jamaican revivalism are based on Simpson, "The Acculturative Process," 335–37; Moore and Simpson, "A Comparative Study," 84–85; and Simpson, *Jamaican Revivalist Cults,* 417–28. Retentions here mean valuational or behavioral elements which show the least degree of change. Syncretisms represent a degree of synthesis "where old and new are merged into a functioning unified entity of clear bi-cultural derivation" (Herskovits, "Introduction," 57). Reinterpretation is "the process by which old meanings are ascribed to new elements or by which new values change the cultural significance of old forms" (Herskovits, *Man,* 553–55).

14. Edward Brathwaite, *Folk Culture of the Slaves in Jamaica* (London; Port of Spain, 1970), 7. Among other African cultural elements in Jamaican folk culture discussed by Brathwaite are birth customs, domestic unions, child rearing, music and dance, musical instruments, private and public entertainments, dress, house types, and language. (This publication is abstracted from Brathwaite's *The Development of Creole Society in Jamaica,* [Oxford, 1970].)

15. J. H. K. Nketia, *Funeral Dirges of the Akan People* (Achimota University, Accra, Ghana, 1955, 15) refers to the 8th, 15th, 40th, and 80th day "of the funeral." See also, Geoffrey Parrinder, *West African Religion* (London, 1949), 119.

16. See G. E. Simpson and P. B. Hammond, Discussion of M. G. Smith, "The African Heritage in the Caribbean," in Vera Rubin, ed., *Caribbean Studies: A Symposium* (Kingston, Jamaica, 1957), 46–53.

4. REVIVALIST AND OTHER CULTS

17. Bascom ("The Focus," 67) states that the Yoruba word *iproni* refers to "the material object which represents the power of a deity and to which its sacrifices are actually presented" and also that "the real power of the *santos* (divinities in Cuban *santeria*) resides in the stones."

18. Blood sacrifices are common in traditional West African religious rituals (Bascom, "The Focus," 67) and biblical references to the ritual use of blood are well-known (for example, Exodus 24: 5–8).

19. Simpson, "The Acculturative Process in Jamaican Revivalism," 336–37.

20. *Ibid.*

21. Jeannette H. Henney, "Spirit-Possession Belief and Trance Behavior in Two Fundamentalists Groups in St. Vincent," in Felicitas D. Goodman, Jeannette H. Henney, and Esther Pressel, *Trance, Healing, and Hallucination: Three Field Studies in Religious Experience* (New York, 1974), 25.

22. G. E. Simpson, *Cult Music of Trinidad,* Folkways Ethnic Library, Album FE 4478 (New York, 1961), 2.

23. *Ibid.,* 3.

24. *Ibid.,* 3. For a detailed account of the Shouters ritual as observed by the Herskovitses in a village in northeastern Trinidad in 1939, see M. J. Herskovits and F. S. Herskovits, *Trinidad Village* (New York, 1947), 218–23.

25. G. E. Simpson, "Baptismal, 'Mourning,' and 'Building' Ceremonies of the Shouters in Trinidad," *Journal of American Folklore,* 79 (1966), 537–50.

26. *Ibid.,* 543–48.

27. Herskovits and Herskovits, *Trinidad Village,* 305.

28. Herskovits (*The Myth,* 223) describes the singing of the Sankey hymn: "Jesus, Lover of My Soul" at a Shouters meeting as follows: "The song begins in its conventional form, sung, if anything, with accent on the lugubrious measured quality that marks hymns of this type. After two or three repetitions, however, the tempo quickens, the rhythm changes, and the tune is converted into a song typically African in its accompaniment of clapping hands and foot-patting, and in its singing style. All that is left of the original hymn is the basic melody which, as a constant undercurrent to the variations that play about it, constitutes the unifying element in this amazingly illuminating music."

29. Herskovits and Herskovits, *Trinidad Village,* 305–9.

30. This interpretation is based on James W. Fernandez's "Symbolic Consensus in a Fang Syncretist Cult," *American Anthropologist,* 68 (1965): 902–29, an analysis of symbolic consensus (social consensus, based on signs, and cultural consensus, based on symbols) in his study of the Bwiti cult in northern Gabon.

31. Talcott Parsons, *The Social System* (New York, 1961), 6.

32. Jeannette H. Henney, "The Shakers of St. Vincent: A Stable Religion," in *Religion, Altered States of Consciousness, and Social Change,* edited by Erika Bourguignon (Columbus, Ohio, 1971), 224; Jeannette H. Henney, "Spirit-Possession Belief and Trance Behavior in Two Fundamentalist Groups in St. Vincent," in Felicitas D. Good-

4. REVIVALIST AND OTHER CULTS

man, Jeannette H. Henney, and Esther Pressel, *Trance, Healing, and Hallucination: Three Field Studies in Religious Experience* (New York, 1974), 21, 23.

33. Henney, "Spirit-Possession Belief," in Goodman, Henney, and Pressel, *Trance,* 23.

34. *Ibid.,* 36–38.

35. *Ibid.,* 30, 38–39, 50–58.

36. This account of the Streams of Power cult in St. Vincent is based on *Ibid.,* 41–48.

37. *Ibid.,* 48.

38. L. H. Rogler and A. B. Hollingshead, *Trapped: Families and Schizophrenia* (New York, 1965), 8, 16–17, 46, 62–63, 248, 255.

39. L. H. Rogler and A. B. Hollingshead, "The Puerto Rican Spiritualist as a Psychiatrist," *American Journal of Sociology,* 67 (1961): 19–20.

40. Rogler and Hollingshead, *Trapped,* 260. On spiritualist cults in Cuba, see Armando Andrés Bermúdez, "Notas para la Historia del Espiritismo en Cuba," *Etnología y Folklore,* Núm. 4 (1967): 5–22, and A. A. Bermúdez, "La Expansión del 'Espiritismo de Cordón'," *Ibid.,* Núm. 5 (1968): 5–32.

41. Theodore G. Vincent, *Black Power and the Garvey Movement* (Berkeley, 1971), 134.

42. Vincent, *Black Power,* 134–35. In the 1950s there was at least one congregation of Black Jews in Jamaica (I attended one of the Saturday afternoon services in 1953). The founding date of this group is not known, and I do not know whether groups of Black Jews have existed in the Caribbean other than in Barbados and Jamaica.

43. Hamilton gives the approximate number of African Orthodox churches in the United States at present as 25 or 30, and the approximate number of members as 6,000. Charles V. Hamilton, *The Black Preacher in America* (New York, 1972), 75.

44. Amy J. Garvey, *Black Power in America* (Kingston, 1968), 38.

45. E. David Cronon, *Black Moses, The Story of Marcus Garvey and the Universal Negro Improvement Association* (Madison, 1955; 1969), 177.

46. *Ibid.,* 179, 180, 182.

47. George E. Simpson, "Political Cultism in West Kingston," *Social and Economic Studies,* 4 (1955): 133–49. For an account of the history of the movement, see M. G. Smith, Roy Augier, and Rex Nettleford, *The Ras Tafari Movement in Kingston, Jamaica* (Kingston, Jamaica, 1960), 8–14.

48. George E. Simpson, "Social Stratification in the Caribbean," *Phylon,* 23 (1962): 43. For accounts of Ras Tafari rituals, see G. E. Simpson, "Political Cultism," 135–43; Sheila Kitzinger, "Protest and Mysticism: The Rastafari Cult of Jamaica," *Journal for the Scientific Study of Religions,* 8 (1969): 247–51.

49. George E. Simpson, "The Ras Tafari Movement in Jamaica in Its Millenial Aspects," *Comparative Studies in Society and History,* Supplement II (1962): 160–65.

50. Rex M. Nettleford, *Mirror Mirror: Identity, Race and Protest in Jamaica* (Kingston, Jamaica, 1970), 43, 218–19. Concerning the number of Rastafarians in Kingston

4. REVIVALIST AND OTHER CULTS

in 1960, Smith, Augier, and Nettleford (1960, 21) wrote: "If the declared Ras Tafari brethren are estimated at between ten and fifteen thousands, the undeclared but closely integrated sympathisers may be an equal number, and the sum of these two may be somewhat less than the numbers of people in Kingston who might take the side of the Ras Tafari brethren if circumstances seemed favourable. Since many Ras Tafari brethren are beardless, and live dispersed through the City, the actual strength of the movement is hard to estimate, while its penetration among the disaffected urban lower class is correspondingly easy." According to these authors, cleavages within the movement include "those who belong to Locals of the Ethiopian World Federation Inc., and those who do not; those who grow beards and long hair, those who also plait their locks, and those who do neither; those who have adopted the Niyabingi ethos [of violence] and those who have not; those totally alienated from Jamaican society, and those who are not; those with a definite Marxist framework of ideas, and those without. There are also important divisions between rural and urban brethren, between the young and the old, between those who regard a firm social organization as a necessary instrument for the achievement of their aims, and those who reject this idea totally; between the unemployed and the employed brethren; between those who are addicted to ganja and those opposed to it; between those for whom the Emperor has special importance as a spiritual force, and those who conceive of him in racial-political terms primarily." *Ibid.*, 28.

51. Nettleford, *Mirror Mirror*, 108.

52. *Ibid.*, 108–9.

53. Vincent, *Black Power*, 226–27.

54. *Ibid.*, 222–23.

55. Garvey, *Black Power in America*, 7.

56. This report on the Dreads is based on articles on this group in *Caribbean Monthly Bulletin*, 9 (May–June 1975): 43–49, and 9 (September 1975): 29.

57. Erika Bourguignon, "Divination, Transe et Possession en Afrique Transsaharienne," in A. Caquot and Marcel Leibovice (eds.), *La Divination* (Paris, 1968), 332. Quoted in Esther Pressel, "Umbanda in São Paulo: Religious Innovation in a Developing Society," in E. Bourguignon (ed.), *Religion, Altered States of Consciousness, and Social Change* (Columbus, Ohio, 1973), 308; Erika Bourguignon, *Culture and the Varieties of Consciousness* (Menlo Park, Calif., 1974), 11.

58. Henney, "The Shakers," in E. Bourguignon, ed., *Religion*, 249.

59. F. M. Davenport, *Primitive Traits in Religious Revivals* (New York, 1905), 78–81; Simpson and Hammond, Discussion of M. G. Smith, "The African Heritage," 48–49.

60. Erika Bourguignon, "Ritual Dissociation and Possession Belief in Caribbean Negro Religion," in Norman E. Whitten, Jr. and John F. Szwed, eds., *Afro-American Anthropology* (New York, 1970), 93.

61. Raymond Prince, "Can EEG Be Used in the Study of Possession States?" in R. Prince (ed.), *Trance and Possession States* (Montreal, 1968), 127. On preparation for trance, induction of trance, length and termination of trance in the Umbanda cult in São

4. REVIVALIST AND OTHER CULTS

Paulo, Brazil, see Pressel, "Umbanda in São Paulo," 310–11. Lee comments that the amount of hard work involved in trance induction among the !Kung Bushmen is manifested "in the performer's heavy foot-stamping, forced breathing, muscular tension, abundant perspiration, and subsequent signs of exhaustion. It is clear that a considerable mobilization of adrenalin occurs during the trance episode, as evidenced (in some cases, but not in all) by aggressive behavior (punching and kicking), by flight reactions (running away), and by constant shivering and muscular spasms." Richard B. Lee, "The Sociology of !Kung Bushman Trance Performances," in R. Prince (ed.), *Trance,* 49. Since many features of the "unit utterance" of glossolalia (vocalization pattern uttered at one stretch) frequently associated with trance are identical cross-culturally, Goodman hypothesizes "the presence of a common denominator, which must be physiological rather than cultural." She writes: "What happens, it seems, is that the person going into trance does so by relinquishing a certain measure of central control, at which point other brain structures take over, and it is their processes that we see reflected in the vocalization during trance. In other words, the glossolalia utterance is an artifact of the trance; it results from, and is shaped by, the way the body acts in this particular mental state." Felicitas D. Goodman, "Disturbances in the Apostolic Church: A Trance-Based Upheaval in Yucatan," in Goodman, Henney, Pressel, *Trance,* 264.

62. E. Bourguignon, "The Self, the Behavioral Environment, and the Theory of Spirit Possession," in M. E. Spiro (ed.), *Context and Meaning in Cultural Anthropology,* (New York, 1965), 56; Ruth Landes, "Fetish Worship in Brazil," *The Journal of American Folklore,* 53 (1940) 261–70; M. J. and F. S. Herskovits, "The Negroes of Brazil," *Yale Review,* 32 (1943): 278–79; Octavio Da Costa Eduardo, *The Negro in Northern Brazil: A Study in Acculturation* (New York, 1948), 96; René Ribeiro, "An Experimental Approach to the Study of Spirit Possession, Recife, Brazil" (unpublished ms.), 2; Roger Bastide, *Les Religions Africaines au Brésil* (Paris, 1960), 520; Pressel, "Umbanda in São Paulo," 309; G. E. Simpson, "The Shango Cult in Nigeria and in Trinidad," *American Anthropologist,* 64 (1962): 1211–12; Personal communication from Roger D. Abrahams, May 21, 1973.

63. Henney, "Spirit-Possession Belief," in Goodman, Henney, Pressel, *Trance,* 61–64.

64. M. J. Herskovits, *Man and His Works: The Science of Cultural Anthropology* (New York, 1948), 67.

65. Ribeiro, "An Experimental Approach," 2.

66. Simpson, "Jamaican Revivalist Cults," 354; J. G. Moore, "Religious Syncretism in Jamaica," *Practical Anthropology,* 12 (1965): 64–65. Such a pattern of induction is not found in all of the Protestant-derived religions of the Caribbean. In St. Vincent, for example, hyperventilation occurs during but not before the trance. The Shaker trancer "jerks, rocks, trembles, but there is no patterned choreography and he does not move far from the spot on which he was standing or sitting when the trance began. He sings hymns and he shouts and speaks in tongues but his range of actions is restricted." Bourguignon, "Ritual Dissociation," 92, 94. See J. H. Henney, *Spirit Possession Belief*

4. REVIVALIST AND OTHER CULTS

and Trance Behavior in a Religious Group in St. Vincent, British West Indies (Ph.D. dissertation, The Ohio State University, 1968). On the beach in Barrouallie, St. Vincent, in April, 1966, however, Abrahams observed an elaborate hand-touching choreography leading up to the trance in an outdoor Shaker meeting. Personal communication from Roger D. Abrahams, April 16, 1973.

67. Esther Pressel, "Umbanda Trance and Possession in São Paulo, Brazil," in Goodman, Henney, and Pressel, *Trance,* 198.

68. Bourguignon, "Ritual Dissociation," 91–92.

69. Pressel, "Umbanda Trance," 194.

70. *Ibid.,* 194–95; Goodman, "Disturbances in the Apostolic Church," 361.

71. E. Bourguignon, "World Distribution and Patterns of Possession States," in R. Prince (ed.), *Trance,* 12; Bourguignon, "The Self," The Behavioral Environment," 44–45, 50; René Ribeiro, *The Afrobrazilian Cult-Groups of Recife, a Study of Social Adjustment* (Evanston, Illinois, 1949, M.A. Thesis in Anthropology), 119–20. Bourguignon points out ("The Self," 45) that dissociational states of this type differ from those in societies where more stereotyped behavior leaves little room for individual differences.

72. Henney, "The Shakers," 249–50.

73. Henney, "Spirit-Possession Belief," in Goodman, Henney, and Pressel, *Trance,* 104–5. Henney concludes that hallucinating under certain conditions is a biological capacity common to all human beings, but "the probability of hallucinating and the content of the hallucinations will vary with the experiences of the people involved, their belief system and other similar factors." *Ibid.,* 105. See also, Henney, "The Shakers," 247–49. For a comparison of the results of sensory-deprivation experiments and mourning-room experience, see Henney, "Spirit-Possession Belief," 70–79.

74. Bourguignon, "The Self," 50, 54–55.

75. Bourguignon, *Culture and the Varieties of Consciousness,* 22–23.

76. Gardner Murphy, *Personality: A Biosocial Approach to Origins and Structure* (New York, 1947), 326, 435, 449; Herskovits, *Man and His Works,* 67; J. M. Yinger, *Toward a Field Theory of Behavior* (New York, 1965), 270; Ioan M. Lewis, *Ecstatic Religion, An Anthropological Study of Spirit Possession and Shamanism* (Middlesex, England, 1971), 185–86.

77. Lewis, *Ecstatic Religion,* 186. Pressel makes the same point: "The data in the study clearly suggest that the possession-trance states in the early stages of Umbanda mediumship are usually due to some inability of the individual to operate successfully in his specific sociocultural environment. Generally, the personal difficulty of the novice does not make him totally dysfunctional and is one that can be successfully treated over a period of several weeks up to possibly a year. If the disorder extends much beyond this period of time, it is likely that the disturbance is 'psychological' or 'physical,' instead of 'spiritual.' What is being emphasized here is that Umbanda is not a repository for psychologically disturbed people unable to operate in their social environment" (Pressel, "Umbanda Trance," 204). Gerlach and Hine *People, Power, Change,* xxii) report that

4. REVIVALIST AND OTHER CULTS

recent studies by qualified psychologists revealed no difference between Pentecostals and non-Pentecostals in incidence of emotional disorder. Although a psychiatrist's study of West Indian Pentecostals in England found "no evidence that emotional instability is a necessary ingredient for participation in the services, behavioral patterns institutionalized in the meetings are sufficiently broad as to provide suitable channels for the expression of a variety of needs and personality traits. For the depressed and guilt-ridden the sin-cathartic basis of the ideology and services provides a useful guilt-reducing device; for the hysteric a socially acceptable model for acting out; and for the obsessional the encouragement of a reduction of inhibitions and increased emotionality. For such accompaniments of neurotic and real suffering as feelings of inferiority, self-consciousness, suspiciousness and anxiety, the social aspects of the movement would seem of value" (Ari Kiev, "Psychotherapeutic Aspects of Pentecostal Sects Among West Indian Immigrants to England," *British Journal of Sociology*, 15 [June 1964]: 135).

78. Bourguignon, "The Self, The Behavioral Environment," 56.

79. Bourguignon, "Ritual Dissociation," 91.

80. T. K. Oesterreich, *Possession: Demonical and Other* (New York, 1930), 158–72, 176–90, 199–203.

81. Ribeiro, "An Experimental Approach," 17.

82. Edward Stainbrook, "Some Characteristics of the Psychopathology of Schizophrenic Behavior in Bahian Society," *American Journal of Psychiatry*, 109 (1952): 334.

83. Bourguignon, "The Self, The Behavioral Environment," 56–57.

84. Arnold M. Ludwig, "Altered States of Consciousness," in Prince, ed., *Trance and Possession States*, 85–86. See also Goodman, "Disturbances in the Apostolic Church," 345–46.

85. Lewis, *Ecstatic Religion*, 32, 134–35, 143–44; 128–29. Lewis also argues (pp. 120–21) that peripheral possession "ventilates aggression and frustration largely within an uneasy acceptance of the established order of things" while witchcraft accusations represent a strategy which "seeks to discredit, sever, and deny links, and ultimately to assert separate identity."

86. Erika Bourguignon, Introduction, to Bourguignon (ed.), *Religion, Altered States*, 26–27.

87. Bourguignon, *Ibid.*, 328–29. Henney says that women in Shaker groups "do not seem to be any more deprived than men, if as much." Henney, "The Shakers," in *ibid.*, 258. I think that this comment applies equally well to Jamaican revivalists and to the Shouters in Trinidad.

88. Walter and Frances Mischel, "Psychological Aspects of Spirit Possession," *American Anthropologist*, 60 (1958): 254

89. Bourguignon, "The Self, The Behavioral Environment," 57.

90. Erika Bourguignon, "Importante papel de las mujeres en los cultos afroamericanos," *Montalban*, 4 (1975): 433–36.

91. Pressel, "Umbanda in São Paulo," 295–296. Pressel remarks that in our cul-

4. REVIVALIST AND OTHER CULTS

ture, social identity is emphasized almost to the exclusion of personal identity or spiritual self. A belief in a spiritual self may make it easier to accept the related concept of spirits than can possess.

92. Ari Kiev, "The Study of Folk Psychiatry," in *Magic, Faith, and Healing,* edited by A. Kiev (New York, 1964), 9.

93. This summary of Paul's personal experiences is based on M. G. Smith, *Dark Puritan* (Kingston, 1963), 9–21, 41–42, 55, 61, 74–80, 84, 100–101, 109.

94. Bourguignon, "The Self, The Behavioral Environment," 57.

95. See Ludwig, "Altered States of Consciousness," 85–86.

96. Lewis, *Ecstatic Religion,* 185–186.

97. Elton C. Fax, *Garvey: The Story of a Pioneer Black Nationalist,* New York (1972), 11–12.

98. On these matters and other points mentioned in the preceding paragraphs, see Cronon, *Black Moses,* 4–7, 11–16, 107; and Vincent, *Black Power,* 92–93, 98, 197, 212.

99. Cronon, *Black Moses,* 70. Detailed accounts of Garvey's philosophy, and of his triumphs and defeats, are readily available. See Amy J. Garvey, *Philosophy and Opinions of Marcus Garvey* (London, 2nd ed., 1967); Amy J. Garvey, *Garvey and Garveyism* (Kingston, 1963); Amy J. Garvey, *Black Power in America;* Cronon, *Black Moses;* Vincent, *Black Power;* Fax, *Garvey.*

100. Fax, *Garvey,* 120–121; 173–174, 202.

101. Vincent, *Black Power,* 115.

102. Fax, *Garvey,* 128.

103. Quoted from the December, 1920, and January, 1921, issues of *The Crisis* in *Ibid.,* 134.

104. Fax, *Garvey,* 134–135.

105. *Ibid.,* 153.

106. Quoted in Cronon, *Black Moses,* 136–137.

107. Fax, *Garvey,* 271.

108. Weston La Barre, "Materials for a History of Studies of Crisis Cults: A Bibliographic Essay," *Current Anthropology,* 12 (1971): 20.

5. South America

1. Philip D. Curtin, *The Atlantic Slave Trade* (Madison, 1969), 88–89.

2. Roger Bastide, *African Civilisations in the New World* (New York, 1971), 19–22.

3. Roger Bastide, *Les Religions Africaines au Brésil* (Paris, 1960), 54–55; 152; 160; 166; 172.

4. *Ibid.,* 166.

5. *Ibid.,* 219; Emilio Willems, *Followers of the New Faith: Culture Change and the Rise of Protestantism in Brazil and Chile* (Nashville, Tennessee, 1967), 25.

6. Bastide, *Les Religions Africaines,* 477–478, 483–484; Willems, *Followers of the New Faith,* 37–38.

4. REVIVALIST AND OTHER CULTS

7. Willems, *Followers of the New Faith,* 35–37.

8. *Ibid.,* 34–35.

9. W. J. Hollenweger, *The Pentecostals* (Minneapolis, 1972), 96.

10. Charles Wagley, *An Introduction to Brazil* (New York, 2nd ed., 1971), 216.

11. *Ibid.,* 229.

12. Hollenweger, *The Pentecostals,* 105–6; T. Lynn Smith, *Brazil: People and Institutions* (Baton Rouge, 4th ed., 1972), 519.

13. Willems, *Followers of the New Faith,* 3–4.

14. Wagley, *An Introduction to Brazil,* 226–28.

15. Willems, *Followers of the New Faith,* 122–26.

16. No Baptist congregations were included in this sample; otherwise, the proportion of lower-class membership presumably would have been higher. The Presbyterian Church in Chile has had little appeal to the middle-class and has been notably unsuccessful. *Ibid.,* 206.

17. *Ibid.,* 216–18; 249.

18. *Ibid.,* 219–20.

19. Hollenweger, *The Pentecostals,* 107. An estimate of the number of Protestants in Brazil in 1970 other than Pentecostals was: Baptists, 235,000; Presbyterians, 167,000; Lutherans, 70,000; Methodists, 57,000; and Episcopalians, 13,000. *Christian Century,* 88 (1971): 7.

20. Willems, *Followers of the New Faith,* 121–22.

21. John Thomas Nichol, *Pentecostalism* (New York, 1966), 164.

22. Willems, *Followers of the New Faith,* 207–8.

23. Quoted from John Van Dyke Saunders, "The Social Organization of a Protestant Congregation in the Federal District, Brazil," unpublished M.A. thesis, Vanderbilt University, Nashville, Tennessee, 1955, 150–51; in *Ibid.,* 208.

24. Willems, *Followers of the New Faith,* 118–19.

25. *Ibid.,* 120–21. Immediate Salvation means that Jesus saves here and now from sickness and the social evils of this world.

26. *Ibid.,* 130–33.

27. *Ibid.,* 133–34.

28. *Ibid.,* 134–35.

29. Bastide, *Les Religiones Africaines,* 515.

30. Willems, *Followers of the New Faith,* 136. See summary of Calley's conclusions on glossolalia among West Indian Pentecostals in England in chapter 8 of this book.

31. *Ibid.,* 137.

32. *Ibid.,* 138.

33. *Ibid.,* 140; Bastide, *Les Religiones Africaines,* 514–515.

34. Willems, *Followers of the New Faith,* 145, 149, 168. Goodman states that the principal attractions of Pentecostalism are the enhanced status it offers to the disadvantaged, and strong group cohesion, but she feels that "the availability of trance behavior needs to be accorded more attention than it has hitherto received." Felicitas D. Good-

5. SOUTH AMERICA

man, "Disturbances in the Apostolic Church: A Trance-Based Upheaval in Yucátan," in F. D. Goodman, J. H. Henney, and E. Pressel, *Trance, Healing, and Hallucination* (New York, 1974), 351.

35. Raymond T. Smith, "Religion in the Formation of West Indian Society," in *The African Diaspora: Interpretative Essays,* edited by Martin Kilson and Robert I. Rotberg (Cambridge, 1976), 319.

36. *Ibid.,* 327–32.

37. Emilio Willems, "Religious Mass Movements and Social Change in Brazil," in Eric Baklanoff, ed., *New Perspectives in Brazil* (Nashville, Tennessee, 1966), 210.

38. *Ibid.,* 206. Official figures show 488,017 Spiritualists in 1953; 680,511 in 1960 (*ibid.,* 206–207); and 758,209 in 1967 (T. Lynn Smith, *Brazil,* Baton Rouge, 4th ed., 1972, 723).

39. Willems, "Religious Mass Movements," 207. In São Paulo, Esther Pressel ("Umbanda Trance and Possession in São Paulo, Brazil," in Goodman, Henney, and Pressel, *Trance, Healing, and Hallucination,* 116) found "the more African forms of Umbanda, heavily influenced by Candomblé and Macumba" at one end of Camargo's "continuum of spiritualism" and "the European spiritualism of Allen Kardec" at the other pole. In the middle band were "just about every type of mixture of African and European spiritualism as well as admixtures with Catholic and indigenous Indian elements."

40. Quoted in T. L. Smith, *Brazil,* 723.

41. Esther Pressel, "Umbanda in São Paulo: Religious Innovation in a Developing Society," in *Religion, Altered States of Consciousness, and Social Change,* edited by Erika Bourguignon (Columbus, Ohio, 1973), 276.

42. *Ibid.,* 270; Willems, "Religious Mass Movements," 220; C. P. F. de Camargo, *Kardicismo e Umbanda* (São Paulo, 1961), 35. Quoted in Willems, *ibid.,* 220; Pressel, "Umbanda in São Paulo," 295.

43. Bastide, *Les Religions Africaines,* 436–42; 472.

44. *Ibid.,* 470. See the section on "The Urban Macumba in Brazil" in chapter 6 of this book.

45. Bastide, *African Civilisations,* 86–87. In São Paulo, Camargo failed to discover any indication of a cultural continuity between the macumba and Umbanda. Cited in Willems, "Religious Mass Movements," 209–10. Willems believes that Umbanda must be considered the result of secondary diffusion in São Paulo, and, perhaps, in other parts of Brazil.

46. Pressel, "Umbanda in São Paulo," 281–83; 284–85. On the Exus of the Batuque cult in Belém, see Seth and Ruth Leacock, *Spirits of the Deep* (New York, 1972), 150–55, and the section on the Batuque in chapter 6 of the present work. On other beliefs about Eshu and the *exus* see the section on Trinidadian shango in chapter 3 and the section on Bahian candomblés in chapter 6.

47. Pressel, "Umbanda in São Paulo," 286. This classification is taken from Camargo (1961, 38). Pressel comments: "One should note that in this particular arrangement, two of the major divisions—Linha do Oriente and Linha Africana—are not com-

5. SOUTH AMERICA

manded by *orixás*. Many umbandists would argue against including the former. The latter, however, is very popular and most of the *preto velho* spirits are included in this subdivision. The *caboclo* spirits are found in various parts of the spiritual organization, but they are most frequently thought of as belonging to the hunter, Oxóce. Some umbandists believe that one of the seven major divisions is headed by saints Cosmas and Damian, and they think the *criança* spirits to this *linha.*" *Ibid.,* 286.

48. Pressel, "Umbanda in São Paulo," 287. Theory of fluids has been borrowed mainly from Kardecism. *Ibid.,* 281.

49. *Ibid.,* 287–91. This classification was made by Camargo (1961, 100–102).

50. Bastide pointed out in 1970 that, in spite of the existence of federations tending to unify the sect, two opposing tendencies create an ambiguity in the umbandist world. Innovations contribute to the progressive deafricanization of the cult, but, on the other hand, reafricanization is occurring due to the urging of some leaders that umbandists be initiated in the candomblés so that they can bring knowledge more authentically African to their devotees. Roger Bastide, "The Black Americans," a paper presented to a conference on Continuities and Discontinuities in Afro-American Societies and Cultures, sponsored by the Committee on Afro-American Societies and Cultures, Social Science Research Council, New York City, at the University of the West Indies, Mona, Jamaica, April 12, 1970, p. 14.

51. Edison Carneiro, *Candomblés Da Bahia* (3rd ed., Rio de Janeiro, 1961), 165–66. For a description of typical Umbanda ritual activities in São Paulo, see Pressel, "Umbanda Trance," 142–46.

52. Erika Bourguignon, *A Cross-Cultural Study of Dissociational States* (Columbus, Ohio, 1968), 27.

53. Bastide, *African Civilisations,* 87.

54. Angelina Pollak-Eltz, "Panorama de estudios afroamericanos," *Montalban* (Caracas, no. 1, 1972), 272.

55. Angelina Pollak-Eltz, *Cultos Afroamericanos* (Caracas, 1972), 207.

56. Angelina Pollak-Eltz, *María Lionza, Mito Y Culto Venezolano* (Caracas, Instituto de Investigaciones Historicas, Universidad Catolica "Andres Bello" [1972], 37.) For the most part, this account of the cult of María Lionza is based on Pollak-Eltz, *Cultos Afroamericanos,* 196–207.

57. Pollak-Eltz, *María Lionza,* 26–27.

58. Pollak-Eltz reports the presence in Caracas of an authentic Cuban diviner who consults the orishas through invocations and animal sacrifices. Venezuelan clients, as well as Cubans of all levels of society, visit his establishment. Thus far this *babalawo* has not sponsored any dances in honor of African deities. There is also in Caracas a spiritualist who has received African spirits for ten years. Formerly a medium in the cult of María Lionza, this lower-middle-class white woman became interested in santeria after trips to Cuba, Trinidad, Puerto Rico, and Santo Domingo. Widely read in the realm of Afroamerican religions, she has adapted parts of many rituals in devising her own ceremonies. Her altar is decorated with lithographs of the Catholic saints whom she can identify

5. SOUTH AMERICA

with African deities in Cuban santeria. Sacred objects of the orishas are kept in a special room where she holds consultations. For a description of a ritual in honor of Chango on St. Barbara's day in the home of this priestess, see Pollak-Eltz, *Cultos Afroamericanos,* 208–9.

59. Pollak-Eltz, *María Lionza,* 49. This attitude toward Catholicism is similar to that held by Batuque cultists in Belém (see section on Batuque earlier in this chapter).

6. Neo-African and African-Derived Religions of South America

1. This discussion of the socio-economic context of religious cults in South America is based on Roger Bastide, *Les Religions au Brésil* (Paris, 1960), 215–37.

2. Everett V. Stonequist, *The Marginal Man: A Study in Personality and Culture Conflict* (New York, 1937).

3. Roger Bastide, *African Civilisations in the New World* (New York, 1972), 93.

4. *Ibid.,* 96.

5. *Ibid.,* 97–99.

6. *Ibid.,* 99.

7. Octavio Da Costa Eduardo, *The Negro in Northern Brazil* (New York, 1948), 5, 7, states that the term *encantado* is used in the Angolan-derived cult houses in Bahia and Rio de Janeiro where Indian, Angolan, and Yoruban deities and the spirits of deified ancestors are worshipped. This term is used also in African-derived cults of Belém. These cults, brought to that city from São Luiz, are discussed later in this chapter.

8. *Ibid.,* 57–58. Eduardo points out that in Haiti, spiritual beings similar to the *encantados,* the *loa,* are called *Zanges,* a contraction of "les anges" (angels). On the Zanges, see Simpson, 1945, 38.

9. Eduardo, *The Negro,* 58, 62.

10. *Ibid.,* 51–53.

11. *Ibid.,* 53.

12. *Ibid.,* 53–54.

13. *Ibid.,* 47.

14. *Ibid.,* 48.

15. *Ibid.,* 76.

16. *Ibid.,* 80. Eduardo cites Herskovits (*Dahomey,* 2: 223) on the role of Legba, the trickster, as the messenger of all deities and their spokesman. See Bastide (*Les Religions,* 520) on *tokhoueni* possessions in Brazil, and Simpson (1962, 1211–12) on *rété* possessions in Trinidadian *shango.*

17. In the vodun cult in northern Haiti, the *loas* (*Zanges;* gods) are said to live "under the water" in their capital (Ville au Camp). (G. E. Simpson, "The Belief System," 39).

18. Eduardo, *The Negro in Northern Brazil,* 81.

19. *Ibid.,* 81.

20. *Ibid.*, 82. In Trinidadian *shango*, Eshu must be dismissed before the other powers can be summoned to a ceremony (Simpson, *The Shango Cult in Trinidad* (Rio Piedras, Puerto Rico, 1965), 42–43).

21. Eduardo, *The Negro in Northern Brazil*, 82–83.

22. *Ibid.*, 84.

23. *Ibid.*, 85.

24. *Ibid.*, 85–86.

25. *Ibid.*, 90. It is of some interest that the sacrificing of animals occurs at daybreak in São Luiz, Brazil and in Trinidadian *shango* (Simpson, *The Shango Cult*, 46). In Bahia, Brazil, Carneiro reported that the candomblé feast started with the sacrifice of animals and was followed by singing and dancing (Carneiro, *Candomblés*, 2nd ed., 55). In *vodun* ceremonies in northern Haiti, animals are sacrificed more or less continuously from nine or ten o'clock in the evening until dawn (Simpson, "The Vodun Service," 242–52).

26. Eduardo, *The Negro in Northern Brazil*, 95.

27. Ibid., 110. For comments on the reinterpretation of the West African multiple soul concept, see the sections on Haiti and Trinidad in chapter 3, and the section on Jamaica in chapter 4.

28. *Ibid.*, 114–16.

29. *Ibid.*, 116.

30. It is interesting to compare the situation in São Luiz with that in Grenada. M. G. Smith (*Dark Puritan*, 34) asserts that the displacement of the Big Drum Dance in Grenada shows the importance of group cohesion in the perpetuation of a culture complex. Although Shango was a late arrival in Grenada, it very largely succeeded the Big Drum Dance because it had a priesthood and a formal organization.

31. Eduardo, *The Negro in Northern Brazil*, 104–105. Eduardo quotes Ramos, *O Negro* (99–100, 111) as saying that survivals of the religions of Congo-Angola peoples in Brazil have been almost totally absorbed by those of Dahomean-Yoruban origin. Later in this chapter I cite evidence from Bastide's work (*African Civilisations*, 105 ff) concerning Bantu influence on New World religions.

32. *Ibid.*, 105–6, 49.

33. Edison Carneiro, *Candomblés da Bahia* (2nd ed., Rio de Janeiro, 1948), 32, 48. Bastide's comprehensive study of African religions in Brazil includes accounts of African religious survivals preceding the candomblé (Bastide, *Les Religions*, part I, ch. 6.)

34. Carneiro, *Candomblés da Bahia*, 2nd ed., 15. Wagley (*An Introduction*, 222–23) points out that at one time African cults were limited largely to the Northeast Coast of Brazil, the area of the largest Negro population. Today they exist up and down the east coast of the country. According to Wagley, the cults were "once very discreet in Rio de Janeiro," but "they may be found today in any district of the city and in the suburbs. Nowadays some of the most famous leaders of the African cults of Bahia reside in Rio, where their income is higher and where they can enjoy the attractions of the great city. Their major temples are still in Salvador, but they have 'branches' in Rio de Janeiro.

6. NEO-AFRICAN RELIGIONS

Nowadays one can see candles and offerings of a syncretic nature almost any night in fashionable Copacabana Beach in honor of Yemanjá, a goddess of water."

35. Carneiro, *Candomblés da Bahia,* 2nd ed., 65–66.

36. *Ibid.,* 66–67.

37. *Ibid.,* 68–70; Edison Carneiro, *Candomblés da Bahia* (3rd ed., Rio de Janeiro, 1961), 77–79.

38. Carneiro, *Candomblés,* 2nd ed., 71–72.

39. *Ibid.,* 23, 73–76.

40. *Ibid.,* 77–78, 88.

41. *Ibid.,* 78–80.

42. Roger Bastide, *African Civilisations in the New World* (New York, 1972), 105–106.

43. Carneiro, *Candomblés da Bahia,* 2nd ed., 80–81.

44. Bastide, *African Civilisations,* 109.

45. Carneiro, *Candomblés da Bahia,* 2nd ed., 43, 81–82.

46. *Ibid.,* 82–85.

47. Bastide, *African Civilisations,* 105.

48. Carneiro, *Candomblés da Bahia,* 2nd ed., 44–46.

49. *Ibid.,* 55, 75–76.

50. *Ibid.,* 56–57.

51. *Ibid.,* 100.

52. René Ribeiro, *Cultos Afrobrasileiros do Recife* (Recife, 1952), 139.

53. *Ibid.,* 58.

54. *Ibid.,* 54–58.

55. *Ibid.,* 43–44. These accounts of the orisha are based mainly on *ibid.,* 44–58. Ribeiro also includes data on the colors, favorite foods and drinks, symbols, and the behavior of devotees who are possessed by these deities. For descriptions of Shango ceremonies in Recife, which are similar to Nago candomblé rituals in Bahia, see *ibid.,* 63–97.

56. René Ribeiro, "Novos Aspectos do Processo de Reinterpretação nos Cultos Afro-Brasileiros do Recife," *Anais Do XXXI Congr. Internacional De Americanistas* (1955), 476.

57. For an interesting analysis of beliefs about Shango in the New World, see William Bascom, *Shango in the New World* (Austin, Texas, 1972).

58. See the comments on Eshu in the Bahian candomblés in the preceding section of this chapter.

59. Ribeiro, "Novos Aspectos," 481–82.

60. Bastide, *Les Religions Africaines,* 288; Melville J. Herskovits, "The Southernmost Outposts of New World Africanisms," *American Anthropologist* 45 (1943): 495.

61. Herskovits, "The Southernmost Outposts," 502–4.

62. Bastide, *Les Religions Africaines,* 288, 290.

63. Herskovits, "The Southernmost Outposts," 500–501.

6. NEO-AFRICAN RELIGIONS

64. *Ibid.*, 500, 505. On *réré* possession in Trinidad, see the section on "Spirit Possession" in chapter 4. See also the section on Bahia in chapter 6 for an account of the Ibeji (twin deities), collectively called *érés* or *meninos,* and the section on San Luiz, Brazil, on *tabosa* possession.

65. Bastide, *Les Religions Africaines,* 295.

66. *Ibid.*, 293–97.

67. *Ibid.*, 298. See also, Roger Bastide, "Le Batuque de Porto Alegre," in Sol Tax, ed., *Acculturation in the Americas* (Chicago, 1952), 195–206.

68. Seth and Ruth Leacock, *Spirits of the Deep: Drums, Mediums, and Trance in a Brazilian City* (Garden City, 1972), 48, 318–19. This account of the Batuque cult in Belém is based on the Leacocks' excellent study.

69. *Ibid.*, 329.

70. *Ibid.*, 150. The resemblance between these ritual acts and those performed in honor of Esu in Trinidadian *shango* is noteworthy (G. E. Simpson, *The Shango Cult in Trinidad,* Rio Piedras, Puerto Rico, 1965, 42–43). See Eduardo, *The Negro in Northern Brazail,* 82, on the Yoruban group in São Luiz that sends away Lebara or Eshu before a *vodun* dance is started. See also Carneiro's observations earlier in this chapter on Eshu in the *candomblés* of Bahia.

71. Leacock and Leacock, *Spirits of the Deep,* 167.

72. *Ibid.*, 82, 85. There are no official statistics on the membership of Afro-Brazilian cults. All cult members are recorded by the Census as Catholics. *Ibid.*, 94.

73. *Ibid.*, 85, 87.

74. *Ibid.*, 52.

75. *Ibid.*, 55.

76. *Ibid.*, 126.

77. *Ibid.*, 58–59.

78. *Ibid.*, 130, 156–58, 161.

79. *Ibid.*, 130.

80. *Ibid.*, 129–46.

81. *Ibid.*, 156.

82. *Ibid.*, 317.

83. *Ibid.*, 167–69.

84. *Ibid.*, 168.

85. *Ibid.*, 90–92.

86. *Ibid.*, 284–85, 290.

87. *Ibid.*, 292–93.

88. *Ibid.*, 170–71, 181, 187–88, 212–14.

89. *Ibid.*, 314.

90. *Ibid.*, 111.

91. *Ibid.*, 111–13, 121. Bastide's view is given in his *Les Religions Africaines au Brésil,* 525.

92. Leacock and Leacock, *Spirits of the Deep,* 113–14, 123.

6. NEO-AFRICAN RELIGIONS

93. For a discussión of the behavior of *rérés* (lesser spirits) in Trinidadian *shango*, see G. E. Simpson, *The Shango Cult in Trinidad*, 30–31.

94. Leacock and Leacock, *Spirits of the Deep*, 323–24.

95. Bastide, *Les Religions Africaines*, 410–12. In a later work, Bastide cites with approval Arthur Ramos' definition of the *macoumba* of Rio de Janeiro as "a syncretistic mixture of Gêge (Fon), Nago (Yoruba), Muslim (Black Islam), Bantu, Caboclo (Indian), spiritualist and Catholic elements." Roger Bastide, *African Civilisations in the New World* (New York, 1972), 168. Despite this extensive syncretization, the Bantu influence appears to be the strongest in these cults, as evidenced in the names of the deities worshipped, the terms for the priests in the cult's hierarchy, and the survival of the ancestor cult through the spirits of the dead who possess the mediums. These dead, however, are no longer family ancestors, but those of the entire enslaved Negro people, for example, Old John, Old Joaquim, Aunt Marie, and others (Bastide, *African Civilisations*, 108).

96. Bastide, *African Civilisations*, 169.

97. *Ibid.*, 86.

98. Bastide, *Les Religions Africanes*, 414–18.

99. Melville J. and Frances S. Herskovits, *Suriname Folk-Lore* (New York, 1936), 44–70; M. J. and F. S. Herskovits, *Trinidad Village* (New York, 1947), 291–92; M. J. Herskovits, *The Myth of the Negro Past* (New York, 1941), 218–19, 256–58.

100. Charles J. Wooding, "The Winti-Cult in the Para-District," *Caribbean Studies*, 12 (1972): 51–55. A member of the Department of Political Science, Institute of Advanced Social Education, Leiden, The Netherlands, Wooding did field work in Surinam in 1962.

101. *Ibid.*, 59–60. Other instances of the reinterpretation of the West African multiple soul complex are given in chapter 3 (Haiti and Trinidad), chapter 4 (Jamaica), and chapter 6 (São Luiz, Maranhão, Brazil).

102. *Ibid.*, 63–70.

103. *Ibid.*, 72–73.

104. Silva W. De Groot, *Djuka Society and Social Change* (Assen, The Netherlands, 1969), 1, 5–6, 23–27. The data in this book were obtained in Surinam in the period 1917 to 1926.

105. *Ibid.*, 27–28.

106. *Ibid.*, 21–22.

107. Jean Hurault, *Les Noirs Réfugiés Boni de las Guyane Française* (Dakar, 1961), 9–11.

108. *Ibid.*, 191.

109. *Ibid.*, 194.

110. *Ibid.*, 194–95.

111. *Ibid.*, 196. On beliefs concerning magical forces among the Boni, including *wisi* (sorcery) and *wisimã* (sorcerers), and *obia* (positive magic) and *obiamã* (one who performs good magic), see *ibid.*, 238–53. Like the Boni in French Guiana, the Winti cultists of the Para region of Surinam, as well as the Djukas of Surinam, believe that the

6. NEO-AFRICAN RELIGIONS

obia-man is one who can offset the evil deeds of the *wisi-man* (conjurer). In Jamaican folk belief, *obeah* refers to harmful magic (Simpson, *Jamaican Revivalist Cults,* 389–94.

112. Hurault, *Les Noirs Réfugiés,* 214. On avenging spirits among the Saramaka, another "Bush Negro" tribe, see Richard Price, "Avenging Spirits and the Structure of Saramaka Lineages," *Bijdragen tot de Taal—, Land, en Volkenkunde,* 129 (1973): 86–107.

113. Hurault, *Les Noirs Réfugiés,* 203–4.

114. *Ibid.,* 206.

115. *Ibid.,* 209.

116. *Ibid.,* 210–11.

117. For a discussion of the ancestor cult among the Boni, including beliefs about and possession by the *yorka,* see *ibid.,* 216–21.

118. *Ibid.,* 199.

119. *Ibid.,* 201–2.

120. *Ibid.,* 198.

7. North America

1. W. E. B. Du Bois, *The Negro Church* (Atlanta, 1903), 10.

2. *Ibid,* 14; E. Franklin Frazier, *The Negro Church in America* (New York, 1963), 6–7.

3. Carter G. Woodson, *The History of the Negro Church* (Washington, 1921), 133.

4. Du Bois, *The Negro Church,* 11.

5. *Ibid.,* 11–12.

6. *Ibid.*

7. *Ibid.,* 16, 20.

8. W. E. B. Du Bois, "Religion in the South," in Booker T. Washington and W. E. B. Du Bois, *The Negro in the South* (Philadelphia, 1907), 141–43; Gayraud S. Wilmore, *Black Religion and Black Radicalism* (New York, 1972), 108–109.

9. Frazier, *The Negro Church,* 22–23.

10. Joseph R. Washington, Jr., *Black Sects and Cults* (New York, 1972), 38.

11. Frazier, *The Negro Church,* 23.

12. Harry V. Richardson, "The Negro in American Religious Life," in *The American Negro Reference Book* (New York, 1966) 397–400; Washington, *Black Sects,* 37–38.

13. Arthur H. Fauset, *Black Gods of the Metropolis* (Philadelphia, 1944), 4.

14. Du Bois, *The Negro Church,* 26.

15. Eugene D. Genovese, *Roll, Jordan, Roll: The World the Slaves Made* (New York, 1972), 211.

16. *Ibid.,* 233–34, 238–40.

17. M. J. Herskovits, *The Myths of the Negro Past* (New York, 1941), 242, 253–54; Genovese, *Roll, Jordan, Roll,* 219.

18. George P. Rawick, *From Sundown to Sunup: The Making of the Black Community* (Westport, Conn., 1972), 47.

19. Genovese, *Roll, Jordan, Roll,* 217.

20. Newbell Niles Puckett, *Folk Beliefs of the Southern Negro*. Chapel Hill, The University of North Carolina Press, 1926, 110.

21. Rawick, *From Sunup to Sundown*, 34–37, 39–43.

22. Zora Neal Hurston, *Mules and Men*, (Philadelphia, 1935), 242, 248, 253, 299–300.

23. Puckett, *Folk Beliefs, passim;* Herskovits, *The Myth*, 235–45; Genovese, *Roll, Jordan, Roll*, 217–32; Robert Tallant, *Voodoo in New Orleans* (New York, 1946, 1962), *passim;* Harry M. Hyatt, *Hoodoo-Conjuration-Witchcraft-Rootwork* (Hannibal, Mo., 1970, 1973) 3 vols.

24. Genovese, *Roll, Jordan, Roll*, 220.

25. *Ibid.*, 232.

26. Du Bois, *The Negro Church*, 22.

27. Du Bois, "Religion in the South," 166–67.

28. Kenneth M. Stampp, *The Peculiar Institution* (New York, 1956), 156–62. Quoted in Hart M. Nelsen, Raytha L. Yokley, and Anne K. Nelsen, eds., *The Black Church in America* (New York, 1971), 55.

29. Charles C. Jones, *The Religious Instruction of the Negroes in the United States* (Savannah, 1842). Chs. 3–4.

30. Genovese, *Roll, Jordan, Roll*, 188.

31. Nelsen, Yokley, and Nelsen, *The Black Church*, 56–57.

32. Frazier, *The Negro Church*, 11; Wilmore, *Black Religion*, 52. Genovese (*Roll, Jordan, Roll*, 252) comments that the slaves merged Moses and Jesus into "the image of a single deliverer, at once this-worldly and other-worldly."

33. Benjamin E. Mays and J. W. Nicholson, *The Negro's Church* (New York, 1933); Frazier, *The Negro Church*, 8; Vincent Harding, "Religion and Resistance Among Ante-Bellum Negroes, 1800–1860," in *The Making of Black America*, edited by August Meier and Elliott Rudwick (New York, 1969), Vol. I, 181.

34. Wilmore, *Black Religion*, 69–70. For an interesting discussion of the tactics of black preachers during the period of slavery, see Genovese, *Roll, Jordan, Roll*, 255–79.

35. Wilmore, *Black Religion*, 72–73.

36. *Ibid.*, 63.

37. *Ibid.*, 74–77.

38. *Ibid.*, 83; Du Bois, "Religion in the South," 156–57.

39. Du Bois, "Religion in the South," 158–60; Vincent Harding, "Religion and Resistance Among Anti-bellum Negroes, 1800–1860," 187. For Harding's source, see *ibid.*

40. Harding, "Religion and Resistance," 187–88.

41. *Ibid.*, 188.

42. Herbert Aptheker, *Negro Slave Revolts in the United States, 1526–1860* (New York, 1939), 48–51. For accounts of other slave revolts in the United States, see *ibid.*, 16–60; Harvey Wish, "American Slave Insurrections Before 1861," *Journal of Negro History*, 22 (1937): 299–320; Marion D. de B. Kilson, "Towards Freedom: An Analysis of

Slave Revolts in the United States," in Meier and Rudwick, eds., *The Making of Black America*, 1: 165–78.

43. Genovese, *Roll, Jordan, Roll*, 594–96.

44. Du Bois, *The Negro Church*, 18.

45. *Ibid.*, 19–22, 111.

46. *Ibid.*, 21–22.

47. *Ibid.*, 17–21; 29.

48. Woodson, *The History of the Negro Church*, 196–98.

49. Wilmore, *Black Religion*, 125; Woodson, *The History of the Negro Church*, 94.

50. Du Bois, *The Negro Church*, 16, 22.

51. Du Bois, "Religion in the South," 134–35.

52. Du Bois, *The Negro Church*, 26–27.

53. Genovese, *Roll, Jordan, Roll*, 187.

54. Woodson, *The History of the Negro Church*, 97–98.

55. *Ibid.*, 99.

56. Wilmore, *Black Religion*, 126.

57. Joe R. Feagin, "Black Catholics in the United States: An Exploratory Analysis," in Nelsen, Yokley, Nelson, eds., *The Black Church*, 247.

58. In 1963 Frazier wrote: "Very often after joining the Catholic church with the expectation that they will escape from their status as Negroes they find that they are still defined as Negroes by whites. Some middle-class Negroes in their seeking to find escape from the Negro identification have gone from the Catholic church to the Christian Science church and then to the Bahaist church. Moreover, there is a tendency among middle-class Negroes to be attracted to Moral Re-Armament, hoping that they would find a group in which they could lose completely their identification as Negroes and escape from their feelings of inferiority and insecurity. A small intellectual fringe among middle-class Negroes have affiliated with the Untarian church. But most of them may still attend more or less surreptitiously the Methodist and Baptist on Friday nights" (Frazier, *The Negro Church*, 80).

59. Feagin, "Black Catholics," 252–253.

60. Wilmore, *Black Religion*, 109–110.

61. Du Bois, *The Negro Church*, 30; Wilmore, *Black Religion*, 125.

62. August Meier and Elliott M. Rudwick, *From Plantation to Ghetto* (New York, 1966), 76; Frazier, *The Negro Church*, 26–27; Du Bois, *The Negro Church*, 30; Wilmore, *Black Religion*, 125.

63. Washington, *Black Sects*, 43.

64. Fauset, *Black Gods*, 6.

65. Robert Anderson, *From Slavery to Affluence: Memories of Robert Anderson, Ex-Slave* (Hemingford, Nebraska, 1927), 22–23. Quoted in Frazier, *The Negro Church*, 16.

66. Du Bois, ed., *The Negro Church*, 41–42.

67. *Ibid.*, 45.

68. Wilmore, *Black Religion*, 133.

7. NORTH AMERICA

69. Richardson, "The Negro in American Religious Life," 402.

70. Du Bois, ed., *The Negro Church,* 47. According to Du Bois, with the exception of a few ministers of the A.M.E. and the A.M.E.Z. churches in the border states, it is likely that there were less than a score of black pastors in full control of Negro churches in the South before the war. *Ibid.,* 33.

71. Meier and Rudwick, *From Plantation to Ghetto,* 78.

72. Du Bois, *The Negro Church,* 111.

73. Mays and Nicholson, *The Negro's Church,* 37.

74. *Ibid.,* 36–37.

75. Wilmore, *Black Religion,* 126–27; Meier and Rudwick, *From Plantation to Ghetto,* 79.

76. Wilmore, *Black Religion,* 145–150.

77. Woodson, *The History of the Negro Church,* 287–91.

78. *Ibid.,* 249–56.

79. John Dollard, *Caste and Class in a Southern Town* (New Haven, 1937), 240.

80. *Ibid.,* 241.

81. *Ibid.,* 239; Gunnar Myrdal, *An American Dilemma* (New York, 1944), 866.

82. St. Clair Drake and Horace R. Cayton, *Black Metropolis* (New York, 1945), 412–13.

83. Wilmore, *Black Religion,* 221–24.

84. Charles V. Hamilton, *The Black Preacher in America* (New York, 1972, 71–73. In this book, Hamilton's special concern is with the "middle minister," not with the mass-movement type of leader nor the leader of small cults.

85. Myrdal, *An American Dilemma,* 866.

86. Washington, *Black Sects,* 55, 69.

87. Frazier (*The Negro Church in America,* 79) pointed out that middle-class Negroes who retain their membership in Baptist and Methodist churches select churches whose ministers are well-educated and which are made up largely of middle-class members.

88. Kenneth B. Clark, *Dark Ghetto* (New York, 1965), 178.

89. About 90 percent of Negro Protestants are in separate denominational organizations. Perhaps 10 to 15 percent of northern and western Protestant churches are interracial to some degree. Probably no more than one or two percent of blacks are in interracial churches. See G. E. Simpson and J. M. Yinger, *Racial and Cultural Minorities* (New York, 1972), 532–533.

90. Woodson, *The History of the Negro Church,* 272–73; Myrdal, *An American Dilemma,* 938–39.

91. Clifton F. Brown, "Black Religion—1968," in *In Black America,* Patricia Romero, ed. (Washington, 1969), 348.

92. Frazier, *The Negro Church,* 44, 85–86; Myrdal, *An American Dilemma,* 877.

93. Drake and Cayton, *Black Metropolis,* 423–24.

94. Wilmore, *Black Religion,* 106.

7. NORTH AMERICA

95. Woodson, *The History of the Negro Church,* 303–4.

96. Mays and Nicholson, *The Negro's Church,* 291; Wilmore, *Black Religion,* 194; Myrdal, *An American Dilemma,* 861.

97. Myrdal, 862; Woodson, *The History,* 304.

98. Wilmore, *Black Religion,* 143–85; Gary T. Marx, *Protest and Prejudice* (New York, 1967), 94–96.

99. Clark, *Dark Ghetto,* 164; Hamilton, *The Black Preacher,* 112.

100. Wilmore, *Black Religion,* 238.

101. *Ibid.,* 71; Hamilton, *The Black Preacher,* 134; Clark, *Dark Ghetto,* 182–85.

102. Clark, *Dark Ghetto,* 177.

103. Myrdal, *An American Dilemma,* 873–74; Clark, *Dark Ghetto,* 144.

104. Charles V. Hamilton, "An Advocate of Black Power Defines It," *The New York Times Magazine,* Apr. 14, 1968, p. 79. An analysis of the "conservative-moderate-militant continuum" for the Black Power movement as of the years 1965–1969 is given in Luther P. Gerlach and Virginia H. Hine, *People, Power, Change* (Indianapolis, 1970), 17–32.

105. Hamilton, "An Advocate," 79.

106. Washington, *Black Sects,* 15–16, 111.

107. Brown, "Black Religion—1968," 347–48.

108. *Ibid.,* 349.

109. *Ibid.,* 352.

110. Albert B. Cleage, Jr., *The Black Messiah* (New York, 1968), 3.

111. *Ibid.,* 20, 38.

112. Quoted in Washington, *Black Sects,* 129.

113. *Ibid.,* 130.

114. James H. Cone, *Black Theology and Black Power* (New York, 1969), 16–17.

115. *Ibid.,* 33, 38, 48–49.

116. *Ibid.,* 39–40.

117. James H. Cone, *A Black Theology of Liberation* (Philadelphia, 1970), 27–28. In Chapter 4, I cite Mrs. Amy Garvey's assertion that her husband had taught all peoples of African descent "to visualize Christ . . . the Redeemer of all Mankind, as a man of color," and her question concerning "who can best portray 'the man of sorrow, and acquainted with grief,' but the down-trodden Negro in modern times." Amy J. Garvey, *Black Power in America* (Kingston, Jamaica, 1968), 38.

118. Cone, *Black Theology and Black Power,* 40–41. Cone says that theologically Malcolm X was not far wrong in calling the white man "the devil."

119. Joseph R. Washington, Jr., *Black and White Power Subreption* (New York, 1969), 121; 141–42. Washington quotes, apparently with approval, Harding's statement on the anger of black youth: "Give us no pink, two-faced Jesus who counsels love for you and flaming death for the children of Vietnam. Give us not a blood-sucking savior who condemns brick-throwing rioters and praises dive-bombing killers. That Christ stinks. We want no black men to follow in his steps. Stop forcing our poor black boys

into your legions of shame. We will not go. If we must fight, . . . let it be on the streets where we have been humiliated. If we must burn down houses let them be the homes and stores of our exploiters. If we must kill, let it be the fat, pious white Christians who guard their lawns and their daughters, while engineering slow death for us. If we must die, let it be for a real cause of black man's freedom as black men define it. And may all the white elders die as well as the causes they defend.' This is Black Power—the response to the American Christ." Vincent Harding, "Black Power and the American Christ," *Christian Century,* January 4, 1967, p. 10. Quoted in Washington, *Black and White Power Subreption,* 141–42.

120. *Ibid.,* 206. This statement by Washington, as well as the preceding one by Harding, must be seen in the context of the rhetoric of the "black rebellion" of the late 1960s.

121. Washington, *Black Sects,* 17. Washington claims that millenarianism or the intervention of supernatural forces is "a very minor and inconsistent theme in black cults. A singular feature is the concern for participation in those benefits of society which symbolize power (e.g., land, money, buildings, etc.) rather than upon eschatology. A cataclysmic transformation of this world is generally viewed as the coming of blacks into power as opposed to the second coming of Christ." *Ibid.,* 12.

122. *Ibid.,* 142.

123. *Ibid.,* 149.

124. Wilmore, *Black Religion,* 184.

125. Simpson and Yinger, *Racial and Cultural Minorities,* 524.

126. Frances Henry, *Forgotten Canadians: The Blacks of Nova Scotia* (Toronto, 1973), ix–xi.

127. Walker, James W. St. G., "The Establishment of a Free Black Community in Nova Scotia, 1783–1840," in Martin L. Kilson and Robert I. Rotberg, eds., *The African Diaspora: Interpretive Essays* (Cambridge, 1976), 214–15.

128. Robin W. Winks, *The Blacks in Canada* (New Haven, 1971), 338–339.

129. Walker, "The Establishment," 215–17.

130. Winks, *The Blacks,* 338.

131. Walker, "The Establishment," 221–26.

132. *Ibid.,* 229, 231, 236.

133. Winks, *The Blacks,* 340.

134. *Ibid.,* 341–42, 345–46.

135. *Ibid.,* 346–47, 351–52.

136. *Ibid.,* 352–53.

137. *Ibid.,* 354–55, 358–59.

138. Henry, *Forgotten Canadians,* xiii, 29.

139. *Ibid.,* 122–23.

140. *Ibid.*

141. Winks, *The Blacks,* 361. Matthew 18: 4—"Whosoever therefore shall humble himself as this little child, the same is greatest in the kingdom of heaven."

142. Walker, "The Establishment," 236.

7. NORTH AMERICA

8. Sect and Cult

1. An earlier version of this discussion of Pentecostalism in the United States appeared in *Phylon,* 35 (1974): 203–11. Used by permission of the publisher, Atlanta University.

2. Malcolm J. C. Calley, *God's People: West Indian Pentecostal Sects in England* (London, 1965), 10.

3. Nils Bloch-Hoell, *The Pentecostal Movement* (Oslo: Universitetsforlaget, 1964), 16. Frodsham reports manifestations of the Holy Spirit and speaking in tongues in Florida in 1854, in New England in 1873, in Providence, Rhode Island in 1875, in Arkansas in 1879, in Delaware, Ohio in 1890, in Moorhead, Minnesota in 1892, in Greenfield, South Dakota in 1896, and in Cherokee County, North Carolina in 1896 (Stanley Howard Frodsham, *With Signs Following: The Story of the Pentecostal Revival in the Twentieth Century,* Springfield, Mo., 1941, 9–12, 14–16). On January 1, 1901, the Pentecostal blessing supposedly fell in Bethel Bible College, directed by Charles Fox Parham in Topeka, Kansas, and, as in Apostolic times, students spoke in other tongues (John Thomas Nichol, *Pentecostalism,* New York, 1966, 18).

4. Liston Pope, *Millhands and Preachers: A Study of Gastonia* (New Haven, 1942), 129. There were only 12,392 Negroes in Gaston County in 1930, and they were employed in the factories. Because Pope's study dealt with the interaction of churches and cotton mills in the county from 1880 to 1940, the Negro population and Negro churches were largely excluded from it. *Ibid.,* x.

5. W. J. Hollenweger, *The Pentecostals: The Charismatic Movement in the Churches* (Minneapolis, 1972), 22–24; Frodsham, *With Signs Following,* 31–32.

6. Bloch-Hoell, *The Pentecostal Movement,* 54.

7. Hollenweger, *The Pentecostals,* 29, 47. The two-stage way of salvation includes: (1) Baptism or rebirth, and (2) Baptism of the spirit, usually but not always associated with speaking in tongues. The three-stage way of salvation includes sanctification, a second blessing or "work of grace"—also referred to as "Christian perfection" or "full holiness" (Nichol, *Pentecostalism,* 5–6, 87). In addition to these two categories of Pentecostals, W. J. Hollenweger ("A Black Pentecostal Concept: A Forgotten Chapter of Black History—The Black Pentecostals' Contribution," in *Concept,* no. 30 [June 1970], Geneva, Commission on World Mission and Evangelism, World Council of Churches, 4–5, 18; and Hollenweger, *The Pentecostals,* xix, 22, 67) distinguishes three other groups: (1) Oneness or Jesus Only organizations (God appeared in the Old Testament as Father, in the New Testament as Son, and appears now as Holy Spirit; (2) baptism is "in the name of Jesus"), including the large and important black Pentecostal Assemblies of the World, Inc.; and (3) Father Only groups which baptize only "in the name of the Father;" and Pentecostal groups "which cannot be identified."

8. Nichol, *Pentecostalism,* 57. Hollenweger (*The Pentecostals,* 59) points out that the white Church of God has developed into a middle-class church, and Calley (*God's People,* 11) observes that many religious groups that began as sects have become established churches characterized by a strong central organization, the ownership of a great deal of property, and considerable influence in public affairs. Of the latter, three of the largest

are the Assemblies of God, the Church of the Nazarene, and the Church of God, all of which have large fellowships outside the United States. All of these denominations are white. According to Hollenweger (*The Pentecostals,* 462), the successful campaign of Pentecostalism among the poor and the intellectually deprived has been followed in recent years by "a wave of Pentecostal revivals amongst high officials, managers in big businesses, scientists and scholars in every subject, artists, diplomats and officers." This author remarks that there are "more people than it is usually supposed who suffer from a real or imaginary disadvantage because of the color of their skin, their education, their sex, their temperament, their outward appearance, a contradiction in their status, and so forth, and wish to compensate for this disadvantage." Hollenweger (*Ibid.,* 8) refers also to the prayer meetings since 1962 of Catholic Pentecostals in the United States.

9. Nichol, *Pentecostalism,* 55.

10. *Ibid.,* 54; Hollenweger, "A Black Pentecostal Concept," 9.

11. Hollenweger, "A Black Pentecostal Concept," 11, and Hollenweger, *The Pentecostals,* xvii. Predictions such as the one mentioned above assume that the children and grandchildren of present adherents will follow in the footsteps of their forebears. Pentecostalism has appealed especially to the lower socioeconomic classes, but if there is considerable social ascent in the Third World by 2000, such predictions will not hold. See Emilio Willems, *Followers of the New Faith: Culture Change and the Rise of Protestantism in Brazil and Chile* (Nashville, Tennessee, 1967, 219–20, 247–48, 249), on the social class aspects of Protestantism (including Pentecostalism) in Brazil and Chile.

12. Calley, *God's People,* 12. Among the Biblical passages cited on the speaking in other tongues are: Acts 2: 4; 1st Corinthians 12: 10; and Mark 16: 17 (Frodsham, *With Signs Following,* 14–15, 31). Concerning the apostles on the day of Pentecost, Acts, 2: 4 states: "And they were all filled with the Holy Ghost, and began to speak with other tongues, as the Spirit gave them utterance." Hollenweger ("Charismatic and Pentecostal Movements") defines glossolalia of Pentecostals as "a meditative, non-rational form of prayer." Gerlach and Hine (*People,* 13–16) give an excellent brief explanation of glossolalia and its role in the Pentecostal movement in the United States.

13. Hollenweger, *The Pentecostals,* 291.

14. *Ibid.,* 315, 321, 370, 377; Block-Howell, *The Pentecostal Movement,* 154.

15. Hollenweger, *The Pentecostals,* 413. A commentary on James 5: 7 states: " 'The early rain fell at sowing time, about November or December; the latter rain about March or April, to mature the grain for the harvest. The latter rain that shall precede the coming spiritual harvest will probably be another Pentecost-like effusion of the Holy Ghost (quoted in Frodsham, *With Signs Following,* 3).' "

16. Hollenweger, *The Pentecostals,* 399–410.

17. *Ibid.,* xviii.

18. Nichol, *Pentecostalism,* 131.

19. Hollenweger, "A Black Pentecostal Concept," 11.

20. *Ibid.,* 16–17. In the early 1960s, the Pentecostal style, including speaking in tongues, began to take root in predominantly white middle-class denominations in the

8. SECT AND CULT

United States. "Neo-Pentecostals" attempted to "avoid anti-intellectualism, stopped short of describing tongues as the test of true Christianity, and . . . sought to relate the Pentecostal style to their denominational traditions rather than to establish indepedent Pentecostal churches." The first "neo-Pentecostals" were Protestant, but the movement first became a major force in the Catholic Church. Now there are approximately half a million Catholic charismatics in the United States and abroad. Charismatic renewal has begun to establish itself in major Protestant denominations—Presbyterian, Episcopal, Lutheran, Baptist, and Methodist. Leaders of this movement in these denominations assert that the movement is a reaction against the "sterility" or the "intellectualism" of their churches. Edward B. Fiske, " 'Charismatics' Gain in Churches," *The New York Times,* September 8, 1974, pp. 1, 42. For an account of the rise of the Catholic Pentecostal Movement in the United States after 1966, see Walter Hollenweger, *Pentecost Between Black and White* (Belfast, 1974), 76–97.

21. Hollenweger, "A Black Pentecostal Concept," 60; Nichol, *Pentecostalism,* 129.

22. Block-Howell, *The Pentecostal Movement,* 60; Hollenweger, "A Black Pentecostal Concept," 16. A conservative estimate for the former church is 1,000, 000 members, but some adherents estimate the membership at 3,000,000 (*Ibid.,* 27). In 1964, the latter church gave an estimate of 3,000,000 members in 300 congregations (*Ibid.,* 43)—probably a greatly inflated estimate.

23. *Ibid.,* 4–5. See note 7 for an explanation of the main categories in this listing.

24. *Ibid.,* 18; Nichol, *Pentecostalism,* 102–4.

25. Hollenweger, "A Black Pentecostal Concept," 118–19. Biblical references to support this exegesis include: Psalms 119: 83; Job 30: 30; Jeremiah 8: 21; Numbers 12: 1; Jeremiah 13: 23; and Galatians 3: 28. *Ibid.,* 35. According to Jeremiah 8: 21—"For the hurt of the daughter of my people am I hurt; I am black; astonishment hath taken hold on me."

26. *Ibid.,* 34.

27. *Ibid.,* 43–44. Undoubtedly, this is an exaggerated estimate, even if followers is used loosely here to include a core membership plus sympathizers.

28. Nichol, *Pentecostalism,* 148.

29. Pentecost is a Christian festival celebrated on the seventh Sunday after Easter, commemorating the descent of the Holy Ghost upon the Apostles.

30. Hollenweger, "A Black Pentecostal Concept," 59–60.

31. Luther P. Gerlach and Virginia H. Hine, *People, Power, Change: Movements in Social Transformation.* Indianpolis, Bobbs-Merrill, 1970, 7–8.

32. *Ibid.,* xix.

33. Hollenweger, "A Black Pentecostal Concept," 59–60.

34. Arthur M. Brazier, *Black Self-Determination* (Grand Rapids, 1969). Concerning the Woodlawn and similar activities, Hollenweger (*Pentecost Between Black and White,* 15) says: "In addition to the charismas which are known in the history of Pentecostalism, such as speaking in tongues, prophecy, religious dancing, prayer for the sick, they prac-

tise the gift of demonstrating, of organizing and publicizing as another kind of prophecy."

35. Bloch-Hoell, *The Pentecostal Movement,* 156.

36. Hollenweger, *The Pentecostals,* 465–66.

37. Emilio Willems, *Followers of the New Faith,* 131–34, 140–44, 168.

38. Hollenweger, *The Pentecostals,* 462; and see footnote 8, above; Willems, *Followers,* 219–20.

39. Gerlach and Hine, *People, Power, Change,* xxii-xxiii, 195. These investigators assert that five key factors must be present and interacting before a collectivity becomes a true movement: a segmented, reticular organization; face to face recruitment; personal commitment; an ideology which codifies values and goals; and real or perceived opposition from the society at large. *Ibid.,* xvi-xvii.

40. Melvin D. Williams, *Community in a Black Pentecostal Church* (Pittsburgh, 1974), 17–19.

41. *Ibid.,* 28–44.

42. *Ibid.,* 103–6.

43. *Ibid.,* 109, 175.

44. *Ibid.,* 115–16, 173.

45. See Benton Johnson, "Do Holiness Sects Socialize in Dominant Values?," *Social Forces,* 39 (May 1961): 309–16.

46. Williams, *Community,* 111–12, 115.

47. *Ibid.,* 96, 178.

48. *Ibid.,* 155, 157–58, 162, 172.

49. Cult, sect, established sect, and church as used in this book are defined in chapter 1. Washington finds the church-type less clear-cut among blacks than among whites, and refers to black Methodist and Baptist groups as church- and sect-types or sectarian church-types. He sees the black sect-type, including black Pentecostals and Holiness groups, as less ambiguous. According to Washington, the black cult-type "seldom emphasizes individual conversion; all blacks are by birthright members and need only to be awakened to that commality to become full participants." Joesph R. Washington, Jr., *Black Sects and Cults* (New York, 1972), 8–9, 11, 111.

50. A. H. Fauset, *Black Gods of the Metropolis* (Philadelphia, 1944), 59–60.

51. *The New York Times,* Nov. 18, 1962, p. 124.

52. Washington, *Black Sects,* 126; Gayraud S. Wilmore, *Black Religion* (New York, 1972), 215–16.

53. Wilmore, *Black Religion,* 215. Reference is made to Daddy Grace's cult in the section of this chapter on Black Pentecostalism. For a discussion of the religious aspects of Marcus Garvey's Universal Negro Improvement Association, see section on "A Religio-Political Cult" in chapter 4.

54. Richard R. Mathison, *Faiths, Cults and Sects of America* (Indianapolis, 1960), 246; Quoted in Wilmore, *Black Religion,* 216.

8. SECT AND CULT

55. Howard N. Brotz, *The Black Jews of Harlem* (New York, 1964), 15, 22–23, 26–27; Washington, *Black Sects,* 134.

56. Brotz, *The Black Jews,* 35–36.

57. *Ibid.,* 44, 88, 99.

58. Harry A. Ploski and Ernest Kaiser, eds., *The Black Almanac* (New York, 1971), 908–9.

59. Wilmore, *Black Religion,* 218.

60. Fauset, *Black Gods,* 77; Wilmore, *Black Religion,* 219–20.

61. C. Eric Lincoln, *The Black Muslims in America* (Boston, 1961), 11–16.

62. E. U. Essien-Udom, *Black Nationalism* (Chicago, 1962), 4.

63. *Ibid.,* 14–15; Gerlach and Hine, *People, Power, Change,* 211.

64. Essien-Udom, *Black Nationalism,* 124–41.

65. *Ibid.,* 250, 261–62, 286.

66. *Malcolm X Speaks,* edited by George Breitman (New York, 1965), 18–22, 58–59; Wilmore, *Black Religion,* 259.

67. Essien-Udom, *Black Nationalism,* 337. Watson sees the basic issue in the Ras Tafari movement in Jamaica and the Black Muslims in the United States as the lack of meaning in the lives of the cultists. Estranged from the larger society, members of both movements reply to rejection by rejection. In both cases, the need for help in coping with difficult life situations has led to the creation of make-believe worlds which seem to devotees to represent betterment. G. Llewellyn Watson, "Social Structure and Social Movements: the Black Muslims in the U.S.A. and the Ras-Tafarians in Jamaica," *The British Journal of Sociology,* 24 (June 1973): 197–99.

68. Wilmore, *Black Religion,* 235–36.

69. Washington, *Black Sects,* 112–13; St. Clair Drake and Horace R. Cayton, *Black Metropolis* (New York, 1945), 642–46. In a discussion of Afro-American naming practices, Dillard lists the names of thirty-eight ghetto store front churches from the Washington, D.C. area (J. L. Dillard, "On the Grammar of Afro-American Naming Practices," *Names,* 16 [1968]: 230–37).

The Bible Way Church of Our Lord Jesus Christ World Wide, Inc., Bethel Commandment Church of the Living God, Bethlehem Fire Baptize Holiness Church of God of the Americas, Brookland Union Baptist Church, Brown Memorial AME Church, Cannanite [*sic*] Temple of the Church of God, Chester Graham Rescue Mission, Church of God of True Holiness, Deliverance Church of God in Son, Emmanuel Church of God in Christ, East Friendship Baptist Church, First Rising Mount Zion Baptist Church, Full Speed Gospel Church, Georgetown Psychic Healing Church, Gospel Union Church of Christ, Gospelite Full Gospel Church, Holy Mount Olive Church of Christ of the Apostolic Faith, International Constitutional Church Organitional, Marantha Gospel Hall, Montell Avenue Baptist Church, Mount Calvary Holiness Church of Deliverance of the Apostolic Faith, Mount Pleasant Baptist Church, Inc., Mount Tabor Baptist Church, Mount Zion United Holy Church, New Bethel Baptist Church, New Mount

8. SECT AND CULT

Nebo Baptist Church, Old Way Baptist Church, Peoples Church, Royal Fellowship Center, Second Eureka Baptist Church, The Church of God Universal Holiness No. 1, The Full Gospel Baptist Church, The Holy Evangelistic Church No. 2 of North America, The Old Samaritan Baptist Church, The Refuge Church of Our Lord Jesus Christ of the Apostolic Faith, The Sacred Heart Spiritual Church of Jesus Christ, Inc., True Baptist Church, United House of Prayer.

70. Robin W. Winks, *The Blacks in Canada* (New Haven, 1971), 353, 354.

71. Calley, *God's People* 1–2, 12, 14, 28; Tables 1 and 2, p. 14, 1965 Institute of Race Relations, by permission of the Oxford University Press. In a white Pentecostal group in England, the Elim Foursquare Gospel Church, there are usually more women present than men, but the degree of involvement in the ecstatic part of the services is significantly disproportionate to the sex ratio of the congregation. In Pentecostal meetings, Wilson observes, "the emotionally unstable have more opportunity to express their feelings in a socially and divinely sanctioned circumstance, to the complete approbation of the community and with the possibility of earning considerable prestige" (Bryan R. Wilson, *Sects and Society,* Berkeley, 1961, 103, 112–13).

72. Calley, *God's People,* 25, 31, 42, 96.

73. *Ibid.,* 60–64, 74–75.

74. *Ibid.,* chap. 7.

75. *Ibid.,* 77–78, 80, 83.

76. *Ibid.,* 93–95. Kiev points out that it is difficult to assay the value of healing procedures in the Pentecostal churches of West Indians in England. The healing occurs in an emotional and supportive setting which creates and reinforces favorable expectancies for curing. He notes that modern medicine and Divine healing are not thought to be mutally exclusive. Ari Kiev, "Psychotherapeutic Aspects of Pentecostal Sects Among West Indian Immigrants to England," *British Journal of Sociology,* 15 (June 1964): 135–36.

77. Calley, *God's People,* 69–70, 126. Calley's study revealed large proportions of West Indians in Seventh Day Adventist congregations, ranging from 6 percent in Liverpool to 20 percent in Gloucester, 33 percent in Derby, 60 percent in Bedford and in Birmingham, and 75 percent in Huddersfield.

78. *Ibid.,* 121, 137–41, 145.

79. Roswith Gerloff, "Black Christian Communities in Birmingham: The Problem of Basic Recognition," in Alan Bryman, ed., *Religion in the Birmingham Area: Essays in the Sociology of Religion,* Institute for the Study of Worship and Religious Architecture, University of Birmingham, 1975, pp. 64–65. On p. 66, Gerloff cites with approval Calley's *God's People,* 57) statement that conflict and fission are an essential integrative part of West Indian Pentecostalism in England, as well as Gerlach and Hine's (*People,* 78) assertion that splitting and multiplication of units in a social movement make it difficult to suppress, permit it to penetrate different socioeconomic and cultural groups, and encourage social innovation.

80. For the Birmingham area, 34 names (96 churches) were listed in the first ver-

sion of this classification, *ibid.*, 76–82. By 1975 the names of more than 50 sects had been listed for the area and the list was still not exhaustive. (Personal communication from Pastor Roswith Gerloff, July 14, 1975.) The addresses of the headquarters or the national overseer of 73 Black-Led Churches are given in Roswith Geroloff and Others, *Partnership in Black and White*, The Methodist Church Home Mission Division (London, 1977), 35–77.

81. Gerloff, "Black Christian Communities," 69.

82. *Ibid.*

83. *Ibid.*, 70.

84. *Ibid.*, 73, 75.

85. Walter Hollenweger, "The Morning Is Full," *Pentecost and Politics* (Bristol, 1975), 5–6.

86. James Tinney, "Black Origins of the Pentecostal Movement," *Christianity Today*, October 8, 1971, p. 4. Quoted in R. Gerloff, "Theory and Practice of the Holy Spirit," *Quaker Religious Thought*, 16 (Summer 1975): 10.

87. Gerloff, "Theory and Practice," 10–12.

88. Kiev "The Study," 134–35; makes the interesting observation that "the gift of 'tongues' provides the inarticulate with an opportunity to speak in a patterned way to an applauding audience."

89. Hollenweger, "The Morning Is Full," 6.

9. Conclusion

1. Philip D. Curtin, *The Atlantic Slave Trade* (Madison, 1969), 128–30.

2. *Ibid.*, 89.

3. Eugene D. Genovese, *Roll, Jordan, Roll: The World the Slaves Made* (New York, 1972), 179; Carl N. Degler, *Neither Black Nor White: Slavery and Race Relations in Brazil and the United States* (New York, 1971), 65, 75; Robert William Fogel and Stanley L. Engerman, *Time on the Cross: The Economics of American Negro Slavery* (Boston, 1974), 232; David Brion Davis, *The Problem of Slavery in Western Culture* (Ithaca, 1966), 229.

4. See chapter 2 of this book on the situation in the Caribbean, and the sections on "Catholicism in Brazil," "Social Class and Protestantism in Brazil and Chile," and "Race and Latin American Protestantism" in chapter 4.

5. Edison Carneiro, *Candomblés Da Bahia* (3rd ed., Rio de Janeiro, 1961), 43, 81–82; Roger Bastide, *Les Religions Africaines au Brésil* (Paris, 1960), 414–18. C. P. F. Camargo, *Kardicismo e Umbanda* (São Paulo, 1961), 35. (Quoted in E. Willems, "Religious Mass Movements and Social Change in Brazil," in *New Perspectives in Brazil*, ed. E. Baklanoff [Nashville, Tennessee, 1966], 210); Seth and Ruth Leacock, *Spirits of the Deep* (New York, 1972), 108, 321; Angeline Pollak-Eltz, *María Lionza, Mito Y Culto Venezolano* (Caracas, 1972), 37.

6. For a discussion of vodun and Protestantism in Haiti, see Alfred Métraux, *Voodoo in Haiti* (Paris, 1959), 351–58.

9. CONCLUSION

7. L. A. A. de Verteuil, *Trinidad: Its Geography, Natural Resources, Present Condition and Prospects* (London, 1858), 175.

8. Carr reports that groups of Rada, Ibo, Congo, and Mandingo peoples lived at the northeastern corner of Port of Spain around 1870. Andrew T. Carr, "A Rada Community in Trinidad," *Caribbean Quarterly*, 3 (1953): 36.

9. Jeanette H. Henney, "Spirit Possession Belief and Trance Behavior in Two Fundamentalist Groups in St. Vincent," in *Trance, Healing, and Hallucination*, edited by F. D. Goodman, J. H. Henney, and E. Pressel (New York, 1974), 24, 81.

10. G. E. Simpson, "Cult Music of Trinidad," Folkways Ethnic Library, Album No. FE 4478 (New York, 1961), 3; G. E. Simpson, "The Acculturative Process in Trinidadian Shango," *Anthropological Quarterly*, 37 (1964): 25–26.

11. G. E. Simpson, *The Shango Cult in Trinidad* (Rio Piedras, 1965), 113.

12. *Ibid.*, 113–15.

13. *Ibid.*, 114.

14. *Ibid.*, 114.

15. Simpson, *Cult Music of Trinidad*, 3; Simpson, *Shango Cult*, 115.

16. Joseph G. Moore, "Religion of Jamaican Negroes: A Study of Afro-Jamaican Acculturation," University Microfilms Publication 7053, Doctoral Dissertation Series, Ann Arbor, 1954, 63–66, 114–19, 189–275; and Donald Hogg, "The Convince Cult in Jamaica," *Yale University Publications in Anthropology*, Number 58 (1960), 3–24.

17. P. D. Curtin, *Two Jamaicas* (Cambridge, Mass., 1955), 32—34, 171.

18. J. G. Moore and G. E. Simpson, "A Comparative Study of Acculturation in Morant Bay and West Kingston, Jamaica," *Zaire*, nos. 9–10 (1957): 984.

19. Hogg, "The Convince Cult," 3–.

20. Moore and Simpson, "A Comparative Study," 989; G. E. Simpson, "Political Cultism in West Kingston, Jamaica," *Social and Economic Studies*, 4 (1955): 135–42.

21. Leacock and Leacock, *Spirits of the Deep*, vi. The ceremonies of this cult are called *batuques* (*ibid.*, 2). Bastide (*African Civilisations*, 124) called batuques "Negro dances, secular as well as religious." On the Neo-African religions in Brazil, see discussion of Brazil, Cuba, and Haiti in a later section of this chapter.

22. This account of the Batuque in Belém is based entirely on Leacock and Leacock, *Spirits of the Deep, passim.*

23. Esther Pressel, "Umbanda Trance and Possession in São Paulo, Brazil," in F. D. Goodman, J. H. Henney, and E. Pressel, *Trance, Healing, and Hallucination* (New York, 1974), 116.

24. According to Pressel, in São Paulo "the *orixás* of Candomblé have changed in that they now send spirits of the dead to possess Umbanda mediums. In a sense, these spirits have been moved upstairs and are more removed from the everyday ritual activities in Umbanda. The fact that they were retained signifies the great importance Umbandists attach to their African cultural heritage even though today Umbandists view themselves as Brazilian, not as Afro-Brazilian." E. Pressel, *ibid.*, 213.

25. Roger Bastide, "The Black Americans," a paper presented to a conference on

9. CONCLUSION

Continuities and Discontinuities in Afro-American Societies and Cultures, sponsored by the Social Science Research Council, New York City, at the University of the West Indies, Mona, Jamaica, April 12, 1970, p. 14.

26. Erika Bourguignon, *A Cross-Cultural Study of Dissociational States* (Columbus, Ohio, 1968), 27.

27. Pressel, "Umbanda Trance and Possession," 210.

28. Leacock and Leacock, *Spirits of the Deep,* 323, 326.

29. *Ibid.,* 322–323.

30. Roger Bastide, *African Civilisations in the New World* (New York, 1971), 221.

31. In his study of the Rastafarians in the early and middle 1960s, Barrett lists no identification with Africa except blackness, long hair, authentic African dress, and African names. Ten years earlier, there was no drumming during meetings; "rhumba boxes," rattles, and, occasionally, a tambourine, provided the accompaniment to singing. At that time there was no dancing during meetings. In the 1960s, drumming and dancing became important in some Ras Tafari meetings. These Africanisms should be added to short list given by Barrett. M. G. Smith, Roy Augier, and Rex Nettleford, *The Ras Tafari Movement in Kingston, Jamaica* (Kingston, 1960), 18–19; L. E. Barrett, *The Rastafarians: A Study in Messianic Cultism in Jamaica* (Rio Piedras, Puerto Rico, 1969), 169–71; Simpson, "Political Cultism," 146.

32. Henney, "Spirit Possession Belief," 84. Concerning the Shakers of Grenada, Smith writes: "Occupying the folk pole of extreme Protestant sectarianism are the Shouters, Shakers or Spiritual Baptists, who combine spirit-possession, divination, the use of cabalistic signs and other ritual differentiae with a liturgy and ethic of recognisably Protestant derivation." M. G. Smith, *Dark Puritan* (Kingston, Jamaica, 1963), 7.

33. Henney, "Spirit Possession Belief," 85–87; G. E. Simpson, "Jamaican Revivalist Cults," 375, 381; Henney, "Spirit Possession Belief," 83, 94.

34. Simpson, *The Shango Cult,* 17–50; Angelina Pollak-Eltz, "The Shango Cult in Grenada, Westindies," *Proceedings, VIIIth International Congress of Anthropological and Ethnological Sciences,* 3: 59–60; Smith, *Dark Puritan,* 7–8.

35. This summary concerning African cults in the state of Maranhão, Brazil, is based entirely on Octavio Da Costa Eduardo, *The Negro in Northern Brazil* (New York, 1948).

36. Carneiro, *Candomblés Da Bahia,* 77–79.

37. *Ibid.,* 43, 81–82.

38. William Bascom, "The Focus of Cuban Santeria," *Southwestern Journal of Anthropology,* 6 (1960): 64–68; Fernando Ortiz, *Los Bailes y el Teatro de los Negros en el Folklore de Cuba* (Habana, 1951), 199–253.

39. Métraux, *Voodoo in Haiti,* 359–60.

40. *Ibid.,* 360–61. Reprinted by permission of Editions Gallimard, Paris, 1959.

41. G. E. Simpson, "Vodun Cult in Haiti," *African Notes,* 3 (1966): 21; Métraux, *Voodoo in Haiti,* 362.

42. This point is developed in James W. Fernandez, "Symbolic Consensus in a

9. CONCLUSION

Fang Syncretist Cult,," *American Anthropologist,* 67 (1965): 902–9. On the value of two analytic perspectives—cultural and social—see also Talcott Parsons, *The Social System* (New York, 1961), 6; and Clifford Gertz, "Ritual and Social Change: A Javanese Example," *American Anthropologist,* 59 (1957): 32–54.

43. Erika Bourguignon, "The Self, The Behavioral Environment, and the Theory of Spirit Possession," in *Context and Meaning in Cultural Anthropology,* ed. M. E. Spiro (New York, 1965), 57. Pressel asserts that *umbanda's* great significance in modern society "lies in its role of meditating macrochanges in the larger society and microchanges at the level of the individual" (Pressel, 1973, 312–13); Arnold Ludwig, "Altered States of Consciousness," in *Trance and Possession States,* ed. Raymond Prince (Montreal, 1968), 89–90.

44. Métraux (1959, 363) wrote: "From a strictly economic point of view it is undeniable that Voodoo heavily burdens the resources of the peasant population." A similar comment could be made about most of the religious cults we have considered. Genovese points out that "there have been few revolutionary-prophetic religious movements among black Brazilians, but adherence to religious cults that separated them from the ruling class retained its revolutionary potential. From time to time, the potential became realized under the leadership of charismatic militants and rebellion became holy war. Here as everywhere, religion proved a two-edged sword for the enslaved. It enabled them to accommodate with some measure of cultural autonomy and personal dignity, and, more rarely but ominously, it provided the war cry for determined insurgents." Genovese, *Roll, Jordan, Roll,* 182.

45. Courlander, "Vodoun in Haitian Culture," 24–25; Bastien, "Vodun and Politics in Haiti," in Courlander and Bastien, *Religion and Politics,"* 48.

46.Rex Nettleford, *Mirror Mirror: Identity, Race and Protest in Jamaica,* Kingston, William Collins and Sangster, Ltd., 125, 218–19.

47. Métraux, *Voodoo in Haiti,* 339–44, Bastien, "Vodoun and Politics, 56–62.

48. Bastide, *African Civilisations,* 132.

49. *Ibid.,* 132; Sidney W. Mintz, Introduction to the Second English Edition, Alfred Métraux, *Voodoo in Haiti* (New York, 1972), 13.

50. Métraux, *Voodoo,* 365.

51. *Ibid.,* 56–57.

52. *Ibid.,* 57; Bastien, "Vodoun and Politics," 66.

53. Charles Wagley, *An Introduction to Brazil* (New York, 2nd ed., 1971) 222–23; Carneiro, *Candomblés Da Bahia,* 44–46.

54. René Ribeiro, "Novo Aspectos Do Processo De Reinterpretaçao Nos Cultos Afro-*Brasileiros* Do Recife, *Anais Do XXXI Congr. De Americanistes* (1955), 481–82.

55. Bastide, Les Religions, 235–37.

56. Hogg, "The Convince Cult," 21–22; J. G. Moore and G. E. Simpson, "A Comparative Study," *Zaire,* no. 1 (1958): 72—73; G. E. Simpson, "The Kele (Chango) Cult in St. Lucia," *Caribbean Studies,* 13 (1973): 110–16.

57. *Eighth Census of Jamaica and Its Dependencies* (Kingston, 1945), lxiv.

58. Simpson, "Jamaican Revivalist Cults," 338–339.

9. CONCLUSION

59. Smith, Augier, and Nettleford, *The Ras Tafari Movement*, 17–18; Donald Hogg, *Jamaican Religions: A Study in Variations*. Unpublished Ph. D. Dissertation in Anthropology, Yale University, 1964, 337–38; 390–91.

60. Henney, "Spirit-Possession Belief and Trance Behavior," 24, 84; Simpson, *Shango Cult in Trinidad*. 96.

61. Emilio Willems, *Followers of the New Faith* (Nashville, 1967), 130–33; 247–48.

62. During a visit to Kingston in 1975, a theology lecturer from Ghana pointed out that some of the "Africanicity" of the Rastas is "unacceptable and, indeed, offensive to Africans on the continent of Africa." Specifically mentioned were some of the hair styles, lack of cleanliness, and some dress styles. John Pobee, "Africa and the Rastas: Basic Differences," *The Jamaica Daily News*. May 6, 1975. 8–9.

63. The effects of Selassie's downfall on the beliefs of Rastafarians are not yet clear, but among the early reactions were denials that reports in white newspapers were true, and the assertion that Selassie chose humiliation in order to redeem his people. Personal communication from George Cumper, Kingston, March 16, 1975.

64. Nettleford, *Mirror. Mirror*. 108–109.

65. In a discussion in the Jamaican press concerning Rastafarians, John Pobee, a visiting theology lecturer from Ghana praised some of the things that the brethren have done—some of the farms they have established, and some of the music, poetry, and arts and crafts they have produced. Although he favors visits to Africa, and even the taking of citizenship in African states by some people, he asserted that "no African Government will accept a mass exodus from Jamaica to Africa. For that will add to the already existing problem. Those who go must have some expertise because we cannot afford to add to the already acute problem of unemployment and all its attendant problems." Pobee told the Rastafarians that the Back-to-Africa campaign amounted to opting out of their obligations to Jamaica, and argued that injustice anywhere has to be fought by the nationals. According to Pobee, inequalities in life exist in Africa, and people who think they are going back to Utopia are deceiving themselves. John Pobee, "Africa and the Rastas," 8.

66. Nettleford, *Mirror. Mirror*. 218–19.

67. *Ibid.*, 127.

68. *Ibid.*, 218–19.

69. Personal communication from George Cumper, Kingston, Jamaica, March 16, 1975.

70. *Caribbean Monthly Bulletin*. 9 (September 1975): 29.

71. Bastide, *Les Religions*. 525; Pressel, "Umbanda Trance and Possession," 113.

72. Pressel, *Umbanda Trance*. 212–25.

73. Leacock and Leacock, *Spirits of the Deep*. 111–12.

74. Angelina Pollak-Eltz, "Panorama de estudios afroamericanos," *Montalban*. Caracas, no. 1 (1972): 272.

75. W. J. Hollenweger, *The Pentecostals*. (Minneapolis, 1972), 96, 107.

76. Willems, *Followers*. 130–133.

9. CONCLUSION

77. Anthony L. La Ruffa, "Cultural Change and Pentecostalism in Puerto Rico," *Social and Economic Studies*, 18 (1969):276–77.

78. Willems, *Followers*, 131, 149; Hollenweger, *The Pentecostals*, 8.

79. Bastide, *Les Religions*, 405–418.

80. Willems, *Followers*, 149.

81. George E. Simpson and J. Milton Yinger, *Racial and Cultural Minorities* (New York, 1972), 532–33.

82. Kenneth B. Clark, *Dark Ghetto* (New York, 1965), 177.

83. Joe R. Feagin, "Black Catholics in the United States," in H. M. Nelsen, R. L. Yokley, and A. K. Nelsen, eds., *The Black Church in America* (New York, 1971), 249; E. Franklin Frazier, *The Negro Church in America* (New York, 1963), 80; Feagin, "Black Catholics," 242–53. On the question of the range of racial prejudices among Catholics compared with Protestants, see Simpson and Yinger, *Racial and Cultural Minorities*, 252–53.

84. C. Eric Lincoln, *The Black Muslims in America* (Boston, 1961), 251–52.

85. The Denver Post, August 16, 1975, 3BB. In October, 1976, Wallace D. Muhammad announced that the Nation of Islam's name had been changed to the "World Community of Islam in the West." A spokesman for Muhammad said: "We are not Black Muslims and never have been. We're a world community—a community that encompasses everybody." *Plain Dealer*, October 20, 1976, 12a.

86. Fogel and Engerman, *Time on the Cross*, 20–21.

87. *Ibid.*, 116.

88. *Ibid.*, 23.

89. *Ibid.*, 24–25.

90. Bastide, *Les Religions*, 54–55.

91. Esther Pressel, "Umbanda in São Paulo," in Erika Bourguignon, ed., *Religion, Altered States of Consciousness, and Social Change* (Columbus, 1973), 295.

92. L. H. Rogler and A. B. Hollingshead, *Trapped: Families and Schizophrenia* (New York, 1965), 16–17, 46, 62–63, 248.

93. St. Clair Drake and Horace R. Cayton, *Black Metropolis* (New York, 1945), 642.

94. E. U. Essien-Udom, *Black Nationalism: A Search for Identity in America* (Chicago, 1962), 124–141, 337.

9. CONCLUSION

Glossary

Abakoso: Another name for Shango.

Abakwa: (1) A secret society in Cuba that is a lineal descendant of the Egbo society of the Ekoi and Efik peoples of the Calabar Coast of West Africa. (2) A class of spirits (also known as *diablitos, nánas, nánigos, írime* or *íreme*) capable of harming human beings; members of the Abakwa impersonate this type of spirit.

Abe: An *encantado* (spirit) in the Yoruban "house" in São Luiz, Brazil. Derived from Abe, a Yoruban deity.

Aduda: An *encantado* (spirit) in the Yoruban "house" in São Luiz (Maranhão), Brazil. Probably derived from Oduduwa, the royal deified progenitor of the Yoruba.

African Diaspora: The dispersals of population out of sub-Saharan Africa to other parts of the world; in this work, to the New World.

African Feast: A variety of the shango cult in Grenada.

Áfurugu: One of three spiritual entities ("souls") possessed by a living individual in Black Carib (Belize, formerly British Honduras) belief. Approximate meaning: "spirit-double."

Anamburuku: An *orisha* in the candomblés of Bahia, Brazil. See *Nana Buruko.*

Aninino: A serpent god in the winti cult of Paramaribo, Surinam. Derived from *Onini,* the sacred python of the Ashanti.

Arrêt: (drogue, garde, point): A magic charm to ward off evil.

Asase: A god in the winti cult of Paramaribo, Surinam. This is the Ghanian name for Earth Deity.

Averkete (Verekete): An *encantado* (spirit) in the religion of blacks in Santo Antônio, Brazil, and in the Batuque cult of Belém, Brazil. Derived from a Dahomean thunder deity.

Babalawo: A diviner in the Ifa religion of the Yoruba.

Baba Oke: A name for Obatala in candomblés of Bahia, Brazil. Also called *Orisha Baba.*

Babaluaiye: See *Shapana.*

Bade (Badé): The thunder deity of Dahomey. Identified with Shango in Yoruban "house" in São Luiz, Brazil, and in the Batuque cult of Belém, Brazil. And found in Haitian vodun.

Baka: (1) A term applied to a variety of evil spirits in Haiti. (2) An evil *loa.*

Batuque: (1) A dance performed by black people in Brazil during the colonial period. (2) A highly syncretized Yoruban-derived cult in Belém, consisting of a mixture of Yoruban and Dahomean beliefs and practices, as well as elements of Indian shamanism, folk Catholicism, Iberian and local folklore, concepts and rites from the Umbanda cult of Rio de Janeiro, and ideas from Brazilian spiritualism (in part also derived from Umbanda).

Béji: The orisha of twins in Trinidadian shango; Ibeji in the Yoruba religion of Nigeria.

Big Drum (Nation) Dance: An ancestral cult of Grenada and Carriacou.

Bocor: One who deals in harmful magic.

Bongo men: Devotees of the Convince cult of Jamaica.

"Building": An advanced ritual among the Shouters in Trinidad and the Shakers in St. Vincent. Purpose: to increase spiritual understanding and to obtain a new "gift" (higher position in the cult).

Cabildos: Societies or associations organized along ethnic (African tribal) lines in the colonial period in Colombia, Bolivia, Venezuela, Peru, Uruguay, Argentina, and Brazil, under the patronage of black saints such as St. Benedict the Moor, or devoted to Our Lady of the Rosary.

Caboclos: Persons of American Indian ancestry in Brazil.

Caboula: A religious cult in Brazil of Bantu origin.

Cachaca: Brazilian rum.

Caloundus: African religious cults in Brazil during the colonial period.

Candomblé: The Neo-African ceremonies given by blacks in Bahia, Brazil, and the sanctuaries where the rites are celebrated.

Chac-chac: Rattle used in Trinidadian shango ceremony.

Changó: Shango's name in Cuban santeria and in the kele cult of St. Lucia.

Chapelle: A small cult house in Trinidadian shango.

Congo: A subordinate *loa* in Haitian vodun.

Convince: An ancestral cult in the two easternmost parishes of Jamaica.

Creole: (1) Native to the country. (2) French patois in Haiti.

Cromanti (Kromanti): An Ashanti (Ghana) people or tribe.

Cumina: An ancestral cult in parts of Jamaica; probably descended from the religion of the Maroons, runaway slaves of the early eighteenth century.

Da (Danbira): A "family" of deities worshipped in the Dahomean "house" in São Luiz, Brazil. Same attributes as the Sagbata (Earth) pantheon in Dahomey.

Dagowe: A god in the winti cult of Paramaribo, Surinam; the equivalent of Dagbe (Ewe-Fon of Ghana).

Dahomean: Persons, groups, or cults of Dahomean (Benin) origin.

Damballa (Damballah): A loa of floods and serpents in Haitian vodun. Derived from Damballah, the serpent god of Dahomey. Also the god of lightning.

Degradation: A ceremony for the removal of the "loa" (talent) from a dead person.

Dernière prière: Final prayer for the dead, which is nine days after the funeral.

Diablesse: A female ghost or demon.

Dilogun: A system of divination which employs sixteen cowrie shells; known as *elegba* in southwestern Nigeria.

Dogó: The most important ancestral rite of the Black Carib of Belize.

Dosu: An *encantado* (spirit) worshipped in the Neo-African cults in São Luiz, Brazil. Derived from the Dahomean god Dosu (literally, the child born after twins).

Duppy: The "shadow" which remains behind after death in Jamaican folk belief.

Egungun: The orisha who symbolized all of the dead ancestors of a lineage in traditional Yoruba belief. *Egun* in Cuban santeria.

Emanja (Omanja): The term in Trinidadian shango for the Yoruban water goddess Yemanja. See *Yemanjá* and *Yemayá*.

Emi: One type of "soul" in traditional Yoruba belief in southwestern Nigeria; sometimes thought of as "the breath" of a person. See also: *ojiji* and *ori*.

Encantado: Supernaturals in the Batuque cult of Belém, Brazil.

Engagement: Pact which binds a person to an evil spirit.

Eowa: An *encantado* (spirit) in the religion of blacks in Santo Antônio (Maranhão), Brazil. Derived from a Dahomean deity of that name.

Erelay (Erile): Erinle is a god of medicine in traditional Yoruba belief; associated with healing and magical help in Trinidadian and Grenadian shango.

Erinle: See *Erelay.*

Erzilie: A Dahomean deity who reigns like a queen in Haitian vodun.

Eshu (Esu). The divine messenger among Yoruban deities and a trickster. Also known in West Africa as Elegba or Elegbara. In Trinidadian shango, Eshu is identified to some extent with Satan.

Exu (Bahian candomblés): See *Eshu.*

Garveyism: The philosophy and teachings of Marcus Garvey, founder of the Universal Negro Improvement Assciation in Jamaica and the United States.

Gédé (Guédé): The loa of death in Haitian vodun. Derived from a Dahomean deity.

Gedensu (Djukas of Surinam): See *Gédé.*

Gros-bon-ange: In Haitian folk belief, one of the two "souls" a human being possesses; similar to the soul in the Christian sense.

Gun (Gu): Same as Ogun in Bahian *candomblés.*

Gurun: Another name for Shango in Trinidad and Grenada.

Houmfort: A vodun temple in Haiti.

Houngan: A priest in the vodun cult of Haiti.

Iaua: One of the three spiritual entities ("souls") possessed by a living individual in Black Carib (Belize, formerly British Honduras) belief. Approximate meaning: "shadow," "reflexion," "image."

Ibedji (Cuban santeria). See *Béji.*

Ibeji (Bahian condomblés): See *Béji.*

Ibo (Haitian vodun): A secondary loa.

Ifa (Orunmila): God of divination in traditional Yoruban belief and in Cuban santeria (*Ifá* or *Orúnla*).

Image: Chromolithograph of a Catholic saint.

Imanjá (Belem batuque): See Yemanjá, Yemayá, and Emanja.

Inkices: Deities in the Angolan and Congolese candomblés of Bahia, Brazil.

Iroko (Bahian candomblés): See *Loko.*

Iuani: One of three spiritual entities ("souls") possessed by a living individual in Black Carib belief. See *áfurugu* and *iaua.*

Jorka: (1) One of the soul's two parts in winti belief in Para, Surinam. After death the *jorka* leaves the body and leads an independent existence in the realm of the dead. May be a good or a bad spirit in relation to the living. (2) A spirit of a deceased person in the winti cult of the Djukas of Surinam.

Kardecist Spiritualists: Devotees of a Brazilian spiritualist movement based on the writings of Allan Kardec.

Kele: An ancestral cult in St. Lucia; also known as Chango (Shango).

Kevioso: A "family" of thunder deities worshipped in the Dahomean "house" in São Luiz, Brazil.

Kolanut: A brownish seed, about the size of a chestnut, of the kola nut tree of West Africa, the West Indies, and Brazil. Nuts are cast in divinatory ritual of Trinidadian and Grenadian shango.

Kra: One of the soul's two parts in winti belief in Pará, Surinam—the source of a person's energy; corresponds to the concept of *kra* among the Akan in Ghana.

Legba: In Dahomey, Legba acts as interpreter to the gods. In Haitian vodun, he is the guardian of the crossroads. Called Lebara in the religion of the blacks in Santo Antônio, Brazil, and Lebara or Elebara in the Yoruban "house" in São Luiz, Brazil. He is called Lêba in Bahia and in the Para region of Surinam.

Loa: A deity of the vodun cult in Haiti; synonyms are: *zanges* (contraction of les anges); *les mystères; les saints.*

Lemba: Same as Obatala in Bahian candomblés.

Lisa: An *encantado* (spirit) in the Yoruban "house" in São Luiz, Brazil. Lisa is the sun god of Dahomey.

Loko: An *encantado* (spirit) in the Yoruban "house" in São Luiz, Brazil. Derived from Loko, a god of healing in Dahomey; an orisha in Bahian candomblés.

Loup garou: A werewolf.

Lua: Deity of the vodu cult in the Dominican Republic.

Lucumi: Afro-Cubans of Yoruba extraction.

Luku-man: A seer or diviner in the winti cult of Para, Surinam.

Macoumba: A syncretistic cult in Brazilian cities consisting of elements from African and American Indian religions, popular Catholicism, and the spiritualism of Allan Kardec (a form of French spiritualism introduced into Brazil in the nineteenth century).

Mambo: A priestess in the vodun cult of Haiti or the shango cult of Trinidad.

Mangé mort: a vodun feast for the family dead in Haiti.

Marassa: Twins; spirits of dead twins (Haiti).

María Lionza: The Queen, or principal spirit, in the spiritualist cult known as María Lionza in Venezuela.

Meninos: Inferior spirits in the candomblés of Bahia, Brazil. See *rérés.*

"Mourning": A rite of isolation among the Shouters of Trinidad and the Shakers of St. Vincent. Shangoists in Trinidad also "mourn" and "build" under the direction of a Shouters pastor. Purpose: to obtain a spiritual "gift." See *"Building."*

Myalism: Positive magical rites performed in Jamaica in the nineteenth century.

Nago: One of the three "lines" of *encantados* (spirits) in the Yoruban "house" in São Luiz, Brazil.

Nanã: (Nanan; Anamburuku): A water goddess in Bahian candomblés. See *Nana Buroko.* In winti cult of Djukas of Surinam, *Nana* or *Nina Kediampon* or *Nijankapon,* the supreme God and creator. The supreme God of the Boni Bush Negroes of French Guiana is called Nana, Masu Gadu, Kedi Amu, or Kediampon.

Nana Buroko: An *encantado* (spirit) in the Neo-African cults of São Luiz, Brazil. Derived from *Nananbukulu,* a member of the Sky pantheon in Dahomean belief and creator of the universe. Important in Neo-African cults of Recife and Bahia, Brazil.

Nine-night ceremony: A rite of dismissal held nine days after the death of a person.

Oba: A deity who is one of Shango's wives.

Obatala (Obatalá or *Orishanlá* in Cuban santeria): The Yoruba god who fashions the form of human beings in the womb. An important deity in Haiti, Cuba, Trinidad, Grenada, and Brazil.

Obeah: A term in Jamaica for harmful magic.

Obi: The kolanuts cast during a rite in Trinidadian and Grenadian shango to determine whether a deity is satisfied with the offerings which have been presented by a devotee.

Obia-man: (1) a person in winti belief in Para, Surinam, who has the power to offset the evil deeds of the wisi-man (conjurer); (2) A healer in the winti cult of the Djukas of Surinam.

Ochosí: The Yoruba god of the hunt. A deity in Cuban santeria. Same as *Oshossie.*

Ochun: See Oshun.

Ode: (Bahia and Porto Alegre, Brazil): A god of hunting.

Ogun (Ogoun): In traditional Yoruban belief, the god of war and of iron. Important deity in Haiti, Trinidad, Cuba, and Brazil.

Ojiji: One kind of "soul" in traditional Yoruba belief in southwestern Nigeria (sometimes thought of as a person's shadow). See also: *emi* and *ori*.

Okó: A god of agriculture in traditional Yoruba belief, and a deity in Cuban santeria.

Olorun: A deity in the shango cult of Recife, Brazil. *Olorun (Olodumare)* is the supreme God of the Yoruba in southwestern Nigeria.

Olufon (Alufon): A Yoruban deity of the shango cult in Trinidad.

Omolu: The god of smallpox and other contagious diseases in Bahian candombles; a doctor of the blacks.

Opele (kpele): A Yoruba divining chain made with halves of fruit seeds. Used in Ifa divination in Nigeria and in Neo-African cults in Brazil and in Cuba.

Opete: A god in the winti cult of Paramaribo, Surinam, derived from Twi (Ghana) belief.

Ori (eleda, olori): Guardian spirit—one of several "souls" of a person. See also: *emi* and *ojiji*.

Orisha (orisa; orixa): A deity in the traditional religions of the Yoruba people, in the Shango cult of Trinidad and in the Neo-African cults of Brazil and Cuba.

Orishanala (Bahia, Brazil): See *Obatala*.

Osain (Osanyin): A Yoruba god of medicine. Found in Trinidadian shango and in Neo-African and other religious cults in Brazil.

Osanyin: See *Osain*.

Oshala (Xango cult of Recife, Brazil): Same as *Obatala*.

Oshossie (Bahian candomblés): Same as *Ochosí*.

Oshumare: A servant of Shango who takes the form of a serpent; the rainbow deity in Bahian candomblés.

Oshun (Osun): A Yoruban river goddess and one of Shango's wives; in Trinidadian shango, mistress of the ocean. *Ochun* in Cuban santeria.

Ouanga (wanga): An evil charm.

Oxalá (Bahian candomblés and Belém batuque): See *Obatala* and *Oshala*.

Oxosse (Bahian candomblés): See *Oshossie* and *Ochosí*.

Oya: A female deity in Trinidadian shango; one of Shango's wives in southwestern Nigeria.

Oyo: An ancient Yoruba kingdom; the city of Oyo in southwestern Nigeria.

Pagelança (cura): Indian magic which has been added to the "African-derived" cults of São Luiz (Maranhão), Brazil; *pagelance*: a syncretistic cult of Indian origin, but supplemented with Damomean and Yoruban deities—centered on Amazonia.

Palais: A shelter where shango ceremonies are held in Trinidad.

Pará: Neo-African cult center in the southern Brazilian city of Porto Alegre.

Pessie: A ceremonial whip used in Trinidadian shango ceremonies.

Petro: (1) A group of vodun deities; (2) dances and rites supposedly derived from the name of Don Pedro, a powerful vodun priest of the pre-Revolutionary era in Haiti.

Pierre-tonnerre (thunder-stone): Small, smooth stone which vodunists and other cultists believe contains a spirit; some are neolithic celts made by Indian aborigines of Haiti, Trinidad, and St. Lucia.

Power (*orisha*): A deity in the shango cults of Trinidad and Grenada.

Prêt' savane: A "bush priest" who recites Catholic prayers in a vodun service.

Rada: Name of a group of vodun deities mainly of Dahomean and Nigerian origin. The word is a corruption of the name of the Dahomean town of Allada.

Rainha Eowa (Belém batuque): See *Eowa.*

Ras Tafari: The name of an anti-white, back-to-Africa movement in Jamaica.

Réré (*éré, wéré*): A messenger-servant of an *orisha* who mildly possesses a Neo-African cultist in Trinidad and Brazil before the major deities have arrived or after they have departed.

Revivalist: In Jamaica, revivalist cults, known as Revival Zion, Zionist, Revival, and Pocomania, are descendants of the Afro-Christian religions of the late eighteenth century. Shakerism in St. Vincent seems to be a blend consisting of a Methodist base, plus some elements of Anglicanism, Catholicism, and Pentecostalism; some modified Africanisms; and some elements of local origin. The Shouters cult (Spiritual Baptists) in Trinidad seems to be a diffusion of Shakerism from St. Vincent. Because the Shouters have borrowed from Trinidadian shango, this cult is more African than St. Vincent's Shakerism.

Santeria: The Afro-Cuban religious cult of the Lucumi people (descendants of the Yoruba and Nupe people who were brought to Cuba as slaves).

Sapata: An *encantado* (spirit) worshipped in Neo-African cults in São Luiz, Brazil. Derived from Sapata, an earth god in Dahomey.

Shaker: See Revivalist.

Shango: (1) Shango is the god of thunder in traditional religious belief among the Yoruba people of southwestern Nigeria and eastern Benin (Dahomey).

(2) The name of a Neo-African syncretistic religious cult in Trinidad, Grenada, and Recife, Brazil (Xango). (3) A powerful deity in Neo-African cults in Haiti, Trinidad, Brazil (Xango), Cuba (Changó), Grenada, and Dominican Republic (Changó). (4) The name by which the stone axes (Chango) which symbolize the African ancestors of St. Lucians who participate in the *kele* cult are known. Also known in Trinidad and Grenada as Abokosa and Gurun.

Shapana (Sopono; Sonponna; Sapana): An earth god in traditional Yoruban belief in Nigeria; more recently the deity of smallpox. In Cuban santeria, Babaluaiye; in Recife, Brazil, the god of smallpox. In Trinidadian shango, a deity of medicine.

Shayshay (sheshere): Ceremonial broom in Trinidadian shango.

Shouter (Spiritual Baptist): See *Revivalist*.

Sobo: An *encantado* (spirit) in the religion of blacks in Santo Antônio, Brazil. Derived from the Dahomean deity, Sobo, mother of the Thunder god Kevioso. In Bahian *candomblés,* Sobo or Sogbo.

Stool: An outdoor or indoor shrine for an *orisha* (power, deity) in Trinidadian shango.

Taipa: One of three "lines" of *encantados* (spirits) in the Yoruban "house" in São Luiz, Brazil. Derived from a Nupe (southern Nigeria) deity of that name.

Tambor de mina: Ceremonies given in Neo-African religious cults known as *tereiros* or *casas de mina* in São Luiz (Maranhão), Brazil, by groups of Dahomean descent.

Ti-bon-ange: A second "soul" in vodun belief; a guardian spirit.

Tomada: Possession by the Holy Spirit in the Pentecostal groups of Brazil.

Umbanda: An Afro-Brazilian cult that originated in Rio de Janeiro in the 1920s, representing a fusion of *macoumba* with spiritualism.

Verver: symbolic designs traced for the gods on the ground by the priest in Haitian vodun in white flour and ashes.

Vodun: (1) Rites and beliefs of a Neo-African syncretistic religious cult in Haiti. (2) A deity in the religion of the Arada "nation" of Benin (Dahomey).

Winti: Gods in the Neo-African winti cult of Paramaribo, Surinam.

Wisi-man: (1) A conjurer who has the power in winti belief in Para, Surinam to injure others. (2) A witch in the winti cult of the Djukas.

Xango: See *Shango.*

Yansã (Yansan): In Bahian candomblés, a deity who is also one of Shango's wives. In Recife, Brazil, Xango cults, she is also called *Yamessan, Oya,* or *Oba.* An important deity who exerts control over wind and lightning, but is also in charge of the souls of the dead.

Yemanjá: A water goddess in Bahian candomblés. Derived from Yoruba religion. See *Emanja* and *Yamayá.*

Yemayá: A water goddess in Cuban santeria. See *Emanja* and *Yamanjá.*

Yoruba: A major tribe or ethnic group of southwestern Nigeria and eastern Benin (Dahomey).

Zange: A contraction of les anges—deity of the vodun cult in Haiti; synonyms: loa; les mystères; les saints.

Zaniapombo: The supreme god in Angolan, Congolese, and American Indian candomblés in Bahia, Brazil.

Zombi: A deceased human being whose soul has been stolen by a *bocor* and who is resurrected after burial and used by the sorcerer to further his evil ends.

Bibliography

Ages, Arnold. *The Diaspora Dimension*. The Hague: Martinus Nijhoff, 1973.

Anderson, William A. and Russell R. Dynes. *Social Movements, Violence, and Change: The May Movement in Curaçao*. Columbus: Ohio State University Press, 1975.

Aptheker, Herbert. *Negro Slave Revolts in the United States, 1526–1860*. New York: International Publishers, 1939.

Banton, Michael. *Racial Minorities*. London: Fontana, 1972.

Barreal, Isaac. "Tendencias Sincreticas de los Cultos Populares en Cuba." *Etnologia Y Folklore*, Núm. 1 (1966): 17–24.

Barrett, L. E. *The Ras Tafari Movement in Kingston, Jamaica*. Rio Piedras, Puerto Rico: Institute of Caribbean Studies, University of Puerto Rico, 1969.

Bascom, William R. "The Focus of Cuban Santeria." *Southwestern Journal of Anthropology*. 6 (Spring 1950): 64–68.

———. "The Yoruba in Cuba," *Nigeria*. No. 37 (1951): 14–20.

———. "Two Forms of Afro-Cuban Divination." In Sol Tax, ed., *Acculturation in the Americas*. Chicago: University of Chicago Press, 1952.

———. "Yoruba Concepts of the Soul." In Anthony F. C. Wallace, ed., *Selected Papers of the Fifth International Congress of Anthropological and Ethnological Sciences*. Philadelphia: University of Pennsylvania Press, 1960, 401–410.

———. *Shango in the New World*. Austin, Texas: African and Afro-American Research Institute, The University of Texas, Occasional Publication, 1972.

Bastide, Roger, "Le Batuque de Porto-Alegre." In Sol Tax, ed., *Acculturation in the Americas* (Chicago, 1952), 195–206.

——. *Les Religions Africaines au Brésil.* Paris: Presses Universitaires de France, 1960.

——. "The Black Americans." A paper presented to a conference on *Continuities and Discontinuities in Afro-American Societies and Cultures,* sponsored by the Committee on Afro-American Societies and Cultures, Social Science Research Council, New York City, at the University of the West Indies, Mona, Jamaica, April 12, 1970.

——. *African Civilisations in the New World.* New York: Harper & Row, 1971.

Bastien, Rémy. "Vodoun and Politics in Haiti." In Harold Courlander and Rémy Bastien, *Religion and Politics in Haiti.* Washington, D.C.: Institute for Cross-Cultural Research, 1966.

Beckwith, Martha W. *Black Roadways: A Study of Jamaican Folk Life.* Chapel Hill: University of North Carolina Press, 1929.

Bell, Wendell. "Equality and Attitudes of Elites in Jamaica." *Social and Economic Studies,* 11 (December 1962): 409–432.

Bermúdez, Armando Andrés. "Notas para la Historia del Espiritismo en Cuba." *Etnologia y Folklore,* Núm. 4 (1967): 5–22.

——. "La Expansión del 'Espiritismo de Cordon.'" *Etnologia y Folklore,* Núm. 5 (1968): 5–32.

Bloch-Hoell, Nils. *The Pentecostal Movement.* Oslo: Universitetsforlaget, (Scandinavian University Books) 1964.

Bourguignon, Erika. "The Self, the Behavioral Environment, and the Theory of Spirit Possession." In M. E. Spiro, ed., *Context and Meaning in Cultural Anthropology.* New York: The Free Press, 1965.

——. *A Cross-Cultural Study of Dissociational States.* Columbus, Ohio State University Research Foundation, 1968.

——. "World Distribution and Patterns of Possession States." In Raymond Prince, ed., *Trance and Possession States.* Montreal: R. M. Bucke Memorial Society, 1968.

——. "Ritual Dissociation and Possession Belief in Caribbean Negro Religion." In Norman E. Whitten, Jr. and John F. Szwed, eds., *Afro-American Anthropology: Contemporary Perspectives.* New York: The Free Press, 1970.

——. *Religion, Altered States of Consciousness, and Social Change.* Columbus, Ohio: Ohio State University Press, 1973.

——. *Culture and the Varieties of Consciousness.* Menlo Park, Cal.: Cummings Publishing Co., Inc., 1974.

———. "Importante papel de las mujeres en los cultos afroamericanos." *Montalban*, 4 (1975): 423–38.

Braithwaite, Lloyd. "Social Stratification in Trinidad: A Preliminary Analysis." *Social and Economic Studies*, 2 (October 1953): 5–175.

Brathwaite, Edward. *The Development of Creole Society in Jamaica*. London: Oxford University Press, 1970.

Brazier, Arthur M. *Black Self-Determination: The Story of the Woodlawn Organization*. Grand Rapids, Mich.: W. B. Eerdmans Pub. Co., 1969.

Breen, Henry H. *St. Lucia: Historical, Statistical, Descriptive*. London: Longmans, Brown, Green & Longmans, 1844.

Breitman, George, ed. *Malcolm X Speaks*. New York: Grove Press, 1965.

Broom, Leonard. "The Social Differentiation of Jamaica." *American Sociological Review*, 19 (April 1954): 115–25.

———. "Urbanization and the Plural Society," *Annals of the New York Academy of Sciences*, 82(1960): 882–84.

Brotz, Howard N. *The Black Jews of Harlem*. New York: Schocken Books, 1964.

Brown, Clifton F. "Black Religion—1968." In Patricia Romero, ed., *In Black America*, Washington D.C.: United Publishing Corporation, 1969.

Burns, Sir. Alan. *History of the West Indies*. London: George Allen & Unwin Ltd., 1969. 2nd ed.

Cabrera, Lydia, *El Monte*. Miami: Rema Press, 1971. 2nd ed.

Caldecott, Alfred. *The Church in the West Indies*. New York: E. & J. B. Young & Co., 1898.

Calley, Malcolm J. C. *God's People: West Indian Pentecostal Sects in England*. London: Oxford University Press (for Institute of Race Relations) 1965.

Camargo, C. P. F. de. *Kardicismo e Umbanda*. São Paulo: Biblioteca Pionera de Ciencias Socias: Livraria Editôra, 1961.

Carneiro, Edison. *Candomblés da Bahia*. 2nd ed., Rio de Janeiro: Editorial E. A. Andes, 1948; 3rd ed., Rio de Janeiro: Conquista, 1961.

Carr, Andrew T. "A Rada Community in Trinidad." *Caribbean Quarterly*, 3 (Spring 1953): 35–54.

Clark, Kenneth B. *Dark Ghetto*. New York: Harper & Row, 1965.

Clarke, Edith. *My Mother Who Fathered Me*. London: George Allen & Unwin, 1966. 2nd ed.

Cleage, Albert B., Jr. *The Black Messiah*. New York: Sheed and Ward, 1968.

Cohen, Yehudi. "Four Categories of Interpersonal Relationships in the Family and Community in a Jamaican Village." *Anthropological Quarterly*, 3 (October 1955): 121–47.

Cone, James H. *Black Theology and Black Power.* New York: Seabury Press, 1969.

——. *A Black Theology of Liberation.* Philadelphia: Lippincott, 1970.

Cook, Scott. "The Prophets: A Revivalistic Folk Religious Movement in Puerto Rico." *Caribbean Studies,* 4 (January 1965): 20–35.

Courlander, Harold. "Abakwa Meeting in Guanabacoa." *The Journal of Negro History,* 29: (1944): 461–70.

——. *The Drum and the Hoe: Life and Lore of the Haitian People.* Berkeley: University of California Press, 1960.

——. "Vodoun in Haitian Culture." In H. Courlander and Rémy Bastien, *Religion and Politics in Haiti.* Washington, D.C.: Institute for Cross-Cultural Research, 1966.

——. *Tales of Yoruba Gods and Heroes.* New York: Crown, 1973.

——. *A Treasury of African Folklore.* New York: Crown, 1975.

Cronon, E. David. *Black Moses, The Story of Marcus Garvey and the Universal Negro Improvement Association.* Madison: University of Wisconsin Press, 1955; 1959.

Crowley, Daniel J. "Supernatural Beings in St. Lucia." *The Caribbean,* 8 (June–July 1955): 241–44; 264–65.

Curtin, Philip D. *Two Jamaicas: The Role of Ideas in a Tropical Colony, 1830–1865.* Cambridge: Harvard University Press, 1955.

——. *The Atlantic Slave Trade: A Census.* Madison: University of Wisconsin Press, 1969.

Davenport, F. M. *Primitive Traits in Religious Revivals.* New York: Macmillan, 1905.

Davidson, Lewis. *First Things First: A Study of the Presbyterian Church in Jamaica.* Edinburgh: Wm. Blackwood & Sons, Ltd., 1945.

Davis, David Brion. *The Problem of Slavery in Western Culture.* Ithaca: Cornell University Press, 1966.

——. "Slavery and the Post-World War II Historians." *Daedalus,* 103, no. 2 (Spring 1974): 1–16.

Davis, J. Merle. *The Church in the New Jamaica.* New York: International Missionary Council, 1942.

De Groot, Silva W. *Djuka Society and Social Change.* Assen, The Netherlands: Van Gorcum & Co., 1969.

Degler, Carl N. *Neither Black Nor White: Slavery and Race Relations in Brazil and the United States.* New York: Macmillan, 1971.

Deive, Carlos Estaban. *Vodu y Magia en Santo Domingo.* Santo Domingo: Taller, 1975.

Delany, Francis X. *A History of the Catholic Church in Jamaica, B.W.I., 1494 to 1929.* New York: Jesuit Mission Press, 1930.

Denis, Lorimer and François Duvalier. "L'Evolution stadiale du vodou." *Bulletin du Bureau d'Ethnologie,* 2nd ser., no. 12, 1955, 1–29.

Deren, Maya. *Divine Horseman, The Living Gods of Haiti.* London: Thames & Hudson, 1953.

Devas, Raymund. *Conception Island: Or The Troubled Story of the Catholic Church in Grenada, B.W.I.* London: Sands & Co., 1932.

de Verteuil, L. A. A. *Trinidad: Its Geography, Natural Resources, Present Condition and Prospects.* London: Ward and Lock, 1858.

Dillard, J. L. "On the Grammar of Afro-American Naming Practices." *Names,* 16 (1968): 230–237.

Dollard, John. *Caste and Class in a Southern Town.* New Haven: Yale University Press, 1937.

Drake, St. Clair. "The African Diaspora in Pan-African Perspective." *The Black Scholar,* 7, no. 1(September 1975): 2–13.

——. and Horace R. Cayton. *Black Metropolis.* New York: Harcourt, Brace, and Co., 1945.

Du Bois, W. E. B. *The Negro Church.* Atlanta: The Atlanta University Press, 1903.

Easton, Wilfred. *West Indies: What of the Church?* London: Edinburgh House Press, 1956.

Eduardo, Octavio Da Costa. *The Negro in Northern Brazil: A Study in Acculturation.* New York: J. J. Augustin, 1948.

Edwards, Bryan. *History, Civil and Commercial, of the British Colonies in the West Indies.* London: John Stockdale, 1801. 3rd ed. Vols. 1–2.

Edwards, Paul and James Walvin. "Africans in Britain, 1500–1800." In Martin L. Kilson and Robert I. Rotberg, eds., *The African Diaspora: Interpretative Essays.* Cambridge: Harvard University Press, 1976, 174–204.

Elder, J. D. "The Yoruba Ancestor Cult in Gasparillo." *Caribbean Quarterly,* 16 (September 1970): 5–20.

Elkins, Stanley M. *Slavery: A Problem in American Institutional and Intellectual Life.* New York: Grosset & Dunlap, 1963.

Ellis, J. B. *The Diocese of Jamaica: A Short Account of Its Growth and Organization.* London: Society for Promoting Christian Knowledge, 1913.

Essien-Udom, E. U. *Black Nationalism: A Search for an Identity in America.* Chicago: University of Chicago Press, 1962.

Fauset, Arthur H. *Black Gods of the Metropolis.* Philadelphia: University of Pennsylvania Press, 1944.

Fax, Elton C. *Garvey: The Story of a Pioneer Black Nationalist.* New York: Dodd, Mead & Co. 1972.

Feagin, Joe R. "Black Catholics in the United States: An Exploratory Analysis." In Hart M. Nelsen, Raytha L. Yokley, and Anne K. Nelsen, eds., *The Black Church in America.* New York: Basic Books, 1971.

Fernandez, James W. "African Religious Movements—Types and Dynamics." *The Journal of Modern African Studies,* 2, no. 4 (1964): 531–49.

——. "Symbolic Consensus in a Fang Syncretist Cult." *American Anthropologist,* 67 (August 1965): 909–29.

Findlay, G. G. and W. W. Holdsworth. *The History of the Wesleyan Methodist Missionary Society.* London: The Epworth Press, 1921. Vol. 2.

Fiske, Edward B. " 'Charismatics' Gain in Churches." *The New York Times,* September 8, 1974, pp. 1, 42.

Fogel, Robert W. and Stanley Engerman. *Time on the Cross: The Economics of American Negro Slavery.* 2 vols. Boston, 1974.

Foner, Laura and Eugene D. Genovese, eds. *Slavery in the New World: A Reader in Comparative History.* Englewood Cliffs, N.J.: Prentice-Hall, 1969.

Forde, Daryll. *The Yoruba-speaking Peoples of South-western Nigeria.* London: International African Institute, 1951.

Franklin, John Hope. *From Slavery to Freedom: A History of American Negroes,* New York: Knopf, 1947.

Frazier, E. Franklin. *The Negro Church in America.* New York: Schocken Books, 1963.

Frobenius, Leo. *The Voice of Africa.* London: Hutchinson & Co., 1913. Vol. 1–2.

Frodsham, Stanley Howard. *With Signs Following: The Story of the Pentecostal Revival in the Twentieth Century.* Springfield, Mo.: Gospel Publishing House, rev. ed., 1941.

Garvey, Amy J. *Garvey and Garveyism.* Kingston: Amy J. Garvey, 1963.

——. *Philosophy and Opinions of Marcus Garvey.* London: Frank Cass & Co., Ltd., 1967. 2nd ed., Part I.

——. *Black Power in America.* Kingston: Amy J. Garvey, Publisher, 1968.

Geertz, Clifford. "Ritual and Social Change: A Javanese Example." *American Anthropologist,* 59 (February 1957): 32–57.

Genovese, Eugene. "The Treatment of Slaves in Different Countries: Problems in the Application of the Comparative Method." In Laura Foner and Eugene D. Genovese, eds., *Slavery in the New World: A Reader in Comparative History.* Englewood Cliffs, N.J.: 1969, 202–10.

——. *Roll, Jordan, Roll: The World the Slaves Made.* New York: Pantheon, 1972.

Gerlach, Luther P. and Virginia H. Hine. *People, Power, Change: Movements of Social Transformation.* Indianapolis: Bobbs-Merrill, 1970.

Gerloff, Roswith. "Black Christian Communities in Birmingham." In Alan Bryman, ed., *Religion in Birmingham,* Institute for the Study of Religious Architecture and Worship, University of Birmingham, 1975.

——. "Theory and Practice of the Holy Spirit," *Quaker Religious Thought,* 16 (Summer 1975): 2–17.

Gerloff, Roswith, et al. *Partnership in Black and White.* London, The Methodist Church Home Mission Division, 1977.

Goodman, Felicitas D. "Disturbances in the Apostolic Church: A Trance-Based Upheaval in Yucatan." In F. D. Goodman, J. H. Henney, and E. Pressel, *Trance, Healing, and Hallucination.* New York: John Wiley & Sons, 1974.

Goveia, Elsa. *Slave Society in the British Leeward Islands.* New Haven: Yale University Press, 1965.

Gutman, Herbert G. *Slavery and the Numbers Game: A Critique of Time on the Cross.* Urbana: University of Illinois Press, 1975.

——. *The Black Family in Slavery and Freedom, 1750–1925.* New York: Pantheon, 1976.

Hamilton, Charles V. "An Advocate of Black Power Defines It." *The New York Times Magazine,* April 14, 1968, p. 79.

——. *The Black Preacher in America.* New York: William Morrow & Co., 1972.

Harding, Vincent. "Black Power and the American Christ." *Christian Century,* January 4, 1967, p. 10.

——. "Religion and Resistance Among Ante-Bellum Negroes, 1800–1860." In August Meier and Elliott Rudwick, *The Making of Black America: Essays in Negro Life and History.* New York: Atheneum, 1969, 179–97.

Harris, Joseph E. *The African Presence in Asia: Consequences of the East African Slave Trade.* Evanston: Northwestern University Press, 1971.

Henney, Jeannette H. *Spirit Possession Belief and Trance Behavior in a Religious Group in St. Vincent, British West Indies.* Unpublished Ph.D. thesis, The Ohio State University, Columbus, Ohio, 1968.

——. "The Shakers of St. Vincent: A Stable Religion." In Erika Bourguignon, ed., *Religion, Altered States of Consciousness, and Social Change.* Columbus: The Ohio State University Press, 1971.

——. "Spirit-Possession Belief and Trance Behavior in Two Fundamentalist Groups in St. Vincent." In Felicitas D. Goodman, Jeannette H. Henney and Esther Pressel, *Trance, Healing, and Hallucination: Three Field Studies in Religious Experience.* New York: John Wiley & Sons, 1974, 6–111.

Henry, Frances. *Forgotten Canadians: The Blacks of Nova Scotia.* Toronto: Longman Canada Ltd., 1973.

Herskovits, Melville J. *Life in a Haitian Valley.* New York: Alfred A. Knopf, 1937.

———. *Dahomey: An Ancient African Kingdom.* New York: J. J. Augustin, 1938. 2 vols.

———. *The Myth of the Negro Past.* New York: Harper & Brothers, 1941.

———. "The Southernmost Outposts of New World Africanisms." *American Anthropologist,* 45 (October-December 1943): 495–510.

———. *Man and His Works: The Science of Cultural Anthropology.* New York: Alfred A. Knopf, 1948.

———. Introduction to Sol Tax, ed., *Acculturation in the Americas: Proceedings and Selected Papers of the XXIXth International Congress of Americanists.* Chicago: University of Chicago Press, 1952, 48–63.

———. "Some Psychological Implications of Afroamerican Studies." In Sol Tax, ed., *Acculturation in the Americas: Proceedings and Selected Papers of the XXIXth International Congress of Americanists.* Chicago: University of Chicago Press, 1952, 152–60.

———. *Cultural Anthropology.* New York: Alfred A. Knopf, 1955.

———. *The Human Factor in Changing Africa.* New York: Alfred A. Knopf, 1962.

Herskovits, M. J. and F. S. Herskovits. "An Outline of Dahomean Religious Belief." *Memoirs of the American Anthropological Association,* Number 41, 1933.

———. *Suriname Folk-Lore.* New York: Columbia University Press, 1936.

———. "The Negroes of Brazil." *Yale Review,* 32 (December 1942): 263–79.

———. *Trinidad Village.* New York: Alfred A. Knopf, 1947.

Hoetink, Harry. *The Two Variants in Caribbean Race Relations: A Contribution to the Sociology of Segmented Societies.* London: Oxford University Press, 1967.

———. "Race Relations in Curaçao and Surinam." In Laura Foner and Eugene D. Genovese, eds., *Slavery in the New World,* Englewood Cliffs, N.J.: Prentice-Hall, 1969, 178–88.

Hogg, Donald. "The Convince Cult in Jamaica." *Yale University Publications in Anthropology,* Number 58 (1960): 3–24.

———. *Jamaican Religions: A Study in Variations.* Unpublished Ph.D. Dissertation in Anthropology, Yale University, 1964.

Hollenweger, W. J. "A Black Pentecostal Concept: A Forgotten Chapter of Black History—The Pentecostals' Contribution." In *Concept,* No. 30 (June, 1970). Geneva, Department on Studies in Evangelism, World Council of Churches, 4–5, 18.

———. *The Pentecostals: The Charismatic Movement in the Churches.* Minneapolis, Augsburg Publishing Co., 1972.

———. *Pentecost Between Black and White.* Belfast, Christian Journals, Ltd., 1974b.

———. "Charismatic and Pentecostal Movements." In D. Kirkpatrick, ed., *The Holy Spirit,* World Methodist Council, Tydings, 1974a.

———. "The Morning Is Full: Charismatic Movements Today." *Pentecost and Politics,* Bristol, 1975, 5.

Horowitz, Michael M. *Morne-Paysan: Peasant Village in Martinique.* New York: Holt-Rinehart-Winston, 1967.

Huguet, Lydia González. "La Casa-Templo en la Regla de Ocha." *Etnologia Y Folklore,* Num. 5 (Enero-Junio, 1968), 33–57.

Hurault, Jean. *Les Noirs Réfugiés Boni de la Guyane Française.* Dakar: Ifan, 1961.

Hurston, Zora N. *Mules and Men.* Philadelphia: J. B. Lippincott, 1935.

Hutton, J. E. *A History of Moravian Missions.* London: Moravian Publishing Office, 1922.

Hyatt, Harry Middleton. *Hoodoo-Conjuration-Witchcraft-Rootwork: Beliefs Accepted by Many Negroes and White Persons, These Being Orally Recorded Among Blacks and Whites.* Memoirs of the Alma Egan Hyatt Foundation, Vols. 1–2, 1970; Vol. 3, 1973. Hannibal, Mo.: Western Printing, Inc.

Inikori, J. E. "Measuring the Atlantic Slave Trade: An Assessment of Curtin and Anstey." *Journal of African History,* 17 (1976): 197–223.

Jesse, C. "Du Tertre and Labat on 17th Century Slave Life in the French Antilles." *Caribbean Quarterly,* 7 (December 1961): 153–155.

Johnson, Benton. "Do Holiness Sects Socialize in Dominant Values?" *Social Forces,* 39 (May 1961): 309–16.

Jones, Charles C. *The Religious Instruction of the Negroes in the United States.* Savannah: T. Purse, 1842.

Kami, Peter. "Revolutionary Cuban Pentecostals." *Pentecost and Politics* (Bristol, 1975), 15.

Kerr, Madeline. *Personality and Conflict in Jamaica.* Liverpool: Liverpool University Press, 1952.

Kiev, Ari. "Psychotherapeutic Aspects of Pentecostal Sects Among West Indian Immigrants to England." *British Journal of Sociology,* 15 (June 1964): 129–38.

———. "The Study of Folk Psychiatry." In A. Kiev, ed., *Magic, Faith, and Healing.* New York: The Free Press, 1964.

Kilson, Marion D. de B. "Towards Freedom: An Analysis of Slave Revolts in the United States." In August Meier and Elliott Rudwick, eds., *The Making of Black America.* New York: Atheneum, Vol. 1., 1969.

Kilson, Martin L. and Robert I. Rotberg, eds. *The African Diaspora: Interpretive Essays*. Cambridge: Harvard University Press, 1976.

Kitzinger, Sheila. "Protest and Mysticism: The Ras Tafari Cult of Jamaica." *Journal for the Scientific Study of Religions*, 8 (Fall 1969): 247–51.

La Barre, Weston. "Materials for a History of Studies of Crisis Cults: A Bibliographic Essay." *Current Anthropology*, 12 (February 1971): 3–44.

Landes, Ruth. "Fetish Worship in Brazil." *The Journal of American Folklore*, 53 (October–December 1940): 261–70.

Larsen, Jens P. M. *Virgin Islands Story: A History of the Lutheran State Church, Other Churches, Slavery, Education, and Culture in the Danish West Indies, Now the Virgin Islands*. Philadelphia: Muhlenberg Press, 1950.

La Ruffa, Anthony L. "Cultural Change and Pentecostalism in Puerto Rico." *Social and Economic Studies*, 18 (1969): 273–81.

Latortue, Gérard R. "The European Lands." In *The United States and the Caribbean*, ed. Tad Szulc, New York, American Assembly Service, 1971.

Leacock, Seth and Ruth Leacock. *Spirits of the Deep: Drums, Mediums, and Trance in a Brazilian City*. Garden City, N.Y.: Doubleday, 1972.

Lee, Richard B. "The Sociology of Kung Bushman Trance Performances." In Raymond Prince, ed., *Trance and Possession States*. Montreal: R. M. Bucke Memorial Society, 1968, 48–50.

Lewis, Bernard, "The African Diaspora and the Civilization of Islam." In Martin L. Kilson and Robert I. Rotberg, eds., *The African Diaspora: Interpretive Essays*. Cambridge: Harvard University Press, 1976, 37–56.

Lewis, Gordon K. *The Growth of the Modern West Indies*. New York: Monthly Review Press, 1968.

Lewis, Ioan M. *Ecstatic Religion, An Anthropological Study of Spirit Possession and Shamanism*. Middlesex, England: Penguin, 1971.

Leyburn, James G. *The Haitian People*. New Haven: Yale University Press, 1941.

Lincoln, C. Eric. *The Black Muslims in America*. Boston: Beacon Press, 1961.

Lowenthal, David. *West Indian Societies*. London: Oxford University Press, 1972.

Ludwig, Arnold M. "Altered States of Consciousness." In Raymond Prince, ed., *Trance and Possession States*. Montreal: R. M. Bucke Memorial Society, 1968, 69–95.

McNeill, Reverend George. *The Story of Our Missions in the West Indies*. Edinburgh: Foreign Mission Committee at the Office of the United Free Church of Scotland, 1911.

Marcelin, Milo. "Les Grands Dieux du Vodou Haitien." *Journal de la Société des Americanistes de Paris*, n.s. 36 (1947): 51–135.

Marx, Gary T. *Protest and Prejudice*. New York: Harper & Row, 1967.

Mathison, Richard R. *Faiths, Cults and Sects of America*. Indianapolis: Bobbs-Merrill, 1960.

Mays, Benjamin E., and J. W. Nicholson. *The Negro's Church*. New York: Institute of Social and Religious Research, 1933.

Meier, August, and Elliott Rudwick. *From Plantation to Ghetto*. New York: Hill and Wang. 1966.

——. *The Making of Black America*, vol. 1. New York, Atheneum, 1969.

Mennesson-Rigaud, Odette. "The Feasting of the Gods in Haitian Vodu." *Primitive Man*, 19 (January–April 1946): 1–58.

Messenger, John C., Jr. "Reinterpretations of Christian and Indigenous Belief in a Nigerian Nativist Church." *American Anthropologist*, 62 (1960): 268–78.

Métraux, Alfred. *Voodoo in Haiti*. Paris: Editions Gallimard, 1959.

——. "The Concept of Soul in Haitian Vodu." *Southwestern Journal of Anthropology*, 2 (Spring 1946): 84–92.

Mintz, Sidney W. "Caribbean Society." In *International Encyclopedia of the Social Sciences*. New York: Macmillan and Free Press, 1968. Vol. 2, 311–14.

——. Introduction to the Second English Edition, Alfred Métraux, *Voodoo in Haiti*. New York: Schocken, 1972.

Mischel, Frances. "African 'Powers' in Trinidad: The Shango Cult." *Anthropological Quarterly* 30 (April 1957): 45–59.

Mischel, Walter and Frances Mischel. "Psychological Aspects of Spirit Possession." *American Anthropologist*, 60 (April 1958): 249–60.

Moore, Joseph G. *Religion of Jamaican Negroes: A Study of Afro-Jamaican Acculturation*. Ann Arbor: University Microfilms; Doctoral Dissertation Series, Publication 7053, 1954.

——. "Religious Syncretism in Jamaica." *Practical Theology*, 12 (March–April 1965): 63–70.

Moore, J. G. and George E. Simpson. "A Comparative Study of Acculturation in Morant Bay and West Kingston, Jamaica." *Zaire*, nos. 9–10 (November–December 1957): 979–1019, and no. 1 (January 1958): 65–87.

Murdock, G. P. *Africa: Its Peoples and Their Culture History*. New York: McGraw-Hill, 1959.

Murphy, Gardner. *Personality: A Biosocial Approach to Origins and Structure*. New York: Harper & Brothers, 1947.

Myrdal, Gunnar, with the assistance of Richard Sterner and Arnold Rose. *An American Dilemma: The Negro Problem and Modern Democracy*. New York: Harper & Brothers, 1944. 2 vols.

BIBLIOGRAPHY

Nelsen, Hart M., Raytha L. Yokley, and Ann K. Nelsen, eds. *The Black Church in America*. New York: Basic Books, 1971.

Nettleford, Rex. *Mirror Mirror: Identity, Race and Protest in Jamaica*. Kingston: William Collins and Sangster, Ltd., 1970.

Nichol, John Thomas. *Pentecostalism*. New York: Harper & Row, 1966.

Niehoff, Arthur and Juanita Niehoff. *East Indians in the West Indies*. Milwaukee: Milwaukee Public Museum, Publications in Anthropology Number 6, 1960.

Nketia, J. H. K. *Funeral Dirges of the Akan People*. Accra, Ghana: Achimota University, 1955.

Oesterreich, T. K. *Possession: Demoniacal and Other*. Trans. D. Ibberson. New York: Richard R. Smith, Inc., 1930.

Ortiz, Fernando. *Hampa Afro-Cubana: Los Negros Esclavos*. Habana: Revista Bimestre Cubana, 1916.

——. *Los Bailes y el Teatro de los Negros en el Folklore de Cuba*. Habana: Ediciones Cardenas y Cia, 1951.

Parrinder, Geoffrey. *West African Religion*. London: The Epworth Press, 1949.

Parsons, Talcott. *The Social System*. New York: The Free Press, 1961.

Patterson, Orlando. *The Sociology of Slavery: An Analysis of the Origin, Development and Structure of Negro Slave Society in Jamaica*, London: McGibbon & Kee, 1967.

Payne, Ernest A. *Freedom in Jamaica: Some Chapters in the Story of the Baptist Missionary Society*. London: The Carey Press, 1933.

Pearse, Andrew C. *The Big Drum Dance of Carriacou*. New York: Folkways Records and Service Corp., 1956. Ethnic Folkways Library Album No. P 1011.

Peel, J. D. Y. *Aladura: A Religious Movement Among the Yoruba*. London: Oxford University Press, 1968.

Pilkington, Frederick. *Daybreak in Jamaica*. London: The Epworth Press, 1950.

Ploski, Harry A. and Ernest Kaiser, eds. *The Black Almanac*. New York: The Bellwether Co., 1971. 2nd ed.

Pollak-Eltz, Angelina. "The Shango Cult in Grenada, British Westindies." *Proceedings, VIIIth International Congress of Anthropological and Ethnological Sciences*, 3 (1968): 59–60.

——. *Cultos Afroamericanos*. Caracas: Universidad Católica Andrés Bello, 1972.

——. *María Lionza, Mito Y Culto Venezolano*. Caracas: Instituto de Investigaciones Historicas, Universidad Catolica Andrés Bello, 1972.

——. "Panorama de estudios afroamericanos." *Montalban* (Caracas, No. 1, 1972), 259–317.

Pope, Liston. *Millhands and Preachers: A Study of Gastonia.* New Haven: Yale University Press, 1942.

Population Council, *Country Profiles: Jamaica.* New York, 1971.

Pressel, Esther. "Umbanda in São Paulo: Religious Innovation in a Developing Society." In Erika Bourguignon, ed., *Religion, Altered States of Consciousness, and Social Change.* Columbus: Ohio State University Press, 1973.

——. "Umbanda Trance and Possession in São Paulo, Brazil." In F. D. Goodman, J. H. Henney, and E. Pressel, *Trance, Healing and Hallucination: Three Field Studies in Religious Experience.* New York: John Wiley & Sons, 1974.

Price, Richard. "Avenging Spirits and the Structure of Saramaka Lineages." *Bijdragen tot de Taal-, Land, en Volkenkunde,* 129 (1973): 86–107.

Price-Mars, Jean. *Ainsi Parla L'Oncle.* Paris: Impr. de Compiègne, 1928.

Prince, Raymond. "Indigenous Yoruba Psychiatry." In Ari Kiev, ed., *Magic, Faith, and Healing: Studies in Primitive Psychiatry.* New York: The Free Press, 1964.

——. "Can EEG Be Used in the Study of Possession States?" In R. Prince, ed., *Trance, and Possession States.* Montreal: R. M. Bucke Memorial Society, 1968, 127–35.

Puckett, Newbell Niles. *Folk Beliefs of the Southern Negro.* Chapel Hill: University of North Carolina Press, 1926.

Ragatz, Lowell J. *The Fall of the Planter Class in the British Caribbean, 1763–1833.* New York: American Historical Association, The Century Co., 1928.

Ramos, Arthur. *O Negro Brasileiro.* 2nd ed., Rio de Janeiro, 1940.

Rawick, George P. *From Sundown to Sunup: The Making of the Black Community.* Westport, Conn.: Greenwood Publishing Co., 1972.

Ribeiro, René. *The Afrobrazilian Cult-Groups of Recife, a Study of Social Adjustment.* Unpublished M.A. thesis in Anthropology, Northwestern University, Evanston, Illinois, 1949.

——. *Cultos Afrobrasileiros do Recife: Um Estudo de Ajustamento Social.* Recife: Boletim do Instituto Joaquim Nabuco, Número Especial, 1952.

——. "Novos Aspectos do Processo de Reinterpretação nos Cultos Afro-Brasileiros do Recife." *Anais Do XXXI Congr. Internacional de Americanistas,* 1955, 473–91.

——. "An Experimental Approach to the Study of Spirit Possession, Recife, Brazil." Unpublished ms., n.d., 1–24.

Richardson, Harry V. "The Negro in American Religious Life." In John P. Davis, ed., *The American Negro Reference Book.* New York: Prentice-Hall, 1966.

Rogler, L. H. and A. B. Hollingshead. "The Puerto Rican Spiritualist as a Psychiatrist." *American Journal of Sociology,* 67 (July 1961): 17–21.

——. *Trapped: Families and Schizophrenia.* New York: John Wiley & Sons, 1965.

Rotberg, Robert I. *Haiti: The Politics of Squalor.* Boston: Houghton, Mifflin Co., 1971.

Rycroft, W. Stanley, "The Contribution of Protestantism in the Caribbean." In A. Curtis Wilgus, ed., *The Caribbean: Its Culture* (Gainesville, Florida, 1955), 159.

Sherlock, Philip, *Shout for Freedom: A Tribute to Sam Sharpe,* London: Macmillan Caribbean, 1976.

Simmons, Harold F. C. "Notes on Folklore in St. Lucia." In Edward Brathwate, ed., *Iouanaloa: Recent Writing from St. Lucia.* Department of Extra Mural Studies, St. Lucia (June 1963): 41–49.

Simpson, George E. "Haitian Magic." *Social Forces,* 19 (October 1940): 95–100.

——. "The Vodun Service in Northern Haiti." *American Anthropologist,* 42 (April–June, 1940): 236–54.

——. "Haiti's Social Structure." *American Sociological Review,* 6 (October, 1941): 640–49.

——. "The Belief System of Haitian Vodun." *American Anthropologist,* 47 (January 1945): 35–59.

——. "Four Vodun Ceremonies." *Journal of American Folklore,* 59 (April–June 1946): 154–67.

——. "Magical Practices in Northern Haiti." *Journal of American Folklore,* 67 (October–December 1954): 395–403.

——. "Political Cultism in West Kingston." *Social and Economic Studies,* 4 (June 1955): 133–49.

——. "Jamaican Revivalist Cults." *Social and Economic Studies,* 5 (December 1956): 321–442.

——. "The Nine Night Ceremony in Jamaica." *Journal of American Folklore,* 70 (October–December 1957): 329–35.

——. "The Acculturative Process in Jamaican Revivalism." In Anthony F. C. Wallace, ed., *Selected Papers of the Fifth International Congress of Anthropological and Ethnological Sciences: Men and Cultures.* Philadelphia: University of Pennsylvania Press, 1960, 332–41.

——. *Cult Music of Trinidad.* New York: Folkways Records and Service Corp., 1961. Folkways Ethnic Library, Album FE 4478.

——. "The Ras Tafari Movement in Jamaica in Its Millenial Aspect." *Comparative Studies in Society and History,* Supplement II (1962): 160–65.

———. "The Shango Cult in Nigeria and in Trinidad." *American Anthropologist* 64 (December 1962): 1204–19.

———. "Social Stratification in the Caribbean." *Phylon*, 23 (First Quarter, 1962): 29–46.

———. "The Acculturative Process in Trinidadian Shango." *Anthropological Quarterly*, 37 (January 1964): 16–27.

———. "Shango Cult in Trinidad." *African Notes*, 3 (October 1965): 11–21.

———. *The Shango Cult in Trinidad.* Rio Piedras, Puerto Rico: Institute of Caribbean Studies, University of Puerto Rico, 1965.

———. "Baptismal, 'Mourning,' and 'Building' Ceremonies of the Shouters in Trinidad." *Journal of American Folklore,* 79 (October–December 1966): 537–50.

———. "The Vodun Cult in Haiti." *African Notes*, 3 (January 1966): 11–21.

———. *Religious Cults of the Caribbean: Trinidad, Jamaica, and Haiti.* Rio Piedras, Puerto Rico: Institute of Caribbean Studies, University of Puerto Rico, 1970.

———. "Afro-American Religions and Religious Behavior." *Caribbean Studies,* 12 (July 1972): 5–30.

———. "The Kele (Chango) Cult in St. Lucia." *Caribbean Studies,* 13 (October 1973): 110–16.

———. "Black Pentecostalism in the United States." *Phylon*, 35 (June 1974): 203–11.

———. "Religions of the Caribbean." In Martin L. Kilson and Robert I. Rotberg, eds., *The African Diaspora: Interpretive Essays.* Cambridge: Harvard University Press, 1976, 280–311.

———. *Yoruba Religion and Medicine in Ibadan.* Ibadan: Ibadan University Press. In press.

Simpson, George E. and Peter B. Hammond. Discussion of M. G. Smith, "The African Heritage in the Caribbean." In Vera Rubin, ed., *Caribbean Studies: A Symposium.* Kingston: Institute of Social and Economic Studies, University of the West Indies, 1957, 46–53.

Simpson, George E., and J. Milton Yinger. *Racial and Cultural Minorities: An Analysis of Prejudice and Discrimination.* New York: Harper & Row, 4th ed., 1972.

Singham, A. W. *The Hero and the Crowd in a Colonial Polity.* New Haven: Yale University Press, 1968.

The Sixth and Seventh Books of Moses: Moses' Magical Spirit-Art. Chicago: The de Laurence Co., 1916.

Smith, M. G. "The Plural Framework of Jamaican Society." *The British Journal of Sociology,* 12 (September 1961): 249–62.

——. *Dark Puritan.* Kingston: Department of Extra-Mural Studies, University of the West Indies, 1963.

——. *The Plural Society in the British West Indies.* Berkeley: University of California Press, 1965.

——. "A Note on Truth, Fact, and Tradition in Carriacou." *Caribbean Quarterly,* 17 (September–December 1971): 128–38.

Smith, M. G., Roy Augier, and Rex Nettleford. *The Ras Tafari Movement in Kingston, Jamaica.* Kingston: Institute of Social and Economic Research, University of the West Indies, 1960.

Smith, Raymond T. "Religion in the Formation of West Indian Society." In M. L. Kilson and R. I. Rotberg, eds., *The African Diaspora: Interpretive Essays.* Cambridge: Harvard University Press, 1976, 312–41.

Smith, Robert W. "Slavery and Christianity in the West Indies." *Church History,* 19 (September 1950): 173–86.

Smith, T. Lynn. *Brazil: People and Institutions.* Baton Rouge: Louisiana State University Press, 1972. 4th ed.

Snowden, Frank M., Jr. *Blacks in Antiquity: Ethiopians in the Greco-Roman Experience.* Cambridge: The Belnap Press of Harvard University, 1970, 11–36.

Stainbrook, Edward. "Some Characteristics of Schizophrenic Behavior in Bahian Society." *American Journal of Psychiatry,* 109 (November 1952): 330–35.

Stampp, Kenneth M. *The Peculiar Institution.* New York: Alfred A. Knopf, 1956.

Stonequist Everett V. *The Marginal Man: A Study in Personality and Culture Conflict.* New York: Scribner's, 1937.

Talbot, P. Amaury. *In the Shadow of the Bush.* London: Heinemann, 1912.

——. *The Peoples of Southern Nigeria.* London: Oxford University Press, vols. 2–3, 1926.

Tallant, Robert. *Voodoo in New Orleans.* New York: Macmillan, 1946; Collier Books, 1962.

Tannenbaum, Frank. *Slave and Citizen: The Negro in the Americas.* New York: Alfred A. Knopf, 1947.

Taylor, Douglas M. *The Black Carib of British Honduras.* New York, Wenner-Gren Foundation for Anthropological Research, Inc., 1951. Viking Fund Publications in Anthropology, Number 17.

Van Dusen, Henry P. "Caribbean Holiday." *The Christian Century,* 72 (August 17, 1955): 946–48.

Vincent, Theodore G. *Black Power and the Garvey Movement.* Berkeley: The Rampart Press, 1971.

Wagley, Charles. *An Introduction to Brazil.* New York: Columbia University Press, 1971. 2nd ed.

399

Walker, James W. St. G. "The Establishment of a Free Black Community in Nova Scotia, 1783–1840." In Martin L. Kilson and Robert I. Rotberg, eds., *The African Diaspora: Interpretive Essays*. Cambridge: Harvard University Press, 1976, 205–36.

Wallace, A. F. C., "Revitalization Movements." *American Anthropologist*, 58 (April 1956): 264–81.

Washington, Booker T., and W. E. B. Du Bois. *The Negro in the South*. Philadelphia: Jacobs, 1907.

Washington, Joseph R., Jr. *Black and White Power Subreption*. New York: Beacon Press, 1971.

——. *Black Sects and Cults*. Garden City, New York, Doubleday, 1972.

Watson, G. Llewellyn. "Social Structure and Social Movements: the Black Muslims in the U.S.A. and the Ras-Tafarians in Jamaica," *The British Journal of Sociology*, 24 (June 1973): 188–204.

Willems, Emilio. "Religious Mass Movements and Social Change in Brazil." In Eric Baklanoff, ed., *New Perspectives in Brazil*. Nashville, Tennessee: Vanderbilt University Press, 1966.

——. *Followers of the New Faith: Culture Change and the Rise of Protestantism in Brazil and Chile*. Nashville, Tennessee: Vanderbilt University Press, 1967.

Williams, Melvin D. *Community in a Black Pentecostal Church: An Anthropological Study*. Pittsburgh: University of Pittsburgh Press, 1974.

Wilmore, Gayraud. *Black Religion and Black Radicalism*. Garden City, New York: Doubleday, 1972.

Wilson, Bryan R. *Sects and Society*. Berkeley: University of California Press, 1961.

Winks, Robin W. *The Blacks in Canada*. New Haven: Yale University Press, 1971.

Wish, Harvey. "American Slave Insurrections Before 1861." *Journal of Negro History*, 22 (July 1937): 299–320.

Wooding, Charles J. "The Winti-Cult in the Para-District." *Caribbean Studies*, 12 (April 1972): 51–78.

Woodson, Carter G. *The History of the Negro Church*. Washington, D.C.: The Associated Publishers, 1921.

Yinger, J. Milton. *Toward a Field Theory of Behavior*. New York: McGraw-Hill, 1965.

——. *The Scientific Study of Religion*. New York: Macmillan, 1970.

Index of Names

INDEX OF NAMES

Index of Subjects